James Joule

Other books by the same author

Organization of Science in England (1957, 1972)
Steam Power in the Eighteenth Century (1963)
From Watt to Clausius: the Rise of Thermodynamics in the Industrial Age (1971)
Technology, Science and History (1972)

Books edited by the author

John Dalton and the Progress of Science (1968)
Artisan to Graduate (1974)

Frontispiece J. P. Joule
(from the portrait by the Hon. John Collier, the Royal Society)

James Joule
A biography

DONALD S. L. CARDWELL

Manchester University Press
MANCHESTER AND NEW YORK

Distributed exclusively in the USA and Canada
by St Martin's Press

Copyright © Donald S. L. Cardwell 1989

Published by
Manchester University Press
Oxford Road, Manchester M13 9PL, UK
and Room 400, 175 Fifth Avenue,
New York, NY 10010, USA

Distributed exclusively in the USA and Canada
by St. Martin's Press, Inc.,
175 Fifth Avenue, New York, NY 10010, USA

British Library cataloguing in publication data
Cardwell, Donald S. L.
 James Joule
 1. Physics. Joule, James P. – Biographies
 I. Title
 530′.092′4

Library of Congress cataloging in publication data
Cardwell, D. S. L. (Donald Stephen Lowell)
 James Joule: a biography / Donald S. L. Cardwell.
  p. cm.
 Includes index.
 ISBN 0–7190–3025–0
 1. Joule, James Prescott, 1818–1889. 2. Physicists – Great
Britain – Biography. I. Title.
 QC16. J68C368 1989
 530′.092′ – dc 19
 [B]

ISBN 0 7190 3025 0 *hardback*

Photoset in Linotron Ehrhardt
by Northern Phototypesetting Company
Printed in Great Britain
by Billings and Sons Ltd., Worcester

Contents

Illustrations

Preface

The biography of a scientist, or man of science as he was commonly called before 1914 (there were too few of them to form a conspicuous class before then), presents certain difficulties unless the scientist's achievements are reasonably familiar to most people. In the latter category, for example, Charles Darwin's ideas, no doubt in simplified form, are part of the common understanding of every educated man and woman. A major difficulty has therefore been cleared before the biographer begins. In sharp contrast, a biographer of Darwin's near contemporary, James Clerk Maxwell, has no such advantage. An understanding of Maxwell's work requires a competent knowledge of mathematics, and a reasonable familiarity with some subtle problems that had developed with the advance of physical science up to 1865, when Maxwell published his immensely important paper on the dynamical theory of the electromagnetic field. No bishop, indeed no curate, denounced it; it led to no crises of belief. There was not even a question in Parliament; there was no *Times* leader, no cartoon in *Punch*. And yet Einstein's theories of relativity were a consequence of that paper; so, too, were radar, radio and television. The full scientific and technological implications of a notable scientific advance are often, perhaps usually, possibly always, delayed by thirty-five or forty years. No biography of Maxwell could hope to do full justice to the consequences of his achievements.

Another difficulty is that the typical scientific career is marked by minor experiments, dead ends and false starts that litter the interludes between the grand discoveries or the all-revealing experiments. And yet to concentrate on the triumphs and to ignore the fruitless endeavours and the individual minor works would be to distort the picture of the man of science; a picture that, at best, can only be partial. But this is a problem that the scientific biographer has in common with all other biographers. All careers have their outwardly unrewarding passages. The problem here is, in short, not so much conceptual, or philosophical, as literary.

A third difficulty concerns the emphasis to be put on the scientist's role as a bridge figure. A danger confronting the biographer is the temptation to exaggerate his subject's – or his hero's – achievements as innovator, as bridge figure. Of course a scientist with a major record of achievement *is* necessarily a bridge figure; his work has to a greater or lesser extent changed the world. The temptation to exaggerate this must be resisted, or at least moderated. If, however, full justice is done to his contemporaries, working in the same or proximate fields, the result will be a treatise on the history of science and not a biography. For this reason I have mentioned only briefly the debate between Joule's champions, Thomson and Tait, and Mayer's champion, Tyndall, concerning priority in the discovery of the conservation of energy. It has, in any case, been very adequately discussed. And I have not mentioned Kronig's work on the kinetic theory of gases. His claim seems to me to be suspect and, clearly, he had no influence whatsoever on Joule and his associates. As regards local aspects of Joule's career I have omitted, as far as possible, material that has been mustered and ably discussed by Robert Kargon in his *Science in Victorian Manchester* (Manchester University Press, 1977).

Another recent historian of nineteenth-century Manchester, Gary Messinger, has described it as the 'half-known city'. As Messinger does not mention him it might be inferred that Joule is entirely unknown. But this is not the case. The internationally accepted name for the unit of energy is the joule and his name, or at least his initial J, commonly appears on such familiar items as packets of breakfast cereal. What cannot be denied is that Joule is a shadowy figure for most people.

Fifty years ago George Sarton, an influential historian of science, wrote a short paper on the discovery of the conservation of energy. He divided the credit very fairly between Mayer and Joule, but he expressed the view that 'As opposed to Mayer who was primarily a philosopher, Joule was a metrologist. His main interest lay in exact measurement, and his special genius showed itself at its best in the invention of methods enabling one to obtain more and more accuracy in quantitative experiments.'

This is seriously misleading. Joule was not a metrologist nor was his main interest in exact measurement. But Sarton was doing no more than repeating a view that was common at the time and that has persisted in some quarters to the present day. In fact Joule was a highly original man of science and, undeniably, a bridge figure. This was – and is – confirmed by the judgement of his peers. But he was also a bridge figure in quite a different sense. When he was a young man, carrying out his first researches, science in Britain was still substantially an affair of the gentlemen devotee. The appeal that led to the formation of the British Association (BA) was addressed to the 'cultivators of science'. Appropriately, Morrell and Thackray entitled their exhaustive study of the early days of the BA *Gentlemen of Science*. Things, of course, had been different on the Continent, and particularly in France, for some years. There, the State was far more directly concerned with science. There were words, such as *savant*, *physicien*, *Naturforscher*, that had no counterpart in English. By the end of Joule's life science as a social institution had changed in Britain to such an extent that he could fairly be called a bridge figure, linking the old with the new. Science degrees had been instituted; new colleges and universities with science faculties and laboratories had been established; the gentleman devotee was being replaced by the professional scientist (although by 1914 there were notably fewer professional scientists in Britain than in, for example, Germany). Joule was, arguably, not the last of the notable 'gentlemen of science'. Norman Lockyer and Oliver Heaviside can claim to belong to that company. But in their day the professional scientist was already dominant and the change during their lives was quantitative, not qualitative.

In the last hundred years the social revolution in science that began in Joule's lifetime has been completed; the gentleman devotee has disappeared and the affluent world enjoys the benefits of applied professional science on a scale that Joule and his contemporaries could hardly have imagined. Over the same period the energy principle, of which he was a leading pioneer, has had a dominant role in physical science. In a different context it has come to be a leading factor, perhaps *the* leading factor, in determining the future of the economically advanced countries. This Joule foresaw 130 years ago; the first prognosis (by W. S. Jevons) of an 'energy crisis' necessarily depended on Joule's prior work. There are, therefore, good reasons for a commerative biography dealing with all the main aspects of the life and work of this often misunderstood, sometimes misrepresented and almost always underestimated man.

The extent to which I have avoided the above-described pitfalls of the scientific biography is for the reader to judge. For my part I am well aware of gaps, ambiguities, and unanswered questions in my account. I can only plead in mitigation that had I sought to deal with these (and others that would no doubt have appeared), I should never have finished by task. There comes a point when every writer has to decide that he must close the account although he is well aware that there is more to be done.

Acknowledgements

I am grateful to Robert Fox, Ed Layton, David Wilson, Joe Marsh, Joan Mottram, John Pickstone, Mrs Joan Savage and Mrs Raj Williamson, as well as to others mentioned below, for their help, encouragement and advice. I am particularly indebted to Eric Mendoza, who has read the typescript, and to Alan Pate for his fine Joule bibliography. They are not, of course, responsible for errors and shortcomings in this book. I am also grateful, for their unfailing courtesy and help, to the librarians and staff of Chetham's Library, Manchester Central Reference Library, the Library of the Royal Society, the National Library of Wales, the University Libraries of Cambridge, Johns Hopkins, Glasgow, Manchester (John Rylands), St Andrews, the UMIST Library and the Public Record Office. Finally I wish to thank my colleagues at UMIST for granting me a sabbatical year to complete this work and my fellow members and the staff of the Manchester Lit & Phil for use of the Society's facilities on so many occasions.

1

Three steps to fame

Manchester, in the middle of the eighteenth century, was a pleasant and prosperous little town. Lying to the east of the meandering river Irwell, it was intersected by trout streams, the Irk and the Tib, and flanked to the south by the River Medlock, a tributary of the Irwell. It had orchards and boasted a huntsman with a pack of hounds. A feeling of the rural past is evoked by the names of the streets: Market Street, Withy Grove, Fountain Street and Hunts Bank. Manchester had neither a Member of Parliament nor a mayor and corporation. Under the Lord of the Manor, municipal government was by the Court Leet whose officers, the Boroughreeve and Constable, ran the affairs of the town. The combined population of Manchester and its sister town, Salford, on the other side of the Irwell, was about 20,000.

To the north of the town centre stood a Collegiate Church (now the Cathedral), together with Chetham's School and Library. Originally a baronial hall, 'Chetham's' had been rebuilt in 1427 to accommodate the warden and fellows of the Collegiate Church. It had been secularised in 1547 and subsequently endowed as a school and public library under the terms of Humphrey Chetham's will of 1653. 'Chetham's' is the oldest library open to the public in the English-speaking world and the school is one of the two leading music schools in Britain. Nearer the centre of Manchester, on the site of the present Piccadilly Gardens, stood the impressive Infirmary with its fine Ionic portico, opened in 1755. Mosley Street and Portland Street, on either side of the Infirmary and running south-west, had elegant houses occupied by wealthy merchants, lawyers and, particularly, honorary surgeons and physicians at the Infirmary. It was a clubbable age and it was quite natural that a number of these gentlemen who were like-minded should come together to form an academic society: the Manchester Literary and Philosophical Society, or the 'Lit & Phil' as it has always been called, in 1781. The Lit & Phil was remarkably successful.

In 1785 it published the first issue of its journal, the *Memoirs and Proceedings of the Manchester Literary and Philosophical Society*, which can claim to be the oldest scientific journal in the United Kingdom after the *Philosophical Transactions of the Royal Society*. By 1799 the Lit & Phil was affluent enough to buy its own house, 36 George Street, conveniently close to the Infirmary.

To the west and south of Manchester the orchards gave way to the rich farming lands of Lancashire and Cheshire, with little villages like Ardwick, Chorlton-on-Medlock, Didsbury, Sale and Eccles, while to the east and north the crescent of hills – Rossendale Forest, the Pennine Chain, Kinder Scout and the Peak – sheltered the twin towns from the cold northerly and easterly air. The hills caught the abundant rain from the grey clouds carried by the prevailing Atlantic winds. This gave Manchester and Salford a mild, humid climate while ensuring that the many rivers and streams flowing to the west – the Mersey and the Irwell with their tributaries, the Irk, the Roch, the Medlock, the Tame, the Bollin, the Goyt – never ran dry. Everything favoured the growth of the cotton textile industry.

Manchester should have been a happy town, for it had no history. Generally, Manchester's leading citizens had been, at best, of second rank. The great affairs of Church and State had neither honoured nor troubled Manchester. The first indication of change was in 1764 when the Bridgewater Canal was completed, linking the Duke of Bridgewater's mines at Worsley, eight miles west of Manchester, to Castlefield, just to the south of the town. In itself the construction of a few miles of canal was a minor matter. Two things, however, made the Bridgewater Canal memorable. In the first place, the Duke's engineer and agent, John Gilbert, together with the famous James Brindley, carried the canal over the river Irwell by means of the Barton aqueduct. This was regarded as a contemporary marvel: that a boat could sail or be towed *over* a river was surely a paradox, almost a contradiction in terms. In the second place, even before the canal reached Castlefield a much grander enterprise was under way. This was the construction of a spur taking the canal to Preston Brook, near Runcorn on the Mersey estuary; and at Preston Brook the extended Bridgewater Canal was to join the Trent and Mersey, or Grand Union Canal, for which Parliamentary approval was given in 1766. This was soon followed by the construction of an extensive network of canals linking the northern counties with the Midlands, London, Bristol, and the Severn estuary. Canal transport was slow, judged by the standard of the best roads, but it was cheap, reliable and could cope with heavy and bulky loads.

The building of the canal network had begun from Manchester. But it had no immediate or direct connection with the contemporary transformation of the textile industry that had begun with Richard Arkwright's

.patent of 1769. Arkwright succeeded in breaking down the skilled pro-cedure of manual cotton-spinning into a number of relatively simple operations, each one of which could be performed by largely wooden machines driven by water-wheels.[1] These machines could be installed in mills – an old word borrowed to denote a new-style factory – and could be tended by relatively unskilled men, women and children. The great increase in production the new machines brought about led to bigger mills powered by more efficient water-wheels. Fortunately John Smeaton (1724–92) had already worked out the rules for the most efficient exploi-tation of water power. As bigger mills were put up so their structures had to be stronger to carry the weight and withstand the vibration of the machines. Again, it was fortunate that the price of iron fell towards the end of the century so that iron-framed and therefore very strong cotton mills could be built by the beginning of the nineteenth century. Iron was also replacing wood in the manufacture of textile machines where its rigidity, the ease of casting and the much greater precision it made possible had significant advantages over wood.

Before long all the best water-power sites were fully exploited – every last drop of water falling the last inch had to be made to give up its full 'effort' to the water-wheel. Accordingly, the steam-engine was called in, at first to supplement the power of the water-wheel and then, finally, to take over almost completely.[2] Iron textile machines and steam-engines led to the development of a new industry: the design and manufacture of machines to make machines, or, simply, machine tools. The steam-engine made it possible for the textile mills to come in from the countryside and settle in the towns where labour, transport, engineering facilities and financial services were available. Manchester and Salford became engi-neering and commercial centres as well as cotton towns. But this did not end the matter. After it had left the mills the fabric had to be washed, bleached, mordanted and dyed or printed before it could be marketed. Consequently a great chemical industry sprang up in towns like Wigan, Northwich, Runcorn and Widnes.

The eighteenth century had seen many notable inventions, beginning with the Newcomen engine of 1712. But they had been individual innova-tions, unrelated to other developments. The textile revolution that began with Arkwright's first patent and his mill at Cromford, in Derbyshire, changed a wide range of associated industries and brought new industries and technologies into being. At the same time it had profound social consequences, for it stimulated the growth of industrial cities and new economic organisations. This was what is now called the Industrial Revolution.

The country town of Manchester became a great industrial city. The population increased fourfold in the last forty years of the eighteenth century and fourfold again in the next forty years. Great numbers of people were drawn to the new industrial area. Some were peasants or landless labourers from Ireland, Scotland, Wales or others parts of England. Some, like blacksmiths, millwrights, wheelwrights, and carpenters, had practical skills that could earn them good wages in the new mills, foundries and workshops. Others had entrepreneurial abilities that they hoped would win them fortunes to rival that of Arkwright. For most of the immigrants the mills and factories offered jobs, a living wage and freedom from the petty tyrannies of the squire and the parson, the seasons and the harvests. Unfortunately, Manchester was not equipped to cope with the huge increase in population; its civic resources were those of an English village. Housing arrangements were chaotic; there were virtually no provisions for public health, water supply, or sewerage. Slums were created on an unprecedented scale with the result that the mortality rates were appalling. Visitors were horrified. Liebig likened the place to an inferno,[3] while de Tocqueville described it as a stinking sewer.[4] Engels was no visitor – he was a resident – and his views about Manchester helped to change the course of history. Contemporary observers who praised or defended Manchester have generally been dismissed as blinkered philistines or worse. But this is a rather limited assessment. The slums were unquestionably appalling, but the impression given by novelists of a community composed solely of ruthless and greedy capitalists and a great mass of exploited, suffering wage-slaves must be a distortion. The mills and factories could not have functioned for one day without the services of a large class of highly-skilled men – fitters, turners, millwrights, draughtsmen, boilermakers – who were proud of their skills and who knew how important they were to the new industries. When Dickens dismissed steam-engines as 'melancholy, mad elephants' – he was presumably thinking of beam engines – it was probable that he knew nothing of the men who designed, built and serviced these fine machines. The existence of this large class was confirmed by the success of the Manchester Mechanics' Institution, founded in 1824. From the beginning this was one of the largest in the country, only those of Leeds, Liverpool and London being of comparable size. And the Manchester Institution was certainly one of the most successful.*

As early as 1792 the members of the Lit & Phil undertook the establishment of a Manchester Academy in which science was to occupy a

---

*The Manchester Mechanics' Institution is now, after several changes, the University of Manchester Institute of Science and Technology (UMIST).

prominent place in the curriculum. The Academy was intended for the education of dissenting ministers and of young men who intended to go into commerce. In 1973 they appointed John Dalton, a young and largely self-taught schoolmaster from Cumberland, to teach mathematics in the Academy. In that same year Dalton joined the Lit & Phil, one of his sponsors being Robert Owen, the pioneer socialist. Dalton was, by inclination, a meteorologist and a keen student of what would now be called the physics of gases. The great problem that intrigued him was why, or by what mechansim, did the two main constituent gases of the atmosphere, shown by Lavoisier to be elements, remain mixed in constant proportions at sea level, on the highest mountain tops, at the greatest heights reached by balloonists? According to Archimedean principles they should separate out, like oil and water, with the ligher gas, nitrogen, on top and the heavier gas, oxygen, underneath. He sought an explanation in terms of what he believed to be the atomic structure of gases. This led him to consider, first, relative atomic sizes and then relative atomic weights. It is probable that he was greatly helped in these researches by his friends Thomas Henry and his son William Henry, fellow members of the Lit & Phil,[5] and manufacturing chemists with considerable practical and manufacturing experience. Having determined the relative atomic weights of oxygen and nitrogen, it must have occurred to Dalton that the concept of atomic weight and the laws that could be deduced therefrom – the laws of multiple and reciprocal proportions – were of immense importance to chemistry. In fact, they enabled chemistry to become a quantified science.

Dalton, in spite of his humble origins, had little difficulty in getting his ideas accepted by the scientific world. The reason was simple. The basic laws worked; they were easily understood and they formed an unquestionable extension to knowledge that at no point and in no way challenged or contradicted accepted ideas, theories or treasured beliefs in which intellectual capital had been invested to mature over the years into emotional attachment. And Dalton was successful in another respect. He established, or was the first representative of, a Manchester school of science. This was something quite new. Since the scientific revolution in the seventeenth century the advance of science had been associated with the great capital cities, the ancient universities and the national academies of Europe. Now a parvenu industrial city was to start a scientific tradition of its own, thanks to the commanding, if tactiturn, figure of John Dalton. His atomic theory was first publicised in Thomas Thomson's *System of Chemistry* (1808), and then in his own *New System of Chemical Philosophy* (1808 and 1827), as well as in many papers in the *Memoirs and Proceedings* of the Lit & Phil and in other journals.

On one key point Dalton failed to carry scientific opinion with him. Only his friends, the Henrys, readily accepted his 'common-sense' picture of atoms as extremely small, round particles. All men of science could accept and use his laws of chemical combination. But what proof could he offer of the reality of his 'billiard ball' atoms? No proof, they argued, could be given. Daltonian atoms, in themselves, were mere speculations, mere metaphysical fancies. But for Dalton they were real; they had led him, via the physics of gases, to discover the laws of chemical combination. And, furthermore, as a Manchester man, if only an adoptive one, the simple common-sense approach, free of sophistry, was the natural one to take; particularly for a dedicated teacher, as Dalton certainly was. It was so easy to explain the atomic theory and its implications by referring to the tiny, hard particles that form the individual elements and that come together in pairs or triplets to form compounds. Dalton was a practical man. His friends and associates were the manufacturers, the businessmen, the engineers and industrial technologists of the rapidly growing town.[6] This extraordinary combination of circumstances – social, scientific, practical – together with Scottish influence, strong in Manchester at that time and for some time to come, goes some way to explain why the scientific atomic theory was born in the outwardly unpromising intellectual milieu of Manchester and not in one of the established centres of scientific thought. It was certainly unlikely soil for a scientific revolution, for it has been recorded that when Carl Jacobi visited Manchester in 1842 he wrote back to his brother, M. H. Jacobi, to say that[7] 'I had the courage there to say that it is the honour of science to be of no use, which provoked a powerful shaking of heads.'

Dalton came to occupy a remarkable place in the life of Manchester. It seemed that Mancunians had come to realise the unfavourable impression their town made on visitors. The squalor, the permanent cloud of smoke from innumerable chimneys, the polluted rivers, the pallid faces of the inhabitants, did not require the eloquence or the authority of a de Tocqueville or a Liebig to make people aware of the less admirable aspects of industrialisation. What better champion than John Dalton to prove that Manchester stood for something more than noise, dirt, smoke, endless miles of woven fabric and great wealth?

Dalton was a Quaker; nevertheless it seems surprising that he was able to work, unperturbed, through a long period of great national stress. The revolutionary and Napoleonic wars raged during the years when he was formulating the atomic theory. The peace of 1815 was followed by massive unemployment as demobilised soldiers and sailors sought work, while the accelerating pace of mechanisation meant that semi-skilled men, like the handloom weavers, found their livelihoods destroyed by the new machines and themselves faced with the option of unemployment and deprivation or unskilled work as a machine-minder in a huge, impersonal mill.

The pot boiled over on Saturday 16 August 1819. A public meeting was called in St Peter's Field, near the town centre, to hear Henry 'Orator' Hunt, a noted radical, deliver an address calling for universal adult suffrage, annual parliaments, the abolition of sinecures and placemen and the repeal of the combination laws. Crowds came marching in from all over Manchester, Salford, Bolton, Oldham, Rochdale, Stockport and other towns and villages. They were orderly and disciplined, with bands playing, flags flying and the girls in gay summer dresses. Peaceable they probably were, lawful they were not, for the magistrates had forbidden the meeting. Listening to wild talk in public houses, fearful of revolution and mindful of the feeble resources for the maintenance of law and order, the magistrates had summoned the military. Units of the regular army were on hand, as were the militia and the Manchester and Salford Yeomanry Cavalry. The order to arrest Hunt and his colleagues was issued as the address began, but the Deputy Constable, Joseph Nadin, the senior paid law officer, complained that he had not enough men to do the job. The Yeomanry Cavalry, under Major Trafford, with Captain Hugh Hornby Birley as second in command, was ordered to make the arrest. What followed has become known as the Peterloo massacre. Eleven people were killed, hundreds injured and the meeting dispersed in panic and despair. Hunt and his associates were arrested, tried and sentenced to short terms of imprisonment. 'Peterloo' has its place in British social and political history and it has played its part in putting Manchester on the national map. A carefully worded, eminently moderate petition of protest was drawn up and signed by about 4,800 respectable citizens, many of whom did not 'necessarily agree with the objects of the meeting'.[8] Many well-known Manchester names were on the list: Ashton, Axon, Boddington, Brockbank, Crossley, Peter Gaskell, Thomas Kirkman, Richard Potter, Archibald Prentice. Some were members of the Lit & Phil. But Manchester's most distinguished citizen, John Dalton, did not sign the petition; nor did his friend Peter Ewart, the engineer. Hugh Hornby Birley, who later attracted the wrath of most the critics for his part in the sad events of 16 August, had joined the Lit & Phil in 1804. He was to be a pallbearer at Dalton's funeral in 1844.

Peterloo did not halt the growth of Manchester. The poor continued to come to seek work; the ambitious came in search of fortunes; the skilled came looking for better opportunities. A particularly interesting group was composed of men with exceptional skills who came from distant places and countries. The first wave of such men came from Scotland, a country with superior educational institutions and a tradition of exporting talent.[9] The next wave came from the German states, for German education improved rapidly in the nineteenth century until it was commonly accepted as the best in the world. They came from Switzerland and Austria–Hungary and from those parts of eastern Europe where archaic tyrannies and religious and racial persecutions were endemic. They came, too, from Italy, bringing with them the fine skills of the Italian people.

In addition to those attracted by the revolutionary new industries and the opportunities they offered there were ordinary folk, tradesmen and the like, who would go wherever there were big markets. Manchester was a big and rapidly growing market. One of the many families attracted by the Manchester market was the Joule family. According to the first Manchester directory there were no Joules in Manchester in 1772.[10] In the following year the directory recorded a John Joule, a corn dealer of Cock Gate. The 1781 edition of the directory mentions a John Joul (*sic*) a corn dealer of Toad Lane and a Joseph Joul (*sic*), a baker of Withy Grove. And so, in increasing numbers, they came, small tradesmen, shopkeepers, stonemasons, a milkman, a butcher, brewers, a warehouseman, cornfactors, a flymaker, a bookkeeper and a china dealer. The 1788 directory records a William Joule, a brewer of New Bridge Street, Salford. A few years later several other Joules are given as brewers: John Joule, of Collyhurst (1794); Hugh Joule, of Water Street, Salford, whose widow, Helen Joule, seems to have taken over the business and was recorded as donating 10s 6d to St Ann's Church Sunday School in 1810.[11] A James Joule is mentioned as a brewer in 1804 and so was another William Joule, of Ardwick Green, in 1824.

The William Joule who set up a brewery in New Bridge Street (soon to be called New Bailey Street) in or before 1788 had been an innkeeper at Youlgreave in Derbyshire.[12] According to one authority he had kept an inn at Smithy Door (off Cateaton Street) before opening his brewery.[13] The family had connections all over Derbyshire and North Staffordshire, particularly in Bakewell, Elton and Youlgreave. If one genealogist is correct, a Robert Youl of Eyam married 'Ann, his wife' – her maiden name is not given – at Bakewell in 1670. It seems likely, therefore, that the Joules came from the heroic village that voluntarily quarantined itself when, in 1666, the plague broke out there. The neighbouring villages and towns were saved but most of the villagers died.

William Joule, the sixth of the nine surviving children of Joseph and Mary Joule of Youlgreave, was born in 1745.[14] He and his wife Martha had six children and by the time he died in 1799 at Buxton, where he had gone for his health (clearly unsuccessfully), he had established a comfortable style of life and a prosperous brewery in Salford to leave to his heirs. The *Manchester Mercury* of 29 May 1799 carried a most respectful obituary, describing him as a man of the utmost integrity and uprightness whose hand, 'as many could testify', was always open to the distressed. The obituarist added the rather odd compliment that, although he was success-ful in business, he had amassed his fortune through diligence and the most honourable means imaginable. And successful he must have been, for as early as 1798, he had a steam-engine working at the brewery that was next door to his house.[15] Only large breweries could afford steam-engines.[16] By 1829 the brewery was described as the largest in the twin towns.[17] The business continued to be known as William Joule & Son after he died. Quite possibly it was in the hands of his widow, Martha, for his eldest child, his son James, was barely twenty in 1799. Four of William's children died before 1812 and James died in 1816 leaving only Benjamin, the second child, born in 1784, to inherit the business. Benjamin was to marry Alice Prescott, a daughter of Thomas Prescott of Wigan and his wife Grace, neé Bradshaw. They were to have seven children. The first two, who were boys, died in infancy. The first to survive to maturity was Benjamin, born in 1817. He was followed by James Prescott, born on Christmas Eve 1818; Alice, 1820; Mary, 1823; and John Arthur, 1824. The brewery, which carried Benjamin's name from 1817 onwards,[18] was close to the famous prison begun by John Howard, the prison reformer, and completed by Thomas Butterworth Bayley. It received its first prisoners in 1790 and soon acquired a reputation as an almost model prison, for it was said that the prisoners kept in remarkably good health.* Seven years before the prison was completed the bridge across the Irwell was built so that New Bailey Street became a direct link between Manchester and Salford. It was not a fashionable street, like Mosley Street or Portland Street; the prison, with its iron *chevaux-de-frise* and loopholes for muskets, cannot have been a social asset. Equally, it was not a slum. The residents were a fair social mix: tradesmen, craftsmen, shopkeepers, with a leavening of professionals, such as attorneys. A mix of this sort was usual in the days before the suburban railway, the tram, the bus and the private car were to make possible the finely-graded dormitory suburb and to reduce the 'inner city' to a place of work, and work only. It was also usual for manufacturers, even of large

---

*In 1824 a much admired treadmill was installed and used to grind logwood for the dyestuffs industry. Instead of festering in idleness, a prey to evil thoughts and designs, the prisoner now had healthful exercise and the moral benefit of knowing that he was engaged in economically productive labour. The prison acquired grisly fame when the Fenians, Allen, Larkin, and O'Brien, were executed outside its gates. Shortly afterwards it was demolished when Strangeways prison was built (1868).

enterprises, to live next door to their mills or factories.[19] As Cooke Taylor observed, a Manchester manufacturer would rather you admired his mill than his mansion. The Joule family, then, can be taken as fairly typical of many who were attracted to Manchester by the opportunities it offered, who worked hard and prospered, who had their share of family tragedies and who helped to form the city that enabled them to make their fortune.

New Bailey Street was conveniently close to the centre of things. From near the bridge over the Irwell fast 'passage' boats, or passenger barges, provided services to places as far away as Runcorn, Widnes, Warrington, Bolton, Worsley and Wigan. The rapidly developed canal system together with the navigable rivers of Lancashire and Cheshire formed a network for passenger traffic as well as for goods. North of New Bailey Street, just on the other side of the Irwell, were Hunts Bank, Long Millgate and Poet's Corner with, not far off, the appalling slums so passionately denounced by Friedrich Engels. Long Millgate was the little street on which stood Chetham's and the old Free Grammar School, founded by Hugh Oldham in 1515, through whose doors many prominent Mancunians had passed and were to pass. Adjoining the Grammar School and Long Millgate was the Collegiate Church, 't 'Owd Church'. But this was of less consequence to the Joule family, for they were dissenters. Benjamin Joule and his family attended Dr William Roby's Congregational Chapel in Grosvenor Street, on the other side of town. Benjamin was an active and esteemed member of the Chapel and his children were baptised there.[20] Like the Unitarian Chapel in Cross Street, it was a fashionable church. The congregation included bankers, solicitors, and cotton masters. Among them were the Armitage family, a member of which, Sir Elkanah Armitage, was to be one of the best known of nineteenth-century mayors of Manchester.

Between Grosvenor Street and New Bailey Street was the Manchester Mechanics' Institution in Cooper Street, near the site of the modern Town Hall and Central Reference Library. Scattered round this central area were numerous mills, foundries and workshops. Not far from the present Oxford Road railway station was a large mill owned by the Birley family. It was a progressive establishment, socially as well as technologically, for the Birleys made proper arrangements for the education of mill children.[21]

Next door to the Birley mill was another in which they had an interest; this one was founded by Charles MacIntosh in 1823 for the manufacture of his newly invented rubberised waterproof textiles (whence 'mackintoshes' *sic*). Just off Oxford Road was Peter Ewart's foundry and in Faulkner Street was the great engineering works of Sharp, Roberts. Richard Roberts was one of the most creative of nineteenth-century engineers. He introduced the stroboscope and the industrial electromagnet; he invented the self-acting mule, the back-geared lathe, the radial drill and, quite probably, the planing machine; in addition he can claim to have invented the first digital-controlled machine tool.[22] Peel, Williams & Peel had their Soho Foundry at Ancoats, to the east of the town centre, where McConnell & Kennedy had their mill and William Fairbairn one of his works, the other one being on Canal Street. Galloway, Bowman & Glasgow, makers of steam-engines, were on Bridgewater Street. In Salford were the Philips & Lee mill, the first factory in the twin towns to be iron-framed and to have gas lighting, and the engine building firm of Bateman & Sherrat. In between these major establishments were the many small workshops of independent mechanics, millwrights and the like; the men who bridged the gap between mill-owners and operatives. There were also skilled instrument makers, like the Italian families of the Ronchettis and the Casartellis, who were closely related by marriage. C. J. Ronchetti became a close friend of Dalton, for whom he made instruments. Much later on the Very Revd L. C. Casartelli became the first Catholic Bishop of Salford.[23] Another well-known instrument-maker was John Benjamin Dancer, of Cross Street.[24]

Manchester was a town of the busy. Even the churches had to work hard to keep up with the demand. Such was the rush of weddings just before Lent (when the fee went up) that 't'Owd Church' introduced mass marriages. The couples were arranged in a semi-circle about the officiating clergyman who, it was noticed, was remarkably accurate in getting the names right. But if, by chance, Phoebe found she had exchanged vows with John and not with her William, while Mary had vowed herself to William and not to John, then all was made right at the end of the service by a general declaration that the right couples were married to each other.[25]

'The habits of Manchester men of business', it was said, 'are marked with the utmost perseverance and energy . . . with the exception of a weeks's or a fortnight's holiday at Southport or a trip to Wales, during the year, nothing but sickness is allowed to interfere with a daily attendance to the business of commerce or manufactures.'[26] And these, it was plain were matters that demanded attention from early morning until late at night. Characteristic, and another thing for visitors to wonder at, was the custom of Manchester men, in all walks of life, of taking their dinner at one o'clock in the afternoon, when the workplaces were all deserted and the streets full of men rushing out to take their main meal of the day.[27]

This was the Manchester in which young James Prescott Joule grew up. The evident effects of industry, the reports of Peterloo and the achievements of Dalton and his industrial contemporaries made Manchester conspicuous in the different worlds of social thought, politics and science.

It was a different place to different people. To the fastidious it was a barbarous manufacturing town with nothing to commend it; to the tender-hearted it was a place with terrible social problems arising from precipitate growth; to the practical, the energetic, the scientifically minded it was a uniquely interesting town where there were outstanding opportunities and where unprecedented changes were taking place.[25] People looked at things, and did things, differently in Manchester.

Many, perhaps most, of the changes were spawned locally and were *sui generis*. One that was not was the technological revolution represented by the Royal Mail stage-coaches that, running over the vastly improved roads built by Metcalfe, Telford and Macadam, kept to strict timetables and charged passengers a standard fare per mile. The drivers and guards were held in great respect; some were former army officers, demobilised after the wars, responsible men, accustomed to accurate timekeeping and careful organisation. On 15 September 1830, a new technological revolution began. The Liverpool and Manchester Railway was opened with passenger trains running to a timetable and with fares charged at so much per mile. Both passenger and freight trains were hauled by steam locomotives, the most famous of which was George Stephenson's 'Rocket', although 'Planet' was to be the prototype of all subsequent locomotives. The Manchester terminus of the line – the station still stands and forms part of the Greater Manchester Museum of Science and Industry – is only a few yards from the Castlefield basin of the Bridgewater Canal, the building of which was the first major event in what we call the Industrial Revolution.

2

Backgrounds

Shortly before his daughter Mary was born in 1823 Benjamin Joule moved his family from New Bailey Street to Swinton, a more congenial locality where the air was far cleaner than in the increasingly smoky heart of Manchester. From 'Broom Hill', his new house, he could see, on a clear day, as far as Runcorn, about twenty miles away. The health of his second son may have prompted him to make the move: James Joule later wrote that he was 'in poor health' between the ages of five and twelve and that his education made slow progress.[1] He had a spinal weakness, the effect of which was to make him a hunchback although, to judge from photographs taken in later life, it was not a conspicuous deformity. For treatment he was taken to Todmorden where the Taylor brothers had one of their surgeries. The Taylors belonged to a remarkable family of unqualified bonesetters and surgeons – practical craftsmen of medicine – who had begun as horse doctors but whose patients eventually included royalty.[2] It seems that they had some success for James enjoyed a normal, healthy youth, although he was under treatment by the Taylors up to his twentieth year. But it is also possible that the minor deformity, which certainly persisted, had an effect on the development of his personality, making him unassertive and shy in company. He was, he said, fond of sketching and reading, particularly books of travel.[3]

Although their interests differed, for Benjamin was to become an accomplished and dedicated musician, James's closest ties were with his elder brother. John was more than four years younger and separated by two sisters, the elder of whom died, to the great grief of the family, at the age of fourteen. Benjamin and James were not sent to school. This may have been because James was considered too delicate and that 'as they were constant companions and greatly attached to each other',[4] it was thought better not to separate them. Instead they were tutored at home, first by their mother's half-sister, Frances Prescott, and then by a resident tutor, T. S. Porter, who was associated with Dr Roby's Chapel and who later became a minister at Westhoughton. It was during this time, when James was eleven, that the brothers went down, one Saturday afternoon, to a field near Eccles, not far from home, to watch the first trains running on the Liverpool and Manchester Railway.[5] This was an experience that would endure in the memory, quite possibly to influence the course and form of future thoughts. The steam-engines of the eighteenth century, revolutionary though they were, made little impact on the wider public consciousness; they were mostly hidden away in engine-houses in remote parts of the country, in west Cornwall, in the North-East coalfield, in the Midland coalfield where the first one had been built in 1712. But as Osborne Reynolds was to point out, the rapid spread of the railway network after 1830 brought the power, the efficiency, and the mode of working of the steam-engine to the attention of all and the understanding of many. The Joule brothers were witnesses from the beginning. The ponderous old engine in the brewery could be taken for granted; the shining modern locomotives were something new.

In December 1832 they had a new tutor, Frederick Tappenden, who came from Ashford in Kent and had been at a 'military school' in the south of England. He stayed for two years until in December 1834 he married Frances Prescott, who was five years his senior, and took her south to start a 'boarding school for young gentlemen' at Sutton Court, Chiswick. James was to remain in close touch with the Tappendens throughout his life. In the meantime their father had decided that the brothers should study chemistry under Dr Dalton who, by permission of the Council of the Lit & Phil, gave private lessons and tutorials at the Society's House. Among Dalton's pupils at the House were to be several, besides the Joule brothers, who later achieved distinction. They included William Henry's son, William Charles Henry FRS; Eaton Hodgkinson, FRS, the engineer; Samuel Clegg, engineer and inventor of the gas meter; Samuel Hibbert Ware, physician, historian and antiquarian, Richard Potter, FRS, professor of Natural Philosophy at the University College, London, and Bennet Woodcroft, who was later to establish the London Science Museum.[6]

The brothers reported that Dalton ignored Tappenden when he introduced them[7], but this was probably no more than an adolescent misunderstanding of the ways of men, and of Dalton in particular, for the latter was later to give Tappenden a generous testimonial in support of his school. Dalton followed his usual procedure with the brothers who attended for hourly sessions, twice a week. He required them to be thoroughly grounded in arthmetic and geometry, beginning with Euclid, Book 1. They found this discouraging, but Dalton was following a most effective syllabus, one that he had undergone when he had been taught by blind John Gough of Kendal.[8] Gough had had great success in tutoring young men for Cambridge mathematical scholarships, men who often went on to become high wranglers, the most distinguished of them being the Revd Dr Whewell, Master of Trinity College. In fact, Dalton and Gough belong to the class of Lancashire geometers. Enthusiasm for the active study of Euclidean geometry – the setting and solving of geometrical problems – was widespread in the North-West.[9] As early as 1718 a mathematical society had been set up in Manchester and, before the end of the century, there was another, very active, one in Oldham. Indeed, interest in geometry transcended class levels and, it was said, was particularly marked among the 'operative classes'.[10] Elizabeth Gaskell wrote (in *Mary Barton*) that

> In the neighbourhood of Oldham there are weavers, common handloom weavers, who throw the shuttle with unceasing sound, through Newton's *Principia* lies open on the loom, to be snatched at in working hours, but revelled over at meal times or at night. Mathematical problems are received with interest, and studied with absorbing attention by many a broad spoken, common looking, factory-hand.

Dalton's insistence on preliminary geometrical studies and the high place Whewell gave to competence in geometry before Newtonian mechanics or the 'progressive sciences' should be tackled[11] sprang, we may infer, from the common culture of the Lancashire geometers.

Whatever brought about the diffusion of a taste for geometry, and whatever the ultimate effect, there can be no doubt that Dalton strongly influenced Joule's scientific method, his acceptance of certain key concepts and, lastly, his personal commitment to science. 'Dalton', Joule wrote later, 'possessed a rare power of engaging the affections of his pupils for scientific truth; it was from his instruction that I first formed a desire to increase my knowledge by original research.'[12] And it was fortunate for Joule that he was under Dalton's personal influence for three years. In April 1837, Dalton had a serious stroke that compelled him to give up teaching. He had taken the brothers through his syllabus of mathematics and on to study Cavallo's textbook and his own *New System*.[13] Thereafter Joule was tutored by John Davies, a lecturer at the Pine Street Medical School, at the back of the Infirmary. But relations between the Joule brothers and John Dalton remained close and cordial to the end.

Joule's scientific interests developed during and after these years of tutelage. He began the informal, spontaneous experimentation, as we may call it, that he carried on throughout his career. It was characterised by numerous unrelated, unco-ordinated experiments and observations, noted down but not usually published. They are of twofold interest in that they confirm his commitment to science and they give some indication of factors that helped to determine his main researches. Early on we find the brothers watching a thunderstorm from 'Broom Hill' and later discussing it with Dalton. They witnessed the aurora borealis – a phenomenon that always fascinated Dalton[14] – from the Lake District and, in 1842, they sounded Lake Windermere, finding the greatest depth to be 33 fathoms, or 198 feet (it is actually 220). Joule made observations from Sca Fell and, to study a particularly fine echo in the mountains, he triple-loaded a pistol that had belonged to his father when a member of the Manchester and Salford Yeomanry Cavalry.* The recoil sent the weapon into the lake. He seems to have been rather dangerous with weapons: on another occasion he blew his eyebrows off. There was some risk, too, in his electrical experiments, which seem to have been his favourite field of study – or entertainment – from the beginning. He flew electric kites and gave himself and his friends shocks from Leyden jars and primitive electric machines. He used 'galvanism' in experiments on a lame cart-horse and, with a powerful voltaic battery, carried out a series of tests on a servant girl. The strength (voltage) of the battery was steadily increased and the subject told to report her sensations until, at last, she became unconscious, at which point it was thought appropriate to conclude the experiments.[15]

The apparent incompatibility between Dalton's high status as a man of science – he was an FRS and held an Honorary DCL from Oxford when he was tutoring the Joule brothers – and his vocation as a teacher at a junior, even an elementary level has often been noted by historians. The surprise expressed by distinguished visitors at finding Dalton engaged in teaching boys usually finds a place in popular histories of science. That such a great man should have had to earn a living by teaching children proved, it was said, that science was not valued in England at that time. But this was to judge the situation by modern British, and contemporary Continental, *academic* standards. According to these a great man of science must be a professor who teaches only advanced students. He can no more be expected to teach children than a general can be expected to drill the awkward squad. But why should it be inappropriate for a scientific man to teach children if he has a talent and a taste for it? A due regard for status, characteristic of the academic everywhere, had no place in the British

---

*It is not known whether Benjamin Joule was present at Peterloo.

industrial city of the 1830s.* Dalton, for his part, was a straightforward man. He thought in simple terms, making things as uncomplicated as he could. Such qualities of mind are surely ideal in a teacher of the young and, at the same time, valuable in a pioneer man of science.[16]

This was consistent with the fact that the institutions, and therefore the forces, making for uniformity were far weaker in those days than they were to become later in the century. Several new scientific journals were launched in the early years of the nineteenth century, but most coalesced with the *Philosophical Magazine* which was, for many years, substantially a journal for the gentleman devotee. There remained only the *Philosophical Transactions of the Royal Society*, then at a rather low ebb, the *Manchester Memoirs* and the *Transactions of the Royal Dublin Society*. There were no science degrees awarded at any university and no science courses in schools; there were no professional scientific qualifications; there was nothing, in short, to differentiate the man of science from other men. Only a small minority of those who published papers in the scientific journals were gainfully employed in science.

The situation corresponded to what we should now regard as the uneven development of science. At the heart of things was the Newtonian achievement. Rational mechanics, planetary astronomy and optics comprised what Whewell was to call the finished sciences; that is, those with developed mathematical structures of theory and concept together with well-tested laws. In contrast were the progressive sciences: botany, physiology, zoology, geology, chemistry, heat, electricity and magnetism. Whewell's finished, or perfected, sciences were commonly grouped together as 'natural philosophy' and lecture courses under this title were given in Scottish universities, invariably as a component of general degrees, and in the two university colleges in London. There were, however, several different interpretations of the scope of natural philosophy. In addition, there was a catch-all subject, 'experimental philosophy', that could include Newtonian mechanics as well as various technologies. Electricity was often, and heat invariably, regarded as part of chemistry. The scientific study of heat had been virtually monopolised by chemists and medical men throughout the eighteenth century. Perhaps this was why, at the beginning of the next century, the substantial theory of heat was so readily accepted. According to this, thermal phenomena were to be ascribed to the presence and action of a 'subtle fluid' called 'caloric'. In

*Dalton gave lecture courses at the Manchester Mechanics' Institution as well as elsewhere in Manchester and in Birmingham, Edinburgh, Kendal and London (Royal Institution). The courses were well received and well remunerated.

much the same way electrical phenomena were considered to be due to a
fluid, or sometimes two fluids. These theories were plausible; after all,
electricity can be stored in a bottle (the so-called Leyden jar, or condenser);
and repeated efforts were made to find a connection between the fluids of
heat and of electricity; perhaps they were particular manifestations of a
common or truly fundamental fluid?

At the end of the eighteenth century Benjamin Thompson, Graf von
Rumford, claimed to have disposed of the caloric theory by showing that an
apparently limitless amount of heat could be generated by metallic friction.
His protégé, Humphry Davy, said that by rubbing two ice cubes together he
had caused them to melt. But he gave no details of the experiment and it is
difficult to see how he could have carried it out in an unexceptionable way.
These attempts to establish a kinetic theory of heat were noted but not
accepted by the scientific community which continued to find the caloric
theory to be, on balance, more plausible.

Over the years 1790–1830 France was, unquestionably, the leading
scientific nation in the world. French physical science was dominated for
much of the time by P. S. de Laplace, whose great triumph had been to
perfect Newton's system of planetary astronomy. Laplace and his able
disciples sought to extend Newton's principle of central forces to other
branches of what, from the beginning of the century, was called 'physics'.
As exemplified in the early textbooks of Haüy and Biot, physics included
mechanics, sound, light, electricity, magnetism and heat. These subjects
were, as Whewell put it, 'brought within the jurisdiction of mathematics',
and this distinguished physics from other sciences. France's imperial
ambitions were defeated by Britain and Prussia in 1815; but France
enjoyed a triumph over her former enemies when the French approach to
'physics' was generally adopted.[17] This was particularly true of the mathematical schools of the universities of Cambridge, Dublin and Edinburgh.
By 1834 the British Association formally recognised physics and in 1840
Whewell, admitting that the French word *physicien* was unacceptable,
coined the word *physicist*.* But although the range of physics was
determined by the extent to which mathematics was involved, conceptual
unity was lacking, the range over which theory could extend was very
limited, and there was doubt as to the boundaries of the subject.[18]

Fourier's *Analytical Theory of Heat* (1822) illustrates the last points. It was
a work characterised by elegant mathematics, clear argument and complete
self-confidence. Fourier clarified the concepts of specific heat capacity and

---

*According to Whewell the word 'scientist' was suggested at an early meeting of the British
Association. It was proposed on the analogy of 'artist' but it did not find immediate favour.

conductivity, introduced the idea of boundary conditions and, with his powerful mathematics, was able to claim that he had completed the science of heat. 'Tell me', he said in effect, 'the thermal properties, state and form of a body and I can predict its thermal state at any time in the future.' Fourier explicitly denied the possibility of a common link between heat and mathematics. He recognised the practical importance of the science of heat, but only under the restricted conditions that the process began and ended with heat; as, for example, in dealing with thermal insulation and the distribution of heat in buildings. He was not interested in the steam-engine, in which heat was applied and by which mechanical work was done. And he was indifferent about the ultimate nature of heat. It was unimportant, he said, whether heat phenomena were caused by caloric or by the rapid motion of the ultimate particles of matter (atoms), an idea that was popular in the later seventeenth century and that had been advocated by Daniel Bernoulli in 1738. Fourier was influential. His book was studied appreciatively, deeply and profitably by an obscure German schoolmaster named Ohm and an equally obscure Irish–Scottish schoolboy named William Thomson.

Despite Fourier's assertion, vitally important contributions to the new science of physics, and particularly to the study of heat, were to come from the work of the mechanical engineers. Galilean mechanics had provided engineers with a quantitative means of measuring and comparing the work done by prime movers. The 'effect' (*effet*), or work done by an engine, could be measured by the weight it raised to a given height. The available, or potential 'effort' (*effort*) could, in turn, be measured by a weight falling from a given height (in the case of a water-wheel, for example, the effort was measured by the head of water from the dam or mill-pond multiplied by the weight of water falling). The ratio of these two was the efficiency of the engine.[19] These engineer's measures were evidently consistent with Leibniz's measure of *vis viva*, or the 'living force' of a moving body. The *vis viva*, proportional to the mass of the body and the square of its velocity, measured its capacity to overcome resistance; for example, the height to which it could rise against gravity. In 1811 the French engineer J. N. P. Hachette suggested that the engineer's measures could be used outside the realms of industrial mechanics and applied, for example, to meteorology, a branch of general physics.

The most fruitful instance of the application of these measures was in Sadi Carnot's highly original *Reflexions on the Motive Power of Fire* (1824)[20] a work that was widely different in assumptions, scope and style from Fourier's near-contemporary *Analytical Theory*. Sadi Carnot set out to do for heat engines, such as the common steam-engine, what the hydraulic engineers and mathematicians had done for water power. That is, to establish the circumstances under which the flow of heat from a hot body, such as a furnace, to a cold body, such as a condenser, can be made to do the maximum possible work. His argument was basically simple. He compared the action of caloric in driving a heat engine to the action of water in driving an hydraulic engine such as a water-wheel. Engineers had proved that in order to get the most work out of a stream the driving agent, the water, must enter the engine without wasting any *vis viva* in shock or turbulence and must leave without appreciable speed. All the *vis viva* would then be given up to the engine. Working like this, the engine would be the most efficient possible, for it could be made to drive a perfect pump that could restore all the water to the dam or mill-pond from which it had been drawn. A more efficient engine was impossible, for such a machine would enable more water to be pumped back than was required to drive it and this would imply 'perpetual motion', for the excess water could be used to drive a second engine that could work indefinitely without any depletion of external resources. Applying an analogous argument to heat engines Carnot showed how, for maximum efficiency, the steam – or whatever 'working substance' was used – should be at the same temperature as the furnace (about 1,000°C) when it began to press on the piston and should, by expanding in the cylinder as it drove the piston down, fall to the same temperature as the condenser (about 15°C). Even to approximate to such ideal conditions was far beyond the capacities of contemporary engineering. Largely for this reason Carnot's book was ignored by most of his contemporaries. This was regrettable, for his association of heat with work enabled him to make potentially fruitful contributions to the scientific study of heat. And in much later years, his principles were to guide the development of heat engines. Fortunately his ideas were rediscovered after his death by Emile Clapeyron and, through Clapeyron, came to make a deep impression on William Thomson, by that time a young professor with a brilliant university record as an undergraduate at Cambridge and an even more brilliant academic career in front of him.

Eight years before Carnot published his book a Scottish clergyman, the Revd James Stirling, invented a hot-air engine that, in effect, worked on Carnot's principles.[21] Remarkable as this was, any theoretical study of the heat engine was inhibited in Britain by a strong prejudice on the part of mathematicians and natural philosophers. *Vis viva* did not have the approval of Sir Isaac Newton. Moreover, it was advocated by foreigners, so it was doubly unacceptable. On the other hand the Newtonian concept of central forces was of no use in calculating the work, or effect, that an engine could do. The engineers, therefore, went their own way, measuring work in foot.pounds and power in foot.pounds per minute. In 1783 James Watt standardised the unit of horse power by proposing that 33,000 foot.pounds of work done in one minute equalled one horse power (this is still the international unit of horse power). Besides work and power, engineers made use of one other indispensable measure, that of 'duty'. This was the amount of work that an engine could do for the consumption of a certain amount of fuel, usually a bushel, or sackful, of coal (between 90 and 110 lb).

James Watt's engine yielded more than twice the duty of the previous best 'atmospheric' steam-engine and so was conspicuously successful. By the beginning of the nineteenth century the steam-engine was so important that the gap, in Britain, between the engineer's measures, on the one hand, and the natural philosopher's concepts on the other, was increasingly unacceptable. In 1813 Peter Ewart,[22] an engineer trained under James Watt, published in the *Manchester Memoirs* a long paper,[23] urging the natural philosphers to accept the concepts of work and of *vis viva*. A feature of this paper was a statement of the axiom of the equivalence of heat and work.[24] If we could get rid of all the imperfections in our steam-engines we should find that a certain amount of heat always yielded a fixed equivalent of work. This was not a statement that heat could be *converted* into work – like Dalton, Ewart accepted the caloric doctrine – but it was a step in that direction. Watt thoroughly approved of Ewart's paper, as did Dalton, who had assisted him in writing it,[25] and who dedicated the second volume of the *New System* to John Sharpe and Peter Ewart, jointly. Ewart had been Vice-President of the Lit & Phil for many years during which Dalton had been President. Friendship as well as admiration for the paper of 1813 were the reasons Dalton gave for the dedication. It is therefore reasonable to believe that it was through John Dalton that Joule learned of, and accepted, Ewart's arguments.

If Fourier and Carnot – with, *a fortiori*, Ewart – represented two diametrically-opposed approaches to the scientific study of heat, the study of electricity progressed in a far more coherent manner. When Volta introduced his galvanic cell at the beginning of the century it was realised, almost at once, that 'galvanic electricity', or the continuous production of electricity by chemical means, opened up wide prospects of new discoveries in chemistry and electricity. In 1820 H. C. Oersted found that if a wire with electricity from a battery (it would be premature to talk of a current) was placed over a magnetic compass the needle was deflected. This was an astonishing discovery. Newtonian science and human experience knew only of central forces of attraction (e.g. gravity) and repulsion (e.g. like magnetic poles). Here was an agent that acted through space to *deflect* things. Oersted's discovery was quickly exploited, particularly in France, where Biot, Savart, Arago and Ampère laid the foundations for the development of the new branch of science. Arago showed how a coil of wire, wound in the form of a long cylinder, or solenoid, and carrying electricity from a voltaic cell, could magnetise a steel needle placed inside it. This was part of an attempt to discover whether magnetism was caused by galvanic electricity.

The discovery that galvanic electricity can be made to induce magnetism was taken up by an obscure and now almost completely forgotten Englishman, William Sturgeon. In 1823 he showed that if soft iron was substituted for steel a very powerful attractive force could be obtained. Moreover, the attraction varied, apparently without delay, as the electricity was varied; indeed the polarity could be reversed, again without appreciably delay, if the connections to the cell, or cells, were reversed. He had, in short, invented the electromagnet on which all electrotechnology depends. Sturgeon was born in Kirkby Lonsdale, in north Lancashire, the son of a shoemaker. Hē joined the Royal Artillery, in which regiment he served for twenty-three years in the rank of gunner. During his time with the colours he educated himself and on his discharge, with an exemplary character, joined a small group of instrument-makers and experimentalists at Woolwich. This led to his appointment as Lecturer in Experimental Philosophy at the East India Company's Military Academy at Addiscombe, in Surrey. It was during this period that he invented the electromagnet for which the Society of Arts* awarded him a silver medal and an honorarium of thirty guineas. Sturgeon always retained a strong affection for the army and, in particular, for the regiment in which, as he said, he had had the honour to serve.

If, however, one name personifies the history of electricity during the nineteenth century it is that of Michael Faraday. Self-educated, like Sturgeon, although with the advantage of a research training under Humphry Davy, he was an inspired experimentalist, a hard-working, dedicated man of science and, clearly, a superb lecturer. He was properly devout, in an eccentric but acceptable way, and, to judge by the number of photographs and portraits, a handsome man. From his position at the Royal Institution he could command physical science in London and strongly influence it elsewhere.[26] If he had a weakness it may be that he had a tendency to keep others at a distance. Unlike Dalton he had no distinguished pupils; he did not accept young men as trainees to take his place when he retired and he seems to have been reluctant to act as a referee or to

*The full title was 'The Society for the Encouragement of Arts, Commerce and Manufactures'. It is now the Royal Society of Arts.

give testimonials. Possibly this was a result of his idiosyncratic religious faith; equally, however, the Sandemanian creed may have appealed to someone of his temperament. More plausibly it could have been no more than a result of the organisation of the Royal Institution, which was a place where the professors carried out research and where lectures were given to large, appreciative and fashionable audiences. The Manchester Lit & Phil was different. Men met at the Society's House to hear and discuss the papers that were read. Not until the end of the nineteenth century did the Lit & Phil contemplate providing lectures.

In 1831 Faraday published his discovery of electromagnetic induction and thereby laid the foundations of field theory, a doctrine that was radically anti-Newtonian although its subversiveness was not generally recognised at the time. It also made possible the invention of the magneto-electric engine. In 1835 he announced his laws of electrolysis, which were hardly less important. The passage of a given amount of electricity through electrolytes deposits weights of elements in proportion to their chemical equivalents. Faraday did not have a quantitative mind and this was one of the few quantitative laws that he established.

The magneto-electric engine, or magneto for short, was invented by Hippolyte Pixii in 1831, immediately after the announcement of Faraday's discovery. It originally consisted of a small horseshoe magnet spinning rapidly on its axis of symmetry with a fixed coil of wire between its poles. The electromagnetic engine, or electric motor, was invented in 1830 by the Italian priest Salvatore dal Negro. It was a simple oscillating electromagnetic pendulum, of little more than academic interest. But other inventors in Europe and America quickly realised the possibilities and, by 1832, the rotative electric motor had been invented. This required the additional invention of the commutator, of which Pixii, Sturgeon and several others were independent inventors.

In 1835 M. H. Jacobi, a German professor at the Imperial University of Dorpat, in Russia, published a paper that aroused widespread interest.[27] His thesis was simple. An electric motor consists of a rotating electromagnet (the armature) with two fixed electromagnets disposed around it. The electric current – the word can now be used* – in the rotating and the fixed electromagnets is such that the poles of the armature are attracted to the nearest poles of the fixed electromagnets. but as the poles of the armature

---

*There was considerable doubt for a long time as to the existence of a flow, or current, of electricity in a circuit (or arc, as it was sometimes called) that included a voltaic cell. All the observed effects may have been due, it was suggested, to static electricity. Even Faraday was doubtful about this.

come into line with, or begin to pass, the poles of the fixed electromagnets, the commutator reverses the direction of one of the energising currents so that attraction is replaced by repulsion. In this way the poles of the armature are attracted to, and then pushed away from, the nearest poles of the fixed electromagnets. The armature is thereby accelerated and next time round it will be accelerated again. The process is cumulative and there would seem to be no limit; in the end the armature should be spinning round with infinite velocity. Of course, Jacobi observed, this could only be true in an ideal world. In the real world the friction of the bearings and air resistance would prevent an infinite velocity being reached. But these can be reduced to small proportions so that an enormously great velocity would be possible if two further conditions could be satisfied. Firstly, that the electromagnets respond practically instantaneously to changes in current. Fortunately the experimental evidence was encouraging on this point. And, secondly, that which is now called the back emf be eliminated; for, as the armature revolves, the changing magnetism must, following Faraday's discovery of 1831, induce a counter electromotive force in the motor that will oppose the energising current. The faster the armature spins, the greater the counter electromotive force so that, before long, a balance will be reached and the motor will settle down at a constant speed, far below the infinite. But Jacobi was hopeful that this little difficulty could be eliminated by careful design.

Jacobi's paper was translated into the major European languages and its promise was immediately appreciated. A near-infinite velocity suggested a near-infinite power. With the newly-invented motor the world was, surely, within sight of a power of enormous, immeasurable capacity. Engineers knew, well enough, what power they could get from a stream or river, from the wind or from a sack of coal; but what power was locked up in the voltaic cell to which the new electric motor was the key? And there were other advantages, not so exciting but still very substantial. Since Watt's time engineers had tried without success to develop a directly rotative steam-engine.[28] The electric motor was a directly rotative engine; its construction presented no great problems; it was virtually silent in operation, required no bulky components such as boilers, needed no great heaps of coal and, a notable advantage, was completely clean: no nasty smoke, no ashes and grime.

The authority and the prestige of Michael Faraday had placed electricity at the centre of scientific interest; Jacobi's paper had shown that it promised, thanks to the new electric motor, to provide a virtually limitless source of power, one that was clean, convenient and safe. The old dream of a perpetual motion machine was on the point of being transcended by rational, nineteenth-century science. No wonder a veritable electrical euphoria swept Europe and the United States.[29] Monarchs and ministers readily found money for enthusiastic inventors. Motors were made to drive all sorts of machinery, pumps, boats on rivers and lakes; and then, in 1841, a battery-driven electric locomotive ran on a standard-gauge railway line.* As part of the electrical euphoria societies, such as the London Electrical Society, were formed to further the study of electricity. And in 1836 the first journal to concern itself primarily with electricity appeared, the *Annals of Electricity and Guardian of Chemistry and Experimental Science*. The founder and editor was William Sturgeon, by this time Superintendent of the Royal Gallery of Practical Science, an institution concerned with instructive exhibits and displays for young people and located in Adelaide Street, London. Other journals were started up, such as the *Transactions of the London Electrical Society*, and the *Archives d'Electricité*. The *Annals* was a particularly interesting journal. Its ten volumes, from 1836 to 1843, covered the high point of the electrical euphoria. Apart from original papers, it reprinted major articles from other journals and gave summary accounts of relatively minor developments, some of which were to prove fruitful later on. Joule's first scientific works were printed in the *Annals*.

Among those keenly interested in electricity and contributing to the *Annals* at that time was Father Nicholas Callan, Professor of Natural Philosophy at Maynooth College. Optimistic, like many others, about the future prospects for electric power, Callan built a number of large motors and batteries. He was certainly one of the first, and probably the first, to notice that an electromagnet could be saturated, a discovery that could only have been made by someone who had compared the variation of magnetic attraction with the strength of the energising current. And Callan invented an ingenious device by means of which the current in an electromagnet was interrupted 3,600 times a minute. By putting a coil with many turns of wire round the electromagnet it was possible to get powerful electric shocks.[30] Callan's machine was improved by G. H. Bachhoffner, Lecturer in Chemistry to the Artists' Society. Bachoffner found that if he substituted a bundle of insulated iron wires for the solid bar of iron in the electromagnet the power of the device was doubled.[31] In this way the practice of lamination was introduced into electrotechnology. Father Callan's machine was further improved by Golding Bird, who substituted a magnetic relay for Callan's mechanical interrupter. This represented the perfection of the

---

*The locomotive, due to Robert Davidson, ran for a mile and a half at about 4 mph on the newly opened Edinburgh to Glasgow line. The performance was not greatly inferior to the first flight of the Wright brothers, more than sixty years later.

Fig 1 William Sturgeon, 1783–1850, from a portrait in oils, now lost

popular Victorian toy, the shocking coil.

Two articles in the *Annals* of particular relevance to Joule's career were the translation of Jacobi's paper of 1835 and Sturgeon's paper of 1833, 'On the theory of magnetic electricity.'[32] Jacobi's paper was truly seminal as far as Joule was concerned. The concluding words were a challenge to any enterprising young man: 'I think I may assert that the superiority of this new mover is proved beyond a doubt, as regards the absence of all danger, the simplicity of application and the expense attending it.'

Sturgeon, in his 1833 paper, mentioned a theory, promulgated by Biot, that the action of the voltaic cell was rapidly intermittent; a succession of pulses of electricity was sent around the circuit.[33] This was an attempt to reconcile voltaic with 'ordinary', or frictional, electricity. The cell, or battery, worked by discharging electricity just like a Leyden jar but with this difference: the cell produced a continued succession of discharges which gave the effect of a steady current. Sturgeon mentioned this theory again in a review he wrote of a book by the Secretary of the London Electrical Society.[34] No chemical action, he observed, took place without disturbing the 'equilibrium of the electric fluid'. Respiration is a chemical process in which oxygen combines with carbon in the lungs and produces the bodily heat which is pumped out with the blood from the heart. This was Adair Crawford's theory of animal heat, which was commended by Dalton. Sturgeon modified the theory by adding electricity to the heat generated in the heart–lung system. This hypothetical electricity, it was argued, might increase bodily heat and have other physiological effects. But this was speculation. What, in essence, Sturgeon was proposing was that a voltaic cell, or battery, worked like a pump, analogous to the heart, and that the electricity generated by chemical action in the cell was pumped out, just as blood was pumped out by the heart, taking with it the heat generated by chemical action in the lungs.

The later volumes of the *Annals* are progressively less interesting. Sturgeon was hard-pressed for copy and resorted to reprinting eighteenth-century classics of electricity, in particular the papers of Franklin and Cavendish. It was not enough to keep the journal going and in 1843 it ceased publication. It may be that the peak of the electrical euphoria had already passed; extremely cheap and convenient power was not just around the corner. In any case Sturgeon had taken on a new commitment, with other problems and worries. He had left London and the Royal Gallery of Practical Science to return north, this time to Manchester where he had been appointed Superintendent of the Royal Victoria Gallery for the Encouragement and Illustration of Practical Science.

This grandiloquently named institution was established following a meeting held at the York Hotel in Manchester in 1839. The chairman of the meeting was Hugh Hornby Birley and among the prime movers were the engineers William Fairbairn, Eaton Hodgkinson and Richard Roberts. John Davies, Joule's tutor and a Vice-President of the Mechanics' Institution, was another member of the group.[35] What was proposed was a straightforward imitation of the Royal Gallery in London. The aims were to illustrate the progress made in industry and practical science, to present experimental demonstrations and, in particular, to arouse the interest of young people. Manchester, in short, was to have a science museum.[36] Shares to the value of £12,000 were offered and, on 25 February 1840, the Royal Victoria Gallery opened in the Exchange Ante-Room and Dining Room, adjoining St Ann's Square. A large electrical machine and an electromagnet were obtained, as well as smaller apparatus, and Mr Sturgeon was advertised to give a series of lectures on electricity and magnetism. Conversaziones were organised during which a speaker delivered a lecture to be followed by a discussion. Lecturers included Joule, Lyon Playfair and Joseph Whitworth. Joule had reason to be grateful to the Gallery as well as to the *Annals*; the former for giving him a platform for the first of the few public lectures he was to give, the latter for giving him a prize (1841) for his scientific communications: his first public recognition.[37]

Unfortunately the Gallery soon failed and Sturgeon, although he struggled on for a time with the equally unsuccessful Manchester Institute of Natural and Experimental Science, had to earn a precarious living as a freelance lecturer. The Gallery, it seemed, failed for several reasons. The early 1840s were troubled years; the newspapers reported the arrests of Chartists, accused of plotting, or secret drilling, or just skulking. The Gallery was, to some extent, in competition with the older, bigger, better endowed Mechanics' Institution and the Manchester Royal Institution. And Sturgeon, admirable as he was in so many ways, combined a rather touchy, even abrasive, manner with an unfortunate lack of tact, or to put it lower, awareness of self-interest. These were the weaknesses of a man who having educated himself, had had a hard struggle to make his way in the world. Although he professed the utmost respect for Michael Faraday, who was, by general consent, a truly great man of science, he continually sniped at him from the pages of the *Annals*. And he carried on a long, acrimonious, at times bitter, dispute with Sir William Snow Harris, FRS, who, although almost completely forgotten, was highly regarded in his day. Sturgeon, unlike many less worthy contemporaries, was never made a Fellow of the Royal Society. When his early achievement in educating himself, his brave effort with the *Annals* and, above all, his valuable contributions to knowledge are recalled it seems that there was a certain lack of magnanimity among his contemporaries.

3

First researches

Mature institutions tend to be conservative. Customarily they resist change and reject new ideas from outside, even though valuable, sometimes vital, innovations are often made by outsiders who bring fresh insights to bear on old problems or discover new and unsuspected opportunities. This is the case in the worlds of science, engineering and technology as it is in other social activities. In the development of the heat engine the decisive innovations of James Watt, Sadi Carnot and Nicolaus Otto were due to men who were, at least when they made their major contributions, outside the world of the engine designer and builder.

It is not surprising, therefore, that engineers concerned with steam-engines showed little interest in the electrical euphoria. In this they were justified for, year by year, the steam-engine became more powerful, more economical and more versatile. The perfection of the electric motor was left to the marginal men of technology; to educated amateurs who might be physicians or surgeons, clergymen, lawyers or teachers, bankers or businessmen. Their ideas and methods were, accordingly, anything but uniform.

Young Joule was a businessman. He was later to record that once his tutelage was over he used to attend at the brewery every day, from nine in the morning until six in the evening.[1] This, by Manchester standards, was a far from excessive burden and Osborne Reynolds was later to assert that Joule had little connection with the business.[2] But, while he carried out some of his researches at the brewery (he acknowledged as much in various papers), his correspondence indicates clearly that he was actively engaged in running the business until it was finally sold. On the other hand his brothers showed little interest in brewing. They apparently wanted little to do with a trade that, although worthy, can hardly have enjoyed the same prestige as the great merchant and manufacturing enterprises of the district. The Joules were well thought of in Manchester,[3] and they were undoubtedly affluent; 'Broom Hill' found work for six live-in servants.[4] The touchstone of comfortable circumstances was the conversion of the brothers, one after the other, to the Church of England, a sure indication of respectability and sound income.[5] Benjamin, the musician, was to become closely associated with St Peter's Church, paying for the organ, training the choir and composing hymns and chants.* John, who was often in poor health, was to settle down to the life of a gentleman of leisure.

From a financially and emotionally secure background, Joule, at just nineteen, began his first publication – a letter to Sturgeon's *Annals* – in confident style: 'I am now making an electro-magnetic engine . . .'. He had, he claimed, made a notable improvement in his electromagnets, which were U-shaped, like tuning forks.[6] The stator consisted of twenty identical electromagnets arranged in a ring with their poles fixed close together. Directly opposite these the rotor consisted of another twenty electromagnets, similarly arranged but free to revolve. A commutator, much approved of by Sturgeon, ensured that polarities changed to keep the engine in motion. Mr Joule, wrote Sturgeon, intended to apply the engine to drive locomotives and boats.[7]

Joule interrupted his work on electric motors to send a short letter to the *Annals* on the subject of lightning. He was less confident about this for he wrote anonymously, signing the letter 'P'. Lightning, he noted, commonly appeared to flicker and this, he suggested, was because two distinct flashes, about a quarter of a second apart, took place in the channel. He offered no explanation for this, leaving it to the consideration of the 'more scientific' readers of the *Annals*.[8] The explanation given by Michael Faraday three years later was unsatisfactory.[9] What, in the light of modern knowledge, is more difficult to explain is how Joule could have recognised so accurately the compound nature of the lightning flash long before it could have been established by photography. Can it be that some men of science possess exceptional accuracy of perception? In any case, this remarkable observation was an instance of that strong interest in all natural phenomena that he had manifested before and was to show through the rest of his life. He did not restrict his scientific curiosity to his laboratory or workshop.

Contrary to his hopes, his first electric motor was not a success. Driven by a batter of forty-eight Wollaston cells, it could barely do more than overcome its own friction. The close arrangement of many electromagnets brought no advantage. But probably the main limitation on speed was the slowness with which the iron cores of the electromagnets responded to the

---

*St Peter's Church was demolished at the beginning of the present century. It stood on a site now part of St Peter's Square.

magnetising currents.[10] This could, perhaps, be overcome by substituting a bundle of insulated iron wires, as recommended by Bachhoffner, for the solid iron core. To test this Joule made a small motor consisting of a fixed permanent magnet with a single electromagnet as armature. Four different electromagnets were tried. The results were inconclusive.

Most men, trying to perfect a promising invention, would be secretive about their actual achievement while emphatic about their success. Joule was frank about the progress of his work. Indeed, his next four papers give a good idea of his research procedure.[11] He observed that the magnetism was greatly increased by the 'completion of the ferruginous circuit' and he specified the rules to be followed in making a powerful electromagnet. But further progress required more systematic knowledge of the relationship between the energising current and the power of the electromagnet. He therefore made and calibrated his own galvanometer, standardising it by measuring the volumes of gases (oxygen and hydrogen) evolved when a measured current was passed through dilute sulphuric acid (specified) for seven minutes. His experiments showed that M, the magnetic attraction at a fixed distance (1/8 in) between two electromagnets, was proportional to the square of the electric current and the square of the total length of wire, W. Or, as he expressed it, untypically and inaccurately, $M = E^2 W^2$. It was untypical in that it was customary to express experimental laws in terms of proportions, not equalities; it was inexact in that the equation was dimensionally inhomogeneous. This was probably a young man's error, but not a slip, for he repeated it later. In fact, the expression of an electric current in terms of mass, length and time lay some twenty-five years in the future. Joule remarked that his law did not hold when the electromagnet was saturated. And he relied on this remark a dozen years later to support his claim to have discovered magnetic saturation.[12] But P. M. Roget had already identified the saturation of permanent magnets and Father Callan that of electromagnets.[13] He should have known about this. He could hardly have known that Lenz and Jacobi had published their discovery of the law of electromagnetic attraction two months before him.[14] However, these are quibbles; what was significant was that Joule, at the outset of his scientific career, was so clearly a disciple of Dalton in his use of mathematics. Unlike Faraday, who was suspicious of mathematics, Joule sought to reduce his discoveries to quantitative, or mathematical laws of nature. And the particular law he had discovered encouraged his hopes for electric power:

> I can hardly doubt that electro-magnetism will ultimately be substituted for steam to propel machinery. If the power of the engine is in proportion to the attractive force of the magnets, and this attraction is as the square of the electric

force, the economy will be in the direct ratio of the quantity of electricity, and the cost of working the engine may be reduced *ad infinitum*.[15]

His reasoning was straightforward. The 'economy', or duty, of the engine was the work done divided by the amount of fuel consumed in the same time; coal in the case of a steam-engine, zinc in the case of an electro magnetic engine. Faraday had shown that the amount of zinc consumed in a battery was proportional to the electricity generated. Therefore, the economy of the engine was proportional to the work done divided by the quantity of electricity, or, simply, to the quantity of electricity. The greater the current, therefore, the greater the duty. He added, cautiously, that it remained to be seen whether this sanguine expectation would be realised.

Perhaps he knew of the great hopes that had been aroused when high-pressure steam-engines had been introduced at the beginning of the century. The pressure of steam increases much more rapidly than the temperature and this had led to the hope that the duty of high-pressure steam-engines could be improved indefinitely. A small amount of fuel could generate an enormous pressure of steam and therefore, it was suggested, do an immense amount of work. But these hopes had been disappointed.[16]

His third and last engine was a simple affair. It had an armature of two moving electromagnets, 36 inches long, 3 inches broad and half an inch thick. There were two stationary electromagnets, slightly longer and bent over at each end to bring their poles as close as possible to the moving poles. One of the revolving electromagnets was made of rectangular wire and the other of solid bar iron, the pair being set to rotate horizontally. In the short paper he published in the *Annals* he wrote that he had 'been much pleased with its performance'.[17]

With this motor he carried out seven series of experiments, setting out the results in tables showing how the motor performed when driven by different numbers of voltaic cells and therefore with different 'battery intensities' (voltages) and currents. In each case he began with a load that stopped the motor. He recorded the current that flowed and then reduced the load until the armature rotated with a velocity of 2 feet per second; again he noted the current and, this time, the power and the duty. He repeated this procedure for speeds of 4, 6, 8 and 10 feet per second. As an additional variation he ran the motor series wound in the first four experiments and shunt wound in the last three.[18] The paper in which he described these experiments was of particular interest as much for what he did not say as for the conclusions he drew. Remarkably, in each of the seven series of experiments, as the speed of the motor increased, the current fell as expected but, at the same time, *the power and the duty increased.* This refuted his prediction, made nine months before, that the duty should increase with the current. Plainly, it increased as the current fell. He did not mention, still less rejoice at, this falsification of his inference but went on to say that the fall in current '. . . shows pretty clearly the effects of magnetic electrical resistance [i.e. back emf]. This resistance is the prime obstacle to the perfection of the electro-magnetic engine; and in proportion as it is overcome will the motive force increase. It therefore claims our first attention.'

The claim, however, was not met and the reader is left without any indication of what Joule intended, beyond the assertion that the back emf was proportional to the current multiplied by the velocity, which the experiments approximately confirmed. He conceded that increasing the intensity of the battery by adding further cells did not improve the economy, whatever changes were made to the circuit. His results showed that the power of the engine was proportional to the product of the current and the emf, or battery intensity. This was the first of the two electrical energy laws that he was to discover; but he made no specific claim to originality. The law implied that if, for example, the emf was doubled by doubling the number of cells twice the current would flow and four times as much work would be done. However, four times as much zinc would be consumed in the same time so that the duty would remain the same; no economy would have been made.

It must puzzle the reader why he did not report the performance of the engine at speeds greater than 10 feet per second. Had he done so he would have revealed that at speeds greater than that which reduced the driving current to half its maximum value (when the motor could not move) the power began to fall and that as the speed increased further and the current fell towards zero so did the power; but the duty – paradox of paradoxes! – went on increasing to its maximum. It seems that he did extend his investigations beyond the speed of 10 feet per second and that he had a good idea of the performance of the engine at higher speeds. He would have been reluctant to publish his results as he would not, at that time, have been sure how to interpret them. Plausibility is lent to this speculation by his claim, made thirty years later, that when he wrote his paper he was 'in possession of' the theory of the electric motor. But it is evident that his thoughts were not yet clear. In spite of the fact that the duty, or economy, was the all-important measure, he still quoted the received wisdom concerning the desirability of eliminating the back emf.

In his next paper, of August 1840, he switched his attention from the attractive power of electromagnets to their retaining, or lifting power.[19] He began, however, by criticising the absence of any universally agreed standard or measure of quantity of electricity. He therefore proposed a unit based on Faraday's law of electrolysis and advocated, although not used, by Faraday himself. A degree of static electricity was that quantity that would decompose nine grains, or the chemical equivalent, of water while a degree of electric current was one unit of electricity flowing in one hour. Having defined his units he reported the results of experiments to determine the lifting, or adhesive, power of four different electromagnets under different conditions. He laid down the principle that the maximum power of an electromagnet varied directly as the least transverse sectional area. He had already pointed out that for a good lifting magnet the iron should be well annealed, the bulk large compared with the length, the poles ground true and the armature of the same thickness as the magnet. These observations, together with references to magnetic resistance, the 'ferruginous circuit', and even to 'the magnetic circuit', have led commentators to believe that Joule had arrived at the modern concept of the magnetic circuit. But this is most improbable. He never referred to the number of turns of wire on the electromagnet, restricting himself to the *length* of wire.[20] As Tyndall later pointed out (see below, pp. 164, and note 26), with magnets of different areas of cross-section the same length of wire would result in different numbers of turns. Joule, at this stage, was substantially concerned with practical matters, not with abstract science. His researches had enabled him to design and make a number of powerful electromagnets and two of these were for 'a long time' on display at the Royal Victoria Gallery. Stimulated by Joule's success, Richard Roberts manufactured the most powerful electromagnet in the world, the original of the industrial electromagnets to be seen in every scrap-metal yard.[21]

Joule spent no time pondering the nature of electricity, or indeed on any other speculation. His procedure was that of the engineer, rather than the man of science. It recalls that of John Smeaton, the eighteenth-century engineer, who, for the construction of the Eddystone lighthouse, required a cement that would set under water. The technique of parameter variation that he used meant keeping all the components save one constant and noting the effects when that one component was varied systematically. This procedure, repeated for the other components, gave Smeaton an effective hydraulic cement. He did not need to investigate the complex chemistry of cement to achieve his end. The same procedure was used by Joule in his work on the electromagnet and the electric motor. It was used, too, by Joule's contemporaries, Eaton Hodgkinson and William Fairbairn, when they were seeking the optimum structure for the Britannia Tubular Bridge over the Menai Straits; probably the most revolutionary advance in structural engineering in the nineteenth century.[22]

It is a pity that when Joule came to revise his papers for publication in the collected *Scientific Papers* (1884), he omitted the final paragraph of his paper 'On electro-magnetic forces'. He admitted, in the 1884 preface, that he had amended some early papers in order to clarify certain obsolete expressions. But there was nothing obsolete or obscure about the last paragraph:

> I must apologise to the reader for I have not relieved the tediousness of this paper by a single brilliant illustration. I have neither propelled vessels, carriages, nor printing presses. My object has been, first to discover correct principles and then to suggest their practical development. If I have succeeded in some measure in the first part of that object, my design has been fully realised.

This tells us something about Joule himself and about the style and content of the papers published by his contemporaries. It also tells us that by 1884 science had become a much more serious affair.

One of the variables associated with a working electromagnetic engine is the appearance of heat. In all machines the appearance of heat due to friction had been recognised for many years as indicating wasted power; hence the long-established practice of using lubricants to reduce friction. The electrical heating of motors and associated circuits might well indicate another source of waste. Procedure dictated that this should be investigated even though the connection between this heat and a waste of power was obscure. If the battery and circuit were used to generate heat only, and no work was done, zinc would still be consumed in the battery and that would certainly be wasteful.

At the end of 1840 Joule sent a short paper to the Royal Society. It was rejected for the *Transactions* but a short abstract of it appeared in the *Proceedings* for December 1840. In it he stated that if an electric current is passed through a coil of wire the heat generated is proportional to the square of the current and the resistance of the wire. He claimed that the law held whatever the shape, size or form of the circuit or the type of wire used (J. F. Daniell had said that the heat due to an electric current depended on the kind of metal of which the wire was made). The abstract ended with the cryptic remark that the heat of combustion of zinc in oxygen was 'likewise the consequence of resistance to electric conduction'. This final remark suggests that in addition to concern for practical improvement another motive was present: scientific curiosity.

The late discovery of this law, forty years after Volta announced the invention of the cell, or battery, is partly accounted for by the fact that Ohm's law had only recently become known in Britain and, indeed, generally in Europe; and partly because there was still some confusion about the distinction between an electric charge and an electric current.[23] But whatever the reasons for the delay, the discovery of this, the second of Joule's laws of electrical energy, must have discouraged hopes of cheap electric power. No one knew of, or expected to discover, superconductors. The heating of a circuit was, therefore, unavoidable and clearly implied a waste of zinc in the battery. Two months later Joule gave the first of the few public lectures he was to deliver in the course of his career. It was given at one of the Royal Victoria Gallery's conversaziones on 16 February 1841.[24] After a short resumé of the history of the electric motor, mentioning particularly Professor Henry and Mr Sturgeon, he went on:

> At that period the expectations that electro-magnetism would ultimately super-sede steam, as a motive force, were very sanguine. There seemed to be nothing to prevent an enormous velocity of rotation, and consequently an enormous power, except the resistance of the air . . . the resistance of iron to the induction of magnetism . . . and the inertia of the electric fluid.

He continued:

> We are indebted to Professor Jacobi for the exposition of the principal obstacle to the perfection of the electro-magnetic engine. He has shown that the electric action produced by the motion of the bars operates against the battery current and in this way reduces the magnetism of the bars until, at a certain velocity, the forces of attraction become equivalent to the load on the axle, and the motion in consequence ceases to be accelerated.

At this point members of the audience may have reflected on the apparent similarity between the electric motor and the steam-engine. De Pambour had shown, by theory and by experiments on the Liverpool and Manchester Railway, that when a locomotive ran at a uniform speed, the resistance that it overcame was exactly equal to the force of steam in the cylinders.[25] If circumstances changed – the steam pressure varied or the gradient of the line altered – the speed of the locomotive changed until the resistance and the force of steam were equal again. The hydraulic engineers had known, ever since 1704, that the same principle governed the working of a water-wheel.[26] But an electric motor was supposed to be different in that, according to accepted scientific ideas, the attractive force of an electromagnet was independent of the speed with which it moved relative to another body, or magnet. Joule knew that the only inferences he could draw from his experiments refuted the possibility of almost indefinitely cheap power from a battery and a well-designed electric motor. But he felt, evidently, that he could not directly challenge Jacobi's assertion.

He presented his objection in a way that no abstraction, no theory, could refute:

With my apparatus every pound of zinc consumed in a Grove's battery produced a mechanical force (friction included) equal to raise a weight of 331,400 lbs to the height of one foot, when the revolving magnets were moving at the velocity of 8 feet per second.

Now the duty of the best Cornish steam-engine* is about 1,500,000 lbs raised to the height of one foot by the combustion of a pound of coal which is about five times the extreme duty that I was able to obtain from my electro-magnetic engine by the consumption of a pound of zinc. The comparison is so very unfavourable that I confess I almost despair of the success of electro-magnetic attractions as an economical source of power; for although my engine is by no means perfect, I do not see how the arrangement of its parts could be improved so far as to make the duty per lb of zinc superior to the duty of the best steam-engine per pound of coal. And even if this were attained, the expense of the zinc and the exciting fluids of the battery is so great as to prevent the ordinary electro-magnetic engine from being useful for any but very peculiar purposes.

The duty, or economy, was the deciding factor. As the price of zinc was said to be between sixty to seventy times that of the same weight of coal, the engine would have had to have been improved by between 300 and 350 times to compete with the best Cornish steam-engine. This must have come as a cold douche for poor Sturgeon since the great hope of cheap electric power was one of the main reasons for the electrical euphoria and hence for the continuation of the *Annals*. Perhaps it also explains why there was a delay of more than a year before the paper was published in the *Annals*; and perhaps this was why there was no subsequent discussion, as was customary following conversazione lectures. What was a hard-headed Manchester audience to make of it now? Manchester science, as Jacobi's brother had reported, must be useful. But what use could mill and foundry owners, the proprietors of engineering workshops and countless other industrial establishments have for something that was useful 'only for very peculiar purposes'? The very words suggest something sinister, if not improper and, what was worse, unprofitable. The paper may, unintentionally, have speeded the end of the Royal Victoria Gallery, for soon afterwards it failed. But whatever influence Joule's paper had on the fortunes of the Gallery, Sturgeon had the highest respect for his scientific abilities. At the end of 1841 he wrote to Joule to present a bound volume of the *Annals* in recognition of his 'valuable scientific labours'.[27]

There was one other possible form of electric motor to be considered. Mr Arstall, 'an ingenious gentleman of this town',[28] had suggested that, as a bar of iron increases in length on magnetisation, the increment could, by

---

*The reference was to the famous Fowey Consols engine (Austin's engine) that, under test conditions, achieved a duty of 125 million foot.pounds per bushel (say, 90 lb) of coal.

suitable gearing and linkage, be applied to drive machinery. Joule therefore tested this proposal thoroughly. He found that the increase in length was independent of the thickness of the bar but proportional to the length and the induced magnetism.* Unfortunately, although the increment in length was almost instantaneous, like a hammer blow at the other end when the current was switched on, it was also extremely small; so small that 'an easy calculation on the basis of the modulus of elasticity of iron' showed that such an engine would be very feeble. It would be much less efficient than an ordinary electric motor. And here, too, there was a parallel with the steam-engine. Just over twenty years earlier a suggestion had been made that the conventional steam-engine could be replaced by an engine in which the 'irresistible expansion' of heated metal could profitably be substituted for the expansion of water into steam. Plausible as it seemed, the application of the same argument proved that this, too, was a delusion.[29]

There was, however, another aspect of Mr Arstall's suggestion that interested Joule. It was the speculative possibilities that it raised. As Fox has pointed out, Joule was, at this time, beginning to take on the role of natural philosopher.[30] Accordingly, in the second half of the paper he put forward two possible models of iron atoms to account for magnetism and magnetic saturation in the light of the Arstall phenomenon. The first was the Ampère model with an 'atmosphere' of electricity orbiting round a central iron atom in a plane at right angles to the axis of the magnet. He rejected this for it implied a force overcoming a resistance indefinitely, or the continued performance of work without any obvious source, which would be absurd in the case of a permanent magnet. The model could account for saturation on the assumption that the atmospheres tended to expand as the speed or rotation increased until they interfered with each other and could expand no further. But in this case the bar should shorten and not expand. His preferred model had a central iron atom surrounded by an atmosphere of 'magnetism' with an outer atmosphere of electricity, the space between the atoms being filled by a vibrating 'calorific ether'. As the iron was magnetised, so the magnetic atmosphere tended to one side of the atom until it was all on that side, in which case the iron was saturated. This explained everything, apart from the hypothetical properties which the 'Great Creator' had placed utterly beyond our understanding. The ether vibrations constituted heat, and if they were strong enough they destroyed the arrangement of the atmospheres so that the iron became demagnetised. This was consistent with the fact that heat destroys

---

*The phenomenon is now known, rather unfairly, as the 'Joule effect'.

magnetism.

While he speculated on the nature of magnetism, with ideas that looked forward to the dynamical theory of heat and the conservation of energy, and backwards to the eighteenth-century notions of subtle fluids and atmospheres,[31] he continued with his practical work, although it was becoming less prominent. He wrote a short paper on voltaic batteries, but most important of all, he completed his work on the heat generated by an electric current. This work, published in the *Philosphical Magazine*,[32] was far more comprehensive than the brief note in the *Proceedings* that did little more than lodge a claim for priority. This time he gave details of three sets of experiments in which an electric current passed successively through two different coils of copper wire, a coil of copper wire and a coil of iron wire, and lastly, a coil of copper wire and a column of mercury in a glass tube. In the three cases each pair was placed in a separate glass jar full of water and the rises in temperature recorded. He did not need to guard against, or compensate for, heat losses as he was not concerned with absolute quantities of heat; other things being equal, a comparison of the rises in temperature would indicate the proportional heating effects in each of the pair of resistances. In this way he established that the heating effect of a current was proportional to the resistance, 'whatever the length, thickness, shape or kind of metallic conductor'. By varying the current flowing in a copper wire and noting the heating effect in each instance he showed that it varied as the square of the current. He said that he expected this result on the grounds that the resistance 'would be augmented' by the increased quantity of electricity flowing and its increased 'velocity'. The analogy with heat due to mechanical friction cannot have been far from his mind.

Having confirmed the i^2r law for metallic conductors he extended his research to liquid conductors, beginning with the battery itself. This was more difficult. He first measured the heat generated by a given current flowing in a length of copper wire. After this he used Ohm's law to compute the resistance of the battery in terms of the length of copper wire. The heat due to a current flowing through the battery had to be corrected for that lost by the cooling of the battery and for the different specific heat capacities of the battery liquid and its solid components. Finally, he corrected for the heat due to the solution of zinc oxide in sulphuric acid, which, as Faraday had shown, had nothing to do with the current. When he had made these corrections he found that the net heat generated bore exactly the same proportion to the current and the resistance as the heat did in the preliminary experiment with the length of copper wire. The i^2r law therefore applied to liquid as well as to metallic conductors.

His last experiment was to determine whether the law applied to electrolytic cells. This time he had to make an allowance for the 'resistance to
electrolysis' or the opposing emf of an electrolytic cell. Faraday had shown
that a minimum emf was necessary before an electrolyte would pass a
current and decomposition could begin. Joule used a cell containing dilute
sulphuric acid and fitted with two narrow platinum foil electrodes. He
found that 3½ pairs of his 20-pair zinc-iron battery were needed to
overcome the opposing emf before electrolysis could begin. Thereafter,
having found the ohmic resistance to conduction, he verified that the
heating law applied to electrolytes. He had shown that the law was universal, applying to liquid as well as solid conductors, to batteries and to
electrolytes. And he deduced two corollaries. Firstly, that in any battery
circuit, assuming no local action, the heat generated would be proportional
to the number of atoms involved in generating the current. If, for example,
the total resistance is halved the current will be doubled and, according to
the law, the heat will also be doubled; moreover, following Faraday's laws of
electrolysis, the number of atoms involved in the action must also be
doubled. Secondly, he inferred that the heat generated was – like the work
done by a motor – directly proportional to the emf and the number of
atoms, or, more simply, the current. If an electrolytic cell was part of the
circuit then the total heat was proportional to the number of atoms multiplied by the 'virtual intensity', or the emf of the battery less the opposing
emf of the electrolytic cell.

Towards the end of the paper he amplified the cryptic remark in the
abstract in the *Proceedings*: 'Berzelius thinks that the light and heat produced by combustion are occasioned by the discharge of electricity
between the combustible and the oxygen . . . in the act of combination.'

He added that his experiments on the combustion of zinc and oxygen
would confirm this as, he believed, did Adair Crawford's experiments on
the heat generated by the explosion of a mixture of hydrogen and oxygen.[33]
But the reference to Berzelius was no more than a paraphrase of Faraday's
words: 'the beautiful idea, put forth, I believe, by Berzelius . . . that the heat
and light evolved during . . . powerful combination are the consequence of
the electrical discharge . . . taking place. The idea is in perfect accordance
with the view I have taken of the *quantity* of electricity associated with the
particles of matter.'[34] There remained, however, one problem. When he
substituted, in the electrolytic cell, platinum foil electrodes with surface
areas twenty-eight times greater than the narrow ones, the actual heat
generated was consistently greater than the i^2r law predicted.

This was the first major paper that he published on a strictly scientific
theme and in a journal with an international circulation. It confirmed his

priority as the discoverer of the law of electrical heating.[35] Osborne Reynolds, writing in 1892, believed that it was the original paper submitted to and rejected by the Royal Society in the previous year. Sir Arthur Schuster, writing forty years later, showed that it was not.[36] The original paper was much shorter and had been committed to the archives; moreover, it did not deal with conduction through batteries and electrolytic cells. Schuster had certainly discussed the matter with Joule himself. He had asked Joule how it had felt to have one of his papers rejected by the Royal Society. 'I was not surprised,' Joule replied. 'I could imagine those gentlemen in London sitting round a table and saying to each other, "What good can come out of a town where they dine in the middle of the day?".' However, in this case an elderly gentleman, well over sixty, was evidently gently pulling the leg of a much younger man. But some confusion must be ascribed to Joule. The introductory paragraph of the major paper clearly implied that he intended it for the Royal Society: 'I have hoped, therefore, that the results of my careful investigation . . . are of sufficient interest to justify me in laying them before the Royal Society.' And he began his next paper by stating that he had mentioned Berzelius's theory 'In the papers which [I] had some time ago the honour of communicating to the Royal Society'. A plausible explanation is that Joule had submitted both papers to Roget, Secretary of the Royal Society, who had suggested that the short paper be extended to cover conduction through liquids, such as battery fluids and electrolytes. As far as Joule was concerned Roget was the Royal Society.

In that next paper Joule sought to confirm Berzelius's hypothesis.[37] For the first time he addressed the Lit & Phil and he had a distinguished audience; Dalton was present. Again, his approach was systematic, but now he revealed a deeper insight into the physics of voltaic electricity. He accepted the common view that the current from a battery depended on the difference between the affinity of oxygen for the electropositive plate and its affinity for the hydrogen of the water (or dilute acid). When the plates were first dipped in the dilute acid there was a surge of current, as the oxygen coating the electronegative plate momentarily neutralised the second affinity. This peak current indicated the affinity of oxygen for the positive metal. Comparisons between the measurements of the transient, peak currents and the smaller, steady-state currents to which they subsided allowed him to compute the relative affinities of oxygen for hydrogen and for the electropositive elements, zinc, iron and potassium. The numbers were, respectively, 1, 1.93, 1.27 and 4.06.

The study of the converse process of electrolysis necessitated using four electrolytes, water, zinc oxide, ferric oxide and potash (potassium carbonate). Using a battery of ten identical Smee cells* he measured, with his galvanometer, the current through each electrolyte when one, two, three and up to all ten cells were connected. No current passed with the first two or three cells – the opposing emf was too high – but thereafter the current increased steadily. He then plotted 'graphs' of current against number of cells and, by extrapolation, determined the emf, to a fraction of a cell, at which each electrolyte began to pass current. He found that 2.8, 3.7, 3.3 and 5.74 Smee cells were needed to begin the electrolysis of water, zinc oxide, ferric oxide and potash respectively. Taking the electrolysis of water as 1 the numbers reduced to 1, 1.32, 1.18 and 2.05. The sequence followed that for the affinities; the proportions did not. But in electrolysis an additional emf was, he believed, needed to turn oxygen into a gas; in the generation of a current the oxygen was combined first with hydrogen and then with the electropositive metal. He therefore deduced a (not very accurate) number expressing the emf required just to convert oxygen into a gas.[30]

The third and last step was to measure the heat evolved when equivalent weights of hydrogen, zinc, iron and potassium were burned in an atmosphere of oxygen. The experimental determination of these heats was difficult but the results were satisfactory. Expressed as proportions, taking hydrogen as 1, they agreed well with the numbers obtained from electrolysis. He concluded that the quantities of heat evolved when equivalent weights of bodies were burned were proportional to their affinities for oxygen, as determined by electrolysis. He had already shown that the same law governed the generation of heat by the conduction of electricity; it followed that the heat of combustion was of the same nature. But he did not stop here; to complete the proof he compared the absolute quantities of heat evolved, as measured experimentally, with the amounts predicted by theory.[39] The agreement this time was only moderately satisfactory; the experimental numbers were all about one-quarter less than those indicated by theory. He felt that there must have been some losses of heat during these, admittedly, difficult experiments and considered that these must have caused the discrepancy. He was, he believed, justified in claiming that he had proved the hypothesis. The audience was impressed. Dalton, who was not in the chair, broke the sixty-year-old tradition of the Society by proposing a vote of thanks to the speaker. It was seconded and passed.

*Alfred Smee was a surgeon who had an apartment in the Bank of England. An enthusiastic experimenter and a member of the London Electrical Society, he devised a cell with platinised silver and amalgamated zinc electrodes. The liquid conductor was dilute sulphuric acid.

Nevertheless, he was not satisfied with his explanation of the discrepancy; particularly when he found that his results agreed closely with those of P. L. Dulong.[40] J. F. Daniell had shown that electrolysis was more complex than just the separation of oxygen from its associated element. Besides the affinity between oxygen and the associated element there was affinity between the acid and the water and between the acid and the base (zinc oxide, etc.). All these binding forces had to be overcome in electrolysis, although the latter two had no counterpart in combustion. Joule had not thought to apply the same correction that he had made in his measurement of the heat generated in a battery. In the latter case the heat caused by the solution of zinc oxide was not associated with the current that generated the i^2r heat and, clearly, had to be deducted. But in electrolysis the need to eliminate auxiliary effects was not so obvious. Realisation that it was necessary was, therefore, a step towards the essential idea of conservation. This time, by subtracting the heat evolved by the solution of zinc oxide in dilute sulphuric acid from the heat, calculated by the theory, he was able to bring it into good agreement with the measured heat. Similar corrections applied in the cases of the other three elements brought them, too, into satisfactory agreement with the experimental results. He ended with a new insight. He had wondered whether a certain amount of heat might be absorbed by, or used up in, or diverted to the copious generation of light that usually accompanies combustion. A series of twenty-eight experiments, with and without the generation of light, convinced him that an equivalent of heat was used up in the generation of light, but it was too small to have affected the validity of his previous researches.

His last paper in this, second, series of experiments was also read to the Lit & Phil; just one month after his twenty-fourth birthday and almost a year after his election to membership of the Society.[41] It was a condensed, indeed cryptic, essay but it had its place in the evolution of his ideas. The reason for the work was his desire to find out why, in the electrolysis of water, the theoretical heat (i^2r) was consistently less than the actual heat.

He used a large tangent galvanometer with a six-inch needle and a most accurate scale. He had a standard resistance, kept in a water-bath to ensure that it stayed at a uniform temperature, and he employed six large Daniell cells; the most reliable as well as the most economical of all cells.* The electrolytic cell was filled with dilute sulphuric acid while the electrodes of platinum, platinised silver, platinised platinum and amalgamated zinc were changed for each experiment. Every reading of the current was carried out

---

*A Daniell cell had copper and amalgamated zinc electrodes and two liquids: copper sulphate solution and sulphuric acid.

twice, the second time with the galvanometer terminals reversed so that slight errors due to the position of the instrument were averaged out. This was certainly precise experimental work.

He found that the resistance to electrolysis, or opposing emf, varied with the type of electrode used. In each of six experiments the actual heat generated was greater than the calculated heat; and the greater the resistance to electrolysis, the greater was the difference between the two. Evidently the excess of actual heat over calculated heat was due to the different electrodes. Joule calculated what the difference would have been if, in each case, electrolysis had continued until one grain of hydrogen had been produced. These differences were converted into resistances to electrolysis by dividing them by the heat that a unit of electricity from a Daniell cell would generate, the Daniell cell being taken as the unit of emf.[42] These resistances, or opposing emfs, were subtracted from the measured resistances to electrolysis, the resulting numbers being, to a reasonable approximation, the same; as they should have been. For, with the variations due to the different electrodes eliminated all that was left was the emf necessary to separate the two constituents of water into their two gaseous forms (the extreme variation over the six experiments was between 1.284 and 1.418).

He concluded his experiments by comparing the emfs required to give hydrogen and oxygen their gaseous forms, having already found that the combined requirement was about 1.35. To do this he converted his galvanometer into a high-resistance instrument by substituting 200 turns of thin wire for one turn of thick wire. That is, he turned it into what would now be called a voltmeter.[43] With it he compared the emfs of a Daniell cell, a Grove cell and two forms of the Smee cell. And from these he deduced the emfs needed to give oxygen and hydrogen gaseous forms. They came out as approximately 0.45 and 1.0 respectively; near enough, he remarked, to the combined figure of 1.35. He added that it would be interesting to see if the mechanical condensation of oxygen would yield the same amount of heat as was due to an emf of 0.45.

He had shown that an electrolytic cell offered three 'obstructions' to an electric current: first, the ordinary, ohmic resistance to a current; second, a resistance to electrolysis, or opposing emf, that varied with the 'chemical repulsion' of the different electrodes; and, third, the resistance to electrolysis associated with the separation of the elements and the evolution of gases. In the second case the resistance to electrolysis opposed the battery emf, lowering the heating power, but where this deficit existed (indicated by the difference between the actual and the calculated heat), the loss was fully restored in the cell. In the third case, where the residual resistance to electrolysis was associated with the separation of the elements and the evolution of gases, the heat was lost to the circuit; it became 'latent' but could, of course, be recovered by burning the gases.[44]

In these three papers Joule satisfactorily accounted for the actions of an electric current in a metallic circuit, in a battery and in an electrolytic cell. All anomalies were explained; the account was properly balanced. He had shown, in the first series of researches, that the mechanical and the heating powers of a current were proportional to the emf times the current and were therefore proportional to each other. He now added, flatly, that since the magneto-electric engine could convert mechanical work into heat by means of an electric current, it followed that an electric motor would do more work as the heat generated in the circuit was reduced. And he added a note to say that he was preparing experiments to prove this (18 February 1843). The exact words he used were the key to his thoughts; their significance could be missed. To his contemporaries the magneto-electric engine worked by converting *magnetism* into electricity.

'Electricity', he remarked, 'may be regarded as a grand agent for carrying, arranging and converting chemical heat.' The words could be taken to imply that electricity and heat are 'fluids', but the context and the last three words indicate that this was not his belief. Two examples he gave illustrated his point clearly enough. A pair of Daniell cells connected to a cell containing dilute sulphuric acid would generate little heat since the emf of the Daniell cells was not much greater than the opposing emf, or resistance to electrolysis, of the electrolytic cell (2 as opposed to 1.35). But there would be a substantial transfer of 'latent heat' by the current that did flow. Again, if a big battery was to be connected to a long coil of thin wire whose total resistance was far greater than that of the battery, then nearly all the heat would appear in the coil and the battery would stay cool.

And yet, despite these observations and convincing arguments, he ended by asserting that 'the beautiful electrical theory of chemical heat, first suggested by Davy and Berzelius [is] beyond all question'.

John Dalton, as far as we know, never gave up his belief in the simple 'caloric' or substantial theory of heat. We do not know whether Joule ever accepted the caloric theory or at what stage in his early scientific career – if not before then – he began to believe in a kinetic theory of heat. Rumford's experiment and arguments were well known although his rather vague conclusion was, not unreasonably, rejected by the scientific community. At best they supported the agnosticism, or positivism, of Fourier.[45] More significant was the undulatory theory of light, due to Young and Fresnel, and its extension to radiant heat by Melloni, Forbes, von Wrede and others. If radiant heat is of an undulatory, or kinetic, nature then the other forms of heat should be similar.

To accept a kinetic theory of heat was not, however, to realise the value of the dynamical theory. The kinetic theory provided a plausible outline that men of science could agree about but that had little or no predictive value. It was a profession of faith, not a working hypothesis. And it was a confusion between the two that led, in the past, to unjustified claims by certain investigators to have originated the dynamical theory of heat. Joule had no reason to speculate about the nature of heat until his researches brought the problem to his attention. He had thereupon adopted the second-hand doctrine that heat was caused by the rotation of an 'atmosphere' of electricity round each atom. He was cautious in his speculations and single-minded in his research, refusing to be diverted even though intriguing and unexpected anomalies appeared. He recognised that the role of electricity in metallic corrosion might be a rewarding topic for research, but he passed it by. He realised that the Peltier effect seemed to contradict the i^2r law,* but was confident that it could be satisfactorily explained (he was right; William Thomson explained the thermodynamics of these effects in 1854). 'I hasten to fulfil my principal design' was Joule's response to challenges from the wings. It may be that the art of successful scientific research includes the ability to assess the significance of the anomalous and, deserting the main line of inquiry, to follow it through to a major discovery. In that case we must assume that Joule had already decided on the course he was to follow. But at what point and in what way he came to that decision it is impossible to say.

As Crowther pointed out,[46] Joule's first papers reveal a remarkable independence for a young man in his early twenties. This may have owed something to an environment that encouraged individual initiative but that lacked authoritative scientific personalities (Dalton was a possible exception) of the sort to be found in universities or colleges. The clarity and penetration of his mind owed nothing to outside circumstances. Nevertheless, in spite of the deserved reputation he later acquired for the accuracy and completeness of his experiments, his first papers do not show a great concern for high precision; his conclusions were often based on relatively few results obtained over a modest range of observation. Edmund Becquerel, for one, criticised him for drawing his conclusions from too slim an experimental base.[47] The criticism seems to have been justified. The

---

*T. J. Seebeck found (1826) that if a circuit of bismuth wire and antimony wire was heated at one junction and cooled at the other a current flowed from bismuth to antimony at the heated junction. J. Peltier found (1834) that if a battery current flowed in the circuit the junction at which it flowed from bismuth to antimony was cooled and the other junction was heated.

probable explanation was that Joule was not yet sufficiently practised in the techniques and requirements of writing papers for international journals. He may well have taken good advice (from Roget?) on this and it would be reasonable to suppose that his experimental skills developed over the years and with increasing experience.

To compare James Joule with Michael Faraday may seem to be an individious exercise. It is, however, instructive. Joule was much indebted to the older man, particularly for the laws of electrolysis, but in other respects the two had little in common. Both were completely committed to physical science and both were individualists, although in different ways. Joule's religious faith, although strong, was more conventional and therefore more flexible than Faraday's. But Joule's slight physical deformity may, as has been suggested, have made him sensitive about public appearances. There are few photographs or portraits of him and he was, by common consent, an unimpressive lecturer. Faraday's approach to physical science was that of a contemporary chemist.[48] He distrusted mathematics; instead he directed the richness of his imagination and the discipline of his mind towards an unparalleled series of brilliant discoveries. Joule, on the other hand, used experiment to discover or establish quantitative relationships, or mathematical laws. In this, the influence of his mathematical training under John Dalton is apparent. It is possible that the requirements of brewing technology and the accountancy needed to run a business helped to mould Joule's scientific attitude. What, however, is quite clear is that between James Joule and Michael Faraday there was little common ground.[49]

Other suggestions about influences on the direction and style of Joule's researches can only be tentative. In 1802 Dalton published his complete solution of the ancient problem of hydrologic cycle. A simple solution had been proposed by Edmund Halley, who had ascribed the flow of rivers to the supply of spring water maintained by rainfall and other forms of precipitation. Dalton, with far more data available, completed the solution by showing that, over the same time, the *net* precipitation – rainfall, snow, hail, dew, less evaporation – within the catchment area of a river and its tributaries was equal to the flow of water down the river. Dalton had solved a systems problem in which a number of variables controlled the operation of a relatively complex system.

Another example of the same kind of investigation was Crawford's research into animal, or bodily heat. Dalton thought highly of Crawford's work;[50] and we know that Joule owned a copy of the second edition of *Animal heat* (1788).[51] Sturgeon, we saw, had suggested that a volatic cell worked in the same way as the heart–lung system, essentially as a chemical machine, drawing in oxygen and expelling carbon dioxide, the heat of the 'combustion' being carried away by the blood to maintain the bodily heat of the mammal. Crawford's research was exemplary and, although his conclusions have been superseded, it could be that he had some influence on Joule, the analogy between the battery with its circuit and the heart–lung system with its artery–vein circuit being quite evident.

A third possible analogy that may have influenced Joule's approach to the problems of the battery and the electric motor was with the new industrial system of Manchester. The complex of mills, power sources and transportation networks represented a system of inputs and outputs, of transformations and mutual dependencies. But this, conceivably pervasive, influence is impossible to assess.

Analogies can be fruitful for the development of new scientific theories. An older contemporary of Joule, J. D. Forbes, a man whom he greatly respected, wrote in 1835:

> The importance of analogies in science has not, perhaps, been sufficiently insisted on by writers on the methods of philosophising. A clear conception of *connexion* has been by far the most fertile source of discovery. That of gravitation itself was only an extended analogy. The undulatory theory of light has been pre-eminently indebted to the co-ordinate science of acoustics, which afforded to Dr Young the most plausible basis for his curious and original investigations; and unless that science had existed it may be doubted whether such a speculation would ever have been invented, or if invented would have been listened to . . . The mere reasoner about phenomena could never have arrived at the result . . . The cause of the long postponement of the discovery of electro-magnetism was the complete apparent breach of analogy between the modes of action of the electric and magnetic forces, and any other previously known.[52]

Whatever criticisms could be made of Joule's paper – and standards of presentation were not, in those days, rigorously enforced – it is not immediately easy to understand why his works, up to 1843, were not received with more understanding; and their author welcomed into the community of science. They were positive additions to knowledge and they did not challenge accepted dogmas, doctrines or beliefs. The answer must surely lie with a somewhat torpid scientific establishment and with the personality of the author. Joule did not have the invaluable gift of being able to arouse attention and command respect just by the strength of his personality. He needed the support and advocacy of someone who possessed the gifts he lacked. As the world knows, the reticent Charles Darwin found his champion in T. H. Huxley. Even Dalton, a born teacher and successful lecturer, in London as well as in Manchester, was indebted to Thomas Thomson, of the Scottish school of chemists as well as to Thomas and William Henry.[53] There is no substitute for a really impressive personality. Not until 1847 did Joule find one to accept and to plead his cause.

4

The Lit & Phil
and the British Association

The end of 1842 was an eventful time for Joule. His researches had reached a crucial point and, on 7 December, at St George's Church, Everton, his brother Benjamin was married; which event, Osborne Reynolds observed enigmatically, 'for a short period disturbed the close alliance of the brothers'. Benjamin's bride, Caroline Molyneux, was described as a governess in the family and was, accordingly, listed in the 1841 Census at the head of the six servants in the Joule household. Caroline's age was given as twenty-five; she was actually about twenty-eight. Her father, Thomas Molyneux, of Liverpool, was dead and she was the youngest daughter of the family. That was not a very enviable position in those days. The only respectable occupation, in the absence of adequate private means, for a young, unmarried daughter was that of governess, although what was entailed in the Joule household, the youngest member of which, John, was well over eighteen, is not entirely clear. Perhaps she was retained as a companion for Mary in what would otherwise have been an all-male household. It would be pleasant to think that, for Caroline, marriage to the handsome, cultured, wealthy and eminently respectable Benjamin Joule was to be followed by many years of happiness. Sadly, the marriage was brief; Caroline died at their home in Salford on 28 July 1844.

Joule's election to the Lit & Phil took place on 25 January 1842. Two others elected on the same day were William Edward Binney, a young solicitor and amateur geologist who was later to combine his professional and amateur skills to enable him to make a fortune in the early mineral oil industry, and Dr Lyon Playfair, a member of the distinguished Edinburgh family, who had just taken his Ph.D. under Justus Liebig at Giessen. Playfair had been appointed manager of a print works at Clitheroe, about thirty miles north of Manchester.

Mr Thompson, the owner of the print works, was well-informed and liberal-minded though old-fashioned in his business practices. He gave

Fig 2 Benjamin St J. B. Joule

Playfair a most generous salary (£350 for his first year), as well he might, for Playfair was able and ambitious. He was among the first of a new type of man, the would-be professional scientist who aimed to make a successful career in science. This, and more, he did, for he ended his active life as the Right Honourable the Lord Playfair, with an imposing record of public services; in particular, to the politics and administration of science. His own scientific achievements were relatively modest.[1]

As his correspondence shows, Playfair was a modern young man[2]. There was no hint of the stuffy Victorian. He was greatly interested in various young ladies with whom he lost no time in getting on first-name terms. He dabbled in the fashionable subject of mesmerism, or hypnotism as the Manchester physician, James Braid, was to call it. He described experiments with young women (including a 'robust young servant girl') and recounted the misfortunes of a 'young gent in Manchester (who) mesmerised his "lady love" ' but who panicked so badly when he could not bring her round that he fainted. And he had risqué stories to tell about Prince Albert and the young Queen Victoria: 'What is Prince Albert's pension? – Half-a-crown a day and a sovereign at night – Hee, Hee,'* But all the time his ambitions were never very far below the surface. He was determined to get to the top; to sit on the platform with the leaders of the scientific world. He knew that in Britain success depended on good public relations; that the 'bashful, retiring, unworldly man' would never go as far as those who, like himself, loved to speak out and suit themselves to the minds of their hearers. He spoke of his interests in 'pure science', which revealed the strong influence of his German training. But, at the same time, he directed his ambitions to the growth areas of applied chemistry.[3]

Playfair, Binney and Joule were by no means the only interesting members of the Lit & Phil. Apart from the venerable John Dalton the other members in 1842 included the engineers J. F. Bateman, William Fairbairn, Eaton Hodgkinson, Richard Roberts, Joseph Whitworth and Bennet Woodcroft, each of whom was a leader in his own field;[4] there were the cotton masters Robert Hyde and William Rathbone Greg, H. H. and Richard Birley, James and William McConnell; there were the bankers Sir Benjamin and James Heywood and the industrial magnate, Thomas Ashton, who was later to be instrumental in saving the Owens College (founded in 1851) from premature failure; there were the chemical manufacturers Charles Souchay, William Charles Henry and the calico-printer

---

*Or this: 'Did you hear that Prince Albert is likely to be transported?' 'No – for what?' 'For plugging and sweating a sovereign.' A common crime was to drill a hole in a gold sovereign and plug it with a base alloy resembling gold. The gold filings were carefully collected.

Edmund Potter (father-in-law of Henry Enfield Roscoe and grandfather of Beatrix Potter, author of the Peter Rabbit books). Among the other members were Dalton's friend, Peter Clare, James Crossley and Samuel Dukinfield Darbishire, the journalists Archibald Prentice and John Edward Taylor, founder of the *Manchester Guardian;* the Revd William Gaskell (Elizabeth Gaskell's husband), Edward Schunck, the country's leading organic chemist,[5] and the well-known politician, Richard Cobden. The total membership was 176, having nearly tripled since the beginning of the century. The Society was at a pinnacle of importance and its membership represented the elite of British industry at the time when Britain boasted that it was the workshop of the world. It is doubtful whether such a diverse and talented group of men could have been assembled anywhere else in the country; at least as far as industry, technology and science were concerned.

In 1842 the British Association paid its first visit to Manchester, the President for the year being Lord Francis Egerton, a member of the Lit & Phil. Following its first meeting in York in 1831 it had worked its way systematically and with proper regard to precedence through the university cities before venturing into the outer provinces. Manchester, in spite of its pre-eminence in science and engineering, came seventh on the list of the grimy and unwashed; perhaps because of its reputation, more probably because of the lack of suitable large buildings in which to hold meetings.[6] For example, the Chemical Section, for which Lyon Playfair acted as Secretary, met in the Portico Library, which was one of Dalton's favourite haunts.

It was at this meeting that Joule met Captain the Revd Dr William Scoresby, FRS.[7] The master of a whaling ship* out of Whitby in the days before mechanised killing, when whaling was a hazardous occupation, Scoresby had a trained mind and a scientific instinct. He had attended Edinburgh University where he had been influenced by T. C. Hope and John Playfair[8] (Lyon Playfair's uncle) before deciding to follow his father's calling and go to sea.[9] After the death of his wife he decided to give up the sea and take Holy Orders, becoming, in due course, Vicar of Bradford. In 1820 he published his two-volume *Account of the Arctic Region*, a major work that was, significantly, much praised in France. Scoresby's interest in what would now be called geophysics was one which he shared with many contemporaries, for much effort was being put into exploration and, more

---

*Whale oil was an important lubricant in the days before mineral oil was available. In those days the lubricating oils used for engines and machines generally were of animal or vegetable extraction.

specifically, into what has been aptly called the magnetic crusade,[10] an international movement that was to have an influence on Joule's later career. Magnetism, always important for the navigator, was a particular interest of Scoresby and it was the common interest that brought the two men together. Scoresby's biographers remark that Joule was 'fascinated by the gifted parson who was so very different from the great majority of clergymen he had met'. Relations were cordial. Scoresby and his second wife were entertained at 'Broom Hill' and, at the end of July, Joule and his brother Benjamin paid a return visit to Bradford.[11] According to Osborne Reynolds they travelled by train, on the roof of a first-class carriage, as they frequently did. At Bradford they stayed at the parsonage and attended divine service. But Joule 'did not forget his rule of sleeping through the afternoon sermon, though his host was the preacher'.

On 30 March 1843, Joule wrote to Scoresby to say that further experiments refuted the hypothesis that the heat generated in a circuit would be reduced in proportion to the work done by an electric motor included in the circuit.[12] On the contrary, it seemed that the chemical action always generated exactly the same amount of heat, whether or not work was done by the motor. Evidently the critical experiments he was carrying out were difficult. But less than a month later, on 24 April, he wrote again to Scoresby to retract this conclusion.[13] The experiments had not been accurate enough to detect the differences in heat, with and without the motor. Furthermore, 'My last experiments with a better contrived apparatus have clearly demonstrated that heat *is* evolved by the coils of the magnetic-electrical machine, proving the generation of heat by mechanical action.'

That is to say, the appearance of heat in the coils of a magneto-electric machine, a generator of electricity, proves that the work done to drive the machine has been converted into heat. His account of these and other, associated, experiments was given in his paper 'On the calorific effects of magneto-electricity and on the mechanical value of heat', read later in the year.[14] Everyone, he said, agreed that the current from a magneto had the same heating powers as currents from other sources. If, then, we assume that heat is a *state of vibration* and not a *substance* (his italics) we can easily understand how the mechanical actions of driving the magneto can be turned into (mechanical action in the form of) heat in the circuit. On the other hand, if heat is substantial then the heating effect of a current from a magneto can only be explained by transference; that is, the magneto must act as a kind of pump, transferring heat from the armature to the outside circuit, the armature itself necessarily being cooled in the process (this was akin to Rumford's argument: where *can* the heat come from?). This, he added, 'did not appear untenable without further experiment'. He had already proved that, in the case of a battery circuit, the heat evolved is *definite*; that is, determined by the chemical changes in the battery. In other words, heat is, seemingly, transported by the current from the source, the chemical action in the battery. And, in the case of electrolysis, the heat made 'latent' is at the expense of heat that would otherwise have been evolved freely in the circuit. The experiments with the voltaic circuit could be taken to indicate that arrangement rather than generation of heat takes place, the circuit itself merely evolving heat that was latent in the battery.

He therefore devised an elaborate experiment to settle the question whether or not a magneto acts like a heat pump. First, he made a small armature of laminated soft iron wound with twenty yards of thin insulated copper wire. It was put in a glass tube, 8¾ inches long and sealed at one end. The tube was mounted horizontally in a hole cut through a vertical wooden spindle, the wires from the armature being taken out of the tube and down the spindle, the point of which which stood on a flat wooden base at the centre of two semi-circular grooves filled with mercury. The wires dipped into these grooves which were connected by other wires to a galvanometer, the arrangement forming a commutator. The tube was lagged and screened with foil to minimise heat losses by convection and radiation; it was filled with water and a greased cork was used to seal the open end. Finally the spindle was placed so that it could rotate between the poles of a powerful electromagnet, energised by six Daniell cells. It was rotated by a cord from a pulley worked by hand.

Preliminary tests showed that there was a cooling effect as the tube spun round. This was corrected for after each experiment by disconnecting the battery so that the electromagnet was inoperative and measuring the cooling effect after the tube had been spun round. The amount of cooling was then added to the change in temperature when the battery was connected. The first series of experiments showed a slight net rise in temperature after the tube had been spun round. Joule therefore substituted a larger electromagnet, made of boiler iron, and used ten Daniell cells. In all he carried out six series of experiments, taking the temperature of the water before and after each experiment and rotating the spindle 600 times a minute for a quarter of an hour. He used different battery arrangements, to vary the current and therefore the 'magnetic intensity', and he tried using a steel permanent magnet. In every case the water surrounding the armature was heated. But before he could give a strict, quantitative answer two further corrections had to be made. There was a small correction for an additional loss of heat as the tube spun round at a higher temperature than the surrounding air and there was the correction to be made for the heating due to the induced eddy currents in the metal core of the armature. To measure the second correction Joule disconnected the armature from the galvanometer circuit so that no current could flow and then noted the residual heating effect. In each experiment the core heating effect was deducted from the total heating effect. He could now show that there was a net heating effect and that this was proportional to the square of the current induced in the armature. The magneto, in short, did not work like a heat pump; everywhere in the circuit there was a heating effect proportional to the square of the current. All that had happened was that work had been done, driving the spindle, and heat had appeared. There had been no cooling, anywhere, and no other effect, physical or chemical, to account for the heat.

Next, he measured the heat generated by a continuous voltaic current flowing through the stationary armature for the same length of time. He then calculated the heat that voltaic currents, equal to the magneto currents in each of his six experiments, would generate. In each case the effect of the voltaic current was about 30% less than the observed effect of the magneto current. Of course the voltaic current was continous while the magneto current was pulsed; that is, twice during every revolution of the armature the current was stopped, briefly, while the wires passed from one groove to the other. The period when no current flowed was one-quarter of a revolution. Joule was able to account for this apparently paradoxical result in a way that showed his complete understanding of the process.[15] He assumed that, for a pulse of current of strenth 'i', the galvanometer reading should be $3/4$i, taking account of the $1/4$ 'dead space'.[16] A continuous voltaic current of strength $3/4$i would generate heat proportional to $9/16i^2$. But the heat generated by each pulse of current would be proportional to i^2 and therefore, over the same length of time that the voltaic current flowed, the total heat generated would be $3/4i^2$. The heat generated by the voltaic current must, therefore, be multiplied by $4/3$ to make it strictly comparable with the magneto current. In this way he proved that the heat generated by a magneto current was governed by the same laws as the heat from a voltaic current; and also that the same amount of heat was generated when the circumstances were comparable.

In the subsequent series of six experiments one or two Daniell cells were included in the armature–galvanometer circuit and the armature rotated so that the battery current was augmented and then rotated in the reverse direction to oppose the battery current. In the last two series the magneto, turning at 370 rpm, virtually cancelled-out the battery and practically no current flowed, while in the final experiment the current was actually reversed and the magneto overwhelmed the battery. Once again the square law applied to the heating effect whether the current was agumented or diminished. He concluded that, in magneto electricity, we have *an agent capable by simple means of destroying or generating heat* (his italics). He had established his thesis and confirmed his speculation in his January paper. He had taken full account of the side-effects that would have obscured his results and in doing so had shown his qualities as an experimentalist. The first part of the paper ended with an account of experiments in which a plain iron bar was substituted for the armature in the tube. The current energising the big, fixed electromagnet was varied and the results showed that the heat generated in the bar was proportional to the square of the current; or, as he put it, to the square of the 'magnetic influence'.

The second half of the paper brought the threads together and completed his efforts over the years with a transcendent synthesis. He said: 'Having proved that heat is generated by the magneto-electrical machine and that by means of the inductive power of magnetism we can diminish or increase at pleasure the heat due to chemical change, it became an object of great interest to inquire whether a constant ratio existed between it and the mechanical power gained or lost.' To do this all that was necessary was to repeat some of the first experiments while, at the same time, measuring the 'mechanical force' required to turn the armature. This was a simple matter of calibration. Two fine strings were wound round the axle of the pulley that drove the spindle. These passed over two small pulleys on opposite sides of the axle and thirty yards apart.* Two scale pans were tied to the ends of the strings so that weights could be made to rotate the pulley. He found the 'mechanical force' required to drive the apparatus by adding weights to the pans until the armature rotated at a steady 600 rpm; the strength of the current through the galvanometer was noted. The pulley was then rotated by hand to give the same armature speed for fifteen minutes. The heat generated was measured and all corrections applied, allowance even being made for the heat due to electric sparks at the commutator (he did not explain how he did this: 'previous experiments' were invoked). By using weights to rotate the pulley when the current for the electromagnets was turned off he was able to deduce the 'mechanical force' required just to overcome friction and air resistance. Subtracting this from the first figure gave him the 'mechanical force' required just to generate the current and, accordingly, the heat. The net driving weight (4lb 12 oz) would have fallen through 571 feet in fifteen minutes; comparing

---

*He did not explain why the pulleys were so far apart. Later, he described how he had dug pits in the garden shrubbery to increase the fall available for the driving weights ('Fragment of autobiography': see Ch. 2, note 1).

this with the heat generated he concluded that 896 lb falling 1 foot could be converted into heat that would raise the temperature of 1 lb of water by 1°F. Two other experiments gave values of 1,001 and 1,040 lbs.

Further experiments were carried out with two Daniell cells included in the armature circuit and the magneto run in reverse; that is, as an electromagnetic engine, or motor. The cells were then removed and weights used to rotate the armature at the same speed. In this way the 'mechanical force' expended, the work done by the motor, could be calculated. The loss of heating power in the circuit when the motor was running was also easy to calculate and by comparing these two a figure for the mechanical value of heat was obtained. Finally, the simple iron cylinder was put back in the glass tube and rotated at 600 rpm for fifteen minutes; the work done was then compared with the heat generated. These experiments gave the figures 910, 1026, 587, 742 and 840 foot. pounds for the amount of work that could be converted into the heat that would raise the temperature of 1 lb of water 1°F. He admitted that there was a pretty wide variation in these results but suggested it could be attributed to experimental error. Later, he was to be unfairly criticised (by Helmholtz) for these imprecise results. In fact, he was feeling his way, learning how to evaluate the difficulties and pitfalls in his efforts to establish that there *was* a 'mechanical equivalent of heat'. Accordingly, he intimated that he was going to repeat the experiments with 'more powerful and delicate apparatus'. At least he could claim that his figures were within the same order of magnitude and there was presumptive evidence that an exact and universal figure could be established. He ended by remarking that 'The quantity of heat capable of raising the temperature of a pound of water by one degree of Fahrenheit's scale is equal to, and may be converted into, a mechanical force capable of raising 838 pounds to the perpendicular height of one foot.'

At the close of the paper he came back to the starting point of his researches, the efficiency of engines. Using the figure of 838 and the published data,[17] he computed that the work obtainable from a pound of best Welsh coal amounted to nearly ten million foot.pounds. But the most that a first rate Cornish engine (he was thinking of the Wheal Towan engine[18]) could deliver was about one million foot.pounds per pound of coal. On the other hand a pound of zinc 'burned' in a Daniell or Grove cell would, through a current, generate heat to a mechanical value of just over a million and rather less than ten million foot.pounds respectively. Since it was impossible to convert more than about one-half the heat of a voltaic circuit into useful power* it was clear that the electric motor, driven by available batteries, could never replace the steam-engine. 'Never' is an uncompromising word. The record shows many instances when it was used, apparently entirely justifiably, in circumstances that were later shown to be inapplicable. But in this case it was justified.

A postscript to this paper described, very briefly, an experiment in which water was heated by being forced through narrow tubes. A number of capillary tubes were bound tightly together round a long rod[19] to form a piston and piston rod. By forcing the piston up and down in a glass vessel full of water he was able to produce an appreciable rise in temperature and from it to deduce a mechanical value of heat of 770 foot.pounds, which he took to be strongly confirmatory of his earlier results. Joule published no details of his procedures, but Mendoza, who has repeated the experiment, confirms that it can, indeed, give an accurate result.[20] Although this might seem surprising it should be remembered that it was a simple, straightforward experiment, with fewer possible sources of error than the experiments with the magneto. Joule affirmed that he would lose no time in repeating and extending these experiments, 'being satisfied that the grand agents of nature are, by the Creator's fiat, *indestructible*; and that wherever mechanical force is expended, an exact equivalent of heat is *always* obtained'. This was a qualitative statement of the principle known as the conservation of energy. Joule ended the paper by showing that he understood the range of the new principle for he envisaged that it could be extended to physiology. And he modified his earlier idea about the electrical origin of the heat of combustion. The heat of combustion cannot be traced back to the forces of chemical affinity; rather it is due to the 'mechanical force expended by the atoms in falling towards each other'. This 'mechanical force', he believed, determined the strength of the current and consequently the heat generated. In other words, the mechanical action of combining atoms produces the equivalent amount of heat.[21]

This paper has been discussed at some length, partly because of its importance in the history of science and partly because it gives a good idea of Joule's scientific methods. It shows us the range of his questioning, and, in particular, the completeness with which he explored – in ways that would have occurred to few men – possible objections to his thesis. Not only did he demonstrate that heat is actually created; he took care to demonstrate

---

*This tends to support the hypothesis that, in early 1840, he had extended his investigations of the electric motor beyond the point at which the current fell to half its maximum value (see pp. 33, 236) and reached, correspondingly, its maximum power. He had done – or, at least, he had recorded – no work on the electric motor between March 1840 and August 1843; his interests had been elsewhere.

the converse, that by reversing his magneto to act as a motor, heat can be destroyed, or rather converted into mechanical action (work). And he demonstrated that these actions were independent of the type of magnet used. The very thoroughness of his work suggests that he feared no rival. There was no eager researcher at his heels, or running neck and neck. His was not a world of competitive science in which there might be every incentive to rush into print. He could afford to explore the ramifications and implications of his discovery. He could even afford to hint that he had discovered a new universal constant – a rare and important event in science. His was the remote, leisurely world of men like Charles Darwin and Willard Gibbs.

The paper was read on 21 August 1843, to the British Association meeting in Cork, in Eire. Joule travelled over with his friend and fellow Mancunian, the engineer Eaton Hodgkinson. If they had felt any doubts about travelling to southern Ireland, the *Athenaeum* had assured them that they would be as safe there as anywhere in England or Scotland and much safer than on the Continent. And, the journal added, 'nor will you fail to be struck by the politeness of the people and their wishes to oblige you in every way'. The *Literary Gazette* was equally enthusiastic and drew a favourable comparison between Cork and Manchester as places in which to hold large meetings.

When it came to Joule's turn to read his paper he was, he wrote,[22] asked to read it to Section B, the Chemistry Section, rather than Section A, the Mathematics and Physics Section. This was because the Physics Section was full, while the Chemistry Section was comparatively empty. For some years physics had prospered at the British Association. This was the time when the earlier reform of the Cambridge mathematics school[23] was beginning to return a profit; it was also the period that saw critically important work in support of the wave theory, as opposed to the emission or particle theory, of light; work in which the Irishmen Hamilton, McCullagh and Lloyd were particularly active.[24] The magnetic crusade was well under way and mathematics was being increasingly applied in physical science. These were the years of Ampère, Arago, Babbage, Gauss, Jacobi, Lenz, Neumann and Weber, as well as men like Sir William Snow Harris and Sir James South, who were highly regarded in their day but whose reputations have subsequently wilted. Chemistry, on the other hand, had seen better days. In Britain, leading figures like Dalton, Davy, Prout, Wollaston were past their primes or dead. Faraday was paying much less attention to chemistry, while on the Continent the great German schools were only just beginning to show their strength.

Whether or not Joule felt out of place in the Chemistry Section seems doubtful. The boundary between chemistry and the new, but ill-defined science of physics was far from clear, certainly in Britain. To recapitulate, through much of the eighteenth century and during the first part of the nineteenth century heat had been regarded as a branch – a most important branch – of chemistry.[25] Electricity and magnetism had no generally agreed home while mechanics, optics and planetary astronomy belonged to natural philosophy. However seriously, or lightly, Joule regarded the divisions between the Sections, he had congenial company in Section B; the young Scottish engineer W. J. M. Rankine was there to read his paper on the generation of electricity by the flow of high-pressure steam, a phenomenon first noticed by the engineer W. G. Armstrong. However acceptable the Section may have been, Joule was disappointed with the reception of his paper. He was grateful that his ideas were supported by Lord Rosse, the astronomer, Eaton Hodgkinson and Dr Apjohn, the Dublin chemist.[26] But, converts though they may have been, none of these men took any further part in the development of the dynamical theory of heat and the conservation of energy. These things were outside their fields of interest. They were busy men with other commitments. As for the journals, the *Athenaeum* made a brief, fleeting reference to the paper and refrained from comment.[27] The *Literary Gazette*, with smug pomposity, dismissed the whole meeting: 'We cannot point out one remarkable scientific fact which is entirely novel.'[28] There was a mention of Mr Joule's new galvanometer and the misleading information that 'Mr Joule read his paper on the calorific effects of magneto-electricity and on the mechanical effect of heat.' It amounted to just three lines.

The paper had its weaknesses; in particular there was an almost complete failure to mention contemporary work – only Lenz and Jacobi were quoted – in related fields. But, even taken together with Joule's shortcomings as a propagandist on his own behalf, the relatively minor flaws hardly explain the failure of the scientific world to appreciate the value of the paper. Other, more general, reasons must be found. And, apart from simple ignorance, as in the case of the *Literary Gazette*, the most obvious of these was a lack of interest in the study of heat at that time. As everyone with a claim to competence in mathematics knew, Fourier had, most satisfactorily, completed the science of heat. Joule's experiments and the arguments he based on them would have been hardly intelligible to the right-thinking 'physicist'. Since the nature of heat, like that of gravity, was inscrutable, the conversion of heat into work, or work into heat, was no more conceivable than the conversion of gravity into hydrogen, or hydrogen into gravity. The non-mathematical chemist, for his part, would have been equally unwilling to accept Joule's arguments.

And yet arguments supporting a kinetic theory of heat continued to be heard, or remembered. They included those of von Rumford and Humphry Davy, both influential, Joseph Montgolfier and his grand-nephew, Marc Séguin,[29] August Colding, Friedrich Mohr and, most insistent of all, the tragic Julius Robert Mayer. Sadi Carnot, it was later discovered, had abandoned the caloric theory after he had published his *Réflections*, one of the main reasons being the success of the undulatory theory of light and the similarities between light and radiant heat. For much the same reason Ampère, too, could be understood to support the kinetic theory of heat. But, as a rule, those who supported the heterodox theory were to be found outside the universities and the great national academies. And, like Joule, many of them had an engineering background or interest. An idea of the attitude of what we may call official science towards the kinetic theory of heat was provided by a revealing letter written by Sir John Herschel in 1846. Herschel, who in his time had a very high reputation as a man of science, was replying to J. J. Waterston, a civil engineer and a pioneer of the kinetic theory of gases. Waterston had asked for help, but Herschel was far from encouraging:

I believe the idea of accounting for the phenomena of heat by motion – i.e. by the interchange of molecular motions among particles on the principle of the conservation of the *vis viva* whether by collision or by orbital revolutions . . . has not been without its advocates – at least I well remember having seen at least one such attempt by M. Séguin many years ago . . .

I confess I entertain little hope of the success of any simply mechanical explanation of the phenomena of heat, electricity, magnetism etc. and I am not surprised at scientific bodies or journals declining to give the authority of their approval, implied in the act of publishing them, to such attempts. Of course I speak *in general*, since it is perfectly possible that in your or any other case there may be that degree of ingenuity and mathematical skill displayed in the attempt as shall make *the attempt itself* instructive. Nor would I be understood to deny that (supposing the steps of the deductive reasoning rigorous) there might be an amount of coincidence of results with observed facts which would render it necessary to pause before absolutely rejecting a mechanical theory which was legitimately produced . . .

I trust however that you will excuse me if I say that I have no time for the subject. Should you be disposed to send your paper for reading to the British Association it will of course have a fair hearing if introduced *by any member*.[30]

Comment is not necessary beyond the explanation that Séguin had written to Herschel about his ideas in 1822 and that Herschel had even-tually passed the letter on to Brewster who published it in the *Edinburgh Philosophical Journal*.[31] The principle that Joseph Montgolfier and Marc Séguin 'maintained was that the *vis viva* could neither be created nor annihilated and, consequently, that the quantity of motion on the earth had a real and finite existence'. Séguin gave four instances of the consequences of the principle, the most intriguing of which was the phenomenon of Prince Rupert's drops, made by allowing drops of molten glass to fall into cold water. Great heat was required to make these; if they were fractured, pieces of glass flew off at high velocities.

Seen from today's perspective it seems clear that Joule's next step should be to prove that the mechanical value of heat is, indeed, a universal constant whose value is independent of the processes or materials involved in the generation, or transformation, of heat. After this, he should measure the exchange value, or mechanical equivalent, as accurately as possible. This was, in fact, the actual course of his main researches over the next five years, although he did not call attention to it; his scientific papers confined themselves to immediate problems and usually eschewed forecasts, generalisations or statements of long-term intentions. The result has been that for generations of students Joule has been known as the man who made the most accurate measurement of the mechanical equivalent of heat. They have not, as a rule, been told how he came to establish that heat and work were interchangeable, that the ratio between the two was fixed and that it was entirely independent of the materials or processes involved.[32]

The psychology underlying his researches is rather more elusive. Did he carry out the experiments that involved different materials and processes confident that they would always give the same result; or did he wonder, half fear perhaps, that one particular process would give a value that was obstinately different from the rest? To put the question another way, was he just confirming his discovery by anticipating and removing all objections, or was he seeking to find how far it was valid? The answer to this question cannot be known; perhaps Joule himself never knew it. There was, too, another aspect to these researches, one that he could well have appreciated. They might reveal the best, the simplest, the most accurate way of measuring the equivalent. The first method, by electrical means, had been indirect and complex; the result was relatively inaccurate in spite of the precautions he took and the corrections he made. Whatever his motives and understanding at this time, his facilities for research improved. On 19 March 1843, the family, together with the six servants, moved from 'Broom Hill' to a new house, 'Oak Field', in Upper Chorlton Road, Whalley Range, about a mile and a half south of the city centre. Here Benjamin Joule built a laboratory for his son, giving him greatly 'increased facilities for his work'.[33]

A feature of eighteenth-century physical science was the attention paid to the properties of air and gases.* One discovery was that if air or a gas is compressed it becomes heated; if it is expanded, or rarefield, it is cooled. The compression or expansion is said to be adiabatic if no heat is allowed to escape from or enter the gas while its volume is changing. Erasmus Darwin invoked this phenomenon to explain how the snow fields and glaciers of the Andes of the equator could exist adjacent to the extremely hot coastal plain.[34] John Dalton took the study further and argued that the heating or cooling effect during rapid adiabatic compression or expansion was far greater than could be shown on the sluggish thermometers of the day. He showed that all gases have the same coefficient of thermal expansion at about the same time that J-L Gay-Lussac made the same discovery, although Gay-Lussac's expression of the law was more satisfactory than Dalton's.[35] The adiabatic heating and cooling of gases assumed considerable theoretical interest when it was realised that it could explain away the scandalous anomaly that vitiated Newton's calculations of the velocity of sound. Newton's predicted value and the experimental measurement differed widely. But Newton knew nothing of the adiabatic heating or cooling of air when rapidly compressed or expanded, as happens in the case of sound waves. When allowance was made for this, theory and experiment agreed and Newton was confirmed as the great man who was never wrong.

From Joule's point of view here was a simple way in which mechanical work could be converted into heat; a way that was quite different from the two previous ways.[36] He placed a strong copper cylinder, a foot long and 4½ inches in diameter, in water in a double-walled calorimeter, designed to minimise heat losses. He used a very sensitive thermometer and Mr. J. B. Dancer, the instrument-maker,[37] made an ingenious vernier scale with eyepiece that enabled him to read the thermometer to, he claimed, an accuracy of ½₀₀°F. When the apparatus reached thermal equilibrium he pumped dry air into the cylinder until the pressure reached twenty-two atmospheres. The water was stirred and the temperature read. He carried out six separate experiments, making a number of necessary corrections in each case. The net effect of compressing the air was to raise the temperature of the water, the cylinder and the double-walled calorimeter by an average of 0.285°F. The work done was calculated by measuring the volume of air used at atmospheric pressure and applying Boyle's law to the compression needed to reduce the volume to that of the cylinder. He then

---

*The most important practical consequence of this interest was the invention of the Newcomen engine. Another was the air-gun, a favourite weapon of poachers. Possession of one was a criminal offence.

used the simple, and no doubt familiar, theory of the steam-engine indicator to compute the work done. Comparing the heat generated with the work done he arrived at a figure of 823 foot.pounds for the mechanical equivalent of heat.[38] This was in acceptable agreement with the results given by the electrical methods and the flow of water. A further series of five experiments using only half the volume of air gave 795 foot.pounds for the mechanical equivalent of heat.

This could not be a really accurate method, for the rise in temperature was small, due to the large heat capacities of the water, the cylinder and the double-walled calorimeter. Nevertheless the figures it gave were sufficiently close to those obtained by the other methods that he felt confident that the heat evolved was just the manifestation, in another form, of all the work done in compressing the air. For the public, though, it was necessary to confirm this supposition experimentally. In compressing the air three things had happened: work had been done, the air had become heated and the air had been much reduced in volume. Was he justified in saying that all the work had been expended in generating heat? On the face of it, certainly not; some work, at least, might have been spent in reducing the volume of the air. Work has to be done to wind up a watch spring; its bulk or volume is reduced. As Joule discovered experimentally,[39] no heat appeared when a spring was wound up; all the work was used to wind up the spring. For a positivist that would, presumably, have been the end of the matter; but Joule was a Daltonian atomist and these results had a bearing on the atomic structure of gases. It had been commonly assumed that the atoms of gases repelled each other with a force that diminished as separation increased. In other words, it was thought that atoms behaved like small springs. But, as far as Joule's evidence went, this was not the case. The atoms of gases could not, therefore, be static; they must, somehow, be associated with motion.

To justify his assumption that all the work done in compressing a gas was converted into heat Joule took two identical cylinders, joined by a brass tube fitted with a stopcock (Fig. 3). One of the cylinders was filled with air at twenty-two atmospheres, the other was exhausted. This difficult operation was made possible by the invention of a stopcock that was perfectly airtight under high pressures. The inventor, Mr Ash, 'of this town, a gentleman well known for his great mechanical genius', generously allowed Joule to describe his invention.

The two cylinders were immersed in water in a figure-of-eight-shaped double-walled vessel and the water allowed time to reach thermal equilibrium. The stopcock was then opened, allowing the air to rush from the high-pressure cylinder into the vacuum. The water was stirred and the temperature taken. The experiment was repeated six times, with the

Fig. 3 Cylinders and calorimeter used by Joule in the experiments of 1844 (Greater Manchester Museum of Science and Industry)

consistent result that the temperature of the water was found to be unchanged. The conclusion was that 'No change in temperature occurs when air is allowed to expand in such a manner as not to develop mechanical power.'

In order, as he put it, to 'analyse' the experiment, the two cylinders were inverted and placed in separate containers of water. On repeating the procedure he found that the water surrounding the cylinder with compressed air had been cooled by 2.36° (roughly 0.23°F), while the water surrounding the exhausted cylinder had been heated by 2.38° (or about 0.24°F). There was also a slight 'redundance' of heat due to the 'loss of cold' (*sic*) through the pipes that were not immersed in water. The explanation of these two effects was simple. Work had to be done to push air out of the high-pressure cylinder; accordingly the temperature fell; work was done on the air that had expanded into the void cylinder; its temperature therefore rose. The two effects cancelled each other out. And since no heat is lost, or used up, when air or a gas expands without doing work, it follows that, generally, a change in volume of a gas does not, of itself, cause the evolution or the disappearance of heat, which are both associated with the performance of work, on or by the gas. The measurement of the mechanical equivalent of heat by compressing air was, therefore, acceptable.

In the third and last series of experiments he set out to measure the mechanical equivalent of heat by comparing the heat lost when compressed air expands with the work done in the process. One of the cylinders was filled with air, compressed to about twenty-two atmospheres. It was connected to twelve yards of coiled lead pipe and the whole immersed in water in a double-walled vessel; the other end of the lead pipe was taken to a pneumatic trough. After thermal equilibrium was reached the temperature of the water was taken and the stopcock opened so that the air expanded into a jar inverted over the pneumatic trough. The temperature of the water round the cylinder was taken and the volume of the expanded air was measured; this volume, multiplied by the atmospheric pressure, gave the work done. Again, six experiments were carried out and the mean loss of heat determined. The lost heat had been converted into the work done by the compressed air in raising a column of the atmosphere, or in pushing the surrounding air back to make room for the expanding air. From this converse transformation, the figure for the mechanical equivalent of heat that was deduced was 820 foot.pounds. Two further series each of seven experiments, using only half the volume of air, gave figures of 814 and 760 foot.pounds.

These results were, Joule claimed, inexplicable, on the assumption that heat was due to the presence of a specific substance. For if it were, the quantity lost by expansion against atmospheric pressure would, when the same volume of air was used, be the same as that evolved by compression. But they were not; the loss of heat when air expanded against atmospheric pressure was little more than half the amount evolved when the same volume was compressed to the same pressure. And in the experiments on the unresisted expansion of air there would surely have been a detectable loss of heat.[40] On the other hand these results were what would be expected on the dynamical theory of heat. The air that expanded against atmospheric pressure did less work than was done to compress it; less heat was therefore lost than was evolved by compression. No heat was lost by the air that expanded into a vacuum – and no *net* work was done.

He believed that, averaging out the most reliable results, the most probable figure was 798 foot.pounds, close enough to 838 foot.pounds. As to the cause of heat, he favoured Davy's hypothesis of the rapid rotation of the elementary particles and he tried to unite this with Faraday's electrochemical discoveries. Each atomic element was associated with the same absolute quantity of electricity. 'Let us,' he said, 'suppose that these atmospheres of electricity . . . revolve (rapidly) round their respective atoms, and that the velocity of rotation determines what we call temperature.' It is the centrifugal force of these spinning atmospheres that causes the expansion of a heated gas. And we may suppose that the spinning electric atmospheres can set up isochronal vibrations in the ether and so transmit what we call radiant heat.

Inevitably, or so it seems, the practical bent of his mind showed itself at the end of the paper. His research, he said, led to a very different theory of the steam-engine from the generally accepted one. He denied that the power of the engine was due to the passage, or fall, of heat from a hot body to a cold one, from the furnace to the condenser. 'Mr E. Clapeyron', he remarked, had adopted this view and 'agrees with Mr Carnot in referring the power to *vis viva* developed by the caloric contained in the vapour in its passage from the temperature of the boiler to that of the condenser'.[41] But this was unacceptable, as it led to the view that *vis viva* might be destroyed through imperfect design of the engine. According to Clapeyron, 'there is an enormous loss of *vis viva* in the passage of heat from the furnace to the boiler'. Joule continued: 'Believing that the power to destroy belongs to the Creator alone I entirely coincide with Roget and Faraday[42] in the opinion that any theory which, when carried out, demands the annihilation of force, is necessarily erroneous.' And he was insistent that the heat given out to the condenser was less than that coming from the boiler, the difference being converted into mechanical power in the cylinder. These words suggest that he had read Séguin's letter to Herschel and, quite probably, Séguin's book on the steam-engine.

This passage contains Joule's statement of the principle of the conservation of energy, the key words being *any theory*. Taken in conjunction with his experimental work it leaves no doubt that he realised very clearly the comprehensive nature of the doctrine. The invocation of Faraday's name is, however, at first sight ambiguous, for Faraday did not have a conception of the conservation of *vis viva*, or, more generally, energy.[43] Such a formulation was, if not alien, certainly unfamiliar and probably unacceptable to his mind. But from Joule's point of view, it was a good idea to claim recognised authority in support of his ideas even if the authority in question would not necessarily have accepted his argument. The use of the word 'force', with or without the adjectives 'mechanical', or 'motive', as an alternative expression for *vis viva* should not cause confusion; familiar words usually have to do duty until a new theory is widely accepted and those with an aptitude for such things can hammer out the best expressions.

The paper was duly submitted to the Royal Society through Roget's good offices.[44] Joule wrote to Roget to express the hope that the paper 'will be found worthy of publication in the *Philosophical Transactions*, at any rate I have spared no pains to make it so'. He ended his letter by expressing his gratitude to Roget for his kindness.[45] But the Royal Society declined to be moved. An abstract was printed in the *Proceedings* – Joule believed it was by Roget himself – and, once again he had to turn to a more liberal journal, the *Philosophical Magazine*, to print it.

The paper was open to criticism on the grounds that the language was occasionally imprecise and there were a few mistakes. Boyle's law, for example, does not apply when the temperature as well as the pressure and volume of a gas changes. A small temperature change means that the deviation from Boyle's law is small; but it also means that the accuracy of the experiment is reduced. No doubt this was noticed by the referees. The statement that when a gas expands without doing work there is no net fall in temperature, no net conversion or loss of heat, is strictly correct only for a perfect gas. But this was not known at the time and cannot have been a criticism of the paper.

On the other hand the paper is rigorously argued, the sources of error are identified and corrected and possible objections are answered; in particular Joule was aware of the need of a further and direct demonstration of the converse, and far less evident, process of the conversion of heat into work. When these merits are considered, together with the consistency of the results with those obtained by two quite different methods, the conclusion must be that the paper should certainly have been published in the *Transactions*. An additional commendation was that Joule's discovery of the i^2r law of electrical heating, rejected by the Royal Society, had been confirmed by Becquerel, Botto and Lenz.

It is an unfashionable belief that when men reject new ideas it must be because they are blinkered reactionaries. At the risk of charges of triumphalism, Whiggery and even worse offences, it is arguable that, in this case, the old-fashioned view may well be correct. There is no reason to suppose that the Royal Society, at that particular time, was wholly exempt from the conservatism, lack of enterprise and resistance to new ideas that afflicts all institutions from time to time.

In April 1844 Joule was elected Honorary Librarian to the Lit & Phil. This implied that the Society was playing a bigger part in his life and demanding more of his time. Lyon Playfair, his fellow member, had given up his job in Clitheroe and moved to Manchester to take up an appointment as Honorary Professor of Chemistry at the Manchester Royal Institution.* The post was unpaid, but he could use the laboratory and this enabled him to make a rather haphazard living by taking on research students as well as by giving lectures. Many years later, in 1890, the elderly Lord Playfair wrote to James Dewar, at Cambridge, to give his recollections of Joule and of scientific life in Manchester in the early 1840s. He wrote that

> Joule was a man of singular simplicity and eartnestness. We used to meet at each other's houses at supper to help the progress of our work by discussion. Joule was an earnest worker, and was then engaged with his experiments on the mechanical equivalent of heat. He took me to his small laboratory to show me his experiments and I, of course, quickly recognised that my young friend, the brewer, was a great philosopher . . . I persuaded him to become a candidate for the Professorship of Natural Philosophy at St Andrews. He was on the point of securing this, but his personal slight deformity was an objection in the eyes of one of the electors, and St Andrews lost the glory of having one of the greatest discoverers of our age. When Joule first sent an account of his experiments to the Royal Society, the paper was referred among others to Sir Charles Wheatstone, who was an intimate personal friend. Wheatstone was an eminently fair man and a good judge, but the discovery did not then commend itself to his mind. For a whole Sunday afternoon we walked on Barnes Common discussing the experiments and their consequences, if true, to science, but all my arguments were insufficient to convince my friend, and I fear that the then Royal Society did not appreciate and publish the researches. I wrote from memory only.[46]

To what paper was Playfair referring? It could hardly have been the

---

*The Manchester Royal Insitution, founded in 1823, was modelled on the London Royal Institution. It was not a success and, in 1881, the building was acquired by the city to house its Art Gallery. The Manchester Athenaeum (1835) was also taken over by the city.

paper on the heating effect of an electric current, rejected for the *Transactions* in 1840, long before Playfair had arrived in Manchester and met Joule. The paper on the thermal effects of the compression and rarefaction of air was not, of course, the first of Joule's papers to be rejected by the Royal Society, but Playfair probably knew nothing about the first paper. As for the second paper, that, too, was rejected while Playfair was still in Manchester and it seems unlikely that Wheatstone would discuss a confidential reference from the Royal Society with a young man of twenty-six who was not yet a Fellow. The most likely explanation is, as Playfair hinted was possible, a lapse of memory; in the same letter he mis-spelled the names of Manchester contemporaries: Binsey, for Binney, Schunk, for Schunck. The conversation on Barnes Common may well have taken place after 1845, after the rejection of the paper, but before Wheatstone had been brought to accept the new theory.

There is doubt, too, about the St Andrews Chair. In 1847 Joule wrote to Playfair.

> I begin to see some fruits from my writing for testimonials for the Chair I have declined. I am not sorry I wrote for them because it gives me an insight into the opinions of divers people – Graham gave me a very good one. Faraday refused on the alleged ground that one Johnson cheated him some years ago! I received a letter from Becquerel this morning containing a first rate 'certificat' which is very gratifying to me . . .
>
> I remain however decidedly of opinion after what Major Playfair said that a mathematician ought to hold that Chair.[47]

Such concern about other people's opinions would hardly have bothered a tougher-minded man, like Lyon Playfair. Brought together through their membership of the Lit & Phil, these two contrasting characters, the diffident man of science and the ambitious and worldly young chemist, set out on a long series of researches. The idea behind the researches was due to Playfair; the experimental work was mainly carried out by Joule. The research continued after Playfair left Manchester and was co-ordinated by an extensive correspondence. Joule always wrote from New Bailey Street, but the experimental work was carried out at the new family home, 'Oak Field'. For his part, Playfair, after he moved to London, had a temporary laboratory in Duke Street, Westminster.[48]

The starting-point for the researches was Gay-Lussac's discovery that when gases combine chemically they do so in volumes that bear simple proportions to each other and to the products, if gaseous. The implications of this discovery were far-reaching, and it was natural to wonder whether a similar relationship could be found to hold between solid and liquid bodies. Unfortunately there were complicating factors that made it improbable, *a priori*, that Gay-Lussac's law could be extended to solids and liquids. All gases have the same coefficient of expansion so that the law holds at any temperature; solids and liquids have different coefficients of expansion so if the law held at one temperature it could not hold at another. Another complication was thought to be the cohesion between the particles of solids. In the case of gases the atoms are so far apart that it was thought that there could be no appreciable forces between them. Accordingly it was decided to examine, principally, bodies that could be dissolved in water and whose constitutions were well established.

The number of gaseous compounds formed by the combination of elementary gases is limited; the number of compounds, solid or liquid, formed by the combination of elements is virtually unlimited. Joule and Playfair were, therefore, faced with a laborious, but simple, task. To obtain the atomic volumes of a large number of compounds they divided their atomic weights by their specific gravities, which they measured by putting a known weight of each compound into a saturated solution in cases where the substance was water-soluble. Other liquids, including mercury, were also used.[49]

They worked their way steadily through a long list of compounds, beginning with hydrated salts.[50] In April 1845 Joule wrote to Playfair: '*I find that sulphate of soda does not crystallize with 10 atoms of water as pretended in the works on chemistry!* It crystallizes with 11 atoms. I have repeated the EXPERIMENT TWICE WITH FRESH CRYSTALS [*sic*]. I beg you to repeat it again to make quite sure.'[51]

Nevertheless the published paper made it ten and not eleven; evidently Playfair had been unable to confirm the result. And the letter ended on a note that seems curiously admonitory when it is recalled that Playfair was the senior in years, that he had gained his Ph.D. under Liebig who was properly revered by the Manchester scientific community* and that, above all, he was an able, ambitious and determined Scot.

'Don't [admonished Joule] be afraid of being called rash, it is a natural thing for a successful young theorist to be called so. And remember what Sedgwick said, "The way to make no errors is to write no papers".' Perhaps ambitious young men from north of the border and with foreign degrees were not yet so acceptable in the capital as they were in Manchester?

Joule's next letter raised another point.

I am strongly opposed to long papers, people won't read them. A paper of 30

---

*Liebig had been lavishly entertained by his former student W. C. Henry when he visited Manchester in 1837. He was made an Honorary Member of the Lit & Phil in 1843, in the same year that J. F. W. Herschel was elected.

pages is long enough for anything. I have no time to go on with this epistle now, but will resume when I have a little leisure and have something more to communicate. I have always to thank you for being a capital correspondent. A letter has a good effect in rousing one to exertion.[52]

However, their first paper of the series ran well over the limit of thirty pages. A footnote to the letter added:

I intended to have a little communication for the British Association on the Mechanical Value of Heat. I am anxious to give this equivalent exactly and to set aside all manner of objection – after this we shall begin to introduce mechanical language in our solution and diffusion experiments. Dont hurry me too much in the expansion business; we shall if spared in health wind up that subject by and by and no fear of others running before us.

And so they ploughed on, after the hydrated salts they examined the anhydrous salts, the nitrates, chlorides, bromides, iodides; the chromates, oxalates, carbonates and ammonium salts. This long paper was followed by the studies of the metallic elements, the sulphides, various non-metallic elements and oxides, dimorphism and polymorphism. Joule suggested that all the papers should be entitled 'Researches on specific gravity and atomic volume' and that the new paper should be called '2nd Series' and so on, 'after the manner of Dr Faraday'.

The experiments in Series 1 had, they argued, shown that water in hydrated salts had the same atomic volume as ice. Indeed, in the case of highly hydrated salts the only increase in volume on solution in water was that due to the water of crystallisation, the salt itself occupying no volume at all. The atomic volume of ice they found to be 9.8 and this, or 11, was the divisor of the atomic volumes of salts in the solid state. Joule was delighted with Playfair's discovery:[53] '8 is the cube of 2, consequently the atom of ice (considered as a globe or cube) will have exactly twice the linear dimensions of an atom whose volume is 1.225'; for 9.8/8 equals 1.225. And 9.8 + 1.225 equals 11.025 which was the other factor that occurred as a divisor for many compounds. The fundamental factor, therefore, appeared to be 1.225. The studies of metals in the solid, powdered and liquid forms – the latter states reduce or eliminate cohesive forces – seemed to confirm this. 'There is no longer any doubt', wrote Joule, 'that the volume of the melted metals are multiples of 1.225'.[54]

By now, however, the research was petering out. The last three series dealt with an accurate determination of the temperature at which water reaches its maximum density, the coefficients of the thermal expansion of salts and the disappearance of the acid and, in some cases, the base of hydrated salts on solution. The great majority of these and the other experiments carried out in collaboration with Playfair were routine and repetitive, but in the determination of the maximum density of water Joule's experimental skills were quite apparent and a brief account of these experiments is therefore given in Appendix 1. Joule had one last speculation to offer[55] but it proved fruitless. In fact the whole series of experiments carried out with zeal and effort turned out to be unimportant. J. R. Partington devoted just two-and-a-half lines to them in volume 4 of his magisterial *History of Chemistry*. It may be that the enduring authority of John Dalton – who steadfastly rejected the atomic implications of Gay-Lussac's law – prevented them following the line of thought that led to Avogadro's hypothesis and that enabled Cannizzaro to reform atomic chemistry.[56] On the face of it the research seemed promising, fundamental in fact, but it was to prove one of the dead ends that litter the record of science, that receive little or no mention in the history books and that are completely unknown to the practising scientist. This is, perhaps, a pity.

Playfair gave currency to Joule's theory of heat in the 'First report on the coals suited to the steam navy, addressed to the Right Honourable Viscount Morpeth, Commissioner of Woods etc', written by Sir Henry de la Beche and Dr Lyon Playfair.[57] But Joule and Playfair were now set on diverging courses. Playfair, elected FRS in 1848, went on to achieve fame, influence and the friendship of royalty through his association with the Society of Arts and his contribution to the success of the Great Exhibition of 1851. And from that he progressed to a chair of chemistry in Edinburgh University and thence to success in national politics and a peerage. To the very end of his career he was the keen and far-sighted advocate of State support for science, of the establishment of provincial universities and the endowment of research fellowships for young scientists. Apathy, academic snobbery and philistinism, recurrent features of British, or rather English, public life were the main obstacles he had to overcome in the campaign, of which he was a leader, for the recognition of the national importance of science.

While Joule was carrying on his researches with, or on behalf of, Playfair, he published a short paper jointly with Scoresby that extended the range of his thinking on the new theory of heat. This time he made it clear that the theory was due to him and that Scoresby provided much of the apparatus.[58] They compared the work done by an electric motor, a steam-engine and a horse with the weight of 'fuel' consumed in each case. Their engine incorporated Scoresby's powerful 'magnetic apparatus', described to the 1845 meeting of the British Association. Two types of armature were used and the engine run, first as a magneto, or electric generator, in which capacity it was used to melt a short length of wire. The engine was then run as a motor, driven by three Daniell cells. The current corresponding to a

steady speed was recorded, as was the quantity of zinc consumed in the
battery. The power that was developed was measured by substituting
falling weights, in place of the electric current, to drive the apparatus. With
their data they argued that if 'a' was the current when the motor was
prevented from running and 'b' the current when it was running steadily,
then a–b would be proportional to the heat actually converted into work.

Mr Joule, they pointed out, had shown in 1843 that a grain of zinc
burned in a battery should give enough power to raise 158 lb one foot high.
And so, in the case of any electric motor, the work done, denoted by x,
should be, for the combustion of a grain of zinc,

$$x = 158 \frac{(a-b)}{a}$$

The fraction (a–b)/a denoted the efficiency of the engine; that is the ratio
of the amount of heat actually available for conversion to the amount
theoretically available.* As a result of six experiments they inferred that the
maximum available duty they could get, using six Daniell cells and the
different armature arrangements, was 80 foot.pounds for one grain of zinc;
or about half the theoretical maximum.

The available evidence showed that the best Cornish steam engines
could convert only one-tenth of the heat generated by the burning coals
into useful work. The heat from one grain of burning coal was equivalent to
1,335 foot.pounds of work, but the best engines could deliver only 143
foot.pounds of work from the same amount of fuel. On the other hand they
deduced that an average work-horse, eating an adequate amount of hay and
corn, could maintain a daily average of 143 foot.pounds of work – the same
as the steam-engine – per grain of fodder consumed. But the combustion
of a grain of fodder generates heat equivalent to 557 foot.pounds of work,
from which it follows that the horse can convert one-quarter of the heat
energy of the fodder into useful work, the remainder being required for the
economy of the animal itself. And from this the conclusion is that an animal
is a much more efficient heat-engine than any human contrivance. This
was a point emphasised by Osborne Reynolds in a lecture thirty-six years
later.

*This formula, as W. J. M. Rankine pointed out much later in a letter to Joule, was analogous
to the thermodynamic expression for the efficiency of a heat engine, which is $(Q_1-Q_2)/Q_1$
where Q_1 denotes the heat absorbed by the engine, Q_2 the heat rejected to the cold body, or
condenser, and the difference between them the heat converted into useful work. (Letter
from W. J. M. Rankine to Joule, 'On the mechanical effect of heat and chemical forces',
Philosophical Magazine, vol. 5 (1853), p. 6.)

The joint paper with Scoresby provided the final refutation of the heady suggestion made by Jacobi ten years earlier and so widely and enthusiastically taken up. The work obtainable from a source of electric power is finite and limited by the amount of heat (= energy) in the fuel. The full amount of this work can be obtained when, in the above expression, the driving current 'b' tends towards zero. But in this case as the rate of burning of the zinc is strictly proportional to the current flowing, the power, too, tends to zero and it takes an infinitely long time to do the work! The paper was significant in another respect: it demonstrated yet again that Joule realised the enormous scope of the new principle, ranging, as it did, through mechanics, heat, electricity and magnetism, light and chemistry into the realm of biology.

Joint papers, the outcome of collaborative research by two or more men, were uncommon in British scientific journals of the time; they were particularly rare in the case of the physical sciences.[59] The attitudes and procedures of British science were still those of the independent gentleman, of the devotee, and its status was still amateur. On the Continent the joint paper was far more common. It was associated with officially sponsored science; notably with the academic world and the professor–student relationship. Such arrangements were still substantially absent in Britain.

After the paper on the heating of compressed air Joule published two short articles on the use of electrical heating in the measurement of specific heat capacities. The method was comparative: currents of the same magnitude were used to heat water and to heat the solid or liquid under examination. The relative specific heats could then be deduced from a comparison of the rises in temperature.[60] But these papers were diversions from his main line of research. The 1845 meeting of the British Association was held at Cambridge and there Joule described his next determination of the mechanical equivalent of heat.[61] It was a familiar experiment. A pair of falling weights drove, by means of two light cords, a vertical drum mounted on a shaft at the lower end of which was a brass paddle. This rotated in a copper drum full of water and fitted with brass baffles to counter the tendency of the water to rotate with the paddle. The apparatus was, he agreed, similar to the one used by George Rennie for studies on the friction of liquids.[62] The weights fell through thirty-six feet at a speed of one foot per second. After sixteen descents and sixteen rewinds the temperature of the water was taken, the procedure being repeated nine times. Corrections for heat losses having been made, Joule calculated that the mechanical equivalent was 890 foot.pounds. It has seemed paradoxical to some that, although this was the least accurate average result that he got, the paddle and drum method was to be the one that he subsequently adopted for his most precise determinations. But Joule made it quite clear that he did not have time to perfect the apparatus and that the experiments had to be carried out under unsatisfactory conditions. On the credit side, the drum and paddle apparatus was the best on the score of simplicity; it was open to fewer objections than the other three methods and it offered the simple and obvious advantage that other liquids besides water could be used thus extending the range of the experiments.

Joule now had four quite separate determinations of the mechanical equivalent of heat, with average results ranging from 774 to 890 foot-.pounds. He estimated that the value of the equivalent, whose validity he claimed was proven, was about 817 foot.pounds. He invited those who 'reside amid the romantic scenery of Wales or Scotland' to confirm his results by measuring the temperature of the water at the top and the bottom of a cascade. The theory indicated that the water at the bottom of Niagara (160 feet high) should be about $1/5°F$ higher than at the top. He ended his paper by extending his theory to gases. The pressure of a gas was, on his theory, proportional to the square of the velocity of the spinning atmospheres of electricity surrounding the atoms. From Gay-Lussac's law,* relating the temperature and pressure of all gases, he calculated that, at 480°F below the freezing point of water ($-266°C$), the pressure of all gases must be zero. Therefore, the atmospheres of electricity could not be spinning. And, as the *vis viva*, or living force, was proportional to the square of the velocity, that, too, must be zero and we must have reached the absolute zero of temperature for all bodies.

Joule presented his work and ideas to the British Association meetings in 1843, 1844 and 1845 and through the pages of the *Philosophical Magazine*. The scientific world seemed indifferent. Men of science were thinking of other things and Joule's papers aroused little interest. The magnetic crusade was under way; Whewell and others were deeply interested in the theory of tides; Couch Adams and Leverrier had discovered a new planet (Neptune). No less intriguing was Armstrong's discovery that a jet of steam was electrified. What did it portend scientifically? Were we on the brink of an invention comparable to, or of even greater importance than, the voltaic cell or the magneto-electric engine? What did it mean for the practical man? Everyone was familiar with the immense power of steam; if high-pressure steam could generate electricity directly and simply there were exciting new prospects of revolutionary power sources and new applications. Faraday himself was interested.

*Still wrongly called 'Charles's law' in English-language publications.

There were those who were unconvinced by Joule's arguments and there were those who were hostile. Among the latter was John Goodman, a Manchester surgeon who had joined the Lit & Phil on the same day as Joule and Binney. Goodman was a supporter of the old theory that heat, electricity, magnetism and light are manifestations of one fundamental fluid. 'Caloric', he wrote, 'in a state of repose is the universal, latent and primitive fluid of all undisturbed matter.' If caloric is generated by friction why does it not disappear when friction ceases? If caloric is merely the effect of particles of matter in motion, how do we explain electricity? There was also the problem of latent heat; to describe it as *vis viva* transformed into 'attraction through space' was merely a verbal quibble to avoid an insuperable objection.

Some, in good positions to judge, were beginning to recognise the value of the mechanical theory. One such was Paul Ermann, who realised that the 'future progress of science' was at issue.[63] The frictional heating of metals, which he called the 'tribothermical effect', was much more likely to be effected by a vibratory motion of molecules than by the continuous efflux of a caloric fluid. Unfortunately he was not a follower of Joule. Electricity is involved in the process and, he adds somewhat portentously, 'the great prize in this race of discovery would fall to him who should discover a difference of thermo-electric action, according as a magnetically polarized bar should be rubbed (that is, molecularly heated) at the one or other end of its poles'.

Finally we should not forget the industrious Professor Wartmann and his kind. Wartmann carried out a long and well reported series of experiments on electricity. He tried to detect the influence, if any, of high mechanical pressure on a current flowing in a wire; he found none. He sought the influence of different coloured lights on an electric current; none was apparent. He measured the rates at which electrified and non-electrified bodies cooled, but found no difference. He concluded that electricity is not 'of itself' hot and that it is not propagated along wire in undulations. He found that a current in a wire does not affect the diffraction of light while a current flowing in an electrolyte has no effect on the polarisation of light. He reported many other curious things, most of them negative. And he must have tramped, unseeing, past a dozen discoveries waiting to be made for he had no hypotheses to guide his mind.

How, in short, were – and indeed are – scientific priorities to be decided? The modern belief that they can be settled by politicians, or civil servants, or committees is obviously nonsensical. If Wartmann's and other fruitless researches together with really valuable contributions are added to the series of debates, discussions, and arguments that make up the life of science we can understand how Joule's work passed almost unnoticed. He may have hoped for some encouragement from a very high quarter, for in May 1845 he wrote to Faraday enclosing a complimentary copy of his original paper on the mechanical equivalent of heat, adding: 'I now feel quite certain that the heat which can increase the temperature of a 1lb of water by a degree is equal to about 800 lbs raised a foot high'.[64] The letter ended sadly:

> Perhaps you may recollect that Mr Sturgeon came to Manchester a few years ago in order to superintend the 'Victoria Gallery of Practical Science'. Owing to the pressure of the times that institution failed soon after its establishment. Mr Sturgeon, from this event and from the expenses he incurred in the publication of the 'Annals of Electricity' which he was at length compelled to discontinue, has, you will be sorry to hear, been reduced to great poverty and has no means of supporting his family beyond the precarious proceeds of his lectures. You will be glad to hear that some of his friends in this town are trying to devise something for his support. It would be indeed a great pity if a man who, like Sturgeon, has under singular disadvantages done very much for the promotion of electrical and magnetical science should in old age be allowed to endure the privations of poverty. Perhaps when our designs are matured with respect to him you would feel disposed to give a little assistance?

The next meeting of the British Association was at Southampton* and, although he had no contribution to offer, Joule attended. There he met the Lion of British Science, Sir J. F. W. Herschel, Bt., Copley Medallist and Bakerian Lecturer. On his return to Manchester Joule wrote him a most respectful letter, referring to the 'conversation I had the honour of holding with you while sailing round the Isle of Wight'.[65] It must have been a strange conversation, and the letter makes curious reading, for it was largely about some sadistic experiments to discover whether spiders could survive in sulphuric acid. It turned out that they could not and Joule added a short, obsequious passage that made Herschel look like a character from Gilbert and Sullivan. 'I regret that I mentioned the alleged property to one so eminent as yourself without having previously ascertained the real fact of the case by experiment.' What would Playfair have written in the same circumstances?

Turning to a more respectable subject and one related to his own researches, Joule said he had hoped to give some account of experiments to show whether a change of temperature was caused by pulling out and collapsing perfectly elastic tissue. Caoutchouc and gutta-percha would not

---

*With the exceptions of York, Oxford and Cambridge, the early meetings of the British Association were held in seaport towns. It was relatively easy to travel, carrying baggage and apparatus, to such towns in the days before the railway network was fully established.

do as they were imperfectly elastic.[66] In a postscript he mentioned that he was repeating some old experiments, published in Sturgeon's *Annals*, on the change of length when a bar of iron is magnetised by a current flowing in a surrounding coil of wire. These experiments were later published in the *Philosophical Magazine*.[67]

Joule had now appealed to the two men who, by general consent, stood at the head of physical science in Britain at that time. Herschel had rejected the dynamical theory of heat and Faraday would have had little sympathy for it; it represented a style of science with which he was unfamiliar and a quantitative, or mathematical technique that he distrusted. Joule could count as (nominal) converts his fellow Mancunian, Eaton Hodgkinson, and two distinguished Irish men of science whose interests lay elsewhere. By the begining of 1847, therefore, Joule seemed to have made little or no headway. Perhaps this was why he decided to give the second of his public lectures. He had, in 1846, been elected Honorary Secretary of the Lit & Phil. Here, at least and in spite of some opposition, his views would be listened to with some interest and respect. He could appeal to the people of Manchester.

The graceful little St Ann's Church, in the heart of Manchester, was built in the early eighteenth century through the generosity of Lady Ann Bland, a formidable lady and a strong supporter of the Hannoverian cause. In 1842 St Ann's Church School was opened in nearby Queen Street; and it was in the library, or reading-room, of the school that Joule gave a comprehensive and, what would now be called, popular account of his work and ideas.[68] The chairman for the lecture was the Revd H. W. McGrath who was described as an eloquent, handsome and refined man. Apart from the Curate of St Ann's, those present included Frederick Crace Calvert, professor of chemistry at the Manchester Royal Institution, E. W. Binney and Dalton's old friend, Peter Clare. The lecture was illustrated by experiments with a voltaic battery, an electro-magnetic engine and other apparatus. It was reported at length in two issues of the *Manchester Courier* (5 and 12 May 1847), a Conservative paper owned by Colonel Sowler, a friend of the Joule family. The radical *Manchester Guardian*, under Archibald Prentice, was willing to print a short résumé of the lecture but declined to give it full coverage, although it gave generous reports of other lectures in Manchester at the same time. For the general public, however, the most interesting events over those days were the dreadful wreck of an emigrant ship off Islay with the loss of 240 souls (only three survived), the 'shocking murder' at the 'rural village of Chorlton-cum-Hardy, a sweet, quiet spot' and the 'Horrid murder of three persons at Mirfield'; all this in the stretch of one week.

The lecture was, in effect, Joule's qualitative statement of the principle of the conservation of energy; his quantitative statements being represented by his systematic researches described in his scientific papers. He began by offering a simple definition of matter and followed that by elucidating the related ideas, or concepts, of *vis viva*, or 'living force' and what he called 'attraction through space' (equivalent to potential energy).[69] These are interchangeable; as, for example, when a moving body rises up against gravity or when fingers wind up a watch spring. In each case the *vis viva* of motion is transformed into attraction through space, but the *vis viva* can be recovered in its full amount: the body can fall down, the spring can unwind.

There followed a short, curiously misleading argument. 'The common experience of everyone', he remarked, 'teaches him that living force is not *destroyed* by the friction of collision of bodies.' This was odd because it was entirely inconsistent with his earlier admission that 'until very recently the universal opinion had been that living force could be . . . destroyed at anyone's option'. Living force, he argued, has always been with us; in spite of friction the winds are as strong, the torrents as impetuous as they were 4,000, even 6,000 years ago (how did he know?). Ignoring the vast solar heat received by the earth every day, and of which he was well aware, he concluded 'with certainty' that living force was not annihilated by friction.

However we interpret this inconsistent paragraph what followed was entirely acceptable and straightforward. Wherever living force was apparently destroyed – by friction, percussion or by whatever means – an exact equivalent of heat was restored: this was proved by his experiments. Conversely, the disappearance of heat was accompanied by the production of living force, or of attraction through space. In the case of the steam-engine, for example, heat from the furnace was converted into the living force of the fly-wheel and the machinery. He admitted that this had not yet been demonstrated. But he claimed that a convincing proof of the conversion of heat into living force could be deduced from the performance of the electromagnetic engine. In this machine chemical heat, abstracted from the battery, was converted into living force. In short, heat, living force, attraction through space '(to which I might add *light* were it consistent with the scope of the present lecture)' were all mutually convertible. Nothing was ever lost. And, he continued, the mechanical value of the heat needed to raise the temperature of 1lb water by 1°F was measured by attraction through space: 817 lb raised one foot against the attraction of gravity. From this, the mechanical equivalent of heat, and from the published data, he inferred that only about one-tenth of the available living force from the burning coal was converted into useful living force by the best steam-engines in the world (i.e. the Cornish engines). But the animal body, much more versatile than any steam-engine, could produce more living force than any steam-engine for the consumption of the same amount of fuel (this was a slip of the tongue; he did not mean 'fuel', he meant 'heat').

To illustrate the explanatory power of his new doctrine Joule turned to the puzzling phenomenon of shooting stars. There had been much debate about these. Were they tiny earth satellites, momentarily catching the sunlight while the earth below was in darkness? Did they shine by virtue of some chemical reaction; or because of electric sparks due to atmospheric electricity?[70] Joule's explanation was simple but, on the face of it, implausible and contrary to common experience. Moving with immense speed meteorites suddenly encounter the earth's atmosphere – their height above earth had been determined – and this retarded them so much that their living force was converted into heat of such intensity that they became incandescent and were burned away. What his audience made of this we cannot know; in their experience movement through or by cold air cooled things down. But they would have approved of his observation that this was most fortunate. Without the protection of the atmosphere the ceaseless bombardment of meteorites would have made life on earth impossible. This, they would have reflected, was one more demonstration of the wisdom and beneficence of the Deity. The same divine plan was apparent in the wind systems of the globe; in this case heat was converted into the living force of atmospheric air. In fact,

> the phenomena of nature, whether mechanical, chemical or vital, consist almost entirely in a continual conversion of attraction through space, living force and heat into one another. Thus it is that order is maintained in the universe – nothing is deranged, nothing ever lost, but the entire machinery, complicated as it is, works smoothly and harmoniously.

He ended with a speculation about the nature of heat. *Sensible* heat – apparent to our senses and to thermometers – is due to the living force of atoms moving like tiny projectiles or spinning rapidly on their axes. Latent heat, on the other hand, is accounted for by attraction through space, so that when water boils, for example, the distance between the mutually attracting atoms increases enormously as it becomes steam.* Finally, he pointed out that the new doctrine could account for many other phenomena and he was sure it could resolve many abstruse as well as simple

---

*There was another interesting slip here. Professor Mendoza has pointed out that he failed to recognise that ice, on melting, when the centrifugal force of his atoms should increase, actually contracts on becoming water!

problems in science. His lecture amounted to a statement of the principle of the conservation of energy within the tested limits together with the proposition that it would be found to be of entirely general application. It was unique among similar contemporary and previous statements to much the same effect in that it was supported by a series of authoritative and, so far as such things can ever be final, decisive experiments of his own devising and execution.

Although the lecture was to be a landmark in his career it is doubtful if it had any immediate effect on the local scientific community, much less on the national one. That he was pleased with it is shown by his action in sending copies of the *Courier* to his friends. Binney wrote to acknowledge the receipt of two copies of the newspaper 'containing your very interesting discussion at St Ann's School', but adding: You will be sorry to learn that poor Mr Sturgeon is again very dangerously ill. Do call and see him this evening if you can.'[71]

Later that year Colonel Grey, Private Secretary to the Prime Minister, Lord John Russell, announced that £200 had been awarded to Mr Sturgeon from the Royal Bounty Fund.[72] For William Sturgeon 1847 was to see the first of two tardy and grudging public acknowledgements of his dedicated work on behalf of, and his contributions to, science. In the same year Joule's ideas were to be publicly and decisively discussed for the first time.

The Oxford meeting of the British Association in 1847 was held in June, unusually early in the year. It was evidently a brilliantly successful occasion. Section A (Mathematics and Physics) was particularly prosperous. Those attending including Faraday, Whewell, G. G. Stokes, Sir William Hamilton and J. D. Forbes, together with Herschel, Snow Harris, Nichol and Joule. The Section President, the Revd Professor Baden-Powell, read a paper on meteors in which he pointed out that, since Quetelet had shown that their mean altitude was about 100 miles, they must be just inside the earth's atmosphere and they may, therefore, burn by ordinary combustion which would explain their brightness.

On Thursday 24 June, Joule read his paper on the new theory of heat. It was late in the day and, to save time, the Chairman asked him to confine himself to a brief summary of the principal points of his paper. He exhibited and explained his paddle-wheel apparatus. Experiments using water and sperm oil gave, he claimed, 781.5 and 782.1 foot.pounds respectively for the mechanical equivalent of heat. He had also made some experiments on the compression of steel springs. No heat, he found, was generated; all the living force used to compress the springs had been converted into attraction through space. It was, he believed, analogous to latent heat. These static experiments were not, Mendoza has pointed out,[73] actually included in his brief summary and they were ommitted from his subsequent paper in the *Philosophical Magazine.* They had to be published later.

Joule believed his paper would have passed without notice had not a young man at the back of the hall risen and asked penetrating questions that created a lively interest in the paper. The young man in question – William Thomson, later Sir William Thomson and later still Lord Kelvin, OM – subsequently denied Joule's account, saying that he remained seated and put his questions to Joule after the meeting.[74] But little of this reached the outside world. The *Athenaeum* hardly noticed Joule's paper, merely remarking that Mr Joule had exhibited an instrument whereby the heat developed by fans moving in water, oil and other liquids could be referred to the distance through which weights descended while whirling the fans round, which could be described as the ultimate positivist account of his experiments and the theory on which they were based. The journal did, however, record some discussion of one of the last of the Playfair–Joule papers.[75] The *Literary Gazette* was more generous. Of the seven papers presented to the Section it selected three for commendation: Sir William Hamilton's on quaternions, a paper by the Russian Davidov and 'the only other communication worthy of notice', which was Joule's. It gave a fair account of his experiments; and it recorded a distinguished audience: Airy (Astronomer Royal), Herschel, Hamilton, the Earl of Rosse, Leverrier, J. Couch Adams, Struve, Whewell, Baden-Powell, Peacock, Wheatstone, Stokes, and several other notables. Young Mr Thomson was not listed; he was, presumably, too junior.

William Thomson (1824–1907), son of Professor James Thomson, was born in Belfast and educated first at Glasgow University and then at St Peter's College (now Peterhouse), Cambridge. His mathematical abilities showed themselves early; at sixteen he had mastered Fourier's *Analytical Theory of Heat.* In the Mathematics Tripos of 1845 he came Second Wrangler and, shortly afterwards, was Smith's Prizeman. He was then sent to Paris where he worked for a time in Victor Regnault's laboratory, improving his practical skills under the master experimentalist. Regnault was, at that time, carrying out government-sponsored researches into the properties of steam, essential work in view of the great, and ever growing, importance of the steam-engine. The success of these researches depended, *inter alia*, on accurate and reliable thermometers; and the problems of thermometry cannot have been far from Thomson's mind when he chanced to read Emile Clapeyron's paper of 1834.[76] This introduced him to Carnot's theory of the heat-engine and he realised, as no else with the exception of Carnot himself had done, that the theory made an absolute scale of temperature possible; a scale, that is, that would be entirely independent of the properties of any material substance. The work done by a perfect heat-engine, working on a Carnot cycle, depended solely on the temperatures of the source, or furnace, and the sink, or condenser. It was necessarily independent of the particular working substance, whether it was a vapour, like steam, a gas, like air, or a solid such as a bar of iron. The work done by a unit of heat in a Carnot engine would therefore be a measure of the temperature difference independent of any thermometric fluid or gas.

In 1846 Thomson, at the remarkably young age of twenty-two, was elected Professor of Natural Philosophy in Glasgow University.* Almost at once he began to work out the absolute temperature scale based on Carnot's principle and assuming the caloric, or conservationist, theory of heat. The result diverged from the conventional gas scale. This was not unexpected. Carnot himself had concluded, correctly but from data later shown to be incorrect, that a unit of heat 'falling' from, say, 100° to 99° would do less work than a unit falling from 10° to 9°. If, therefore, the work done by a unit of heat falling 1° was to be taken as the fixed standard the gas scale and the new absolute scale were bound to diverge.[77]

After the British Association meeting Joule published a short paper on the velocity of sound, applying his ideas to Laplace's correction of Newton's formula.[78] And then he went off to Sutton Court, at Turnham Green, to stay with his aunt and her husband, his former tutor, Frederick Tappenden, who was now running his school there.[79] But he was anxious to enlist the support of a man whom he recognised as well informed, interested and potentially sympathetic, if by no means yet a convert. From Turnham Green he wrote to Thomson at the end of June to confirm that he had left offprints of two of his papers with the porter at Pembroke College (one on the 'changes of temperature produced by condensation & c of air' and the other on the 'Calorific Effect of Magneto Electricity'.[80] He was sorry to have missed Thomson before leaving Oxford and begged him to accept the papers that, he hoped, would be of interest. He added:

> I have felt pretty much gratified in meeting at least two (Mr Stokes and yourself) who enter into my views of this subject and hope to be able to cultivate an acquaintance which I found so delightful. Any time you may be going through Manchester, do me the favour of a visit at New Bailey Street, Salford, where I should have great pleasure in showing you my laboratory & apparatus. I shall be in Manchester in a day or two.

*Hamilton, however, had been elected Professor of Astronomy in Dublin while still an undergraduate.

Two days later Thomson wrote to his father from Cambridge, having returned to his old College.[81] The BA meeting had been 'delightful':

> I need not give you any details, as you will of, course, see the *Athenaeum* containing the report (tell James [his brother] to look for an account of Joule's paper on the dynamical theory of heat. I am going to write to James about it & enclose him a set of papers I have received from Joule, whose acquaintance I made, as soon as I have time. Joule is, I am sure, wrong in many of his ideas, but he seems to have discovered some facts of extreme importance, as for instance, that heat is developed by the fric[n] of fluids).

Behind the last sentence lay a problem that Thomson knew about before he heard Joule's paper or had any discussion with him. Four months earlier he had written to J. D. Forbes:

> I have found a Stirling's air-engine in our Augean Stables and got it taken to pieces, as it was clogged with dust and oil, and I expect to have it going as soon as I have time.
>
> I think this consideration will make it clear that there is really a loss of effect, in conduction of heat through a solid. There is neither expenditure nor gain in mechanical effect in melting ice in an atmosphere at 32° as is readily proved. Now we may have a fire or source of heat, in the interior of a hollow conducting shell, spending all its effect in melting ice at 32°. But it seems very mysterious how power can be lost in such a way, but perhaps not more so than that power should be lost in the friction of fluids (a plumb line, with the weight in water, for instance) by which there does not seem to be any heat generated, nor any physical change effected.[82]

Joule's paddle-wheel experiments showed that heat *was* generated by the friction of fluids; but, for Thomson, the problem remained: how could he account for the work that could be obtained if an engine was to be interposed when heat flowed directly from a hot body to a cold one?

On his return to Manchester Joule lost no time in pursuing what he plainly saw to be his advantage with Thomson. On 7 July he wrote to explain that his experiments on compressed air refuted the doctrine that the specific heat capacity of air was changed by compression or expansion.[83] And he made it clear that his experiments on 'the calorific effects of magneto-electricity' showed that there was no compensatory cooling anywhere in the circuit; everywhere heat was generated according to the i^2r law. He accounted for the Peltier effect as the conversion of heat at the bimetallic junction into the 'mechanical force of the current'. And he passed on his suggestion of a simple experiment that Thomson might try:

> With regard to the waterfall experiments I don't think you would find much difficulty and I am anxious that you should make the experiment. I think you might succeed with a sensible thermometer of Regnault's and a rope and bucket

for collecting the water. As for the spray and foam, I think that in a large waterfall the influence of the air must be trivial as the same particles of air are in contact with the water for a length of time and even if the objection held good it might be overcome by examining the effect in summer and winter. I do hope to hear of your success in this experiment which is really a very interesting one.

Three days later he wrote to his convert, George Gabriel Stokes.

I am at present engaged in setting up an apparatus made of wrought iron in order to repeat the experiment on the friction of fluid with mercury. I am not sure that this form of the experiment was not suggested by yourself or whether it had not previously occurred to myself. If the former be true I should be glad to know. I intend also to repeat the expt. with the friction of metal as suggested by Faraday but I do not expect to obtain more heat thereby.[84]

Joule had made good use of his opportunities to discuss his experiments and ideas with some of the scientific leaders of the day. It is particularly interesting that both Stokes and Faraday appear to have made useful suggestions about further experiments, although it may be doubted whether Faraday appreciated the full significance of Joule's experiments and the ideas motivating them. The letter ended with a postscript:

I have inferred from conversation with you that you are entirely in favour of the mechanical theory of heat. I hope to see labours of yours in the same direction. I have not unfortunately had opportunities of studying mathematics sufficiently to follow the subject in its mathematical department. Professor Thomson will, I hope, try the heat of waterfalls. There is an immensity of work in this subject which is enough to occupy a dozen scientific men at least.

Thomson's interest did not, however, imply his conversion to the new doctrine. The influence of Fourier and the deep impression made by Carnot's work were not to be nullified by Joule's experiments. On 12 July Thomson wrote to his brother, James, to tell him that he was just off to London 'where I shall remain for as few days as possible, before starting for Paris'.[85] He continued:

I enclose Joule's papers which will astonish you. I have only had time to glance through them as yet. I think at present that some great flaws must be found. Look especially to the rarefaction and condensation of air, where something is decidedly neglected in estimating the total change effected in some of the cases. Keep all the papers carefully together & give them to me when I return.

Dutifully, James considered that Joule had committed blunders and, following William's hint, identified one in the experiments on the expansion of compressed air.[86] Joule had claimed that no external work had been done during the expansion and therefore no heat had been consumed. But, in fact, there was an external effect: in the 'analysis' of the experiment one vessel was cooled, the other heated, and this effect could have been used to produce external work.* But James was uneasy: 'Some of (Joule's) views have a slight tendency to unsettle one's mind as to the accuracy of Clapeyron's principles. If some of the heat can absolutely be turned into mech. eff. Clapeyron may be wrong.'

James suggested that a more precise definition of what was meant by *quantity of heat* could have settled the matter. Joule might have argued that if a pound of hot water lost a degree of heat to a pound of cold water, the latter gained more heat than the former lost, the increment being due to the mechanical effect, or work, that might have been done by the 'fall' of the heat from the high to the low temperature. This odd suggestion, that tacitly abandoned the axiom of the conservation of caloric, or heat, may have been prompted by the criticisms put forward by Marc Séguin in his book, *De l'Influence des Chemins de Fer,*[87] which Thomson, as an apprentice engineer, had quite probably read. Séguin, an experienced engineer, had been led to doubt the accepted theory of heat. In his book he had put forward a practical problem that, at the same time, implied the theoretical question that William Thomson had proposed to Forbes. If, Séguin suggested, steam from a boiler was passed through a mass of cold water so that it condensed, the water should be raised to a higher temperature than if the same steam had been previously used to drive an engine. Séguin's experiments to prove this were indecisive – such experiments were extremely difficult to carry out (see below, pp. 224) – but the implicit problem he raised – how to account for the work that *could* have been done when heat flowed by simple conduction rather than through an engine – remained unanswered.

In the meantime Joule was writing to Stokes to thank him for his suggestion that mercury be used in the paddle-wheel experiments. The apparatus was similar to that used for water and spermaceti oil but made of iron instead of brass. It weighed nearly 40 kg and held 205 kg of mercury. Stokes's forecast proved correct; mercury was an excellent liquid for the purpose. The expenditure of 5,230 foot.pounds caused a rise in temperature of 4.20° and this gave an equivalent of 782 foot.pounds, aggreeably close to the figures given by the two previous experiments. The paddle-wheel and calorimeter method, simple and open to few sources of error, gave very consistent and accurate results. It may well be that the continued

---

*Joule's experiment showed that when air expanded without doing work the temperature did not fall, which according to the accepted theory it should have done as the specific heat capacity was supposed to increase with the volume. Furthermore, if work had been done then, on the accepted theory, the temperature should have been the same at the end as at the beginning, which would have been contrary to Carnot's fundamental axion.

scepticism of his peers had stimulated Joule to aim for the highest standard of accuracy and the greatest possible consistency between his results. If this was so, the course of his researches between 1843 and 1847 reflected something of the social art of scientific persuasion as well as the logic of research. But for many, if not for most, people the interest of the paddle-wheel experiments was that they led to a novel and quite unexpected result. That water could be heated merely by agitating it seemed quite extra-ordinary.* Even today non-scientific people are surprised to learn this; everyone has been conditioned to accept that in order to heat water a gas, coal or oil flame or an immersion heater is essential.

These points, however, were not prominent in the thoughts of the various parties in August 1847. In his letter to Playfair of 22 May Joule had given, as an additional reason for withdrawing from the competition for the St Andrews Chair, the fact that he would 'have enough to do . . . this half year in furnishing a house and *marrying a wife* without bothering . . . with infinitesimals'. On 18 August, James Prescott Joule married Amelia Grimes, daughter of John Grimes and his wife Janet, at St Peter's Church, Higher Bebbington, Rock Ferry; incumbent, the Revd Thomas Fisher Redhead. John Grimes, who had been Comptroller of Customs for Liverpool, was presumably dead, for the bride was given away by a Mr Dawson. Amelia, who had been born in Leith, was thirty-three at the time of her marriage while her bridgegroom was just under twenty-nine. Like his brother Benjamin, James Joule had married a woman older than himself. It has been said that it is not unusual for a man who has lost a mother to whom he was deeply attached to marry an older woman. In the case of the Joule brothers such a predisposition could have been reinforced by the loss of their younger sister, Alice, two years before their mother had died. It may also be that Joule's slight physical deformity coupled with his shyness made him the sort of man who would, in any case, seek the company of an older and self-assured woman.

Young Thomson was off on a grand tour. On 22 August he wrote to his father from the Hotel des Bergues, Geneva. He had, he said, time only for a short line. Tomorrow he would take the Sallanches diligence as far as Cluses, on the Arve; if the weather was bad he would go straight on to Chamonix where he was to meet the famous August Balmat, of the same family as the great Joseph Balmat who had accompanied de Saussure to the summit of Mont Blanc. A week later he wrote from Chamonix to give a

*In 1808 Joseph Reade reported that a half-pint of water agitated for a few minutes rose in temperature by 8°F (*Nicholson's Journal*, vol. 19 (1808), p. 113). He gave no details of his experiment and evidently no one was able to repeat it. By 1847 it had been forgotten.

graphic account of the journey. The grand spectacle of the mountains had greatly pleased and impressed him. He had walked part of the way, meeting a friendly notary who had chatted to him. He had also been soaked in a rain storm, and an English couple, who had lived there for many years, had taken pity on him and invited him into their home to dry off. A week later he wrote from the Hospice of the Grand St Bernard.[87] He had met an Irish party, two ladies and three gentlemen, with whom he had had a friendly chat. He had sampled and greatly enjoyed *Glühwein*; it had set him up for the passage of the Col de Bonhomme, to the south-west of Chamonix. It had been a doubtful morning so he had started at noon

> for St Gervais (a detour of about three miles). As all the summits were still enveloped in mists we did not go over the Col de Forclaz, but kept by the car road which goes about 2/3 of the way to St Martin (which you have traversed twice). Before leaving the St Martin road I met, walking, Mr Joule, with whom I had recently become acquainted at Oxford. When I saw him before he had no ideas of being in Switzerland [*sic*] (he had even wished me to make some experiments on the temperature of waterfalls) but since that time he had been married and was now on his wedding tour. His wife was in a car, coming up a hill. As we were going different ways we had of course only a few minutes to speak. I was even more surprised by this accidental meeting than the last.

It seems unlikely that, at Oxford, Joule would have told Thomson that he had no idea of being in Switzerland. As he was meeting Thomson for the first time there was no reason why he should tell him he was to be married in two months' time. But the encounter was to have rather more interesting consequences than a chance meeting and geographical confusion might suggest. It was to be the source of one of the best known anecdotes in the history of science. Thirty-five years later Thomson was to say that, when they met, Joule had a thermometer with him and was measuring, or was about to measure, the temperature of a waterfall – and on his honeymoon, too! The story told in 1882[89] was to be repeated ten years further on. But as there was no mention of the thermometer and the waterfall in the letter written only four days later, the conclusion must be that Thomson knew how to recognise and how to improve a good story. At that time, however, the young professor who had such a brilliant career was heading north into Switzerland and the Bernese Oberland.[90] Perhaps he did have the experiences that J. D. Forbes, the pioneer alpinist and notable contributor to knowledge of the conduction and radiation of heat, had hoped for him: 'If you have enjoyed one five hundredth part of the pleasure I have had in those mountains your heart will be overflowing.[91]

5

Consolidation and development

Salford, in P. M. S. Blackett's words, is one of the towns in which so much of the nation's wealth has been made and on which so little of it has been spent. To the south and east of the town centre were the mills, foundries, factories and slums that, according to Leon Faucher, were the scenes and causes of so much human misery. Even in the mid-nineteenth century, however, when the 'grimy hand of industrialism' lay heaviest on the town, it could still show attractive features. The Crescent was, and still is, a broad road, curving round a deeply incised meander of the River Irwell, with affluent, even elegant houses on the south side; to the north, beyond the Irwell, lay open country, interrupted only by occasional collieries and dye-works along the river. Benjamin Joule and his wife Caroline lived at 29 The Crescent until she died in 1844, whereupon he returned to 'Oak Field'. In the following year, on 24 June, St. John the Baptist day, he was baptised and received into the Church of England at Holy Trinity Church, Hulme. Four years later, on 9 April, 1849, James and Amelia moved into a house on The Crescent, just a year before the birth of their first child, Benjamin Arthur, on 18 May, 1850. For the first two years of married life they had lived at 'Oak Field'; house-furnishing seems to have been a lengthy business. Their Salford home, 1 Acton Square, still stands; a relatively modest Georgian house on the corner of The Crescent and a small cul-de-sac that could only by courtesy be called a square. It has a small front garden and the rooms, while reasonable by modern standards, are small for the period. But the neighbourhood was select; the people who lived on The Crescent included solicitors, cotton-spinners, merchants and Joule's friend and supporter, Eaton Hodgkinson. 'Joule House' – now the head office of the Cultural Services Department of Salford City Council – faces Salford City Art Gallery, with its famous collection of Lowrys, and the University of Salford on its fine, open site to the west of the meander in the Irwell.

The year 1847 was another memorable one for Joule. He had married; he had gained the interest, if not yet the support, of a young man who was clearly going to be successful. And in that same year two very different works were published, both urging the case for the energy principle and both indebted to Joule.

John Herapath (1790–1868) was a self-taught man of science, a devotee who put forward a mechanical theory of heat early in the nineteenth century.[1] He accepted the Daltonian theory that the atoms of a gas were arranged in a lattice. But he argued that heat was not due to the presence of a self-repulsive fluid, caloric; it was caused by a rapid vibration, or oscillation, of atoms about mean, fixed points. Temperature was the measure of the momentum of the particles; gas pressure was due to change of momentum. Herapath, who does not seem to have known of Bernoulli's earlier pioneer theory, sent his papers to Sir Humphrey Davy, President of the Royal Society, who was well disposed to the mechanical theory of heat. Davy had suggested that heat was due to the rapid rotation of the atoms and was willing to sponsor a kindred, if rather different, theory. Unfortunately, some of Herapath's ideas were open to serious criticism; his mathematical treatment was obscure and he had a fondness for inventing and using neologisms that increased the difficulty of understanding him. His papers were given fair consideration but, as he refused to make any changes or corrections, they were rejected for the *Transactions*.[2]

Herapath, like Sturgeon, ventured into publishing; unlike Sturgeon his enterprise – the *Railway Magazine and Annals of Science* (1832–), – was a success and he used it to publish occasional articles on his theory of heat. In 1845 he read Joule's paper on the heat generated by the compression of air. Joule's determination of the mechanical equivalent of heat was gratifyingly close to the figure that he found could be deduced from his own theory (he, himself, had no prior conception of the mechanical value, or equivalent of heat). In 1846 he mustered his papers and wrote them up, with additional material, for publication under the title of *Mathematical Physics*.[3] 'One of the great aims of the present work', he wrote, with an eye firmly fixed on a matter of great public interest and concern, 'is to apply its principles to a correct theory of the operation and economy of steam.'

Herapath gave Joule full and generous recognition.[4] One one point they differed. Herapath's theory resulted in a mechanical equivalent of heat of 885 foot.pounds; Joule's figure (817 foot.pounds) was, he claimed, too low.[5] As for Sir Humphry Davy's theory, 'Circular or rotary motions, as suggested by Sir H. Davy, we do not consider. They have no place in the view taken here of heat. If there be any phenomena requiring such motions they are unknown to us.'[6] To what extent these, and Herapath's other views, had an immediate influence on Joule it is impossible to say. Joule had a copy of *Mathematical Physics* and, to judge by pencilled annotations, he had read it with some care. It was published at the beginning of 1847 and the question is whether he had time to read it, or at least the relevant passages, before he wrote his St Ann's Church lecture. As we know from a letter to Playfair, written in 1846,[7] Joule already knew something of Herapath's earlier work and views. And there the matter must rest.

The idea that heat could be explained by the motion of atmospheres of electricity spinning round material atoms was not mentioned in the St Ann's lecture and Joule never referred to it afterwards. It may well be, therefore, that Herapath's writings had convinced him that the hypothesis was unnecessary; that the motion of atoms could adequately account for heat. As for the old idea of electricity as a 'subtle fluid', it progressively disappeared from other communiqués from the front lines of science. Electricity was to be regarded as a form of energy, or at least as an efficient means of transporting energy. Its exact nature was unimportant, even inscrutable. Joule's paper on the electrolysis of water had marked the beginning of the new view: 'electricity . . . the grand agent for transporting . . . chemical heat'. And when he showed that heat, chemical or otherwise, is of the nature of energy the equation was virtually complete. In contrast, Herapath was not interested in electricity; he was therefore out of step with many of the leaders of physical science of his time. But he has an indisputable claim to recognition by posterity as the pioneer, after Bernoulli, of the dynamical theory of gases.

The belief, or hope, that the phenomena of the physical world could be accounted for by a comprehensive yet relatively simple theory is as old as philosophy and science. Newton expressed the hope that his system of mechanics could be found to do this. And what Newton hoped his mechanics could be found to do, most of his successors were quite sure it could do. John Robison, for example, looked forward to the science of 'universal mechanics' that could embrace chemical affinity and mechanics in one system.[8] Herapath expressed a similar view when he wrote: 'It has long been suspected by the most eminent philosophers that the whole phenomena of the universe are connected by some simple and general principle.'[9]

Robison and Herapath worked within a tradition of British Newtonianism that, by their times, had becom arthritic. Momentum and central forces were the key concepts they used while Herapath retained the antique paraphernalia of propositions, scholia and lemmas. There was no direct route from these sets of ideas to the energy doctrine. Joule, on the other hand, was indebted to the engineering tradition of Smeaton, Watt and Ewart. He would have learned to use the concepts of *vis viva* and 'attraction through space' through his Manchester mentors, particularly John Dalton. Others, not connected with Manchester, who accepted these concepts were Davies Gilbert, the MP who had been a good friend to Cornish engineers, such as Richard Trevithick and Arthur Woolf, the chemist W. H. Wollaston and, of course, Scottish engineers like W. J. M. Rankine.

A different approach was taken by Hermann Helmholtz, a young Prussian army surgeon, who in 1847 published his influential memoir, *Uber die Erhaltung der Kraft* ('On the Conservation of Force').[10] Like Joule, Helmholtz used the conjugate concepts of *vis viva* and 'attraction through space', which he called 'tension' (*Spannkraft*).[11] Unlike Joule, his approach is that of an academic, a mathematician, rather than an engineer. The memoir is often regarded as the first comprehensive and scientifically satisfactory statement of the principle of the conservation of energy. It is implied – and sometimes stated – that Helmholtz's understanding was more general, more profound, than that of Joule. But this is misleading; furthermore, the memoir has certain faults, although these are rarely noticed.

Following a short introduction, Helmholtz stated that the problem of physical science 'to refer natural forces to unchangeable attractive and repulsive forces whose intensity depends solely upon distance'. In other words, everything was to be explained in terms of central forces, of which gravity was the most familiar example. The fundamental axiom was that it was impossible to produce, by any means, 'force' from nothing. The context here implied that by 'force' was meant work. Using this axiom Carnot and Clapeyron had, he noted, deduced important laws concerning specific and latent heats, some of which had been confirmed by experiment while others awaited confirmation. The purpose of the memoir was to extend the same principle, the same basic approach, to other branches of physics.

The principle of the conservation of *vis viva* expressed the impossibility of 'perpetual motion'. Having set up the mathematical equations and three basic propositions Helmholtz proceeded to consider the conversion of 'force' into heat. Did a certain amount of 'force' always generate a definite quantity of heat? He quoted Joule's short paper of 1845 (see pp. 75–6) above), but dismissed it, unfairly, on the grounds that the results had little claim to accuracy. He was well aware that the material or caloric theory of heat was refuted by the friction of fluids (he did not mention that Joule was the only one to have done this), by percussion and by the melting of ice by rubbing.[12] Helmholtz then discussed, in some detail, Clapeyron's formulae that had been confirmed experimentally, within limits, even though the caloric theory, assumed by Clapeyron, was inconsistent with the dynamical theory. His next steps were to apply the principle of central forces and the conservation of *vis viva* to electrostatics, voltaic electricity, magnetism and electromagnetism. In all Helmholtz made seven references to Joule. Of these, one could be described as neutral, four were carping or patronising, one was misleading and one could be fairly described as showing, at best, scholarly incompetence (see Appendix 2). The uninformed reader of the memoir would be left with the impression that Joule was a not particularly skilful experimenter who happened to make isolated experiments that chanced to be relevant to the memoir. There was no suggestion that Joule was carrying out a systematic research, endeavouring to explore the generality of the new principle and to determine the exchange value as accurately as possible. No other scientist mentioned in the memoir was criticised in the way that Joule was. The translator of the English edition, John Tyndall, felt called upon twice to explain, in footnotes, that Helmholtz was acquainted with the 'earlier experiments only of Mr Joule'. And Helmholtz was reported to have said that he learned of Joule's work only when he was completing the memoir; in which case it would be interesting to know what the memoir would have been like had he never heard of Joule at all.

There is no reason to suppose that Helmholtz was personally hostile to Joule. The evidence of the references in the memoir suggests, strongly, that he had never read any of Joule's papers and knew of them only through the writings of others who had their own reasons (including jealousy?) for denigrating Joule. But these speculations are outside the scope of this work. Joule and Helmholtz appear to have had little or not contact with each other. *Die Erhaltung der Kraft*, while it helped to establish the dynamical theory and at the same time gave the scientific world a most useful single word – conservation – to sum up a comprehensive theory, belonged, in essence, to a different branch of physical science from that pursued by Joule. What is regrettable is that it presented a misleading picture of Joule. He was to be seen as an uninteresting, rather tedious man concerned with measurements. Helmholtz went on to reach the very top of the scientific tree. He became a world statesman of science; the man who was offered the Cavendish Chair before it was offered to Maxwell, who delivered the Rede Lecture, the Faraday Lecture, the Gifford Lectures; the man who was to be honoured almost as much in Britain and other countries as he was in Germany. It is one of the purposes of this study to correct the misleading impression his youthful work left of James Prescott Joule.

Neither Joule nor Thomson knew of Helmholtz's memoir at the time. Thomson did not learn of it until January 1852, while Joule gave no indication of having read it. After their chance meeting in the Alps Joule and Thomson went on their separate ways for some time. Thomson returned to professorial duties in Glasgow University and to the publication of papers on hydrodynamics and on theories of electricity and magnetism. In the following year he published his paper on an absolute scale of temperature, founded on Carnot's theory.[13] He remarked that 'the conversion of heat (or caloric) into mechanical effect is probably impossible, certainly undiscovered'. A footnote stated that this opinion was nearly universal but that 'Mr Joule, of Manchester, has made some remarkable discoveries concerning the friction of fluids and the operation of magneto-electric machines that seem to indicate the actual conversion of mechanical effect into caloric'. He added: 'no experiment, however, is adduced in which the converse operation is exhibited; but much is involved in mystery with reference to these fundamental questions of natural philosophy'. This foreshadowed, in a crude form, the second law of thermodynamics, or the recognition of a bias in nature: there is no restriction on the conversion of mechanical energy into heat, but the converse operation, thought then to be impossible, is subsequently seen to be possible under restricted conditions.

The twelve months that followed the Oxford meeting brought Joule an agreeable increase in public recognition. While he was on his honeymoon *Comptes Rendus* published a short paper of his on the measurement of the mechanical equivalent of heat using water, sperm oil and mercury with an iron calorimeter and paddle-wheel. The results were satisfactorily consistent: 781.6, 782.1 and 787.6 foot.pounds respectively.[14] As Paris could still claim to be the scientific capital of the world, Joule diplomatically presented the iron calorimeter and paddle-wheel to Regnault. Further international recognition came later in the year when he was elected a Corresponding Member of the Royal Academy of Sciences, Turin, a most distinguished European academy whose membership had included Avogadro and Lagrange. At that time Botto and Menabrea[15] were among its most active members, and Joule was one of only three British Corresponding Members, the other two being Faraday and Herschel.

Joule received further support from Sir Henry de la Beche and Lyon Playfair's report on coals for steam-propelled naval vessels. He wrote to say that his average figure was 782 foot.pounds, adding that 'This is by far the best result I have got and cannot, I think, be 1/100th wide of the truth.[16] De la Beche and Playfair accepted it and also Joule's estimate of the absolute efficiency of the best Cornish engine: roughly one-eleventh of the 'theoretical force' of the heat obtainable from the coal. Joule was, however, unsuccessful in his efforts to convert Sir John Lubbock to his theory of the origin of the light from meteors. He therefore published a short paper proving that a meteorite, travelling at eighteen miles per second (the earth's orbital velocity), would, on entering the atmosphere, be raised to an enormous temperature very rapidly.[17]

Joule was now preparing for the 1848 meeting of the British Association to be held in Swansea. For his latest experiments, to be described there, he made a slight modification to the apparatus; he did not say what it was and his laboratory notebook gives no information. The new result was 771 foot.pounds which he believed to be within 1/200th of the true figure. He did not say what liquid(s) he used in these experiments and he claimed, mistakenly, that he had used water, oil *and* mercury in the experiments described at the Oxford meeting. But the novel part of his short paper, and of the longer account he read to the Lit & Phil two months later, was his development of the kinetic theory of gases. As Brush has pointed out, he was indebted to Herapath for the clarification of his ideas on the kinetic theory although he refused to reject Davy's 'beautiful' idea of spinning atoms. An ingenious calculation enabled him to deduce that the linear velocity of hydrogen atoms at 60°F was 6,225 feet, or just over a mile per second,* a figure close to the present value for the root mean square velocity. Joule's theory indicated that the absolute zero of temperature would be −459°F, or −272.8°C. At this temperature the atoms would be motionless. He ended by using the theory to compute the specific heat capacities of hydrogen and other gases.[18] The assumption had been made, for the sake of simplicity, that at a constant temperature, gas atoms all possessed the same velocity and he did not envisage the equipartition of energy. Nevertheless, with this paper he established himself as a pioneer of the kinetic theory of gases, the succession running from Bernoulli to Herapath and Joule and on to Clausius, Maxwell, Gibbs and Boltzmann.

It is not entirely clear to what extent Joule emancipated his ideas from Herapath's 'lattice' theory. Joule was always discreet about the origins of his ideas and cautious about his speculations. While it is probable that he, like his successors, adopted the 'projectile' theory of atomic motion he did not, as Mendoza has indicated, present so clear and unambiguous a model as did Waterston, who likened gas atoms to a swarm of gnats in the sunlight. One possible key to Joule's ideas is his theory of meteors. It is interesting that the unquestionably high velocity of meteorites and the immense heating of the air that they produce are, *a priori*, consistent with the calculated velocity of hydrogen atoms at 60°F.

Joule's contribution to the Swansea meeting was, once again, ignored by

---

*He had asserted, in the St Ann's School lecture, the previous year, that the velocity of 'water atoms' was at least one mile per second.

the *Athenaeum* as was a short but interesting paper by Thomson.[19] Apparently Joule did not notice this paper, or if he did regarded it as less important than the work he was doing. He wrote to Thomson to say he was sorry to have missed him at Swansea,[20] barely concealing his disappointment that Thomson, in his paper on the absolute scale of temperature, 'still adheres to Carnot's theory'. He thought that Thomson's views about this would be just as valuable even if Carnot's theory should be proved incorrect. Surely his researches on the battery and electric motor showed that 'chemical force is turned into mechanical force instead of into heat', and the cooling of compressed air when it expanded against atmospheric pressure both indicated the conversion of heat into work, which Thomson had denied could take place? He was, he wrote, anxious that the matter should be settled and he proposed to build an air or steam-engine to show how it could be done. As the principles of the experiment he had in mind were similar only the steam-engine need be described.[21] It was to be a simple model in a box that could be evacuated of air. Fuel, in the form of gas, was to be conveyed to the engine through a pipe from outside while another pipe carried away the products of combustion. The box was immersed in a tank of water and a shaft connected the engine, through stuffing boxes, to a pulley outside the water tank. This pulley enabled a weight to be raised; that is, work to be done.

He expected to find that there would be less waste heat from the engine (indicated by the rise in temperature of the surrounding water) when it did work than if it was prevented from working and the steam blown off through the safety valve into the vacuum. Let us suppose, he wrote, that a certain amount of fuel could raise the temperature of 1,000 pounds of water by 1°. According to the current theory the same amount of fuel would enable the steam-engine to raise a weight and, since heat cannot be converted into anything else, to raise the temperature of the water by 1°. But instead of raising a weight the engine could be made to drive paddles that would raise the temperature of, say, 100 pounds of water by 1°. So now we would have 1,100 pounds of water raised 1°, while with the engine stopped we would have had only 1,000 pounds raised 1°, the same fuel being burned and the same heat applied in both cases. This could only mean, on the theory that Thomson accepted, that the steam-engine itself was a *manufacturer* of heat; which, Joule concluded triumphantly, was contrary to all analogy and reason. And what had Thomson to say to that?

With hindsight the argument is convincing to the point of being conclusive. But it was not original. Thomson himself had already acknowledged the force of the argument, the source of which may well have been, as far as he was concerned, Séguin's book. Joule certainly knew of Séguin's work.

He had a copy in his library, relevant parts of which were marked in pencil; as, for example, on page 382; 'it seems to me more natural' (than the current theory) 'to suppose that a certain quantity of heat disappears in the very act of the performance of force or mechanical power, and vice versa'. And, in a passage that seems surprisingly modern, Séguin asserted that enormous quantities of heat were wasted in industry and in domestic use and that modern science should be applied to reduce the loss. But Joule did not mark this passage.[22]

Thomson's reply came on 27 October. Unfortunately, the letter has faded badly and parts of it are illegible.[23] However it is possible to form a good idea of the main points. Thomson apologised for the delay in replying and explained that he could not travel to Swansea. He had just visited Paris where everything was chaotic following the revolution of that troubled year. Regnault had had his salary as a mining engineer stopped and was unable to go on with his researches, on which so much depended. As for Thomson's own work, back in Glasgow,

> I have constructed an apparatus for collecting the heat developed by the friction of water, which consists of a disc of tinplate about 8in in diameter with radial vanes on each side, each of which is about 1/10in broad centered on the end of a spindle held vertical by bearings above the axle of the disc and enveloped in a circular box about an inch deep with an aperture for the spindle in the centre of the cover and having radial vanes similar to those of the disc on its bottom, and on the lower side of the cover.

The box was filled with water which gave an 'immense' fluid friction when the disc was rotated. A thermometer was fitted in the box, close to the edge of the revolving disc. With this apparatus Thomson was able to raise the temperature of water from $45\frac{1}{2}°$ to 56°C in one hour. In a second experiment, starting with the water at 98°C, the temperature reached $99\frac{1}{2}°$C in fifteen minutes, when the gearing broke. He had now, he wrote, had the apparatus modified for drive from the main shafting in a cotton mill. He hoped to boil water by fluid friction alone.

In spite of this he was still unwilling to accept Joule's theory in its entirety. He was working on his paper, 'An account of Carnot's theory',[24] which was to complete the recovery of Carnot's ideas, first undertaken but never completed by Emile Clapeyron. Thomson had already derived a formula for the amount of work required to generate a unit of heat by compressing a gas at 15°C;[25] it involved what he called 'Carnot's function', denoted by the Greek letter μ. This was the work that one unit of heat would yield through a Carnot engine restricted to a 'fall' of one degree. The figure the formula gave was close to Joule's value for the mechanical equivalent of heat. But the same formula showed that the work required to generate a unit of heat must increase as the temperature of the gas increased.* Nevertheless, Thomson had not forgotten the objections to the current theory of heat. He took Joule's point that living force cannot be destroyed,[26] even though this seemed to be implied by Clapeyron: 'I have never seen any way of explaining it although I have tried to do so since I first read Clapeyron's paper.' And he proposed an experiment to test Séguin's idea.

Joule was pleased with Thomson's long letter. He admitted that he had found difficulty 'in persuading our scientific folk' that the heat generated in his paddle-wheel experiments had not come from the friction of the bearings.[27] Thomson's experiments, with their considerable temperature rises, were far less easy to explain away. And he had presumed to read that part of Thomson's letter to a meeting of the Lit & Phil. He confessed that he had always 'found a difficulty in making people believe that fractions of a degree could be measured with any great certainty, but your experiments showing a rise in temperature of 30° or 40° would prove the truth of the fact'. The biggest rises he had been able to get were 2½° with mercury and 0.6° with water. He therefore wanted Thomson to measure the amount of 'force' used to get his big temperature rises; a confirmation of the equivalent obtained in this way would surely be valuable. The letter closed with an expression of sympathy for Regnault in his troubles and with an acceptance of Thomson's invitation to visit him in Glasgow.

A month later, on 9 December 1848, Joule wrote again to thank Thomson for the tables he had sent, setting out the values of 'Carnot's function' from 1° to 0° up to 231° to 230°.[28] From these Joule calculated the work that would have to be done to generate a unit of heat at 20° intervals from 0° to 220°. There was a gradual, but irregular, increase from 427.3 to 484.8 (metric measure) and he wrote: 'I strongly suspect that the experimental data on which the table is calculated are not quite correct even as low as 100°.' He continued:

> I believe that ultimately the mechanical equivalent of heat will come out 423, which is very nearly 427.3, the value of W/Q (work divided by quantity of heat) by your table at 0°. Now supposing you were to take 423 as a datum for calculating μ (Carnot's function). Then at,
>
> | | | |
> |---|---|---|
> | 0° | you will have | 1.548 |
> | 20° | | 1.442 |
> | 40° | | 1.350 |
> | 60° | | 1.270 |
> | 80° | | 1.198 |
> | 100° | | 1.133 |

*This did not falsify the dynamical theory of heat.

numbers inversely as the temperature from zero. Would you think that the limit of experimental errors would not justify such a change in the numbers. I make this suggestion with great difference [*sic*] knowing that I have not yet sufficiently studied your papers.

Joule had therefore maintained, against Thomson, that the work done to generate a unit of heat (the mechanical equivalent of heat) was constant at all temperatures. He gave no reason for believing this and it must be supposed that he was relying on his intuition. He had reversed Thomson's procedure and had calculated Carnot's function at different temperatures on the assumption that the same amount of work always generated the same amount of heat. In justification he pointed out that Thomson himself admitted the values for Carnot's function at higher temperatures might be considerably in error and it was at these temperatures that the biggest increases in the value of the work done to generate a unit of heat (W/Q) took place. Assuming, then, that W/Q had the same value at all temperatures and that this value was 423 metre.kilogrammes per thermal unit, the new calculated values for μ were inversely proportional to the absolute temperature. At this point, perhaps, his intuition was important. Simple arithmetic showed that the above figures implied an absolute zero at $-273°$, a figure satisfactorily close to the one he had inferred from his kinetic theory of gases.*

Joule went on without a break in the paragraph:

I perceive that a German by the name of Mayer has set up a claim for the discovery of the equivalent on the ground that he had asserted in 1842 that the heat produced by compressing air was the equivalent of the force employed although he had made no experiment to prove it. This is disagreeable to me as it has involved the necessity of writing in reply to the *Comptes Rendus* but I will not be drawn into a controversy on the subject of priority beyond one rejoinder. I do not want to monopolise as the merit will belong to all those who have worked out the doctrine.

The acrimonious dispute about the origins of the conservation of energy, a dispute in which Thomson was one of the leading protagonists, lay ten years in the future. More immediately, Thomson had another problem on hand. It was familiar knowledge that when water froze and turned into ice at 0°C it expanded and, in expanding, exerted great pressure if it was constrained in any way. But it was a fundamental axiom of Carnot's theory

---

*It must be stressed that Thomson, at that time, did not envisage an 'absolute zero of temperature'. Such a concept would have been unacceptable to a disciple of Fourier. In any case $-273°$, the temperature at which a perfect gas has zero volume, would have been minus infinity on Thomson's absolute scale.

that wherever there is a difference in temperature there is the possibility of generating motive power. The steam-engine works because the steam is at 100°C or more while the condenser is kept at 15° or 20°. If the condenser were to be kept at 100° or more the engine could not work. In the case of freezing water and ice, both at 0°C, there is no temperature difference but, as water changes from the first state to the second, great pressure can be exerted. Contrary to Carnot's axiom an ice-engine could be made to do work and deliver power without requiring a change in temperature. And this, in turn, implied the possibility of 'perpetual motion'. Thomson's brother James suggested a way out of the dilemma: under pressure the melting point of ice might be lowered. The ice-engine, while feasible, would not therefore violate Carnot's axiom. Thomson was able to confirm his brother's suggestion experimentally.[29]

The lowering of the boiling point of water as the pressure was reduced was well known in the eighteenth century.* Apparently, however, analogy did not prompt any studies of the effects of pressure on the freezing point of water. It might have been supposed that British men of science who had been scrambling about in the Alps for many years before 1848 would have speculated about it; particularly as some of them were interested in glaciers. But for Thomson the surprising novelty of the discovery could be taken as strong confirmation of the essential soundness of Carnot's theory. And this necessarily heightened the dilemma: there was a great deal to be said for both Carnot and Joule.

Sadi Carnot was unfortunate in that his book was too abstract to interest many practical engineers of any nationality. He had sound insights and predictions to offer but most of them were the same as those that engineers were working towards, guided not by theory but by intuition and the logic that economic need imposed on design and development. The men of science, the other main group that Carnot addressed, were equally uninterested for most of them were unfamiliar with the steam-engine and its mode of working.[30] In addition, Carnot's use of the concept of the reversible cycle would have represented a form of reasoning unfamiliar to the natural philosphers, the chemists and the 'physicists' brought up in the traditions of rational mechanics and the chemical–medical theories of heat. By Thomson's day this had changed. The steam-engine was familiar to everyone, thanks to the railways. In little more time than would be required today for a public inquiry into a proposed minor civil engineering project, England had been covered by a complete railway system, the main lines to

*Knowledge of this phenomenon was an essential factor in James Watt's researches that led to the invention of the condensing steam-engine (1769).

Scotland had been built and the railway was pushing on towards Aberdeen. Only a crassly unimaginative individual would have been unimpressed by this achievement. The scientifically minded could not have failed to realise the significance of steam power and to understand the working principles of the steam-engine.

By the time Thomson wrote his 'Account of Carnot's theory' he could expect his readers to be familiar with the operation of the heat-engine. He gave a careful introduction to Carnot's theory and accepted the axiom of the conservation of heat. But he also clearly expressed the problem of the disappearance of mechanical effect when heat flowed by conduction from a hot body to a cold one. He echoed Joule's words of 1845: 'Nothing', Thomson wrote, 'can be lost in the operations of nature – no energy can be destroyed.' He mentioned Joule's paper showing that heat was actually generated by an induced electric current; the heat was not the result of cooling elsewhere in the circuit. This, he said, seemed to overturn the common opinion that heat cannot be generated, that it must be transferred from somewhere else. But, he added, in the present state of knowledge no operation is known by which heat can enter a body without raising its temperature or becoming latent, and that 'the fundamental axiom, accepted by Carnot, may be considered as still the most probable basis for an investigation of the motive power of heat'. Thomson's position, to recapitulate, was that he had accepted Joule's demonstrations that mechanical work can be converted into heat while he denied the converse proposition, that heat can be transformed into work.

The subsequent account of Carnot's theory was simple and practical. Thomson analysed the operation of a steam-engine, working on a Carnot cycle, and followed that with a similar analysis of an air-engine. He showed how Carnot's function could be calculated by a consideration of either the steam-engine or the air-engine.[31] But the former was preferable as Regnault had recently provided reliable data on the pressure and latent heat of steam at different temperatures from 0° to 230°C. Only one assumption had to be made, the apparently very reasonable one that saturated steam obeyed the gas laws of Boyle and Gay-Lussac.* (This was the assumption that Joule had queried in his letter of 9 December, 1848.) Thomson then worked out a table of values of μ for every degree from 1°–0°C to 231°–230°C and a similar table for the work 'due to' a centigrade unit of heat 'falling' to 0°C from every integral degree up to 231°C. In a short appendix, published in April 1849, he gave the formula, previously communicated to Joule, for the work required to generate one unit of heat

*I.e. $p.v = p_0 v_0 (1 + Et)$, where E is the coefficient of expansion of a gas.

by compressing a gas; and also a table showing how the work increased with the temperature. He had rejected Joule's suggestion that W/Q was a constant. Thomson concluded his paper with a comparative assessment of the economies of steam and air-engines, coming down, like Carnot, in favour of the air-engine as it could work at very high temperatures without, at the same time, generating impossibly high pressures. In an interesting footnote he commented on Carnot's suggestion that a two-stage engine might be feasible: an air-engine to work at the high temperature end of the scale and a steam-engine using the waste heat from the air-engine.[32] But, Thomson argued, it might be better and simpler to heat the steam to a high temperature outside the boiler and therefore out of contact with the water. The steam would then be, in effect, a gas. This was, in all probability, the first scientifically-based suggestion of the technique of superheating.

Using Regnault's data and the evidence of Lean's *Monthly Engine Reporter* Thomson showed that the efficiency of the Fowey Consols Engine was 57½% that of a Carnot engine working over the same temperature range. No other engine, in Britain, France or elsewhere, could match the performance of this supreme example of early Victorian engineering. And the assessment of its efficiency that Thomson offered was far more plausible than Joule's figure of 10%.

Thomson had several personal advantages. His academic position gave him good contacts in the active Scottish university circle; his successful career at Cambridge ensured that he was well known and his ideas respected in what was to become a major centre of science; and, finally, his time in Paris had given him influential friends in France. There was, however, more to it than friends and contacts, important though they were. In retrospect it is clear that Thomson had, with skill and insight, hit on the immediate growth points in Carnot's theory. While his two papers were not as abstract as Clapeyron's, his realisation of an absolute scale of temperature, although it may have needed subsequent correction, was, by any standard, a sufficiently original contribution to fundamental, basic or 'pure' science to satisfy the most intellectually austere of academics. At the other end, his invocation of the Fowey Consols engine and his estimate of its efficiency gave a degree of practical realism, of immediate utility, to Carnot's theory that was surely missing from the author's own work and from Clapeyron's paper. In that respect Thomson's paper would appeal to engineers. They were not convinced by Joule's estimate of the best efficiency of the steam-engine; their experience, their gut reactions, told them that Joule was wrong, and in this they were quite right.

In the meantime Joule was completing a paper that, he said, he had pledged to submit to the Royal Society some years earlier.[34] It was to be one of the two papers for which he is, and has been for a long time, best known. The paper is not remarkable, save for the high experimental precision it shows. Joule began with a summary of earlier ideas about the dynamical theory of heat, being careful to pay tribute to Rumford, Davy, the research of Dulong, Faraday – whom he described as 'that great man' (Faraday communicated the paper to the Royal Society) – and the more recent works of Grove and Mayer. He mentioned Séguin's work and his demonstration that the mechanical equivalent of heat could be deduced from the expansion of steam.[35] He credited Rumford, wrongly, with having estimated the work necessary to generate a given amount of heat;[36] and, more reasonably, stated that Mayer was the first to say that heat could be generated by fluid friction. Joseph Reade, of Cork, was by that time, quite forgotten.

The value of the mechanical equivalent of heat, given at the end of the paper, was the average of three separate experiments. In the first set a pair of falling weights drove a brass paddle-wheel revolving between fixed brass vanes and immersed in a copper calorimeter full of water. In the second set the weights drove a wrought iron paddle-wheel with fixed vanes immersed in a cast iron calorimeter full of mercury. In the third set, perhaps following Faraday's suggestion in 1847, the weights drove a cast-iron bevel wheel pressing on a fixed bevel wheel, again immersed in mercury in a cast iron calorimeter. In the last set of experiments allowance was even made for the work wasted in causing the apparatus to vibrate and emit sound, although no details were given of the way in which the wasted work was actually estimated.

The three sets of experiments gave consistent results: 772.692, 774.083 and 774.987 foot.pounds respectively. Joule considered that the first set gave the most reliable results and that, since even in this set it was impossible to prevent some work being wasted in unaccounted for vibration and sound, the final result should have been slightly lower than that given. He therefore proposed that the heat due to friction, whether fluid or solid, was always proportional to the 'quantity of force' expended and that, for one (British) unit of heat, 772 foot.pounds of mechanical force must be expended. His argument that friction consisted in the conversion of 'mechanical power' into heat was, according to a footnote, 'suppressed in accordance with the wish of the committee to whom the paper was referred'. Evidently Joule was sufficiently anxious to see his paper published in the *Philosophical Transactions* to be willing to leave out the all-important conclusion that his previous researches had established. The committee, or perhaps its most influential member, interpreted the paper as giving proof that the performance of a certain amount of work invariably produces a determinate amount of heat, which was an important contribution to knowledge; but that to speculate further about the source or nature of that heat was profitless and out of order. This interpretation was, in some ways, similar to the one that many leading men of science, among them Faraday, put on Dalton's atomic theory when it was first published. They accepted his laws of chemical combination but rejected his ideas of discrete atoms from which he had derived the laws and in which he believed. There was, nevertheless, an element of inconsistency in the committee's requirement for they allowed scattered assertions, direct and implied, of the mutual convertability of heat and work to remain in the body of the paper.

Crosbie Smith has given good grounds for believing that the objection came from Faraday.[37] The referee's report, in all probability written by Faraday, praised the skill and care with which the research had been carried out, criticised and effectively, Joule's failure to define the terms 'difference' and 'interpolation' used in his tables,* and ended with the judgement that with his valid, indeed valuable, results the author had 'mingled up the statement of another proposition which appears to be deduced most illogically from it'. That, because mechanically evolved heat always requires, *ceteris paribus*, 'the same amount of force (measured as *work*); therefore *heat is converted into force and force into heat*. In accordance with this strange conclusion he speaks of "Friction as consisting in the conversion of force into heat" and "a quantity of heat being equal to a mechanical force".' Whether Joule should have mentioned his papers from 1843 onwards in support of his unacceptable conclusion may be doubted; they might have ensured the complete rejection of the paper.

While his paper was causing concern to at least one man of science in London, Joule was carrying on a somewhat desultory correspondence with Thomson. The exciting days of 1847 were over. The prospect of acceptance by the Royal Society may have made Thomson a little less important in Joule's eyes. In addition, Thomson had ignored the suggestion that Carnot's function was inversely proportional to the absolute temperature and, moreover, had mustered strong new evidence in support of Carnot's theory. But Joule was too good a man of science to miss the significance of the lowering of the melting-point of ice. He wrote to Thomson on 8 March 1849[38] to say that 'the analogy of liquefiable gases would rather point to the reverse result'. Carnot's theory predicted, or at least was consistent with, the opposite effect and was by so much strengthened when that effect was experimentally confirmed. He had for some time been puzzled by the anomalous maximum density of water, 'a phenomenon which seems so utterly at variance with all analogy and any theory' (Helmholtz, too, was

---

*These undefined terms were omitted from the published paper.

puzzled about this). He asked Thomson if he could give the problem some attention; and he sent him a copy of his reply to Mayer, printed in *Comptes Rendus* and prompted by the latter's claim to the law of equivalence as 'my law' when he had made no attempt to establish it experimentally. But Joule had 'not the slightest wish to detract from Mayer's real merits and I hope I have said nothing which might be thought acrimonious or unfair'.

Four months later Joule wrote to Thomson to thank him for the proofs of his paper on Carnot's theory and to say that he had done nothing further about 'the equivalent' beyond sending off his paper to the Royal Society. 'Whether it will appear in the *Phil. Trans.* or not, I am not yet aware.'[39] Clearly his pledge to the Royal Society carried no reciprocal obligation. He was planning a new research. It was to be into the law of friction between discs revolving in different fluids under pressures up to 800 pounds to the square inch. Coulomb had found no increase in friction with pressure. Joule wondered if Thomson knew of any researches in this field. The results would be of theoretical interest and of use to shipbuilders. Scott Russell, the leading naval architect of the day, had done much, but nothing on this particular subject. Joule intended to begin with a disc of cast iron revolving in mercury.

The surprising discovery about the melting-point of ice and the support it indicated for Carnot's theory continued to inhibit scientific correspondence between Joule and Thomson. Eight months after the last letter Joule wrote to thank Thomson for a copy of the relevant paper. He had just received it from James Thomson, whom he had met for the first time. The paper had, he wrote, aroused great interest at the Lit & Phil. Like James Thomson he hoped there might be some reconciliation between his position and that of Carnot. 'For my own part', he confessed, the lowering of the melting point of ice 'quite baffles me.'[40] Shortly afterwards he wrote to Stokes enclosing a copy of his Royal Society paper. He explained why he had withdrawn his conclusion about the conversion of 'Force' into 'Heat', adding: 'although I think this view will ultimately be found to be the correct one. I cannot see why it may not be as well asserted that the heat evolved is the cause of the loss of force in friction as vice versa.'[41]

In fact the reconciliation had already been made. A third party, R. J. E. Clausius (1822–88), had published a paper in 1850 showing how, by making a slight alteration to Carnot's theory, it could be brought into harmony with Joule's demonstration that heat and work are interchangeable.[42] All that was necessary was to postulate that, in the reversible cycle as defined by Carnot, a proportion of the heat entering from the hot body was converted into the work done while the remainder was rejected into the cold body. Clausius was emphatic that both processes were essential for the operation of any heat engine. Heat must flow from hot to cold, as specified by Carnot (but ignored by Joule), while some must be converted into work, as insisted on by Joule (but denied by Carnot). The work done was proportional to the heat converted (Joule) and, equally in a reversible cycle, to the heat transmitted from hot to cold (Carnot). For the rest the bulk of Carnot's and Clapeyron's deductions were valid. Clausius had not, at that time, seen Carnot's short book; he had relied on Clapeyron's paper of 1834 and Thomson's paper of 1849. This may well have allowed him to take a more independent position than Thomson whose predilection for Carnot's theory had been reinforced by the recent discovery concerning the melting point of ice.

One other modification to Carnot's theory was required. He had postulated that no heat engine could be more efficient than a reversible one; for if such an engine were possible it could, by driving the reversible engine backwards to act as a heat pump, raise more heat to the hot body than was required to drive it. This, Carnot said, would imply 'perpetual motion'. But the action of a heat engine was now seen to be *not* exactly analogous to an hydraulic engine. A more efficient engine could be conceived. Such an engine could draw heat energy from the 'cold' body, converting it into work which could be used to drive a Carnot engine in reverse with the net effect that heat would flow steadily from the cold body to the hot body. As every heat engine sits, literally, on the vast reservoir of heat that is the earth and its oceans such a super engine could go on working almost indefinitely.[43] An arrangement of this sort would not violate the principle of the conservation of energy. Faced with this difficulty Clausius restated Carnot's postulate. No engine can be more efficient than a reversible one for if such an engine could be built it would imply that heat could be made to flow from a cold body to a hot body *without compensation*. And this, Clausius asserted, was impossible.[44]

6

Technical considerations

Friedrich Engels related how it was his custom to walk to his office every morning in the company of a fellow bourgeois merchant. Usually they talked about business, Manchester affairs and, sometimes, trivia until they reached the place where their paths diverged. One morning, moved by strong feelings, Engels showed his true colours. All the way he denounced capitalism and everything that Manchester stood for until they reached the parting of their ways. His companion, who had remained silent, raised his hat in the usual way and remarked: 'And yet, Sir, there is a great deal of money made here.'

This story has been repeated many times, often to illustrate the gross insensitivity of mid-nineteenth-century Manchester: its obsession with money-making, its indifference to the hardships of industrial society. William Sturgeon might be considered a victim of that society. By 1850 he was destitute and ill, the £200 granted him in 1847 having been exhausted. But a small group that included Dr Lee (the first Bishop of Manchester), Edward Binney and Joule succeeded in getting him a civil list pension of £50 per annum six months before he died on 4 December 1850. He is buried in Prestwich churchyard. There is no commemorative plaque in the Church, the incumbent having refused to sanction one on the grounds that Sturgeon was not of sufficient scientific distinction. Measured by the standards of Dalton and Joule that might have been correct; set besides the achievements of many of his scientific contemporaries it was certainly not true.[1]

There was another side to the industrial society. Many of its leaders were devout Nonconformists. Their faith often impelled them to lead austere personal lives; as frequently it led them to take active parts in schemes of social amelioration and works of personal charity, sometimes at considerable cost to themselves.[2] The advancement of education, public health and science were the main areas that attracted public-spirited men.[3] The Lit &

Phil was only the first of a number of educational and scientific ventures that later included the Manchester Statistical Society and various specialised scientific societies. But besides the Lit & Phil and the Mechanics' Institution, the most important of these ventures was the Owens College, founded in 1851 as a result of a £100,000 bequest in the will of John Owens, a wealthy bachelor who had been in the textile trade. Its historical importance can easily be underestimated if it is seen merely as one of the succession of university colleges founded in the nineteenth century and beginning with University College, London in 1826. Owens College, accommodated originally in Richard Cobden's old house in Quay Street, was to provide an education that incorporated the practices of the Scottish universities and to be of use to young men who intended to enter commerce or industry. It was to be non-sectarian, but not Godless. The courses were based on traditional subjects: Latin and Greek, mathematics, natural philosophy, English and history, chemistry, foreign languages and natural history. In the first year sixty-two students enrolled but numbers fell to thirty-three in the session 1856–57 and it was not until 1862–63 that numbers rose to over 100.[4] There were no faculties of law, medicine, science or technology; the only degrees that could be taken were those of London University, but as these were, from 1858 onwards, open to anyone who could pass the examinations, this was no particular privilege. Soon, the local newspapers, including the liberal *Manchester Guardian*, decided that the venture was a humiliating failure. So did the professor of chemistry, (Sir) Edward Frankland, who resigned in 1857 to go to the Royal School of Mines in London. By a strange turn of fate, Frankland's departure, which might have been disastrous, turned out to be a blessing in disguise for his successor, Henry Enfield Roscoe (1833–1915), did as much as anyone to save the College and put it on a path of rapid development that was to give it a leading place among British universities.

Roscoe came of two distinguished local families. One grandfather, William Roscoe, was a wealthy and cultivated man who was described as the 'founder of Liverpool culture' while the other grandfather, the Revd William Enfield, was a prominent Nonconformist divine, a scholar, an educationalist and the last Rector of Warrington Academy. H. E. Roscoe had been educated at University College, London, and at Heidelberg, where he had taken his Ph.D under Bunsen. He combined, in his academic philosophy, the utilitarian values of the commercial and industrial classes of Lancashire with a German reverence for learning and an awareness of the high importance of research in the life of a university. This combination, allied to a driving personality, was enough to enable him to change Owens from a college for the didactic instruction of young gentlemen in polite subjects to a modern university institution with a bias towards research and an awareness of the needs of the local community, yet with a regard for the essential requirements of higher education. It was largely due to the efforts of Roscoe and Adolphus Ward, Professor of English, 1866–89, that Owens could, by 1900, look back on an academic record of fifty years barely surpassed by any other university in Britain. The rise of Owens was in part the effect and in part the cause of the change from the scientific world of James Prescott Joule to that of today. Roscoe was an experimental scientist. The first professors of mathematics and natural philosophy were not particularly distinguished but the standard rose sharply with the appointments of Balfour Stewart (1870) and Arthur Schuster (1881). Roscoe was joined by Carl Schorlemmer as professor of organic chemistry in 1874. H. B. Dixon replaced Roscoe in 1887 and he was joined by W. H. Perkin, jun., in 1892. Osborne Reynolds was appointed professor of engineering in 1868. Roscoe and his successors consolidated the style and temper of Manchester science.

What Joule thought of the new college is not on record. He did add a postscript to his letter to Thomson of 26 March 1850;[5] would brother James be interested in the post of professor of mathematics and natural philosophy now being advertised by the trustees of the new college? James was not interested; nor was Joule, who was apparently resting on his laurels at that time;[6] he had been elected a Fellow of the Royal Society and made a Vice-President of the Lit & Phil.

Stokes was by no means the only one to receive a complimentary offprint of Joule's Royal Society paper. One was went to Herschel, who replied with a note that combined brevity with verbosity.* Writing to Lubbock on 13 July 1850, Joule pointed out that the friction of blood passing along veins will not increase bodily heat, the frictional heat being due to the chemical heat driving the heart, and that action alone determined the heat, whether caused by friction or not.[7] This was another example of the battery analogy, noticed before: heat was not transported by the medium, whether blood or electricity. The question of frictional heating arose again in correspondence with Thomson; this time it was the frictional heating of high-pressure steam escaping from a boiler through a narrow orifice.[8] According to Rankine's recently published theory the steam should be wet and therefore scalding, but as Thomson noted, it was always dry and did not scald the

*'Allow me to thank you for your obliging attention in transmitting me a copy of your exceedingly interesting paper on the mechanical equivalent of heat the exact numerical relations developed in which appear to me of as much novelty as importance.' (Letter in UMIST, Department of Physics.) Did Herschel recall his letter to Waterston as he wrote this?

hand. Joule agreed with Thomson that the steam had been heated by friction in the orifice and therefore remained dry. But the main point of his letter concerned the power and saturation of electromagnets. He referred Thomson to his paper in Sturgeon's *Annals*, implying that it gave him priority as a discoverer of the saturation of electromagnets. In a postscript he mentioned that he was designing and making a powerful electromagnet to be displayed at next year's Great Exhibition.[9] This was to be a disappointment to him even though his friend, Lyon Playfair, now moving in almost the highest circle of all – that of Prince Albert – was busily engaged in organising the Exhibition. But by that time the electrical euphoria had long since abated and the various electrical machines on display were little more than instructive toys and classified under 'philosophical instruments'. They were no threat to the always triumphant steam-engine.

One of those most closely associated with the study of the steam-engine at that time was W. J. M. Rankine (1820–72). Educated privately and later at Edinburgh University, where he attended J. D. Forbes's lectures, Rankine's first employment was as a railway engineer. On 4 February 1850 he read his paper 'On the mechanical action of heat, especially in gases and vapours' to the Royal Society of Edinburgh. This was the culmination of a dynamical theory of heat that Rankine had formulated in 1842 but had laid aside for want of adequate experimental data. Regnault had now provided the data and Rankine was therefore able to develop his own version of the dynamical theory and thence his own distinctive thermodynamics.[10] He accepted Joule's arguments in general but criticised, much more fairly and reasonably than Helmholtz had done, the accuracy of Joule's determination of the mechanical equivalent of heat. The best, least objectionable method of determining the equivalent, argued Rankine the engineer, was one in which no machinery was involved and that meant by consideration of the velocity of sound. Rankine concluded that the mechanical equivalent of heat must be about 695.6 foot.pounds per thermal unit, or more than 10% less than Joule's figure.

Having recognised the two principal specific heats, Rankine went on to define a third: the specific heat of a saturated vapour, or the quantity of heat that a unit weight of vapour absorbs or gives out as its temperature is changed by one degree, the pressure being altered at the same time so that it remains saturated. Rankine's theory led him to deduce that the specific heat capacity of saturated steam must, paradoxically, be negative; Clausius reached the same conclusion, quite independently, at the same time.

Since Watt's time engineers had been familiar with the fact that the pressure of dry, saturated steam in a boiler increases much more rapidly than the temperature.[11] If the temperature of saturated steam is to be increased the heat generated by the compression necessary for it to remain saturated is greater than the heat required to raise its temperature and therefore the surplus heat must be given out; it must lose heat to rise in temperature *and* remain saturated. Conversely if the temperature of saturated steam, or water vapour, is to be reduced, the cooling caused by the expansion necessary for it to remain saturated is so great that heat must be supplied from outside,' *otherwise a portion of the vapour will be liquified in order to supply the heat necessary for the expansion of the rest'* (Rankine's italics). He continued: 'This circumstance is obviously of great importance in meteorology, and in the theory of the steam-engine. There is, as yet, no experimental proof of it.' He commented that the exhaust steam from a non-condensing expansive steam-engine is wet. But engineers had long recognised 'priming', or the carrying of drops of water by the steam from the boiler into the cylinder and out through the exhaust port. Rankine admitted it was impossible to distinguish his predicted effect from priming.

Joule was impressed by Rankine's paper. He told Thomson that he was not going to do anything more about the mechanical value of heat until he had made some accurate experiments on the 'absorption of heat by the mechanical expansion of air'. This was with the aim of confirming his ideas about the velocity of sound. 'I do not think', he added, 'that the errors in my experiments are such as to cause the great difference between mine and the equivalent deduced by Rankine.'[12] Rankine's authoritative support for the dynamical theory was particularly welcome to Joule, in spite of the criticism of his experiments and Rankine's claim that the value of the equivalent was more than 10% less than his figure. It was doubly welcome when Thomson wrote from Paris on 15 October 1850, taking up the point he had made two months earlier: steam issuing from a narrow orifice is dry and not scalding. This could be reconciled with Rankine's impressive theory only by accepting Joule's discovery of the frictional heating of fluids. Thomson added that he had seen Clausius's paper, although he was 'not yet . . . fully acquainted with it'. It seemed that Thomson's conversion to the dynamical theory was almost complete.

Joule immediately communicated Thomson's letter, with permission, to the *Philosophical Magazine*, adding, in his covering note, that Rankine's 'fact' was 'analogous to that of the production of a cloud when air, saturated with vapour, is rarefied in the receiver of an air-pump'.[13] Furthermore, it explained the 'approach of the economical duty of the steam-engine to that of the air-engine, on which I propose to make a few observations shortly'. This second point was amplified in a letter that he wrote to Thomson on 6 November 1850:

Mr Rankine's fact that a portion of steam is condensed when expanding so as to evolve work would seem to point out that the whole *vis viva* communicated in the shape of 'latent heat' to the steam would be evolved by the utmost possible extension of the expansion principle – for then the whole of the steam would be condensed into water, and no vapour would be left to evolve heat on the return stroke. This is why I believe that neither the air-engine, nor any other will be made to supersede the steam-engine.[14]

This interesting passage shows that Joule differed from the commonly-held opinion of two generations of engineers who believed that the high latent heat of steam meant heat wasted in the condenser. They therefore experimented, with uniform lack of success, on liquids with low latent heats of vaporisation.[15] Joule agreed that latent heat might be wasted but to him it was 'fuel' that, properly used, could ensure continued expansion. The passage also shows that Joule did not, at that time, accept Carnot's theory; indeed, he explicitly rejected it, presumably still believing that Carnot's theory and the dynamical theory were mutually exclusive.[16] The cycle he envisaged (implicitly, the Rankine cycle) necessitated pumping the condensed steam back into the boiler and heating it up again to boiling point. It was an irreversible process and the cycle could not, therefore, have been as efficient as the Carnot cycle between the same two temperatures. Practical men, who might have known little or nothing about Carnot, would have appreciated this shortcoming. The Cornish engineers had long realised the advantage of using waste heat to pre-heat the boiler feedwater. The cylinders of their engines were carefully lagged while the use of the equilibrium valve ensured that condensation in the cylinder was kept to a minimum. But then the most economical working of the Cornish engines was the *sine qua non* for the continued profitability of the Cornish mines; the economy of the steam-engine in Lancashire and Yorkshire was a less critical matter, for coal was cheap and locally abundant while there was still water power available.

A month later Joule had changed his mind about the air-engine. He remarked to Thomson that 'the whole heat might be converted into power by the agency of the air-engine'.[17] His idea was to pump air into a pressure vessel and there heat it up to several hundred degrees after which it was to be made to do work by expanding down to atmospheric pressure in a cylinder fitted with a piston. He asked Thomson if there was a formula to give the 'force' needed to compress air to half its volume, or to any other aliquot part, 'regard having been paid to the heat evolved by the compression'.* In

---

*It will be remembered that the relatively small heating of air on compression was ignored in Joule's experiments of 1845.

the meantime he solved the problem 'empyrically' (i.e. experimentally). He found that as the air in a small cylinder was progressively compressed a reduction in volume in geometrical progression was accompanied by an increase in the absolute (*sic*) temperature that was also in geometrical progression, although not in the same ratio. This allowed him to compute the temperature to any degree of compression. He was very pleased when Thomson sent him the appropriate formula and he found that the theoretical temperatures agreed very well with those he had computed 'empyrically'.[18] Knowing the weights and specific heats of air, he had all the data he needed to calculate the performance of his air-engine. He asked if Thomson would communicate the paper he was writing to the Royal Society of Edinburgh and, furthermore, if Thomson would write a mathematical footnote to it? He was now convinced that the air-engine could be made to supersede the steam-engine as he found 'it theoretically possible to convert into force nearly all the heat communicated to the air'.[19] His change of heart had been brought about, not by an acceptance of Carnot's arguments, but by a comparion of the physical properties of air and steam.

Joule proposed an air-engine working on the simple cycle he had outlined to Thomson. The cycle was not reversible for the air was heated up in a 'receiver'. After it had expanded in the working cylinder it was released at atmospheric pressure although at a higher temperature than the surrounding air. Joule was aiming, not at theoretical perfection, but at a basic engine that was to be robust, practicable in construction and simple in operation. He calculated the work needed to compress and to heat each fresh charge of air to the pressure and temperature of the air already in the receiver. The receiver was to be so large that the overall pressure was not affected appreciably as each new charge of air was pushed in at the same pressure but at a lower temperature. When the new air had reached the temperature of the receiver exactly the same quantity was admitted to the working cylinder and that air drove the piston, expanding down to atmospheric pressure. He calculated the work done by a unit of heat eight times for increasing pressures and temperatures up to a pressure of nearly four and a half tons to the square inch and a temperature of over 1,470°C. The corresponding duty increased from 103 to 629 foot.pounds per heat unit. The last figure was not far short of the theoretical maximum of 772. In addition to these calculations he set out a table, derived from 'Professor Thomson's formula', of the temperature range divided by the absolute temperature of the receiver and multiplied by the mechanical equivalent of heat.* The results were in complete agreement. Thomson, however, was reluctant to give his approval; it would have involved acceptance of what he had begun to call 'Mayer's hypothesis', or the assertion that all the work spent in compressing a gas at any temperature was converted into heat. And this, his investigations in his 'Account of Carnot's Theory' showed, could only be true at one particular temperature. He therefore mentioned the formula in his 'Additional Note' to Joule's paper but carefully refrained from mentioning the temperature from absolute zero.* He did, however, make one innovation that has lasted to the present day and is now universal: he used the letter 'J' to denote the mechanical equivalent of heat.

Joule realised that heating the outside of the receiver was wasteful and he hoped that a way might be found of burning the fuel inside the receiver. This would be economical and would save space and weight. In such a form the engine would be strikingly analogous to the electromagnetic engine and 'present a beautiful illustration of the evolution of mechanical effect from chemical forces'. The cycle he envisaged was later to become known as the Brayton cycle (1872), which was subsequently incorporated into the working of the gas turbine. His recommendation of internal combustion was, of course, far from original. The difficulty was the hot gases that would soon have damaged the pistons, cylinders, and valves and would have carbonised lubricating oils that were still of animal or vegetable origin. In short, the difficulties in the way of an efficient internal combustion engine, able to compete with the triumphant steam-engine, were formidable indeed. Joule and others who may have been thinking along the same lines could hardly have foreseen the future development of the steam-engine, particularly in the form of the steam-turbine that, linked to a highly efficient alternator and a distribution system, was to confirm electricity as the grand agent for the transmission of energy from a power station in which burning coal, oil or gas or nuclear fission yielded the 'chemical heat'.

The development of the steam, or, generally, the heat-engine, had reached a particularly interesting stage by the middle of the nineteenth century. There was a remarkable diversity of ideas and of achievement. In Cornwall the community of highly competent engineers had, by unusually close collaboration and the free interchange of ideas, greatly improved the performance of pumping engines.[20] It was alleged that by the 1830s the profitability of the mines depended on the use of engines that were

*I.e. $J.H. \dfrac{T_1 - T_2}{T_1}$ Where T_1 and T_2 are temperatures from the absolute zero $(-273°C)$ and H the quantity of heat, taken as 1. Thomson wrote the same formula as J. H. $E(S + T)/(1 + ES)$, E being the coefficient of expansion of air, S the temperature of the receiver and T the temperature of the atmosphere, both temperatures taken from 0°C.

markedly more efficient than those employed twenty years earlier.[21] In the 1860s the Cornish engine was described by W. S. Jevons as the most efficient in the world.[22] There was, in effect, a race between the continued improvement of the engines and the increasing depth of the mines on the issue of which the future of the industry depended. Finally, at the end of the nineteenth century, the engines lost.

The Cornish engine, following the lead set by Richard Trevithick and Arthur Woolf, was a high-pressure engine. Railway locomotives were offspring of the mining industry and were of necessity high-pressure engines, but their relative efficiencies were very difficult to assess.[23] A railway locomotive had to cope with different loads under different conditions, at different speeds and for different times. These were not circumstances that allowed of the most economical working. But as the railways had no rivals, apart from canals, for slow, bulk transport, this was not a matter of great importance.

The development of the marine steam-engine lagged behind that of the pumping engine, the mill engine and the locomotive. The reason was simple. High-pressure working was essential for fuel economy. But high-pressure working entailed some risk of a boiler explosion that, while acceptable on land, could be disastrous at sea.[24] Accordingly, marine engines were large, low-pressure machines. To make matters worse, for long voyages sea-water had to be used to replenish the boilers since it had proved very difficult to develop a satisfactory surface condenser to recycle fresh water. As salt water is corrosive, high-pressure working would have been doubly dangerous. Ocean-going ships had, therefore, to be large to accommodate big, inefficient engines. The ultimate in this direction was the *Leviathan*, later called the *Great Eastern.*

In 1855 a vessel put to sea with an efficient surface condenser. John Elder, of the Clyde firm of Randolph & Elder who engined the vessel, was a close associate of Rankine. In the following years Randolph & Elder built a number of ships for the Pacific and West Indies Royal Mail Lines. The engines of these vessels incorporated surface condensers and used high-pressure steam; in some cases the steam was superheated. Fuel economy was essential on the long runs, carrying mail to South America (at that time an Honorary British Colony) and as a regular service was maintained it was possible to monitor the performance of the engines with reasonable accuracy. Their recorded economy was admirable. Accounts of the engines and their performances were reported to the British Association by Elder.[25]* It

*Elder died, prematurely, in 1862. When, later, Rankine's application to Glasgow University for an increased stipend was rejected, Mrs Elder intervened and endowed an increment in salary for the Regius Professor of Engineering.

was said that in the 1860s the performance of the best marine engines doubled; in the next decade, that saw the introduction of the triple expansion engine, the performance was said to have doubled again.[26] The consequent development of sea transport revolutionised world trade and, in particular, Britain soon became dependent on imported foodstuffs.

The difficulties with the marine steam-engine compared with the successful mill engine and locomotive directed attention to the possibilities of the air-engine. The Stirling engine of 1816/1826 worked on a cycle that was, in principle, reversible. The less efficient Ericsson engine was better publicised and, in the early 1850s, was hailed as the solution to the problem of the marine engine. The principle was simple. A volume of air was heated so that it expanded and drove a piston linked to a flywheel. The heat was then abstracted from the air and put in a heat store, or regenerator, consisting of thin strips of metal. The cooled air contracted so that the piston returned to its starting-point, after which the heat was withdrawn from the store and returned to the air so that the cycle could be repeated. Just by shifting a given amount of heat to and fro, into and out of a volume of air, a continuous working cycle could be maintained. The only heat required for steady working would be that needed to make up for losses by conduction, convection and radiation. In other words, the principle implied something like 'perpetual motion'. Extravagant claims were made on behalf of the Ericsson engine and a 'caloric' ship, named the *Ericsson*, was actually built. It was not a success.[27]

In 1850 Willian Poingdestre read a paper to the Institution of Civil Engineers in London, giving an account of Sir George Cayley's air-engine.[28] He pointed out that Ericsson's engine had the advantage that the fuel was burned and the air heated in an enclosed space so that little 'caloric' was wasted. On the other hand this led to serious corrosion and carbon deposit in the engine. Two years later Benjamin Cheverton presented a paper to the same Institution that led to three days of discussion, involving many leading engineers.[29] Cheverton argued that 'caloric' was no more than a 'force' and scornfully dismissed all suggestions of a 'perpetual motion' machine. In the form of heat 'caloric' was always conserved but when mechanical 'force' was involved some 'caloric' was transformed into that force and ceased to be 'caloric'. 'It is', he said, 'in the declination from a higher to a lower degree of temperature – it is in the aspect of a *vis viva* force in caloric, that mechanical action is developed . . . It is in the reduction of temperature that force is elicited.'

He then put a familiar argument in a slightly different form. If a given amount of heat, say X units, was imparted to a large quantity of water there would be a small rise in temperature, say t°. If the same amount of heat was imparted to a small quantity of water there would be a big rise in temperature, say T°, *and* the performance of mechanical work by the steam generated. From whence came the mechanical effect in the second case, for the water and steam can, on the established theory, contain no more and no less heat than the tepid water in the first case? The work must have come from nowhere; it must have been created out of nothing.

This, Cheverton observed, was analogous to the *vis viva* versus momentum, or Newton versus Leibniz, debates in the eighteenth century. Momentum was always conserved but *vis viva* was conserved only in elastic collisions. It was left, he added, to the practical men to show that there was nothing arbitrary about this: 'They forced into recognition the importance of another modification of power besides that of momentum, or quantity of motion, and the names by which it is known bear witness to its practical origin, such as "mechanical power", "work", "duty", "labouring force" etc.'

Just as the engineers of France and Britain pushed the related concepts of *vis viva* and work to the forefront of mechanics so the steam engineers of the time were forcing a new set of concepts of heat to the forefront of that science. Cheverton observed that even if all the 'caloric' from a furnace was absorbed by the boiler of a steam-engine there would still be a big temperature difference between the fire and the water in the boiler; and this difference meant a loss of efficiency unless there was a suitable motive agent to bridge it. The gap, he suggested, could be bridged by using air as a motive agent.

Cheverton, an engineer and inventor who lived near Bristol, was an interesting, if hazy, figure. He claimed that he had had thirty years experience of steam-engines and, in 1826, had described, but did not patent, a gas engine.[30] His other achievements included inventions in printing and coining. But the most intriguing thing about him was the concurrence of his ideas, set out in this paper, with those of Carnot, Clausius, Joule and Thomson. He did not mention them, yet it seems inconceivable that he could in complete ignorance, have put forward a series of ideas that were so similar as to be virtually identical to theirs. Had he, most improbably, not known of their works, had his arguments been original, then he is, indeed, a neglected genius.

With one exception, his distinguished listeners seem to have been quite unfamiliar with the ideas Cheverton was putting forward.* W. G.

---

*Had the audience been fairly familiar with these ideas Cheverton would surely have been careful to give credit where it was due – always assuming that he was not, himself, an original, independent author of the ideas!

Armstrong, Isambard Brunel, Michael Faraday, Captain Fitzroy, George Rennie, C. W. Siemens and Robert Stephenson were far too well informed to give any credence to the possibility of the heat-engine as a source of 'perpetual motion' (or, more accurately, a source of inexhaustible energy). But Brunel confessed that he did not know how to refute the claims that had been made. Of the assembled engineers one, William Siemens, appeared to know something about the new ideas that were relevant to the great problem. He was invited to expound them at a future meeting. This, in due course, he did.[31]

This little episode throws light on three points that are central to this work. In the first place Cheverton's argument supports the thesis that technological advance has often led to scientific progress and that ideas forged from practical experience have later been incorporated into the corpus of scientific knowledge. This may seem close to the position taken by a previous generation of determinist historians who argued that scientific progress was governed by the interests of the ruling economic class. Newtonian science, for example, was said to have been built on the requirements of the trading classes, dominant in seventeenth-century England. This interpretation was strongly criticised by libertarians on the reasonable ground that reductionism of the type science is determined by the economic interest of the dominant class would lead to the subordination of science to the State, and hence its effective destruction. No such view of science is proposed here. What is asserted is no more than the facts warrant. It would have been astonishing if the dramatic increase in powers over nature, associated with the Industrial Revolution of the past 250 years, had had no effect on science. On the other hand it can be argued that the insidious claims of what has been called aesthetic physics[32] can be no less damaging than the crudest of determinist dogmas. To suppose that the elegance of a theory should override hard experimental evidence, to believe that physics can be deduced, *a priori*, from a few axioms by a speculative thinker contemplating the eternal verities, is to ignore the history of science. The aesthetic, or intellectualist, interpretation of science is more dangerous than the economic interpretation for it appeals to the self-esteem of certain scientists, whereas the latter is a dogma imposed on science from without. The evidence shows that experience and experiment are as essential to science as theory; and that experience, for its part, includes a great deal of information, practical skills, techniques and insights gained from technology.

The second point to emerge is, in a sense, a corollary of the first. It is, at first sight, remarkable that so many distinguished engineers and men of science in London should have been ignorant of the new thermodynamics elaborated by Thomson, Rankine, Joule and others. Cheverton might have been an exception, but he was an exception that proves the rule. Partly this is confirmed by the style of his exposition, which is that of a teacher addressing an audience on an unfamiliar subject; partly, it is confirmed by the decision to invite Siemens to enlighten the company on the new theory. In fact the London engineers and men of science were not too familiar with the new power industries. The engineer, William Pole, could complain, with some justice, that Cornish achievements were better understood and appreciated in Paris than in London.[33]

Individual communities of engineers and men of science can be recognised in London, Edinburgh, Glasgow, Manchester and, particularly where science was concerned, in Cambridge and Dublin. They tended to reflect local ideas and interests in addition to the broadly accepted principles of technical knowledge. In London the temper of physical science had been set by Davy and Faraday and the roots of power lay between the Royal Society, the Royal Institution, the engineering institutions and the university colleges. The Glasgow community was the offspring of a rapidly growing industrial complex together with the Andersonian Institution and a distinguished university that had included Joseph Black on its staff in the eighteenth century and Lewis Gordon and William Thomson in the nineteenth century. Manchester had its characteristic industries and the Lit & Phil as well as the Manchester Royal Institution and the Mechanics' Institution. It is not suggested that virtue resided exclusively, or even largely, in any one of these communities or that they were homogeneous in outlook. Not everyone in Manchester accepted Joule's theories,[34] while there was an interesting division of opinion at Cambridge. G. G. Stokes, W. H. Miller and William Hopkins had been among the first to accept the dynamical theory of heat, but the Revd William Whewell, Master of Trinity College, was unconvinced. Mathematician, geophysicist, textbook writer, educationist, historian and philosopher of science, friend and advisor to Michael Faraday, Whewell was familiar with the full range of scientific achievement. If, perhaps, he had a tendency to regard himself as omniscient,* a pillar of sound, established learning,[35] that was hardly enough to account for his reluctance to accept the dynamical theory of heat as late as 1857. In the third edition of his memorable *History of the Inductive Sciences* (vol. 2, pp. 487–8), he mentioned the theory briefly but made it quite clear

---

*Cf. He who the nebular galaxies travelled,
       And the mysteries of science so neatly unravelled,
       Found, when he reached the edge of infinity,
       God's greatest work was the Master of Trinity.

that he regarded it as unproven. He accepted the undulatory theory of radiant heat: it had 'strong arguments and anologies in its favour'. But the dynamical theory of heat was, he added, an hypothesis 'of quite another kind'.

These considerations suggest that British science at that time held no uniform creed or code of practice. Rather there were several indentifiable schools that, while easy to recognise, were more difficult to describe or define. There were very few professional 'scientists'. In a non-professional age a wide diversity was inevitable. It was also an advantage; the number of options was greater than it would otherwise have been; a fruitful idea that might have been inhibited or suppressed in one school or community might be allowed or encouraged to flourish in another.

The third and last point to consider is not directly related to the first two. It is the vexed, and contemporary as well as historical, question: what is the relationship between scientific theory and technological advance? Or, to take a specific example, would the development of the high-pressure steam-engine, up to and including the modern turbine, have been the same had Carnot, Joule, Clausius, Thomson, Rankine, etc., never lived? It is possible to envisage that economic pressures, certainly present all the time, would have brought about the formulation of effective empirical rules, much as the pressures on the Cornish mining industry led to the building of engines of sound thermodynamic design without the guidance of theory.

Put like this the problem can hardly be answered. But this is not a satisfactory conclusion. In fact, once theory has unambigously laid down the laws determining the performance of the engine, designers can confidently work along the lines indicated by those laws. Obstacles can be realistically assessed, either as strictly insurmountable or as accidental hindrances that can be overcome. Theory enables the engineer or technologist to see over the hill, as it were, and to realise the full possibilities of his ideas. This is clearly apparent in the case of the invention of the dynamo. Nineteenth-century power engineers had an excellent exemplar in the eighteenth-century achievements of John Smeaton. He transformed the efficiency of water-wheels, sources of power whose ancestry went back to the earliest times. By using the basic concepts of Galilean–Leibnizian mechanics he was able to lay down the ground rules for the perfection of the water-wheel, in fact of all water-power engines. At the same time his French contemporary, the Chevalier de Borda, was able to use theory to such effect that he was able to specify the advantages offered by the turbine, a machine that was neither made nor even named until some eighty years later. Technology and science are therefore related but autonomous, mutually dependent activities and their values are solely and simply measured in human terms.

7

Coincidences

The incorporation into physical science of the doctrine of the conservation of energy went far towards the fulfilment of an aspiration held since the seventeenth century: the hope that all natural phenomena, at least in the realm of the physical sciences, could be explained by means of rational mechanics, Robison's universal mechanics. It was, therefore, wider in scope than the dynamical theory of heat which, *pace* Herschel, had a number of advocates in the first half of the nineteenth century. Conservation of energy has been quoted as an example of simultaneous discovery[1] and, certainly, a number of individuals can be named as independent discoverers of the doctrine. But it is asserted here that only a small number – a handful – can stand scrutiny. The first of these was Julius Robert Mayer (1817–78).

Trained as a physician, Mayer gained his first insight into the conservation of energy while serving as a ship's doctor in the East Indies.[2] The circumstances were unusual and the motivation indirect but he shared a common faith that there must be a simple, unifying principle to account for all natural phenomena. On his return to Germany and to a medical practice he worked out his ideas, first published in 1842, in his paper, 'Bemerkungen über die Kräfte der unbelebten Natur' (Liebig's *Annalen der Chemie*). Starting from the metaphysical postulate that *causa aequat effectum* he laid down that forces are causes and that, therefore, to every force there must correspond an appropriate effect. *Vis viva* is a force and it can cause 'fall-force' (attraction through space, tension or potential energy). While *vis viva* can cause its equivalent of fall-force and vice versa, very often *vis viva* causes, or seems to cause, no effect at all; as, for example, in inelastic collisions. Something was wrong here; there must be some effect. And that effect, he argued, was heat. He had, he claimed, found that violently moving, or agitating, water raised its temperature from 12° to 13°C. But, like Joseph Reade before him, he gave no details of his experiment. He did not believe that the motion, the *vis viva*, was actually transformed into heat; he believed that the *vis viva* disappeared and the right amount of heat appeared in its place.

This implied that there must be a numerical relationship between *vis viva* and heat. To find this he made the assumption that the reason why the specific heat of air at constant pressure was greater than at constant volume was because in the former case the air had to expand against atmospheric pressure and the measurable fall-force required to do this was correlated with extra heat. From the published data he calculated that one kilocalorie of heat corresponded to 365 kilogramme.metres of fall-force. This was as accurate a value for the mechanical equivalent of heat as possible, given the data he used.[3] He gave no account of his method of calculation in the 1842 paper, nor did he attempt to justify the assumption he had made.

Stripped of redundant metaphysics, Mayer's argument was that the disappearance of *vis viva* must be explained. This can be done by recognising that when *vis viva* vanishes, apparently without mechanical effect, an equivalent amount of heat appears.[4] He then offered an estimate of the amount of heat in terms of fall-force. Regarded like this, and with knowledge of what followed, the argument was brilliant, original and potentially fruitful. But that was not how Mayer's contemporaries saw it. The metaphysics was highly dubious and had no place in a scientific communication, the predictive value was not apparent and the paper failed to address itself to some of the most important questions of the day, particularly in the fields of electricity and magnetism. Undeterred, Mayer extended his ideas to the organic world and to the dynamics of the solar system – his meteoritic theory of the sun's heat was subsequently and independently proposed by Thomson and by J. J. Waterston. But Mayer had great difficulty in getting his papers published, suffering, in fact, something like academic persecution. His life was clouded by tragedy, and although he eventually achieved recognition it was only after the work had been done by others and without reference to him.[5] Mayer, like Carnot, Sturgeon, and Waterston, never enjoyed the fulfilment of seeing his ideas woven into the fabric of physical science. And the reasons for this are fairly clear. He lacked a champion, someone who could have understood, corrected and publicised his ideas. Worse, perhaps, he was outside, conspicuously outside, the academic establishment at a time when that establishment, particularly in Germany, was becoming increasingly important. Finally, the language in which he expressed his ideas was not that of contemporary physical science. As Mendoza has put it, there could be little understanding between two such different men as Joule and Mayer.[6] When Joule, painfully, translated Mayer's first paper for himself he interjected a few disparaging remarks, concluded that there was nothing new in it and added – incorrectly – that Rumford's estimate of the mechanical equivalent of heat had been just as accurate as Mayer's.[7] Von Rumford, of course, made no estimate of the mechanical equivalent of heat. Perhaps the fairest way of summing up these two contrasting men would be to say that Mayer was a speculative thinker, a philosopher's scientist; Joule was a scientist's scientist.

William Robert Grove (1811–96), a barrister and later a judge, was deeply interested in electricity and electrochemistry, being best known for his invention of the Grove cell. From 1841 to 1846 he was professor of experimental philosophy at the London Institution and it was there that he delivered a course of lectures that he published as *The Correlation of Physical Forces* (1846). Early in 1842 he had discovered that the electric "force", resulting from the combination of gases in the gas cell he had invented, was able to electrolyse the liquid formed from the same combination and restore the gases to their gaseous form. This, he said, was a 'beautiful instance of the correlation of natural forces'.[8] This implied that Grove had reached almost the same point that Joule had reached at much the same time, just before the publication of the latter's paper of 1843. Grove did not take the next, crucial, step; possibly because he lacked the engineer's measure of work, perhaps because he lacked the vision. He did, however, enunciate a qualitative version of the principle of the correlation of forces, or the conservation of energy, in his lectures at the London Institution. In later years Grove felt that the scientific world had not given him the credit for his formulation of the new doctrine. Pasted inside Joule's own copy of *The Correlation of Physical Forces** is a letter to *The Globe*, claiming that Grove had taught the correlation of forces, the grand new doctrine, in 1842. The attached initials are 'A. Q. C.' and the letter could well have come from Grove himself (he became a Queen's Counsel in 1853). Rather tartly, the editor commented that Grove must share the credit for 'the greatest scientific theory of modern times' with 'Joule, Mayer etc'. Very much later when, after Joule's death, it was decided to erect a plaque commemorating him in Westminster Abbey, the elderly Sir William Grove complained to the elderly Sir George Stokes about the wording.[9] It stated that Joule had discovered the principle of the conservation of energy and made no mention of Grove.

The last claimant to the title of discoverer of the principle to be

*In the Joule Collection in UMIST Library. The letter was dated 12 May but no year was given. As Joule's copy was from the third edition, 1855, it seems likely that the letter was written after that year.

discussed, briefly, was August Colding, an engineer, who in 1843 carried out experiments in which heat was generated by friction. They seemed to confirm, quantitatively, his theory about the 'transformation of powers to reappear as other powers'. He conceded that Mayer was the first to point this out but said that he had made the first statement of the law in its generality.[10] Unfortunately his theory was expressed in the language of *Naturphilosophie*. This philosophy, or view of nature, would have been quite unacceptable, if indeed intelligible, to Joule. Nevertheless, all these men had one thing in common: they did their work outside the academic and university institutions of the day.

Joule began the year 1851 delighted with the news that Thomson had succeeded in reconciling Carnot's theory with the dynamical theory of heat to his own satisfaction.[11] He begged Thomson to give the implications of this priority over considerations of his forthcoming paper on the air-engine, and he pointed out an error in Richard Potter's paper on the velocity of sound.[12] Potter, of whom it was said (incorrectly) that he could not assimilate developments from later than 1790, was refuted by Rankine, Stokes and others.[13]

Thomson had, by this time, begun work on his first paper on the dynamical theory of heat.[14] In it he magnanimously divided the credit between Carnot, Clausius and Joule. Although this, together with the recognition given him by Clausius, should surely have been sufficient, Joule was worried about Mayer. He wrote to Thomson:

The first intimation I received of Mr Mayer's claim was from the *Comptes Rendus* for Oct 16, 1848 in which he inserted a paper, 'Sur la transformation de la force vive en chaleur et reciproquement'. From this paper it appears that he presented a memoir to the Academy on 27 July, 1846, containing a description of an experiment he had made. He says, 'Je mésurais la chaleur qui se dégage dans la masse à papier des moulins à cylindre.'

In the same number of *Comptes Rendus* (Oct 16, 1848), he refers to what he had written previous to my determination. He says, 'J'ai trouvé, en 1840 à Sourabaya la loi de l'équivalence du travail mécanique et de la chaleur et j'ai publié, pour le premier fois, cette loi dans l'*Annales de Chemie et de la Pharmacie*, mai 1842, que la descente d'une colonne de mercure comprimant un gaz est équivalente à la quantité de chaleur dégagée par cette compression; d'où il s'ensuit que la descente d'une poids d'environ 365 metres d'élévation corre-spond à la chaleur qui hausse la temperature d'une même poids d'eau 1°C'.

Mr Mayer's claim to priority appears to be entirely based upon this last theoretical assertion and in my reply to him in *Comptes Rendus*, Jan 22, 1849 I said that the conclusion . . . was not warranted by the facts known at the time . . . for the general opinion conformably with the experiments of de la Rive and Marcet was that the sp. heat of a gas varied with its pressure. I remarked also that the simple fact of the heat produced by the compression of a gas did not warrant the conclusion that the heat was the exact equivalent of the force employed; because one may conceive of a gas formed of repulsive particles in which part of the force would be employed in forcing the particles nearer and only the remainder in generating heat.[15]

Mayer had responded by mentioning Gay-Lussac's experiment, now well known,[16] that showed that there was no cooling effect when air expanded into a vacuum. Although he had not mentioned it in his paper, he claimed that the experiment justified his assumption. Joule commented:

> I am not, however, of this opinion but shall be quite content to leave Mr Mayer in the enjoyment of having predicted the law of equivalence. But it would certainly be absurd to say he has established it.
>
> I have not pursued the controversy further because the facts are before the scientific world and shall be perfectly satisfied with its verdict whatever it may be.

It is probable that Joule's awareness of a possible spring effect, besides heating, when a gas is compressed led Thomson to ask Stokes: 'Do you think, when air is compressed, any appreciable proportion of the mechanical effect produced by the work is statical?'[17] And he confided to Joule, after agreeing about the assessment of Mayer's arguments, that the question of the work done and the rise in temperature when air is compressed deserved much deeper study. He added:

> Either a confirmation or negation by experiment of Mayer's hypothesis at any two temperatures differing by a considerable interval would be a most interesting and valuable result. I think no so limited series of experiments could do more to advance the theory of heat from the present state of the science than a series to determine the relation between the mechanical effect and the heat in the compression of air at different constant temperatures. I do hope you will be induced to enter upon the subject again.[18]

This exchange of views marked the beginning of the classical series of researches carried out jointly by Joule and Thomson. Joule had been planning to undertake further experiments, specifically of the kind in which air was cooled when it did work in expanding. He wanted to find out whether 'the results would *perfectly* coincide with the equivalents from liquid friction'.[19] The experiments on the expansion of air were, he believed, the most accurate of the series. But the practical difficulties of such experiments compared with the straightforward, uncomplicated procedure of the paddle-wheel experiments may have led to lingering doubts about this. Such doubts did not affect the usefulness of the experiments in the sense that they were indicative of the soundness of the hypothesis that heat and mechanical work were mutually interchangeable. But it would clearly be interesting if it should turn out that the results, using the last method, diverged from the results obtained from the other methods. Any such divergence might, in the first instance, be expected to throw light on the hypothetical watch-spring nature of the atoms of gases.

In the light of the later disputes between the champions of Mayer and of Joule it might be thought that there was an ungenerous motive on the parts of Joule and Thomson in their desire to test what they rather conspicuously called 'Mayer's hypothesis'. This was not the case. Thomson frankly did not believe it, and with good reason. His theory showed that the work required to generate a unit of heat by compressing a gas increased with the temperature; only at one temperature did it coincide with Joule's mechanical equivalent of heat. These calculations, based on impeccable authority and one seemingly most reasonable assumption, were, he showed, valid according to the new theory of heat.[20] And Mayer might well have discredited himself in Thomson's eyes by asking a simple, rhetorical question. Two pieces of ice, Mayer knew, could be melted by being rubbed together; but let anyone try to melt ice by pressure, however enormous! Thomson knew the answer to that one; and it, too, was equally valid on the new theory. On the other hand, despite Joule's doubts about the exactness and scope of Mayer's hypothesis he had one reason for hoping that it would turn out to be not too far from the truth. The Herapath–Joule kinetic theory of gases and the argument he had put to Thomson on 9 December 1848 independently implied the same absolute zero of temperature ($-273°C$). This area of disagreement apart, Joule and Thomson shared an interest in the air-engine. 'The more I look into the subject', wrote Joule, 'the more I feel that air will supersede steam.'[21] Here was another reason for investigating Mayer's hypothesis.

By this time the two men were exchanging visits. Acquaintance had bred friendship and mutual respect. Thomson must have been particularly impressive for he was rising rapidly in the world. He was only twenty-seven but he was, as Joule was quick to inform him, already a successful candidate for Fellowship of the Royal Society;[22] at the same time Joule proposed him for Honorary Membership of the Lit & Phil. Joule, too, found himself in demand. William Hopkins, Thomson's tutor at Cambridge, had started to visit Joule to consult him about experimental details concerning the research into the rigidity of the earth that he was carrying out in partnership with Fairbairn.[23] And Joule found civic duty demanded that he was

'at work all day on the Committee appointed here to investigate 'Staite's electric light' and we had the light uninterruptedly for 6½ hours together. I do not think anything will be made of it in practice. Mr Staite has also got a slip of *iridium* made by Mr Petrie which when traversed by a powerful current gives a light of dazzling brilliancy without melting.[24]

He did not say who convened this municipal committee, nor did he name the other members. It is a pity that neither W. E. Staite nor anyone else realised that a much cheaper and more convenient material could have been substituted for iridium by enclosing it in a small glass bulb evacuated of air.[25]

More importantly, Thomson and Joule were taking preliminary steps towards the experimental testing of Mayer's hypothesis. On his way south to Italy in early May, Thomson stopped off in Manchester to discuss plans with Joule.[26] On reaching London, Thomson at once called on Colonel Sabine, Secretary of the Royal Society, and found him favourably disposed towards their plans.[27] The Royal Society had £1,000 at its disposal to spend every year on research. Thomson and Joule resolved to apply for £100 of this money to pay for the apparatus; the idea for which, due to Thomson, was based on Joule's experiments of 1845. Joule had noticed that when compressed air from one cylinder was allowed to expand through the stopcock into the other, evacuated cylinder, the stopcock was slightly heated. Joule's explanation for this at the time was incorrect;[28] but Thomson, recognising the same effect as the heating of high-pressure steam from a boiler, saw in it the germ of an idea for testing Mayer's hypothesis.

And then, by coincidence, both men found themselves involved in minor disagreements that foreshadowed trouble in the future. Clausius published a short paper in which he criticised Thomson's explanation of the super-heating of steam passing through an orifice. After careful analysis Clausius concluded that the heat generated was not due to friction as Thomson claimed; it was the thermal equivalent of the work expended in driving the steam through the orifice.[29] Thomson's prompt response, written from London on 10 May, was a brusquely dismissive, single-paragraph note.[30] And Clausius's considered reply to the note met with no less cavalier treatment.[31] Joule was not involved in this dispute and the whole affair was hardly more than a quarrel about words. Thomson could, and probably should, have been more courteous, but in private he was surprisingly bitter. He wrote to Stokes to complain:[3]

> It is a bore to have to write a defence of what is as clear as a pikestaff against objections which must be appreciated by all who admit the truth of Newton's first law of motion with *nec* in place of *nisi quaternus* (however I suppose the insult cannot be published so I shall content myself with a shot in the air).

Can it be that Thomson, privately, resented the man who had so quickly and elegantly solved the problem that he had puzzled over for so long? Stokes was too diplomatic to get involved in the matter.

Joule's difference – disagreement would be too strong a word – was with

John Tyndall, a man who was to pay a bigger part in Joule's life than has been recognised up to now. Tyndall (1820–93) was an Irishman, born in Youghal. His first employment, with the Ordnance Survey, ended with his dismissal after a bitter quarrel with his superiors (he was always notably combative). After a spell as a teacher he had saved up enough money to enrol at the University of Marburg where, after two years, he was awarded his Ph.D. (1850). Tyndall was among the first British physicists to go to Germany to get an advanced scientific education. And, like so many subsequent British and American students, he returned deeply impressed by his experiences in Germany. The old university towns, the ease and pace of life, the zeal of the professors and the deep reverence for learning for its own sake combined to leave many men with the fondest memories of their student days. 'To Germany I owe much', he wrote, 'goodbye, dear old Germany.'[33]

On his return to England Tyndall wrote a series of articles for the *Philosophical Magazine* on recent scientific work in Germany. Discussing magnetism and electromagnetism he mentioned Lenz and Jacobi's work at St Petersburg and then announced that, in 1848, Dub had established that there was a saturation point for soft iron beyond which its receptivity for magnetism did not increase.[34] Joule lost no time in replying that he had reached the same conclusion twelve years ago and had published his findings in Sturgeon's *Annals*.[35] In confirmation the magazine republished his old papers from the now forgotten journal. Also forgotten, apparently, was the even earlier paper by Father Callan announcing the same discovery. But the little episode left no ill-will; after all, Tyndall had not made a positive claim for Dub's priority; he was merely reporting on work done. A few months later Joule gave Tyndall a testimonial in support of his application for the Chair of the University of Toronto. Joule said that he sincerely hoped that Tyndall would obtain the position which he was 'so qualified to fill'.[36]

While Joule was reminding the scientific world of his early work in electromagnetism and, at the same time, preparing his paper on the air-engine for publication, he was privately briefing Thomson on his subsequent researches in electrolysis. Thomson had read Wilhelm Weber's paper of March 1851,[37] in which the determination of electrical resistance in 'absolute', or mechanical, measure was described and, with that remarkable flair for recognising the potentialities in other men's works, had seen that the Weber–Gauss system could be extended to electroche-mistry and, generally, to the energy principle. Although Joule was prin-cipally engaged in sending Thomson hard data on electrolysis he did allow one homely note to intrude on his scientific discourse. He wrote to say, at midsummer, that he had not been able to reply promptly as his wife and child were at the seaside and he had therefore not had time to write;[38] which raises an interesting question about the conjugal division of labour among the affluent middle classes of mid-nineteenth-century Manchester. But the rest was prosaic. Mr Dancer was to make a galvanometer for Thomson, presumably for the comparison of electromotive forces. Joule commended his own instrument which with '400 turns of thin wire is useful in ascertaining the intensity of different galvanic arrangements on account of the resistance being immensely greater than that of most couples'.[39] In other words, the galvanometer could be used as an efficient voltmeter. And, also relevant to Thomson's study of electrolysis, they discussed the question whether pure water was a conductor or whether it was a perfect insulator. Joule was doubtful whether a perfect insulator could exist in nature.[40]

In December 1851 Thomson summed up his work in two papers in which he succeeded in putting Joule's and Weber's systems into a common framework.[41] In doing this he helped to lay the foundations of modern electrical science. From then on equalities increasingly replaced the proportions in which the laws of electricity had been commonly expressed. Another advance was indicated by the words with which Thomson began his first paper: 'Certain principles discovered by Mr Joule must ultimately become an important part of the foundation of a mechanical theory of chemistry.' He was right: Joule's work on electrolysis represented a substantial advance in quantified chemistry as a mature physical science, although not towards the realisation of the 'Newtonian dream', as Thackray succinctly put it.[42] Energy, and not Newtonian 'force', was to be the dominant principle.

Thomson, in his first paper, imagined a very simple magneto-electric engine charging a Daniell cell.* Some of the work done in driving the engine generated heat; the remainder was accounted for by the chemical action as the cell charged up. When the cell was fully charged the speed of the magneto could be reduced until its electromotive force was equal to that of the cell, in which case no current would flow from the magneto to the cell. If the speed was reduced still further the current would flow in the reverse direction and the cell would begin to drive the magneto; this time as an electromagnetic engine, or motor. Thomson's analysis showed that

---

*The Daniell cell is reversible. The expressions 'charging' and 'charged' were not used by Thomson, or his contemporaries. His simple magneto was similar to the one described by Faraday in his Bakerian lecture of 1832: a metal disc was spun at right angles to the earth's magnetic field and the resulting emf was developed between brushes pressing on the rim and centre of the disc. The machine should ensure a uniform emf.

when the cell was fully charged and no current flowed, its emf was equal to the product of the electrochemical equivalent of the metal of the cell, the amount of heat absorbed or given out by the metal in electrolysis or combination and the mechanical equivalent of heat.[43] Using the figures provided by Joule he calculated the mechanical value of the emf of a Daniell cell. Much later he showed that it was equal to 1.074 volts; a gratifyingly accurate result. Using Joule's figures for the electrochemical equivalent and the heat of combination, or electrolysis, of hydrogen, he calculated the emf required to electrolyse water; in modern measure it came to 1.416 volts. This confirmed, satisfactorily, why more than one Daniell cell was required for the electrolysis of water.

Satisfactory as this seemed, important as the introduction of the energy principle into electrochemistry undoubtedly was, there was, nevertheless, a defect in Thomson's (and Joule's) reasoning. The emf of the Daniell cell is substantially independent of the operating temperature. But the emf of other cells varies with the temperature. Since heat and temperature are involved in the working of electrochemical cells – in, as Joule and Thomson would have put it, the transformation of chemical heat into mechanical effect, or work – it follows that both laws of thermodynamics apply. Some years later, when the implications of Clausius's and Thomson's works were better understood, Helmholtz worked out a formula showing how the emf of a cell depended on the chemical heat and the temperature.[44] It is ironic that, at the time when Thomson was criticising Mayer for assuming that his hypothesis was independent of the temperature, he himself was, quite unwittingly, making the same unjustified assumption in his analysis of the Daniell cell.

The second paper is, apart from the final paragraph, rather less interesting. Thomson discussed the question, arising from the first paper, to what extent do the different chemical reactions in a cell determine the emf? Did the heat generated by the solution of the oxide in the acid contribute to the emf or was it just the heat of oxidation that was effective? And he put forward two propositions. The first asserted that the mechanical value of the total effect of a current flowing in a circuit was numerically equal to the product of the numbers representing the emf and the current, or $JH = ei$, the law originally established by Joule in the form of a proportional relationship. And the second stated that the resistance of a conductor was, in absolute measure, equal to the product of the mechanical equivalent of heat and the quantity of heat generated in unit time by a current of unit strength; this, too, followed from Joule's original formulation of the law (H is proportional to i^2r). Joule's own standardised measure of electric current – one unit would electrolyse nine grains of water in one hour – turned out to be 'very exactly' one-eighth of Weber's absolute unit in British measures. This coincidence enabled Thomson easily to calculate, from data provided by Joule, Becquerel and others, the specific resistance of various metals in Weber's absolute units. The results showed a clear agreement between Joule's measurement of the resistance of copper and Weber's measurement of the resistance of electrolytically precipitated copper. Elsewhere, with different specimens of copper, there were wide divergencies, indicative of the effects of impurities on the specific resistance. Thomson therefore wrote:

> It is very much to be desired that Weber's direct process, and the indirect method founded on estimating, according to Joule's principles, the mechanical value of the thermal effects of a galvanic current, should be both put in practice to determine the absolute resistance of the same conductor, or that the resistance of two conductors to which the two methods have been separately applied, should be accurately compared.

As Thomson was completing these two papers Joule was preparing to travel to Glasgow, taking with him the long-delayed galvanometer. He intended to travel by train, then he changed his mind and decided to go by ship from Liverpool (he much preferred sea to rail travel) but, finally, had to go by train. Early in December he wrote to Thomson.

> I shall be most happy to become acquainted with Mr Clerk Maxwell and am very glad to avail myself of your kindness; but should it give you the least inconvenience do say so, and I could come at a later time. If nothing to prevent it occurs I hope to arrive by train reaching Glasgow at about 8 pm on Monday the 15th. Your paper in the *Phil Mag* was most gratifying to me. I am only afraid you speak too highly of my researches.[45]

8

Joule and Thomson

Richard Roberts, like other leading engineers, was an active member of the Lit & Phil of which he was, for many years, a vice-president.[1] He was therefore a colleague of Joule and when, towards the end of his active life, he started to wind up his business affairs he asked Joule to dispose of his big electromagnet. He stipulated that he would sell it for five guineas to anyone who could appreciate its originality.[2] Joule wrote to Thomson to suggest that Glasgow University might like to buy it, adding that it would hardly be suitable for class demonstrations!

Robert's big electromagnet was not the only item that Joule offered to Thomson early in 1852. He sent up his maximum density of water apparatus and the big electromagnet he had used in his critical experiments of 1843. Perhaps he was acknowledging a watershed in his career; More prosaically, he may have been clearing out a space in the cellars of 1 Acton Square for the projected joint researches with Thomson. But before these could begin there was another experiment to carry out. W. H. Miller, who had refereed his paper on the air-engine, had pointed out that Joule had relied on an inaccurate figure for the ratio of the principal specific heats of air.[3] The figure he had used had been calculated from Delaroche and Bérard's unreliable value for the specific heat of air at constant pressure and from his own (accurate) value for the mechanical equivalent of heat. In order to determine the specific heat of air at constant pressure he arranged to pump dry air through a spiral lead pipe, immersed in a hot-water tank and thence through an identical spiral in a cold-water tank. The volume of air pumped through was measured and the suitably corrected rise in temperature of the cold-water tank taken. From these the specific heat of air at constant pressure was found; it was reasonably close to the figure that could be deduced from the ratio that Miller had quoted.[4] The experiment was straightforward and the result did not greatly affect the table in which he set out the performance of the air-engine. The interest lies in the

Fig. 4 William Thomson in 1852

outward resemblance of the apparatus to that used in the joint experiments with Thomson; experiments in which the lead piping, the thermometers and the air-pump could all be used.

In Thomson's modification of Joule's experiments of 1845 the two copper vessels were replaced by long coils of metal piping immersed in two water-baths kept at the same temperature as the atmosphere.[5] A pump maintained a continuous stream of air through the pipes and a narrow orifice was fixed in the short section of pipe joining the two coils. The temperature of the air was measured as it emerged on the low-pressure side of the orifice.

Let us imagine, Thomson said, a unit volume of air at high pressure passing through the orifice and emerging on the low-pressure side at the same pressure as the atmosphere and, before long, at the same temperature. It follows from Boyle's law that no net work has been done by the air; all the work has been done by the pump. The temperature of the air as it emerges from the orifice will depend on two things: the cooling effect due to its expansion to a lower pressure and the heating effect due to friction.* The net effect will constitute a test of Mayer's hypothesis. Suppose, said Thomson, that in place of the orifice there is a movable piston with a second movable piston behind the unit volume of air on the high-pressure side. Both pistons slide along the pipe until the second piston reaches the original position of the first piston. At this point the first piston is allowed to move on, driven by the pressure of the air behind it. This piston can be made to do the maximum amount of external work which we can calculate and also the cooling of the air due to its expansion. The next step is to imagine the orifice restored and this time, instead of external work, the passage of the air generates the thermal equivalent of the work done in forcing the air through the orifice and beyond. In both cases the same amount of work has been done and, as far as the air is concerned, the end result is the same. If, therefore, passage through the orifice converts all the work done into heat and that heat is just enough to compensate for the cooling due to expansion, then Mayer's hypothesis is confirmed. Which means that if a gas changes volume without the performance of work its temperature remains the same. But if the net effect is either a heating or a cooling then Mayer's hypothesis is falsified.

This explanation of the theory is that given by Thomson and it is certainly clear enough. But the pedantic student may not be entirely

---

*'Or which', as (probably) Thomson put it, 'is the same, the thermal equivalent of the work done by the air in expanding from its state of high pressure on one side of the narrow passage to the state of atmospheric pressure'. This was similar to Clausius's expression.

satisfied with Thomson's ascription of the source of the idea entirely to Joule's experiments of 1845. Clausius, in his derided note on the efflux of high-pressure steam, calculated the amount of heat required to keep a unit weight of steam saturated when it acted on a piston; in addition he computed the thermal equivalent of the work done to drive the same amount of steam through a narrow orifice, the initial and final conditions being the same as in the first case. He noted that the work was done by the evaporative process in the boiler which drove the steam through the orifice: in Thomson's scheme the work was done by a pump. Finally, the student might point out that the equations derived by Clausius and Thomson are, formally, almost identical.[6] Of course there can be no question that Thomson was entirely competent to think out the principles of the proposed experiments for himself and to derive the relevant equation. He announced the outline of the experiments at almost the same time as the translation of Clausius's note appeared in the *Philosophical Magazine*. Evidently, Clausius has priority of publication in this little affair, and it should go on record that he might have influenced Thomson's thoughts in the matter of what was to become a classic series of experiments.

At the beginning of 1852 Joule seemed to be in no great hurry to get on with the testing of Mayer's hypothesis. He wrote, unenthusiastically, to Thomson: 'I will bear in mind the experiment you mentioned for testing Mayer's hypothesis and will see if I can put together the requisite apparatus'.[7] He was facing a change in his domestic affairs, for Amelia was pregnant again. Furthermore, apart from the need to complete his study of the air-engine in the light of Miller's correction, he had started a new scientific hare. He had been struck by the close analogy between the newly-discovered law governing the proportion of heat converted into work in a perfect Carnot engine and the law that he and Scoresby had discovered relating the work done by an electric motor to the proportionate reduction in current when the engine was working. What, he asked Thomson,

'is the physical condition of a wire carrying a galvanic current? Is there a vibration of the material of the wire itself of a different kind from that which constitutes heat? Or is there merely the flow of a substance (possessing some but not all of the properties of matter) which we call electricity? The latter view explains many phenomena very well but I suspect it will ultimately be overturned.[8]

To this Thomson replied that in his opinion, 'an electric current circulating in a closed conductor *is heat*, and becomes capable of producing thermometric effects by being frittered down into smaller local circuits, or 'molecular vortices'.[9]

Thomson, it seems, had not, at this time, understood or accepted the significance of Joule's work on the kinetic theory of gases. He was at the stage Joule had reached when he had envisaged 'atmospheres' spinning round individual atoms, or the stage Rankine was at when he conceived his vortex theory of heat. It looked as though the ghost of caloric was proving very hard to exorcise. And, for once at least, Thomson's great ability to recognise the growth points in other men's ideas was dormant. The development of the kinetic theory of gases passed from Joule to Clausius, Maxwell, Gibbs and Boltzmann without any assistance from Thomson. Joule, who cannot have been too happy about Thomson's opinion, applied to the Royal Society for a £30 grant to study the effects of currents on the dimensions of conductors.[10] But this trail soon petered out and it was to be a long time before further progress could be made in the study of electric currents.

The extended joint researches of Joule and Thomson began when Thomson travelled down to Manchester in mid-May to spend some ten days with Joule.[11] On May Day Joule had written 'The arrival of this day reminds me of your kind promise and I may soon expect the pleasure of seeing you. I have got my compressing pump here and have prepared the other necessary articles for making experiments on the cold produced by rarefaction and have no doubt we may arrive at good results.[12]

Their first experiments, carried out in the cellar at 1 Acton Square, were inevitably tentative, amounting to a reconnaissance to find out what would be the main problems and difficulties. The apparatus mustered was simple: eight yards of lead piping immersed in a water-bath, a small hand-pump of 10½ inches stroke (the one that Joule had used in his earlier experiments), and a small copper vessel to act as a shock absorber to even out the pressure of the air before it reached the stopcock that acted as orifice. The experiments began by fitting a short length of rubber tubing to the stopcock and arranging it so that the mouth was just above the water level (Fig. 5(1)). With the stopcock almost closed, a thermometer held in the rubber tube showed that the rushing air was perceptibly cooled below the temperature of water. With the stopcock wide open and the rubber tube constricted just below the thermometer the rushing air was still cooled, so any conduction of heat through the metal stopcock cannot have had much effect. The cooling effect was still apparent, although considerably reduced, when the temperature of the water, and therefore of the air passing through the lead pipe, was maintained at 150°F. The explanation seemed to be that the cooling was due to the expansion of the air while the *vis viva* due to the action of the pump was taken up by the rushing mass of air. That is, the *vis viva* imparted by the pump had not yet been transformed into the *vis viva* of

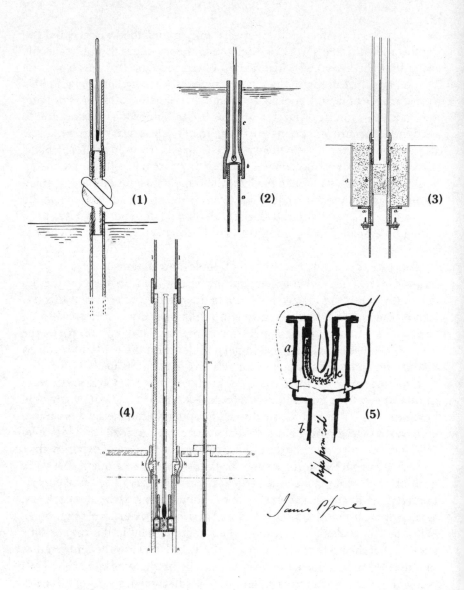

Fig. 5 The development of the porous plug. (1) is a conjectural representation of the initial stopcock experiment; (5), from Joule's letter to Thomson, shows the absbestos plug in which the thick and thin wires (of different metals) form a differential thermocouple

the molecules comprising the gases of the atmosphere; or, in simple language, into heat.

By the time Thomson left to go to Cambridge they had 'not arrived at any quite positive result'.[13] Joule continued on his own, carrying out an analytical experiment in which the stopcock was immersed in a small tin can full of water and the rubber tube, leading from it, was joined at the other end to a spiral of block tin tube immersed in a second tin can full of water. This time Joule found that

> The result is cold in the first vessel containing the stock-cock, heat in the second! which proves that which, if I recollect rightly you thought probable, viz that the principal amount of friction occurs in the axis of the orifice among the particles of air and not as I had imagined at the metallic surface. I will write to you again with the details of the expts shortly. But I have no doubt whatever of the fact being already established.[14]

The candid reader might suppose that this offered a proximate confirmation of Mayer's hypothesis. Joule and Thomson were, apparently, reluctant to accept it as such. For the moment, however, they had other things on their minds. A fortnight later Joule wrote to tell Thomson that

> I am happy to say that the expected stranger arrived safely into the world yesterday morning. It is a little girl, very healthy and strong and is as well as its mother, doing as well as could be expected. It occurs to me that you intend to return to the north about 3 weeks from the present time; if, as I hope, you will make it convenient to be at the christening and stand godfather, we might at the same time endeavour to settle the question of heat and cold from air rushing through an orifice. Using a plug of gutta percha with a small hole I find the air to be cooled from 63 to 61½ when rushing at a pressure of 4 atmospheres but this must be repeated with an orifice of metal.[15]

It seems at first sight strange that Joule, a member of a respected Manchester family and active in the affairs of the Lit & Phil, should choose as the godfather for his only daughter a man whom he had known for barely five years and whom he could have met only occasionally and for relatively short periods. What it surely implies is that Joule was a very private man whose inner life was dedicated to his science. Anyone who could get close to that science was close to Joule himself.

The next letter continued to mingle the christening with the research.

> I feel much gratification in the anticipation of your company as godfather at the christening of my little daughter. I am happy to say that she and her mother are doing remarkably well. We think of 11 or 14 days from this for the christening and hope you will be able to make it convenient to be with us at that time.
>
> I am also desirous of your company on another account. The experiments which I sent an outline of to you convince me that our first conclusion viz, *that*

cold is produced by air rushing at low temperature is correct. Now I am making all the apparatus tight and if you will lend your help a little at the pumping we shall, I doubt not, settle the question for all temperatures we may wish to try.[16]

Thomson, however, could attend neither the christening nor the pumping:

The christening of your little god daughter took place last Wednesday at our own church by Mr Stowell, my brother acted as your proxy. Its name is Alice Amelia, the former after a beloved mother & sister and the latter after my wife. We had a little party of our immediate relations and everything went on pleasantly. I am sure you will not be ashamed of your god daughter when you see her, she is a remarkably healthy and firm child and improves rapidly.

   I have not yet proceeded further with the expts in consequence of a thermometer I had ordered for them not being finished.[17]

Thomson was somewhat blasé about the affair. He remarked to his brother: 'Talking of babies, Mrs Joule has had a second which is a girl, notwithstanding which I am asked to be its godfather, so I have an addition to my family of godchildren which is now tolerably numerous'.[18]

Much more important for Thomson was his engagement, announced shortly after the christening of Joule's daughter, to Margaret Crum, the daughter of Walter Crum, JP, FRS, a calico-printer of Glasgow.

It was in August, while on holiday at Southport for the benefit of the sea air, that Joule described a significant improvement to the apparatus:

I have taken the following plan in carrying out the experiments on the temperature of rushing air. A brass pipe was soldered to the lead coil and a piece of calf skin leather was tightly bound over the open end. Over this a piece of vulcanised india rubber piping was fastened. In the experiments the compressed air rushed through the pores of the leather against the bulb of a very small thermometer placed in the india rubber tube, the bulb being in immediate contact with the leather. The pressure was measured, as before, by a mercurial gauge.[19]

Joule had realised that if, in place of one orifice, many smaller ones are substituted, then the *vis viva* of the proportionately smaller rushing streams of air, or 'rapids' as Thomson called them, will be much more readily transformed into molecular *vis viva*, or heat (Fig. 5(2)). This will occur before any flow of heat from (or to) the surroundings can negate the effect they were seeking. Using the calfskin pores Joule found that there was, indeed, a cooling effect and that this effect was reduced to about half as the temperature of the surrounding water was increased from 61° to 160°F; was this not, he asked Thomson, in accordance with theory?

The answer to that question was: not really. Thomson's theory also indicated that the cooling effect should be proportional to the logarithm of the pressure drop across the orifice.[20] But in ten series of experiments the law was not substantiated, due, they felt, to 'accidental circumstances'. In the first series of experiments the temperature of the water was kept as nearly as possible the same as that of the atmosphere while the pressure was increased. They noticed that there was a 'tendency' for the cooling effect to increase with the pressure.[21] This suggested to Joule that as the pressure increased, so the quantity of air passing also increased, and that the effect of heat absorbed through the rubber tube must be relatively reduced as more cooled air passed through.[22] This might be remedied to some extent by increasing the thermal insulation of the rubber tube; but the best solution would be to increase significantly the flow of air. And that would mean bigger apparatus and a more powerful pump.

The preliminary experiments had distinguished, to some extent at least, the net cooling from the much greater effect before the *vis viva* of the rushing air had been transformed into heat. Joule and Thomson had established that Mayer's hypothesis was not rigorously correct and they had indicated a serious discrepancy in Thomson's theory. He had predicted that the cooling effect would decrease with an increase in temperature. This had been confirmed but the theory also indicated that at about 33°C, or 92°F, the cooling effect would vanish and, at temperatures above that, would be replaced by a heating effect. In fact there was still a slight cooling effect at 171°F. From this it followed that, as Regnault's results could not be queried, saturated steam could not obey the gas laws. Finally, the experiments demonstrated – a modern touch, this – the need for further research. 'I think', wrote Joule, 'it will hardly be necessary to go on with experiments with the present apparatus as I think the results already obtained are about as accurate as can be obtained unless a more powerful current of air can be commanded.'

The experiment was first proposed by Thomson, who hoped that it would lead to the falsification of Mayer's hypothesis. Joule also had doubts about Mayer's hypothesis; they sprang, as Mendoza has argued, from his awareness that gas atoms might incorporate spring-like properties. The introduction of the calfskin leather membrane was due to Joule and it was vitally important. Before then Thomson had spoken only of a small orifice. Furthermore, Joule had identified the need for an increased flow of air to ensure more accurate results. When, therefore, their joint paper was read to the British Association meeting in Belfast on 3 September 1852, the credit belonged in equal measure to both of them.

Joule had not been able to attend the Belfast meeting; he had been too busy at the brewery. But his enthusiasm for the research was now fully aroused. The joint paper had been well received. The Royal Society committee had recommended the award of their grant to cover the cost of the apparatus. Afterwards, wrote Joule, the pump, thermometers, etc., could be returned to the Royal Society 'for subsequent use, or made part of a museum of philosophical apparatus such as I saw with very great interest at the College of France'.*[23] He could now design apparatus on a much bigger scale: an air-pump with a bore of 6 inches and a stroke of 22 inches, compared with 1⅜ inches and 10½ inches, capable of delivering sixteen times as much air as the hand-pump and driven by the steam-engine at the brewery, an oil bath to enable experiments to be carried out at temperatures up to 600°F and apparatus able to withstand pressures of ten atmospheres. This was verging on what we should now call big science.

Thomson was on the eve of his wedding (15 September) but he was not to be spared Mayer's hypothesis. Could he, asked Joule, manage to write a short note for the *Philosophical Magazine* when on his honeymoon in Wales?[24] And could he and the new Mrs Thomson 'make it convenient to return to Glasgow through Manchester? If so, Mrs J and myself would have great pleasure in entertaining Mrs Thomson & yourself in our plain ways for a few days.'[25] And, of course, they could talk about experiments on air and on the effects of currents on the dimensions of conductors.

The cylinder of the pump was to have a spiral piston ring made by Mather & Platt, whose factory was only a hundred yards from the brewery. The piston ring was to be coated with anti-friction metal. The remainder of the apparatus was to have been made by William Fairbairn's works, but they were under such pressure that Mather and Platt had to complete the job.[26] The piston, when finished, was found to be a 'very beautiful piece of workmanship'. It had to be, for the pump would be required to drive air in a closed circuit through more than 120 feet of copper and wrought iron tubing, an air-drier full of quicklime, a gas-holder, three stopcocks, a pair of drop-valves and, finally, the essential 'nozle' incorporating the 'porous plug' through which the expansion took place. This was scientific research on a scale beyond the resources of the traditional devotee with his spare-room laboratory and his reliance on the 'philosophical instrument maker's' shop.

Joule was now among the leaders of British science. This was publicly acknowledged when, in November 1852, he was awarded the Royal Medal of the Royal Society for his work on the mechanical equivalent of heat. In

*On the death of Joule's son, Benjamin Arthur Joule, in 1922, the Manchester College of Science and Technology (now UMIST) bought all the remaining apparatus including some of the oldest and most important pieces. The UMIST Physics Department has presented the apparatus to the Greater Manchester Museum of Science and Industry where it is now on public display.

this way honourable and expeditious amends were made for the Society's earlier neglect of his work. Ironically, at the same time, John Tyndall wrote to Samuel Hunter Christie, Secretary of the Royal Society, to decline the award of the Royal Medal on the grounds that he had learned that certain members of the Council had 'on mature consideration' come to doubt the originality and value of his work.[27] Tyndall, so often pugnacious and, in that respect, quite unlike Joule, may well have made powerful enemies.

Public confidence was confirmed when, on 6 December, Joule wrote to Thomson to say that an interim grant of £50 had been made and that work on the apparatus was proceeding satisfactorily. At the same time he gave a list of the names of the men of science to whom he had sent copies of their paper on the air-engine.[28] By 20 December he had decided that it would be 'very desirable' to experiment on carbonic acid (carbon dioxide), other permanent gases and steam. The last should not offer any great difficulty; all that would be required would be a small, high-pressure boiler.[29] A month later he admonished Thomson: 'I feel much concerned to hear that your health has not been so good since your return to Glasgow. I do trust that you will exert yourself less until you feel quite recovered. We have all of us at times reason enough to rest a while to recruit our strength which otherwise might be permanently impaired.'[30]

He continued, without a break: 'I have ordered our cooper to make three tubs of 4 feet diameter, and 2 feet, 3 feet and 4 feet deep respectively. The two first to hold the coil of pipes, the last to be the lower vessel of the gas holder which will therefore contain some 40 cubic feet.'

Nothing was to interfere with the flow of scientific intelligence. And so Thomson learned that Hopkins had returned to Cambridge. His experiments in Manchester had been unsuccessful but Joule had profited from them: he had been brought to appreciate the importance of perfectly tight soldered joints. However, interest in the details of large-scale experiments was interrupted for a moment by a different matter;

Since I have seen the February no of the Phil[1] Magazine containing your (Thomson's) and Rankine's paper I have felt how much I would have enjoyed a conversation with you on the subjects therein treated of. The term energy employed by you seems admirably suited to the expression of anything which might ultimately by proper transformation be exhibited in the form of, say, heat. The adjectives potential and actual employed by Mr Rankine seem to deserve the approbation you express in reference to them, but still it would be desirable . . . not to confine the terms to any particular state or power, for instance light may be transformed into heat and the heat so transformed to be given out as a chemical force hence if the heat be viewed relatively to the light it is a potential energy, but actual energy in relation to the chemical force and vice versa if the light be produced by the chemical force through the intervention of heat.

... the men have commenced putting up the pump, and I have promises that the copper coils (of 2 inch diameter pipe) will be finished in a fortnight.[31]

Rankine had given memorable names to the conjugate concepts of energy. Thereafter energy, in both its forms, actual (later called kinetic) and potential, could be distinguished from Newtonian force and the mis-understandings of readers ended. Before long energy, in its own right, assumed a general significance that far transcended its Leibnizian forbear, *vis viva*.[32]

Joule was not to be diverted for long.

'I have just been to see the coppersmith to see the progress of our work – the gasmeter and pipes are well advanced. The cylinder is also put up in our engine house . . . I am endeavouring to get the work forwarded simultaneously at the different workshops so as to be all ready near the same time.[33]

He hoped that they would be able to start experiments by about the middle of March. And he was glad to learn that Thomson could join him then. He continued:

You have heard, I dare say, that a testimonial to the memory of Dr Dalton is about to be instituted in Manchester in the shape of a monument and two exhibitions in connexion with Owens College, one for mathematics, the other for chemistry. The scientific people here have subscribed one or two guineas apiece towards the above object and the merchants & c their £50s. Should you know of any chemical or other gentleman who would like to assist in the above I would have great pleasure in forwarding their subs to the Committee. I feel however that this is a work that ought to be supported by those who, like our manufacturers, have reaped pecuniary benefit from Dr Dalton's discoveries and not by the scientific men who are pushing those discoveries further and deserve rather to be rewarded thereby rather than to reward others.*[34]

By mid-March Joule could report that he had tried the pump and it seemed to work well. He tested the apparatus up to about six atmospheres of pressure and he tried to find out if the coils of copper pipe were sufficient to bring the air accurately to the temperature of the surrounding water. To do this he pumped hot air through the pipe and measured the temperature at the outflow end.[35] He was surprised to find that the compressed air leaving the pump was very hot. Although this showed that the pump and valves would have to be water-cooled it also confirmed that an air-engine would be entirely practicable; little heat would be lost through the metal

*This was unfair. As the Farrars and Scott have pointed out, Dalton was, in all probability, much indebted to the chemical manufacturers Thomas and William Henry. Later, the manufacturers of Manchester were to show themselves particularly generous supporters of Owens College and the Victoria University.

sides of the cylinder.

All was now in readiness for Thomson's short visit. This led to one immediately interesting discovery. Thomson noticed that if he held his fingers in a certain way in a rushing stream of air he felt a strong sensation of heat. At the time Joule thought it was not more than a deceptive impression produced by the rushing air.[36] He soon confirmed it from his own experience and investigated further. With air at five or six atmospheres pressure rushing through a small orifice he found that when he tried to put finger and thumb together, squeezing or pinching the jet, it proved surprisingly difficult and as he tried he felt an intense burning. When he fitted a gutta-percha tube round the thermometer bulb, leaving a narrow space all round, he recorded a temperature rise of 100°F, but a slight change in position, away from the main jet, brought the temperature to a fall of 2°F. Pressing his finger over the orifice resulted in burning again. The most dramatic effect was when a piece of rubber was placed over the orifice and pressed down; it soon became intolerably hot and the undersurface started to disintegrate. As Joule explained to Stokes, these experiments confirmed Thomson's prediction that heating and cooling effects would occur in the same high-pressure jet of air.[37] But there was a little more to it than that. The adiabatic heating and cooling of compressed or expanded air was familiar knowledge. Joule, in his speculation about meteors, had argued that a body in rapid motion through the air would be heated, not cooled. Now, for the first time, the effect was demonstrated in practice. There was a slight difference in the two cases; in the first, the energy, or *vis viva*, belonged to the meteorite, in the second it belonged to the moving air; in both cases the heat generated was communicated to the solid body. For those days it was a very surprising phenomenon.

Mr Hopkins, having returned to Manchester to continue his experiments, brought some rather disturbing news. Regnault, it seemed, had written to the Royal Society 'claiming the whole ground' on which Joule and Thomson were working and stating that his investigation of the entire subject was now complete and that the results would be published in a forthcoming volume.[38] The Royal Society decided that it would be quite improper to allow anyone to pre-empt a whole important area of research and that if Joule and Thomson published first the results should and would be theirs. Of course, the testing of Mayer's hypothesis and the study of 'rushing air' were incontrovertibly within Joule and Thomson's established area of interest. But the implication was quite clear. 'I am therefore', wrote Joule, 'disposed to prosecute our experiments with more energy in order that we may not be forestalled by a process not consistent with the spirit of modern investigation.' A few weeks later a letter from Regnault was published in the *Proceedings of the Royal Society*, and shortly after that Joule's reply appeared.[39] Regnault was courteous and respectful (he had been elected a foreign Fellow of the Royal Society). But his account of his (unpublished) researches did suggest that he was staking a large claim to a substantial area of science. And his criticism of Joule's determination of the specific heat of air was misconceived: he selected the lowest figure quoted by Joule ('beaucoup trop faible') and ignored the final figure that was actually used by Joule in his calculations. In his reply Joule corrected the error and made it quite clear that he and Thomson were fully entitled to priority in their own chosen field of research. It was a minor affair but relations between the two parties were cool for some time thereafter.

Alarmed by Regnault's claims Joule and Thomson hastened to get their latest work into print; the result as an uncharacteristically short paper in the *Philosophical Transactions*.[40] A principal object of the research was, they said, to determine the value of Carnot's function;* but, beyond quoting the formula that Thomson had already published, they took this no further.[41] A cotton-wool porous plug (Fig. 5(3)) was substituted for the calfskin leather in order to obviate the effects of 'rapids' and to ensure that the air, on arriving at the thermometer, 'may be reduced to a uniform condition'. To prevent the stream of air blowing the cotton-wool plug along the pipe it was secured by strong threads running across it. It was important to eliminate the effect of the pulsations of pressure due to the action of the pump. Obviously, the gas meter did not fulfil the same task as the copper vessel in the first, reconaissance, study; however, a cotton-wool plug between the iron and the copper pipes evened out the oscillations in pressure satisfactorily and also helped to prevent sperm oil from the pump reaching the porous plug and upsetting the results. Only three short series of experiments were carried out and in each case a net cooling effect was found. The experiments were all carried out at or near normal room temperature, on dry air and at low pressures. At the lowest pressure the cooling effect proved to be erratic, varying between $\frac{1}{10}° \frac{2}{10}°$C. The reason for this was not immediately obvious.[42]

In May Thomson and his wife set off an an extended tour of France and Italy leaving Joule to complete the experiments, identify the source of the problem at low pressures and to apply for the remaining £50 of their initial grant. For Joule it was to be a quiet time, at least in terms of scientific work. The short paper, establishing their priority, was read before the Royal Society in June, his wife and little children went off to the seaside and there was work enough at the brewery. The head of the family, father Benjamin,

---

*Thomson's calculated values on the old theory were, of course, no longer acceptable.

had had a 'slight paralytic stroke' in February and the family was beginning to think of disposing of the business. The eldest brother, Benjamin, long a widower, was still living at 'Oak Field'. Organist, choirmaster, composer of hymns and chants, Benjamin was essentially a gentleman of leisure. John Arthur, the youngest brother, married and moved to the select Victoria Park before retiring to the Isle of Man to live the life of a *rentier*. As for Mary, whoever heard of a lady running a brewery? In other words, the family were in the process of that common metamorphosis whereby, through hard work, commercial enterprise and, no doubt, a modicum of good luck, a considerable fortune is amassed after which the inheritors of the fortune turn their backs on its source and seek to enter the ranks of the gentry. They had already taken the first step when they abandoned the church of their fathers for the Anglican communion. It prompts natural queries. At what size and in what particular kinds of business does, or did, it become acceptable for succeeding generations to carry on the enterprise without feeling that they are, or were, accepting a lower social status?

It was with some relief, for he had been anxious about his friend, that Joule learned of Thomson's return to Britain towards the end of August. He was pleased that Thomson's health had improved, remarking, characteristically:

> On your return I do hope you will make it a rule not, for whatever consideration, to overtax your strength by too much mental work. You will ultimately find this the wisest policy even as regards your scientific investigations; but independently of this no advantage could counterbalance either to yourself or your friends the loss of good health.[43]

The industrious Mr Hopkins had been busy during the summer vacation, calling on Joule's skills to help him with his researches on the fusion of beeswax under pressure and the associated change in the latent heat. But Joule was anxious to see Thomson to discuss the progress of the experiments. Mr Hopkins was to be in Manchester again for the British Association meeting on 7 September, and 'he monopolizes me a good deal when he is here'. He hoped that Thomson could spare a fortnight in September and the whole of October. Mr Hopkins, after all, had the resources of Fairbairn's works and an excellent workman to help him. A good reason why Thomson should come was that Joule had run a pipe to one of the tuns that would soon be in use for fermenting porter, a process that was accompanied by the generation of carbon dioxide.[44] Here was an opportunity to study the effect on carbon dioxide of forcing it through the porous plug. This was fortunate, for when the Earl of Rosse wrote, on behalf of the Royal Society, asking for an account of the work done with the aid of the grant, he could be told that the cooling of air, escaping through a porous plug, had been established with considerable accuracy and that carbon dioxide was, significantly, cooled four times as much.[45] At about this time (mid-October) he found the reason for the erratic cooling of air at low pressures but he did not explain it for some time.

Thomson could not spend six weeks in Manchester. Perhaps this was as well, for Joule admitted that:

> Ever since you left I have been much troubled with boils* which, by the way, are a sort of epidemic just now. I have scarcely been able to go about this week and the requirements of business have been at the same time unusually pressing owing to the rascally conduct of one of our travellers who has defrauded us of £1,200.[46]

Nevertheless he had extended the study of carbon dioxide to two different pressures, and in each case there was a much greater cooling effect than with air. All this cost money and the total expense was now nearly £200, of which the grant covered only £100. There would have to be an application for a further grant.

Further experiments with 94.77% pure carbon dioxide confirmed these results and measurements made with mixtures of air and carbon dioxide showed that the net cooling effect was that due to each gas separately. Joule went on:

> You will find by subtracting the atmospheric pressure from the pressure of the gas numbers will be obtained very nearly proportional to the cooling effects, particularly in the case of carbonic acid. Can it be the fact that the cooling effect is proportional to the excess of the pressure in the receiver above that of the atmosphere?[47]

This ran counter to Thomson's theory according to which the cooling effect should be proportional to the logarithm of the pressure difference. Although Joule may have been reluctant to query Thomson's theories he had good reason to be confident about his inference. For the current series of experiments he used a boxwood 'nozle' enclosed in a tin can filled with cotton wool; the thermal insulation was thereby greatly improved (Fig. 5). On 8 November he wrote: 'I feel pretty certain that the effect is proportional to the excess pressure over the atmosphere.'[48] Two days later it occurred to him that the experiments would 'be more complete' if the exit pressure were to be varied above that of the atmosphere. He added: 'You will observe that the cooling effect is nearly proportional to the excess pressure of the gases as the delicacy of the experiments can warrant us to

*This could surely have been better expressed.

expect.'[49] Experiments with the exit pressure at three atmospheres 'show that the cooling effect is measured by the difference of pressures of confined and escaped air.'[50] In other words, the back pressure of the escaping air did not affect the simple law that the cooling was proportional to the pressure difference across the porous plug. His next step was to examine the variation of the effect with change in temperature. A problem to be overcome here was the drying out of the boxwood 'nozle' with increase in temperature. That surmounted, Joule found that, at about 90°C, the cooling effect for air was reduced but not nearly so much as in the case of carbon dioxide. At a low temperature (about 13°C) the cooling of carbon dioxide was greater than the simple law, of proportionality to pressure difference, implied. 'I think you will agree with me', Joule wrote, 'that the greater cooling is owing to the approach towards the temperature of liquefaction of the gas.'[51]

Joule had other things to think of besides the immediate course of his researches. There was his fear that someone – presumably he had Regnault in mind – would steal a march on them and publish significant conclusions before they could. He was careful to let Lord Rosse know what they were doing in the hope that Lord Rosse would refer to their work in his Presidential Address to the Royal Society and so guarantee their priority;[52] even the postmark could be invoked in support of their claim (this was taking things rather far). To Joule's chagrin Lord Rosse did not mention their work. And, in addition, he had the uncertain future of the brewery to worry about. 'We are still', he wrote to Thomson, 'in a *mist* about the brewery which I will try to prevent giving me too much anxiety.'[53] If and when the brewery was sold they would not be able to use the steam-engine for their experiments. Joule thought it would be quite easy to get hold of a three horsepower engine, either in Manchester or in Glasgow, for about £90, with a resale value of about £40.[54] Fortunately the end-of-term account showed that, although they had been granted an extra £100, they had not exceeded the total £200 allocated them. And the Royal Society was, according to Colonel Sabine, prepared to give them an additional grant. Another agreeable communication to counter Joule's anxieties had been a letter from Stokes asking for guidance on the design and layout of a heat laboratory for Cambridge University.

Both Joule and Thomson had family health problems. Mrs Thomson had been unwell ever since her return from southern Europe and was now virtually an invalid;[55] a misfortune that prevented Thomson visiting Manchester. Joule's problem was less serious. 'My wife', he wrote, 'has been confined to the house by a very severe cold and little Alice has had a trying time with her teeth; we were at one time quite alarmed for her, but she is now picking up her strength again.'[56] Distractions in the first months of 1854 concerning the health of his family and the possible sale of the brewery did not divert his attention from planning – and changing his mind about – the new steam-engine. He was also completing the necessary researches for the forthcoming paper that he and Thomson hoped would unambiguously establish their claim to priority. It is surprising that they had so little idea how original their work was.

As it was impossible to obtain an abundant supply of pure carbon dioxide, Joule had to compute the cooling effect due to this gas by comparing the cooling effects in the case of air with those due to three different mixtures of air and carbon dioxide.[57] Knowing the proportions he was able to eliminate the effect due to air and get consistent results for pure carbon dioxide. At Thomson's suggestion they took the investigation a stage further when Joule showed that as air and carbon dioxide diffused into each other, adiabatically, the temperature of the mixture fell.[58] They intended to continue this study, but failed to do so.* Various other experiments were suggested by Thomson but did not prove important.[59]

In February 1854, Joule wrote to Thomson to say that

> In the meantime my own brewing succeeds, and in fact since I commenced the saving was immediately effected of £2,000 per annum and the beer much better approved of. And I can moreover say that I have actually *more time* than before for scientific pursuits in consequence of working directly and not with the *help* of a self-willed assistant.'[60]

He continued:

> I see that Maxwell has obtained a very high degree at Cambridge, 2nd Wrangler, but Mr Hopkins admitted to me that had the questions been put generally so as to take in the scope of physical science he would have stood first. I feel confident from what I saw of him that a great deal may be expected of him as a scientific investigator.

Joule's comment on Maxwell needs no amplification. His account of the brewery does, however, raise some questions. Exactly what improvements he made to the brewing process cannot now be known. But it seems most probable that since his father had a stroke, he had taken a more responsible part in running the business, even as the family planned to dispose of it. And if the beer was now 'much better approved of' can it be assumed that, up to that time, they had catered for the cheaper end of the beer market? However, there were other matters to attend to. Joule, on behalf of the

---

*This effect was consistent with the demonstration, very much later, that when gases diffuse into each other, isothermally, the entropy of the mixture is increased.

trustees of the Owens College, invited Thomson to let them have his comments on their plan for scholarships.[61] And he asked Thomson to visit him fairly soon as Amelia had promised him 'a little stranger' in the middle of June and 'we should not be able to make you as comfortable as we should wish'.[62] At the same time he found himself marginally involved in a dispute between Thomson on the one hand and Clausius and Riess on the other. Thomson had assumed, through a misunderstanding, that Joule's discovery of the i^2r law had been made before Riess's discovery that the heating power of static electricity was proportional to the square of the charge. The whole affair was no more than a quarrel about words; except perhaps for Snow Harris, who had claimed that the heating power of static electricity was simply proportional to the charge.[63]

As the problems thrown up by the current research became clear and the pattern of the next research more sharply defined, so Joule substantially modified the apparatus. The proposed steam-engine was to have a new and improved governor and a heavy flywheel to ensure uniform pressures; a new, patent boiler was to supply steam of 100 lb psi. The new pump was to be double-acting to reduce the loss of gases: an important consideration if they wished to test gases that might be difficult and expensive to obtain in quantity.[64] All this would cost a great deal. They were going to have to ask the Royal Society for an extra £180. Joule had complete confidence in Mr Millwood, the engine maker, and believed that, without the brewery, the small engine and apparatus could be assembled in the laboratory his father had built for him at 'Oak Field'.*

The sale of the brewery was still unsettled. Towards the end of April Joule reported that

> Mr Smith who, you may recollect came to look at the concern last September, has been making a desperate effort to get it at a very low figure to which we would not agree. The trouble and anxiety caused by his conduct has been very great, of which I have had a considerable share. I perceived from the first that the parties were not so straightforward as they ought to be and although of course I would like to be freed from the business I had no intention of throwing away £5,000 or £6,000 on the brewery and been (*sic*) reduced to a very bad condition by Mr Dix and I have endeavoured to prove its real worth under proper management. The result has proved such as to encourage us to resist the great sacrifice we were invited to make by our *kind friends*. I am glad to say that although an agreement was drawn up for signature I deferred the pulling down of the apparatus so that it is still there.[65]

---

*A high-pressure, and therefore small, engine would be more suitable for a small private laboratory.

It is interesting that nowhere in this letter, or in the others in which he discusses the affairs of the brewery, did he mention his father or his two brothers. The implication must be that he took a major, and quite possibly the whole, share of the burden of selling the business. The affair demonstrated his versatility and energy for, while he was negotiating with Mr Smith (one of two brothers, Thomas and Richard Smith who eventually bought the brewery), he was making the hundreds of careful observations that were to form the basis of the paper they were so anxious to publish. This appeared in June 1854, the second of the four joint papers they were to write for the *Philosophical Transactions*.[66] It confirmed beyond any doubt their priority and it answered some key questions.

The paper began by explaining the main cause of the erratic cooling effects at low pressures. These were due to the considerable pressure changes when air began to flow through the porous plug. The associated sharp temperature changes resulted in heat being conducted through the porous plug and through the boxwood 'nozzle' to the thermometer on the other side of the plug. This process took some time and Joule and Thomson presented graphs – a novel technique for both of them – showing how the transient temperature varied with time until eventually it settled down to the appropriate level. They therefore made it a practice to run the apparatus for an hour and a half or two hours before taking any readings. Then, using different quantities of cotton wool and of silk in the 'nozzle', they carried out seven series of tests on air, requiring some 640 separate observations, and four series of tests on carbon dioxide, needing over 100 observations. These confirmed that in both cases the cooling effect was proportional to the pressure difference across the porous plug. They displayed the results in graphs of pressure difference against temperature drop. Joule was delighted to find that the lines representing air and carbon dioxide were 'wonderfully straight'.*[67] They experimented with hydrogen as well but, as the apparatus was not suitable, they used the old hand-pump with the leather 'plug'. There was, they thought, a slight cooling effect of about one-thirteenth that of air under the same conditions. And they confirmed that for both air and carbon dioxide the cooling effect was reduced as the temperature was raised.

The second half of the paper was concerned with theoretical deductions. It began with the assertion that Mayer's hypothesis could not be justified without the support of theory or experiment. Now their detailed experiments allowed 'precise answers to the questions regarding the heat of

---

*These graphs were an advance on Joule's earlier 'graphs' ('resistance to electrolysis') in that the points were not all joined up; instead, the average lines were drawn.

compression, and to others which rise from it'. They proceeded to analyse the quite complex components of the heating and cooling effects that occur when gas streams through a porous plug from high to low pressure. On the one hand there was the cooling due to expansion, on the other there was the heating effect due to the work done in forcing the air through the orifice; the latter was slightly reduced because of the deviations from Boyle's law, discovered by Regnault. The net heating effect was less than the cooling effect; they derived a formula from their experimental results to express this deficit.[68] With this information and with the help of an empirical law, again due to Regnault, they were able to calculate the proportion of the excess heating to the thermal equivalent of the work done when a gas is compressed – the converse process to the deficiency of heating when a gas expands – and so indicated the deviation from Mayer's hypothesis.[69] The deviation turned out to be small. The amount of heat lost through the departure from Boyle's law was calculated; and they noted, in passing, that the compensation was far less in the case of carbon dioxide; the inference being that 'the more a gas deviates from the gaseous laws, or the more it approaches the condition of a vapour at saturation, the wider will be the discrepancy'. It was hoped to extend the researches to steam 'which will probably present a larger cooling *effect*' (author's italics). This part of the paper was rounded off with a calculation of the cooling effect that would have occurred in Joule's celebrated two-cylinder experiment. It would, they showed, have been far too small to have been detected having regard to the specific heat capacities of the apparatus and the water.

   Their next task was to tackle the key question of the density of saturated steam. The original statement from the 'Account of Carnot's theory' was set out:[70] the work done to generate a unit of heat by compressing a gas increases with the temperature, being equal to the mechanical equivalent of heat only at about 30°C. But, they added, from the experiments described the requisite work must be the same at all temperatures. Accordingly, 'the true density of (saturated steam) increases much more at high temperatures and pressures than according to the gaseous laws, and consequently . . . steam appears to deviate from Boyle's law in the same direction as carbonic acid'. There was no explicit admission, still less rejoicing, that the previous, very plausible, assumption has been falsified.

   The evaluation of Carnot's function, mentioned in the previous paper as a principal objective of the researches, could now be made. It was, in principle, equal to the mechanical equivalent of heat divided by the temperature plus the reciprocal of the coefficient of expansion of air, or

Fig. 6 Joule in 1863 (engraving taken from the original portrait which was destroyed with the Lit & Phil Society's House in the air raid of December 1941)

272.85.* After this an elaborate expression was derived, giving its value when account was taken of the deviations from ideal conditions. A reformed and corrected absolute scale of temperature could now be drawn up; one that was seen to accord very closely to the ideal gas scale, either by constant pressure or constant volume. In short, Carnot's function was equal to the mechanical equivalent of heat divided by the absolute temperature. Joule's suggestion of 9 December 1848 was vindicated and the theory expounded in the 'Account of Carnot's theory' and retained in the 'Dynamical theory of heat' was rejected. At the end of the paper Joule and Thomson remarked that

> In the notes to Mr Joule's paper on the air-engine, it was shown that, if Mayer's hypothesis be true we must have approximately,
> $$K = .2374 \text{ and } N = .1684$$
> because observations on the velocity of sound, with Laplace's theory, demonstrate that,
> $$k = 1.410$$
> within 1/700 of its own value. Now the experiments at present communicated to the Royal Society prove a very remarkable approximation to the truth of that hypothesis . . . and we may therefore use these values as very close approximations to the specific heats of air.

Mayer's hypothesis had, therefore, been discreetly confirmed.

*I.e.
$$\mu = \frac{J}{272.85 + t}$$

9

The middle years

The joint papers written by Joule and Thomson over a period of ten years have been somewhat overshadowed by the establishment of the energy doctrine and the dynamical theory of heat. While the latter are, unambiguously, at the heart of physical science it can be argued that the Joule–Thomson partnership over the years 1852–62 was of hardly less, although rather different, significance. Over the whole period Joule made a full – perhaps the major – contribution to the joint work. He designed and made the apparatus. It was he who developed the porous plug and who insisted that the cooling effect was proportional to the pressure difference and not to the logarithm of that difference. It was Joule who extended the researches to other gases besides air and it was he who realised that the closer a gas gets to the state of a saturated vapour the greater the net cooling effect; a discovery that showed that the gas laws did not apply to saturated steam, contrary to Thomson's assumption. And Joule had argued that Carnot's function was proportional to the reciprocal of the absolute temperature, an insight that Thomson did not accept until 1854. The conclusion must be that their joint researches were the consequence of a close collaboration between two men whose geniuses were equal and complementary.

Style is easy to recognise but very difficult to describe or define. It is commonly associated with literature, art, politics and athletic sports. It is also recognisable in science. Leibniz is said to have recognised Newton's style in an anonymous publication. Everyone who reads Faraday's *Experimental Researches* will recognise a distinctive, very personal style. In the same way Joule's style can be seen in the joint papers with Thomson. There is a common element with the earlier works on electrolysis and on the mechanical equivalent of heat. There is the same progressive, systematic clarification of the issue, the same drive to generalise the research as far as possible and the same concern for increasingly accurate quantification.

Apart from the dubious examples of the BA Committees there were very few precedents for joint research in the annals of British physics prior to the collaboration between Joule and Thomson. Thomson, from his experiences in France and knowledge of French science, would have been familiar with the principle of collaborative research. Joule, it might be thought, had no exemplar, other than his work for Playfair, to guide him. There were, however, similarities between Joule and Thomson's researches and the investigations of Eaton Hodgkinson and William Fairbairn[1] on behalf of the projected Britannia Tubular Bridge. It is sufficient to point out that Hodgkinson provided the theoretical skills, Fairbairn the experimental skills and resources (he had engineering works at Ancoats and at Millwall, near London). Their partnership was a good example for Joule and Thomson to follow. Joule was well informed about Hodgkinson's work for he was a Vice-President of the Lit & Phil at the time when Hodgkinson was President (1848–50). But the nature and extent of the mutual influence, if any, between these two partnerships can only be a matter for conjecture. What is more certain is that most men of science in England were still gentlemen–devotees and would be much less likely to participate in collaborative research than would professional scientists or engineers. The academic men of science of Scotland were technically 'professional' but would, in great measure, have shared the attitudes and outlook of their English colleagues.

If the joint paper was, at that time, a rare event in British physics, a series of joint papers was wholly without precedent. Even in European physics there had been nothing like it. The accurate determination of physical constants was one thing; systematic and continued research into the unknown by two men of complementary abilities was different, and quite new. The publication of what were to be eight joint papers by Joule and Thomson can be taken as one indication that physics was beginning to achieve the rank and status of an autonomous discipline in both intellectual and social or organisational terms. Depending on one's interpretation and viewpoint physics is either a science of great antiquity or barely 130 years old, at least as far as Britain is concerned; in France it could be considered about 200 years old.[2] The problem is that the different branches have very different histories. Geometrical optics began with Euclid while the science of mechanics traces a lineage back to Archimedes. The study of magnetism began in the Middle Ages; heat and electricity first aroused interest at the beginning of the scientific revolution; physical optics started with Newton and other seventeenth-century thinkers and experimentalists. These branches were independent and there was no common link between any of them. Two developments that were to establish the required unions were the energy doctrine and, in part derived from the energy doctrine, electromagnetic field theory. Joule contributed his share to this work of consolidation that was to provide physics with a firm theoretical framework and to confer upon it the autonomy that marks a mature science as distinct from a progressive one (as Whewell put it).

The establishment of a substantial discipline like physics entailed appropriate social institutions. Apart from collaborative research as exemplified by the work of Joule and Thomson and practised in chemistry for many years, textbooks, syllabuses, teaching and research institutions are the distinguishing features of an acknowledged scientific discipline. Mary Somerville's *Connexion of the Physical Sciences* (first edition 1834) was, perhaps, the best of the early British books on physics. An able mathematician, Mary Somerville, published an effective précis of Laplace's *Mécanique Celeste* under the title *Mechanism of the Heavens* (1831). On friendly terms with many leading French scientists, she was particularly well qualified to interpret French physics to the British public.[3] *Connexion of the Physical Sciences* dealt with planetary astronomy, heat, light, sound, electricity and magnetism. The book was immensely popular and went through ten editions, the last being published five years after she died in 1872. Energy had no place, of course, in the earlier editions of her book; and only a subordinate role in the last. In her emphasis on astronomy she followed the historical pattern of the growth of physical science. This was commendable, for astronomy appeals to the imagination and through it the abstractions of mechanics can be more easily understood and accepted. One may regret that astronomy has disappeared from the syllabus. But by the second half of the nineteenth century the marvels of the heavens, so impressive in earlier times, had been surpassed by the marvels of modern industry and technology.

The foundation of teaching and research institutions was associated largely with the rise of the new, and the reform of the ancient, universities. Royal Commissions to inquire into the Universities of Oxford and Cambridge were instituted in 1850. In that year Oxford established the Honours School in Natural Sciences and, a year later, Cambridge followed suit with the Natural Sciences Tripos. The enlightened Prince Consort, as Chancellor of Cambridge University, was greatly interested in reform and wished to see some of the principles and practices of the increasingly successful German universities adopted. But rather less was achieved than he hoped for. The use of apparatus for class demonstrations of the principles of natural philosophy, electricity, or magnetism went back to the eighteenth century. And the Cambridge Natural Sciences Tripos excluded physics, being concerned largely with the biological sciences.[4]

That something quite different was being considered was clear from Joule's letter to Stokes of 12 November 1853. It began:

I am glad to hear that an institution is about to be established which will doubtless be of the greatest value to Cambridge – I have thought a good deal on the subject of your queries, and in the first place I do not think that for experiments on heat it is absolutely essential to have a uniform temperature, although it would be desirable to obviate sudden or uncontrolled changes. If a room were to be built without windows it would be rendered useless for many purposes and I think that for experiments on heat it would be desirable to use a room of considerable size such as might at times be used for different purposes, such as experiments on light, and chemical experiments, probably also for magnetic expts.[5]

He outlined in some detail the requirements for a laboratory, with adjoining apartment, in which experiments on heat could be properly carried out. Stokes, in thanking Joule for his suggestions, was rather cautious: 'With respect to our contemplated building nothing has yet been put into any formal shape as regards the plan. However I hope that before very long something definite will be proposed.'[6] His caution was justified. Twenty years were to elapse before the Cavendish Laboratory was opened. It looks as if the advocates of conservative teaching – that nothing must be taught that is not absolutely certain and true and preferably at least 100 years old – had had their way.[7] Nearly a decade had to elapse before physics was recognised by university institutions.

Joule had other things to attend to besides physics laboratories and the paper for the Royal Society. On 8 June Amelia bore him a son, to be christened Henry James, which were Joule family names. At first things seemed to go well, but by the end of the month came the common little tragedy of Victorian family life.

You [Thomson] will be sorry to hear that I have had much domestic affliction. My dear infant son took a turn for the worse on Sunday and was in such a state on Tuesday that I had him Christened in the house. Monday & Tuesday was a time of great anxiety and every effort was made to save the dear little fellow's life. He, however, sank rapidly and died on Wednesday morning. I have buried him this morning in Mr Stowell's Churchyard. My anxiety has been very greatly increased by the state of my wife's health who has been in imminent danger but is now I am most thankful to be able to say considerably better. She has borne her loss with a spirit of magnanimity and Christian resignation which I could wish to possess to an equal extent myself. As soon as I can contrive it I must take her to her mother's; somewhere where a change of scene may recruit her shattered nerves and health.[8]

Six days later he was still alarmed about his dear wife.[9] 'She requires strength and does not rally properly. However all that can be done has been done in the shape of advice & c and we have simply to resign ourselves into the hands of our all wise & ever compassionate Redeemer.'

For nearly three months hope and despair alternated with extraordinary rapidity. On 22 July he could hope that the worst was over even though 'last Saturday she was given up by her medical attendants and one of them in the evening pronounced that she was actually dying and could not possibly survive till the following morning. However she rallied . . . and has since been gaining strength and I do trust and pray that the improvement may go on continually.'[10] He had felt it necessary to take on many of the duties of a nurse so there had been no time for experiments.

By 10 August there seemed to be good prospects for a satisfactory recovery. She had even been able to get dressed for the first time.[11] It had been very harrassing and the sale of the brewery, now expected by the end of September, had not made things easier. After that he hoped that he would be able to devote his time to 'subjects more consonant with my feelings than the business of brewing, and then I shall be somewhat more able to run in harness with you.' He was even able to talk about the boiler for the steam-engine – it must be a *safe* one – and to remind Thomson of the dates of his papers on the rarefaction of air, on the powers of electricity, steam and horses, and on the nature of shooting stars. On 25 August, an ominous note entered the correspondence.[12] Ten days earlier a 'medical man' had been hopeful of Amelia's recovery but

> almost immediately afterwards a diarrhoea (which is very prevalent now and comes no doubt from the poisonous state of the atmosphere during the cholera season) seized her, which every day undid as much as we had gained in a week previously. The consequence is that she has been literally at the brink of the grave for the last 3 or 4 days. The diarrhoea has now, thank God, considerably abated but she remains in imminent danger from extreme exhaustion. This is the third time since her confinement that we have been led almost to despair of her life and I do trust and pray that in this instance also she will rally.

On 8 September he wrote to Thomson.

> It is a great relief to me to be able to write to one who I know will sympathise with me on the occasion of the terrible blow which has fallen upon me. During the latter part of last week and up till Monday I had hopes of my dear wife's recovery, the diarrhoea having been subdued, but suddenly on Tuesday it returned with very great violence and nothing we could do appeared to have the slightest effect on it. My wife sank rapidly and died at peace at 12½ noon of Wednesday. I have thus lost my dearest earthly friend and no one can fully comprehend the greatness of the loss who has not had the opportunity I have had during our union of 7 years, of estimating her high moral worth and intellectual refinement. How the loss of such a parent can be replaced to my dear children I cannot tell. I must trust in the Almighty to care for them and to

direct me in their upbringing. This event has occurred at a time when owing to the disposal of the brewery I am overwhelmed with duties devolving upon me. I feel happy however in the reflexion that I have not suffered these to interfere with my attendance on my wife during her long illness. And it is a great satisfaction to reflect that death had no terrors reposing as she did on the merits of her Saviour as her title to her heavenly inheritance.[13]

Once again he did not mention his brothers or his sister.

The shock of Amelia's death took a long time to wear off. His friends and contempories agreed that this never very assertive man became more withdrawn. To recover from exhaustion and grief he went with his children to Southport, to the seaside. Although the British Association was meeting in Liverpool that autumn he did not pay a visit, even to see Thomson. He was, he said, on those particular days required to go to Manchester for thirteen or fourteen hours a day to complete the sale of the brewery.[14] He was hoping to do a little research on the dimensions of conductors, for which the Royal Society had granted him £30, but otherwise he was uncertain about the future. His elder brother, Benjamin, had suggested that he should go to Cambridge to read for a degree (presumably to take the Mathematics Tripos) but, while he was well aware of the advantages of such study, he felt that he had his dear little ones to think of; and there was too much research outstanding. In any case he could not break up old plans and connections to form new ones at his time of life.[15] He had decided to join his brother Benjamin and his father at 'Oak Field', on Upper Chorlton Road. He never returned to 1 Acton Square.

On New Year's Day, Joule expressed his feeling to Thomson:

I most honestly wish Mrs Thomson and yourself a happy new year and pray that God may crown it with goodness to us all. The remembrance of 1854 is full of bitterness not only to me but to unusual numbers who have been deprived by the death of the dearest and most important members of their families. God grant that these severe trials may be sanctified to the everlasting good of the survivors.[16]

Joule had compensations that most of the families of Crimean War casualties could hardly imagine. Thomson had already lauded him as a pioneer of the most important advance in physical science since the time of Newton.[17] When told of this Joule could only say: 'I was quite ashamed to see my name in any sort of association with one to whom I have always looked up with the last degree of reverence.' And, in addition to public praise on the grand scale, there was also the emollient of work. There was the outstanding research still to be carried out on gases in motion, there were researches in magnetism and there were minor matters – odd speculations, subsidiary inquiries – that form part of a scientific life. The unquenchable curiosity that characterises the man of science and the diversity of his interests present serious problems to the biographer. In between and sometimes coincidental with the major discoveries, these activities that, from the biographer's point of view, are of minor importance, make awkward interruptions in an otherwise coherent narrative. They cannot be ignored without distorting the picture, inevitably imperfect, of the man and his work.

Work on the steam-engine, with its boiler and pump, continued while Joule began some new researches on magnetism. After the disappointment over the electric battery and motor as a source of power events were again directing attention towards electromagnetism and electricity generally. A network of electric telegraph lines was rapidly being constructed and with it a new breed of engineer had appeared: the telegraph engineer.* By 1851 a submarine telegraph cable had been successfully laid across the English Channel and proposals were being made for a telegraph cable across the Atlantic. Thomson was deeply interested and was soon to be personally involved. Joule, too, was interested, although from a more parochial standpoint. A telegraph cable had been laid from London to Manchester, for some of the way along the beds of connecting canals.[18] Faraday had predicted that there would be a delay in transmission in such cables due to the significant capacity of the lines. There was, in fact, a delay of between a fifth and a quarter of a second in the transmission of a signal from Manchester to London and back.[19] This was consistent with Thomson's experiments and his law according to which the delay should increase as the square of the distance. A later experiment, witnessed by Joule, involved a circuit from Manchester to Rugby and back, a total distance of about 200 miles. When the entire circuit was insulated there was no delay, but when it was earthed through the Manchester water mains there was a delay of not more than a quarter of a second. 'I have not', wrote Joule, 'had much practice in estimating small intervals of time';[20] an aside that throws some light on his powers of self-discipline.

The fascinating problems of the Atlantic telegraph interested Joule and were to lead him into some desultory and not particularly fruitful experimentation. More immediate was the need to transfer the apparatus from the brewery to 'Oak Field', re-erect it and build a small annexe there to

---

*The telegraph engineers were the pioneers of electrical engineering. The Society of Telegraph Engineers (1871) became the Institution of Electrical Engineers in 1888. Electric telegraphs developed rapidly with the spread of the railways. An incidental consequence was the adoption of common, or 'railway time', all over the country. Among the pioneers of the electric telegraph were Gauss, Weber, Cooke and Wheatstone. The immensely important principle of the earth return was due to C. A. von Steinheil.

house the new boiler. This entailed a delay so that experiments on the flow of gases had to be suspended. He could, instead, resume his researches on magnetism that had been laid aside for nearly twelve years, apart from some work, published in 1852, on the measurement of the strength of the big electromagnet he had built for display at the Great Exhibition of 1851.

While Thomson was devising an experiment to demonstrate Joule's discovery that heat is generated by the magnetisation, or demagnetisation of iron,[21] and was exploring the thermodynamics of the cycle of magnetisation,[22] Joule was occupied in extending some earlier experiments on long bar magnets.[23] Using bar magnets, 1 and 2 yd long, 1/8 to ½ in. thick, he claimed to have found that on cutting off the magnetising current the residual magnetism, which he called the magnetic *set*, was proportional to the square of the current. His friend Eaton Hodgkinson had announced, at the memorable Cork meeting of the British Association in 1843, that when iron or any other metal was subjected to strain the permanent change, or the *set* as he termed it, was proportional to the square of the imposed force. The puzzling thing for Joule was that when the magnetic set was subtracted from the overall magnetic effect it appeared that the magnetism increased proportionately more than did the current.

Increasing the current, he found that both the set and the magnetism over and above the set still increased more than the current; the set, indeed, now increased more than the square of the current. This continued until the onset of saturation, when the rate of increase diminished.[24] But an act of faith is needed to accept the validity of the 'square law'. Joule's motive was, apparently, to find a law, or laws, relating magnetism to the energising current and thence to find a way of understanding the molecular changes that, it was believed, must accompany magnetisation. Such changes were implied by the theories of Ampère and Weber. Artstall's and Joule's own observations on the change of dimensions of iron on magnetisation, together with his discovery that iron heats up on magnetisation, both pointed to a relationship between magnetic force and atomic or molecular structure. Hodgkinson's work on elasticity and the strength of materials suggested, by analogy, an ultimately mechanical theory of magnetism. Accordingly, Joule referred to *Magnetic elasticity* and, when the set increased sharply, to the *magnetic breaking point*.[25]

This was another instance of preliminary, ground-clearing research and a statement, on inadequate evidence of what he hoped, would be a new law. This procedure, which had been misunderstood by Helmholtz, characterised the first joint paper with Thomson. Evidently, in the present case, Joule had felt that his explanation of his results justified a short paper for the *Philosophical Transactions*. He admitted that the paper 'can only be

regarded as an introduction and is imperfect in many respects'. And this
was no less than the truth. Tyndall, to whom the paper was referred for
assessment, was respectful but justifiably critical.[26] He pointed out that
Joule had failed to mention work being done in Germany and had mis-
quoted Jacobi and Lenz. Furthermore, Joule's interpretation of his results
had been far too casual; some of them diverged widely from the supposed
square law. The paper was referred back to Joule, who made some corrections on the lines recommended by Tyndall, but the latter was not satisfied.
'I confess my own opinion', he wrote,

> is that the reputation of Mr Joule would not be increased by the publication of
> the paper. To my mind the reasoning appears loose, the conclusions do not
> seem to be in all cases warranted and the mode of experiment seems doubtful. I
> say this with extreme reluctance ... Mr Joule is a far older labourer in the
> domain to which his paper refers than I am.[27]

Nevertheless the paper was published. It was to be his last published
work on the subject. The term *set* was taken up – Maxwell used it in his
Treatise on Electricity and Magnetism – but was soon replaced by *residual
magnetism*. No simple, straightforward law was discovered. Further understanding of the process of magnetisation and of the hysteresis cycle was for
the future; and only obtained after a great deal more work.

In that year (1855), the British Association met in Glasgow and Joule
submitted a short paper. Experiments showed that once an electromagnet
had been strongly magnetised the polarity tended to persist as a bias so that
if it were to be magnetised in the reverse direction and the current then cut
off the original bias reappeared.[28] This, he thought, explained many of the
irregularities previously observed; and the solution, he suggested, was to
start with low intensity and iron previously completely demagnetised by
being made red hot (unfortunately, this would change the properties of the
metal). The complications of magnetisation and demagnetisation were
becoming apparent. But, surprisingly, knowledge of this had been available
for some time. Scoresby seems to have noticed the bias as early as 1824,
and Sturgeon apparently made a similar observation.[29]

The short paper was read by Thomson. Joule had declined Thomson's
invitation to stay with him and had avoided going to Glasgow for he was well
aware that Margaret Thomson was unwell. She had never recovered since
they had returned from the Mediterranean in 1853 and, with her husband,
had had to spend long periods taking the cure at spa towns. Joule, ever
anxious about health – other people's as well as his own – took it upon
himself to give Thomson some good advice:

> With reference to the opening of your house on account of the Meeting you will

forgive me for saying a word or two of advice. On no account take any step which would entail any degree of trouble or anxiety to Mrs Thomson or which would remove her from the air of the country unnecessarily. In such a case always err on the safe side. Mrs Thomson is I hope & believe in a fair way to recovery, but the partial relapse you mentioned in your last proves that improvement in health ought to be an encouragement for further care and not an inducement to any step by which the ground gained might be lost a second time.[30]

Almost at once he regretted the presumptuous tone of his advice and wrote to Thomson to apologise. It is difficult to see how he could, thereafter, have accepted Thomson's invitation. Fortunately the children offered a useful alibi:

I am however advised that it is most desirable that the children should visit the seaside for a time and I have been so situated with business and agents here (with respect to the interminable brewery affair) as to have been unable to take them away before, and now an opportunity offers I must embrace it at once. I could have arranged to leave them at the seaside for a week but my sister in consequence of illness when alone last year is afraid of being left with the children alone again. I thank you for your kind enquiry after myself. I am looking forward to a week or two of perfect quiet which will tend to do me much good. I still feel weak and nervous, but by taking things easily I feel satisfied that I shall ultimately get strong again.[31]

As so many Manchester businessmen had done before, and were to do in the future, he headed for Rhyl on the north Wales coast. There the little family lodged with Mrs Owen at 29 West Parade. The weather was fine, as it is so often in late September. He had two bilious attacks but could report to Thomson that 'My dear children are quite well and much improved by their sojourn at the seaside. Your little God daughter is grown up into a strong romping girl. This gives me great comfort particularly as for a long time it was very doubtful whether we should be able to rear her.'[32]

Although experiments on electromagnetism continued for the remainder of 1855 the results were not satisfactory and were never published.[33] At low intensities the antecedent magnetic state of the iron distorted the results; the onset of saturation had a like effect at high intensities. In consolation, as it were, the little steam-engine with its boiler had been completed and installed at 'Oak Field'. A condenser, based on the principle of the Liebig condenser, was fitted to increase the power and economy of the engine.[34] Joule hoped that he and Thomson could resume their experiments. Two years had elapsed since they had met and spoken together.

The first experiments did not require the engine; only the boiler was needed. A 1½ in. bore pipe was connected to the boiler and a cotton wool plug secured in it by pieces of wood. A fine platinum wire ran through the plug and, after being kinked at each end to reduce the flow of heat along the wire, was connected to two iron wires leading to an astatic galvanometer.[35] The arrangement formed a differential thermo-couple (the idea was Thomson's) to indicate the difference in temperature across the plug. The outside of the short pipe was lagged with felt and steam passed through it until thermal equilibrium had been established. With an excess steam pressure of 27 lb psi the cooling effect was 6.37°C, or as they put it, rather casually, about 0.2°C per pound. The temperature of saturated steam at an excess pressure of 27 lb psi is about 132 °C, so that it would leave the plug at a temperature of about 125½°C and therefore dry and superheated at atmospheric pressure. This, they claimed, confirmed 'the view which we brought forward some years ago' about the non-scalding properties of steam rushing from a boiler. More to the point, it showed that the nearer a vapour was to the temperature of liquefaction, the more it deviated from Mayer's hypothesis.

Early in 1856 Thomson renewed his invitation to Joule to visit him in Glasgow and this time Joule accepted. The only thing that could have prevented the trip was frost. It could – surprisingly – damage the engine and Joule liked to look after it personally. He had hoped to travel up by sea from Liverpool, but the weather was unfavourable and he had to go by rail.[36] The visit was for a few days only; the subjects for discussion were strictly technical. He returned by sea, just before the arrival of a severe westerly gale. Thomson had predicted bad weather, as Joule admitted:

> Your prophecy proved correct as to the weather I should encounter on my voyage. We had a very heavy sea particularly when off the Mull of Galloway. The 'Lynx' is however a splendid sailer so that after all we arrived at L'pool at 12 OC on Wednesday. I am happy to say I find my children quiet well but my sister has not been quite so well.[37]

And, on being told of the hurricane that had hit Glasgow just after he left: 'When I sailed I noticed 8 seagulls which accompanied the boat from the neighbourhood of Greenock as far as Ailsa Craig. They must have been flying at a rate of 50 or 60 miles an hour through the air. About 2 strokes of their wings per " as far as I can recollect.'[38]

It is quite possible that the visit to Glasgow served to stimulate Joule's interest in the problems of the steam-engine and, in particular, those of the surface condenser. The Clydeside engineers were the leaders in marine engineering and in the development of the surface condenser, a refinement that was not needed in mill engines and was therefore unfamiliar to Lancashire engineers.[39] Immediately on his return to Manchester Joule made a minor alteration to the condenser of the little steam-engine that, he believed, amounted to a major improvement. The modification was, essentially, a simple technique for bleeding off air that would otherwise accumulate in the condenser and rapidly impair the performance of the engine. 'I believe this condenser will supersede all those in present use. Its importance in steam navigation cannot be overestimated.'[40] It would be, he thought (mistakenly), the most fruitful practical result of their researches. But the least amount of leakage seriously affected its efficiency and he had great difficulty in making the joints fit properly. This would not have commended it to the marine engineers, who were only too familiar with the testing conditions under which engines worked at sea. Nevertheless Joule took steps to patent his improvement although, in the end, he did not complete the application.[41]

Another innovation that resulted from the visit to Glasgow was the idea of electric resistance welding. Joule had already noticed that

> Mr Nasmyth has given up the welding of his great gun in consequence of the unprofitability of producing the mass free from flaws and crystalline structure. Probably a mass of iron wires brought near the point of fusion by voltaic electricity (under hydrogen) would cement into a homogeneous mass possessing throughout the qualities of the best wrought iron.[42]

In Glasgow he had seen Thomson fuse a bundle of iron wires together by means of a current from a voltaic battery. But, as he explained in a paper he read to the Lit & Phil on 4 March, 1856, the expense of using the same method to join two large sheets of iron would be prohibitive. Calculation showed that to raise a weight of iron to fusion temperature would require the consumption of the same weight of zinc in the battery. A more economical method would be to use a magneto-electrical engine to generate the current:

> This machine enables us to obtain heat from ordinary mechanical force, which mechanical force may again be derived from the conversion of heat, as in the steam-engine.* In a steam-engine it is practically possible to convert one fifth of the heat due to the combustion of coal into force; and one half of this force applied to work a magneto-electrical machine may be evolved in the shape of heat.[43]

Joule did not apply for a patent for electric resistance welding but in that same year one Henry Wilde, whom we shall meet again, did apply for one.[44] Two years later a Manchester artisan named Thomson and his family emigrated to the United States. They had a five-year-old son, Elihu, who was destined to become a founder of the international electrical firm of

*This contains the germ of the idea of the dynamo.

Thomson–Houston. Elihu Thomson has also been credited with the introduction of electrical resistance welding.[45]

Apart from these ventures into the world of technological innovation Joule was anxious to continue with the experiments on the thermal effects of fluids in motion. There was some delay, as Thomson was unwell. Anxious, as always, about health matters, Joule wrote to Margaret Thomson:

> I take it very kind in your writing to inform me how my dear friend is. I fear he is suffering the effects of overmuch exertion lately and trust he will not trouble himself with any scientific matters or class duties until thoroughly *recovered* . . . The beginning of May will be perfectly convenient to me and you must spare Mr Thomson as long as you can.[46]

Thomson was able to spend ten days in May with Joule just before he set off with his wife for Kreuznach where Margaret was to take the waters. She did not accompany her husband to Manchester, however, for Mary Joule was 'so feeble that she feels unable to give the attention which would be necessary for (Margaret's) comfort'.[47] Poor Mary Joule; it is not difficult to feel sorry for her. Possibly she was one of those Victorian women who elevated indisposition into a social art; perhaps she and her weaknesses provided an always available excuse for the family; most probably she was a frustrated Victorian spinster confronting her isolation in a home with a dying father and brothers who were self-indulgent in their own particular ways.

The first thing Joule and Thomson wanted to do was to study in more detail the heating and cooling effects of a jet of air from a very small orifice. They had, in their hurried paper of 1853, noticed the quite different effects when the thermometer bulb was surrounded by a narrow tube over the orifice and when it was not confined. Now they used a thermocouple in place of a mercury thermometer, three small orifices of different diameters and a comprehensive theory* to predict the temperature of air rushing in a jet with a given velocity and a specified initial temperature.[48] The theory was almost certainly due to Thomson; the experiments were carried out by Joule after the Thomsons had left for Germany. Joule found that the velocity of the jet, calculated as if the density in the orifice was the same as on the high-pressure side, reached a maximum when the excess pressure was 50 in. of mercury above the atmospheric pressure. Thereafter, as the pressure increased further, the velocity fell. Joule plotted a curve of velocity against pressure and found that the results from the three different orifices

---

*There are two misprints in the equations as given in Joule's *Joint Scientific Papers*; they do not occur in Thomson's *Mathematical and Physical Papers*, vol. 1.

fitted the same curve.[49]

It was found that the actual fall in temperature of a jet of air was far less than that predicted (a mere 13°C compared with 150°C), from which they concluded that a body round which air was flowing rapidly acquired a higher temperature than the average temperature of the air close to it all round. Evidently there was a stratum of hot air all round the body so that flowing air did not give its temperature to a thermocouple or thermometer bulb immersed in it. It had been customary when taking the temperature of the air to whirl a thermometer round, to cover as wide a sample as possible. On the contrary, they found that if a thermometer was tied to a length of string and whirled sufficiently fast the indicated temperature was invariably higher than if the thermometer was whirled more slowly. In his lecture in 1847 Joule had been careful not to specify the actual mechanism whereby meteorites were burned up; it was enough to say that the *vis viva* of the meteorites was transformed into the equivalent of heat by the retarding effect of the earth's atmosphere. A modern textbook explains the process in more detail:

> Some of the energy (of a rapidly moving projectile) is used to compress the air immediately in front of the object; the rest is used to overcome the viscous effects of the air near the surface. The combination of these two effects is a region of high temperature air immediately surrounding the object. As a result some energy flows back in the object as heat. The heating effect thus experienced is called *aerodynamic heating.*[50]

The general implication of the results of these experiments was that it was impossible to measure directly the temperature of a moving fluid, whether gas, vapour or liquid, since complex thermo-mechanical effects must affect the reading of any thermometer or thermocouple by causing heat to be imparted to it.[51] This was an early example of an uncertainty principle in physics.

After these experiments the research on fluids in motion was put aside for a time. Thomson was increasingly involved in the Atlantic cable project, being made a director of the company in December 1856, while Joule had various other matters to attend to. He was involved in a tedious dispute with Thomas Woods that lasted for most of 1856. Woods had published a paper in which he claimed to have shown that the heat of combination was equal to the heat required for decomposition.[52] In this he was, essentially, repeating Joule's earlier work. Unfortunately he succeeded in misrepresenting, by accident or design, Joule's basic discoveries. Joule was extremely annoyed and expressed the opinion that Woods had behaved 'most abominably', which was strong language indeed.[53] He added, with some charity: 'It is painful to see a man who might do well commence his scientific course by 'running a-muck''.' At the same time, and with considerably less justification, he took issue with Clausius over his interpretation of Thomson's earlier views on Mayer's hypothesis and the law governing the specific heat of saturated steam.[54] In defence of Thomson he considered that Clausius's language 'had a sort of unfairness about it': a somewhat subjective judgement. Why was it that the group to which Joule belonged remained so hostile towards Clausius?[55]

It is, at first sight, surprising that Joule worried about these minor quibbles while ignoring the paper that Rennie had read to the British Association meeting at Cheltenham that September. Rennie had tried to determine 'the law of evolution of heat by fluid friction'. He ascribed the dynamical theory of heat to Mayer and Helmholtz with honourable mentions for William Siemens and Grove. Mr Joule had, according to Rennie, determined an equivalent relation between force and heat but only over a very limited temperature range. Rennie said he wanted to discover whether and in what way the relationship varied over a much wider range.[56] His experiments, spread over two years, were crude and inaccurate, yielding two figures for the mechanical equivalent of heat: 1,030 and 621 foot-.pounds. His conclusion was that the value varied with the quantity of water used and the 'rate of agitation'.[57] Nothing further was heard of this research and it has been, understandably, ignored by historians. This is a pity for the shortcomings of Rennie's experiments and the confusion of his ideas throw into sharp relief Joule's merits as a scientist. Joule was justified in ignoring Rennie and his experiments.

Another diversion from the study of fluids in motion was brought about by Joule's interest in photography. He was by no means alone in this for Manchester was, for some years, the world capital for the art and science of photography. The first flashlight photograph was taken in Manchester; it was of Henry Enfield Roscoe.[58] John Benjamin Dancer, of Cross Street, made some important inventions in photography, including that of microphotography. Joule was active in the Manchester Photographic Society and took a leading part in setting up a Photographic Section in the Lit & Phil. He also invented a new camera. It was a simple affair in which a solution of silver nitrate lay in a gutta-percha tank in the base of the box. When the photograph had been taken the camera was turned on its side so that the solution poured over the plate fixed to the back of the box. The lens could not be focused in the usual way; it had to be calibrated for different distances.[59] Whatever advantages it had in simplicity of construction the camera was suitable for use by careful and skilled individuals only.[60]

In addition to photography and scientific disputes Joule was continuing his work on the steam-engine, particularly on the condenser. In the autumn of 1856 Rankine invited him to submit a description of his condenser to a meeting of the Institution of Mechanical Engineers in Glasgow. He could not attend but Thomson, who had just returned from Germany, was there to act in his place. Joseph Whitworth was in the Chair and proposed the vote of thanks after the discussion.[61]

The variety and depth of Joule's activities in the second half of 1856 suggest that he had, at last, recovered from the shock of Amelia's death and, at the same time, was feeling the benefit of not having to worry about the brewery. (The Smith brothers ran the business for a few years and then left, closing it down as they did so.) Joule found the time to give an account of the life and achievements of William Sturgeon to a meeting of the Lit & Phil.[62] He confirmed that Sturgeon had made the all-important invention of the soft iron electromagnet and he gave a fair, if conventional, account of Sturgeon's character, work and sacrifices on behalf of science. But public recognition of Sturgeon is still to come.[63]

A good reason for the diversion of Joule's interest from the study of fluids in motion was the much improved facility for research in a problem that had interested him ten and more years ago. The improved facility was the thermocouple introduced by Thomson. It made it possible to measure temperatures and temperature differences rapidly and in situations where a glass bulb thermometer could not be used. As part of his justification for measuring the mechanical equivalent of heat by compressing air he had had to show that if the constituent atoms were like springs then no heat would be evolved when air was compressed. His approximate confirmation that this was the case had been simple enough.[64] In the action of a spring, as in the bending of any solid, one side is stretched, the other compressed. The analogy with the air experiments suggested that the heat evolved by one action should compensate the heat absorbed by the other; the analogy with the study of Mayer's hypothesis suggested that the compensation might not be exact. Joule therefore decided to use thermocouples to find out whether or not this was the case.

A thin bar of steel, one yard long, was clamped at one end and cords were tied to the other so that it could be pulled to and fro. Two copper wires were tied by string, one to each side of the bar, while the free ends were connected to what Joule, misleadingly, called a 'thermomultiplier'* (evidently a galvanometer with several turns of wire about the needle). When

---

*The 'thermomultiplier', invented by Nobili and used by Forbes, consisted of a number of thermo-couples in series and used as a sensitive detector of radiant heat. It is now called a thermopile.

the bar was bent there was a slight current through the galvanometer indicating, Joule believed, a heating effect on the stretched side, and a cooling effect on the compressed side. But this was a differential indication. It could just as well have been that the cooling was greater on one side than on the other.[65] More accurate experiments were needed. The next series, carried out on the following day, seemed to confirm that there was an actual cooling effect on the compressed side; but two days later the results were negative. He therefore decided to make the most sensitive galvanometer he could and place it in a vacuum to minimise outside influences.[66] This time he found that a ¼in. diameter iron wire was perceptibly cooled (1/10°F) when stretched by means of a heavy weight. On removing the weight the wire heated up again.[67] Annoyingly, subsequent experiments yielded contradictory evidence until, towards the end of year, he found that the explanation lay with the different metals he had been using. He had experimented with wrought-iron, steel and cast-iron wires and bars. But the thermoelectric properties of these metals were, he discovered, so different from each other that two different combinations with copper could actually reverse the effects he obtained.[68]

The mystery resolved, Joule established that metals, subjected to a stretching load, were cooled and were heated when the load was removed.[69] He had suggested to Thomson that the heating and cooling effects were proportional to the load applied, at least between 200 lb and 1,200 lb. He was now able to confirm the simple formula that Thomson had worked out for him, giving the thermal effect when solids or liquids were subjected to weights or pressures.[70]

Joule had now passed beyond the simple testing of the thermal effects to be expected when springs were put under pressure or load. He was generalising his study of the thermal effects of the compression of air, or other gases, to include solids and liquids. Leaving the metals he found that gutta-percha also cooled on stretching but, anomalously, indiarubber was heated, while it cooled on contraction.[71] Thomson soon had the explanation. Indiarubber, at least when under tension, must have a negative coefficient of expansion and a negative sign in his formula would indicate that heat was given out, not absorbed, when rubber was stretched. A simple experiment, in which a stretched rubber tube was found to contract when heated, confirmed Thomson's explanation.[72] And then Joule made another discovery, but of quite a different nature. He had found that Mr Gough, 'of this town' (he was actually of Kendal), had observed the heating of stretched rubber fifty years earlier. Blind John Gough had made the discovery by stretching a rubber band between his lips. But the properties of rubber are complex; its characteristics change with temperature and pressure and vary disturbingly with time.

At the end of January 1857, Joule travelled up to Glasgow for further discussions with Thomson.[73] But the only immediate scientific result of the visits was negative.[74] Thomson wrote to Forbes:

> We made a thermodynamic expedition to the Falls of Clyde on Tuesday but got no satisfactory result, whether because of the variation of the temperature of the water from time to time, or because the heating effect of the fall, which is about $1/10°$Fahr., is too much interfered with by cooling (or heating as the case may be) occasioned by the air and broken water.

The rest of Thomson's letter to Forbes throws light on events that were to come. It was concerned with the problem of glacier motion. Forbes, with his pioneering interest in and love of the Swiss Alps, was much intrigued by glacier motion and had his own theory to account for it. Glacier motion posed one of those riddles of nature that, like the source of the Nile, greatly intrigued the Victorians. James Thomson's discovery that the melting-point of ice is lowered under pressure could, Joule believed, account for the phenomenon. He was so convinced of this, wrote Thomson, that he

> believes you may knead a piece of clear ice at 32° into any shape; while ice of a degree or two below the freezing point will be quite rigid and elastic. I have no doubt myself that it explains the phenomenon which Faraday & every boy making a snowball & every experimenter taking a handful of snow and pressing it round a thermometer bulb have observed & which Tyndall adopts as the foundation of a new theory.[75]

Thomson's hostility to Tyndall was evidently as personal as it was scientific. He wrote:

> The only new information I can describe is *that there is to be a Tyndall Theory of Glaciers.* I see that all observations on the plasticity of glacial ice which have been made are to be in perfect accordance with the Tyndall Theory and (after the world is convinced that the Tyndall Theory is opposed to yours) will be gradually and completely absorbed into it.[76]

Tyndall may have been at loggerheads with the Scottish natural philosophers at this time; Joule, on the other hand, was in friendly correspondence with him. On 2 May 1857, he wrote to Tyndall to thank him for his 'kind letter' announcing the selection of Robert Angus Smith* for election to Fellowship of the Royal Society.[77] He ended his letter with a characteristic admonition:

*Robert Angus Smith, Ph.D., was the first alkali inspector. He collaborated with Alexander McDougall on the development of the disinfectant 'carbolic acid', later adopted by Lister for antiseptic surgery. Smith was President of the Lit & Phil 1864–5, and wrote the centenary history of the Society.

I much regretted hearing of your illness, but trust that you are now fully restored. I hope you will not be tempted by the ardour of philosophical research to overstep the limit of exertion which your health and strength can accomplish. I have seen so much of this that I always advise my friends to take things easily, which is also an advice I have been obliged to take myself.

Two years later Joule was to tell Thomson: 'Don't plague yourself about Tyndall. Surely he will not get a medal. Nor do I think Forbes will either, although deserving it so much better.'[78] Joule had bent in the strong north wind.

The visit to Thomson had been enjoyable. Joule returned to Liverpool by sea and wrote back to thank Thomson and to confirm the odd information that he, Joule, could diverge the optic axes of his eyes (i.e. squint outwards). It was, he said, a faculty very easily acquired,[79] although he did not explain for what purpose. Eleven days later he expressed his sympathy with Thomson on the death of his sister, Anna (Mrs Bottomley).[80] He hoped that the Almighty would support Thomson and the bereaved family; the loss painfully reminded him of his own wife's death. Nevertheless he could not resist including the observation that ordinary indiarubber is like vulcanised rubber 'in its comportment, but the effects are more marked'.

In March 1857 Joule wrote two letters that were informative in quite different ways. The first, written in the middle of the month, described a homely experiment.[81] During a seasonable, but severe, gale he had decided to try the effect of the wind on a thermometer. Climbing on to the roof of the house he exposed the thermometer some six inches above the topmost ridge, in the full force of the gale. The reading was one-third of a degree Fahrenheit lower than when the thermometer was in the shelter of the roof. Was this, he asked Thomson, because the *vis viva* of the relatively still air had been 'taken out' by rubbing against the walls of the house so that the air could communicate more heat than that arising from air *partially* (his italics) impeded by the thermometer bulb? A second experiment, after he had been nearly blown off the roof and the gale had abated somewhat, showed that a thermometer elevated six feet above the ridge registered about a fifth of a degree higher after a strong gust than after a lull. It may be that this experience helped to direct his attention back to the experiments on the thermal effects of fluids in motion.

The second letter, apart from describing some minor experiments on rubber, gives a fairly clear indication of Joule's political views:

We have been in a considerable ferment here on account of the election which has terminated in a manner little anticipated the night before. People here are however tired of the domineering ring of the League and Bright was never acceptable personally.* I was very sorry to hear of the death of Dr Scoresby. I had not seen him for a long time and did not know that he was ill. I respected him much and considered him a man of great ability, particularly as a seaman and navigator. His voyage to and surveys of the coasts of Greenland and Arctic regions are very interesting and abound with philosophical observation.

My father is still confined in his room and suffers a great deal at times but is not worse (I trust better) than when I wrote last. My sister is about the same. It is quite exhilarating to me to see the blooming health of my children who are as well as they can be.[82]

Thomson was one of eighteen directors of the Atlantic Telegraph Company of which Cyrus Field was the General Manager, Charles Bright the Engineer-in-Chief and O. E. Wilding Whitehouse the Electrician. Early in April Thomson and Whitehouse paid a short visit to Birkenhead where some of the cable was being manufactured. Joule had already arranged to go to Birkenhead; naturally he accepted Thomson's invitation to see the cable at Newall & Co.'s works there.[83] Joule, like other men of science and engineers who were interested in the project, had his own suggestions to offer. In fact he collaborated with Lewis Gordon – a partner in the Newall firm and former professor of civil engineering in Glasgow University – in experimental work on the cable.[84]

Thomson had embarked on the long and ultimately triumphal enterprise that was to earn him a knighthood. Joule was carrying on with his researches into the thermodynamic properties of solids as well as into fluids in motion. Following the problem that he had met, and solved, when he began researches on the cooling and heating of stretched solids, he drew up an extended thermoelectric series of fifty-one common metals and alloys including different forms of cast iron, wrought iron and steel.[85] He was surprised to find that '*pure* bismuth and *pure* antimony are not so far positive and negative as commercial bismuth and commercial antimony'.[86] However, his insatiable scientific curiosity led him momentarily off the subject. He had noticed that the earth's magnetic field had decreased considerably. As the inertia of the instrument at Kew was so great that it could register only slow, gradual changes, he had thought of a sensitive magnetometer that would respond to sudden, sharp changes. Perhaps Thomson would care to make a similar instrument so that they could compare readings? But Thomson had other things in hand.

'Nearly everybody', Joule explained to Thomson, 'has been at the opening of the Art Treas. but you will see that I have been better employed.'[87]

---

*This was the election that resulted in the surprising defeat of the 'Manchester School' of radicals (the League) and the rejection of Cobden, Bright and their followers as well as the group of Peelites. Joule's views were not universally held in Manchester.

The Art Treasures Exhibition, which opened on May 5 1857 in a crystal palace erected specially for the purpose at Old Trafford, was a display of major European paintings and *objects d'art*. It ran for five months and was judged a great success. According to one modern writer, 'the exhibition was by many standards one of the greatest in the history of the world'.[88] Joule thought otherwise and his opinion should not be discounted. He was, on the evidence of his notebooks and letters, an excellent draughtsman and on the evidence of friends and other letters, a good judge of fine art. It may be that his dismissive attitude reflected his dislike of crowds and a not unreasonable opinion that popular taste in art was neither to be trusted nor in the best interests of art.

It is ironic that the particular work on which he thought he was better employed was to prove fruitless. A comparison between measurements of the thermal effects of stretching copper, lead, gutta-percha and three varieties of iron showed that in every case the effect was slightly greater than predicted by theory.[89] Joule believed that this was due to an increase in the coefficient of thermal expansion when the solid was under tension.[90] He had evidence to support this explanation, but it was soon found to be unsatisfactory.

The anomalous behaviour of rubber was not entirely unique. There was the behaviour of water between 0°C and 4°C. According to Thomson's theory, compressing water when its temperature lay between these figures must lead to a cooling effect.[91] This was because the pressure, or compression, had a positive sign in this case while the tension, in the case of rubber, had a negative sign; in both cases the coefficient of expansion was negative. Joule added a note supporting Thomson's theory of the cooling effect between 0°C and 4°C and indicating a heating effect above 4°C. He relied, however, on experimental measures of the coefficient of expansion rather than Thomson's formula to give a 'rough estimate'.[92] Subsequently, Joule confirmed the cooling followed by heating effects experimentally.[93]

Having refined his apparatus, established an extended thermoelectric series, including different forms of iron as well as certain alloys, and explained the anomalous behaviour of rubber and cold water satisfactorily, he set about extending and consolidating knowledge of the thermodynamic properties of solids.[94] Systematically, he listed the results of experiments on the effects of tension on metals, on rubber, on gutta-percha and on different woods, with the grain and across the grain and in different hygrometric states. He examined other organic substances – paper, leather, whalebone – before going on to study the effects of compression on solids. In every case, when the solid was compressed, the result was a rise in temperature. But the effect was consistently slightly higher than the theory predicted. This refuted the suggestion that, in the case of solids under tension, the slight excess was due to an increase in the coefficient of thermal expansion: in the second case, the effect should have been less than the theory predicted.

While Joule was extending his studies on the thermal effects of the performance of work from gases to solid bodies his interest in the thermal effects of fluids in motion had revived. Thomson paid a visit to help with the experiments that were simple and straightforward. Their attention had shifted from air rushing through orifices to air flowing round bodies and bodies moving through air. A simplified theory had predicted that the pressure would be higher in the fore and aft parts of the body and reduced round the equatorial zone. Using Poisson's formula for the adiabatic heating of a compressed gas an expression was derived for the expected heating and cooling effects: heating at the fore and aft parts, cooling round the equator.[95] The theory showed that at speeds low in comparison with the velocity of sound, the change in temperature would be proportional to the square of the velocity.*

Their apparatus consisted of a wheel, driven by hand, connected to an axle with a radial rod at the other end. The thermometer was fixed, bulb outward, to the end of the rod. After Thomson had returned to Glasgow Joule continued the experiments, using two different thermometers.[96] He covered the bulb with folded writing-paper and then cut away paper on the posterior side; after that he turned the bulb round so that the anterior side was exposed. These different experiments showed that there was an increased heating affect at low velocities due, Joule believed, to friction.[97] He therefore wrapped iron wire round the bulb and found the effect, at low velocities, was four or five times greater than when the bulb was uncovered. Experiments using fine brass wire in place of iron wire yielded the same result. At high speeds the effect, in both cases, tended to be the same as if the bulb was quite bare. Joule concluded that this was due to a cushion of air being dragged round with the bulb so that the effect of friction diminished progressively.

In a footnote to the paper that Joule and Thomson submitted to the Royal Society in June 1857, they explained, as far as was possible, Joule's experiences on the roof-top in the light of their whirling experiments (as Joule described them). The actual temperature of a gust of wind was, they concluded, lower than that of the succeeding lull, probably because the relatively still air had had its *vis viva* converted into heat by collision with

*There are two misprints in the equations as given in Joule's *Joint Scientific Papers*; they do not occur in Thomson's *Mathematical and Physical Papers*, vol. 1.

fixed objects. A thermometer in a sheltered position, they pointed out, indicated a higher temperature than it would if exposed to the gale. The heating effect of moving air against the thermometer bulb was not enough to negate this difference. The whole question was, they admitted, most complex.

Two years went by before Joule resumed the whirling experiments and it was not until 1860 that the results of these experiments were published as Paper 3 of the series, 'On the thermal effects of fluids in motion', in the *Philosophical Transactions.*[98] Following the established practice these experiments and the paper that followed represented the systematic establishment of the theories and data presented in the exploratory experiments of 1857. As the innovations in the paper of 1860 were minor and the conclusions confirmatory little violence will be done to historical continuity if a short summary of them is given here.

The main innovation was the use of thermocouples as well as conventional thermometers. On 14 June 1859, Joule wrote to Thomson to say: 'I have set up the whirling apparatus again, and my first proceeding was to break the thread of the galvanometer you left me. I am sure that if you had witnessed my proceedings you would have been confirmed in your opinion of the hatred I had to [*sic*] it'.[99] The hatred was directed at the whirling apparatus, not at Thomson's mirror galvanometer that he had developed for use in connection with the Atlantic cable and that was to become so familiar to generations of students doing 'physics practicals'. Joule surrounded the whirling thermocouple with cotton wool and observed that the heating effect was notably increased. To Thomson he suggested that 'If you have a thermometer in Arran put it in a small basket filled with hay or tow on a windy day and I am sure you will find it a little higher than a thermometer placed in the fresh air.'[100]

A thermometer mounted on a spinning disc of 'millboard' showed a greater heating effect for very low velocities; greater than predicted by the law they had inferred. The effect, Joule suggested, was due to friction similar to that between solids: 'in this way supposing air to have a certain viscosity which enables it to be rubbed against, like a solid at very low velocities'.[101] At higher velocities the friction effect diminished and heating was due to the air being 'stopped'. Finally, he examined the thermal effects on spheres when whirled round or when subjected to a blast of air from a powerful organ bellows. The effect at the equatorial junction (thermocouple) could, by a rather homely anology, 'be accounted for by supposing that the air rushes quicker past the equatorial parts in the same way that water rushes quickly by the side of canal boat as the only means of establishing equilibrium'.

The conclusion from this research was simply that at low velocities the heating effect was substantially due to friction of the air against the solid body and therefore simply proportional to the velocity; but at high velocities the heating effect was due to the air being 'stopped' and therefore proportional to the square of the velocity (adiabatic compression). Joule and Thomson admitted that there was much more to find out, that the effects were complex and that the subject was of great interest to meteorologists.

The long interval of three years between the appearance of the two papers on the heating of bodies in current of air is not easy to account for, particularly as no new, expensive or elaborate apparatus was needed and there were no intellectual problems to solve. It must be supposed that Joule was committed to the tedious and demanding work on the thermodynamic properties of different types of wood, differently cut and in varying states of wetness. For Thomson there was exhausting work on the Atlantic cable; work into which Joule, too, was drawn, supervising the construction of galvanometers at Birkenhead, giving advice on the properties of gutta-percha used in the cable, defending Thomson's contribution against the pretensions of Whitehouse, Bright and others and raging against the aspersions on Thomson's abilities in a letter from Cyrus Field that was soon exposed as a forgery.[102]

Thomson, engaged in one of the most dramatic technological achievements of the nineteenth century, was increasingly in the public eye, particularly after he replaced Whitehouse as Chief Electrical Engineer. Joule, too, had a modest share of publicity. The 1857 meeting of the British Association was held in Dublin. 'I may see you', he said to Thomson, 'at Dublin, at least if something does not interfere, as it has so often done before, to prevent me going.'[103] He could have mentioned that Trinity College was to take the opportunity to award him the Honorary Degree of Ll.D.* It was in an Irish city that he had first announced the dynamical theory of heat; it was appropriate that an Irish university should award him the first of his three honorary doctorates. Now he was Dr Joule, the holder of an honorary doctorate awarded at the remarkably young age of thirty-eight. Further public recognition came when he was proposed for, and accepted, membership of the Council of the Royal Society. As he explained to Thomson:

---

*He was modest about this and his other doctorates. In those days the ancient universities were peripheral institutions, of interest to those whose careers lay in the Church of England, law or politics. Many in Manchester held the Scottish universities in high esteem, while others tended to judge a man solely by his material possessions. 'What's he worth?', as Engels sardonically observed.

I am going to attend the first meeting of the Council of the Royal Society on Thursday next. When it was proposed I, at once, expressed my willingness to serve on the principle that country Fellows should take their share in the business of the Society. Otherwise it would fall into the hands of too few to give personal attention. I am afraid I shall not be able to attend as many meetings as I ought. One thing is in my favour, ie. the competition between the Gt. Northern and L & N.W. Rwys whereby I can go to London on Wednesday and return on Sat for the double journey 1st class £1. 1/-. The only fault I can find is that the Companies compete in speed as well as in price for I think 4¾ hours rather too fast from here to London per narrow gauge.*[104]

Distinctions, however considerable, did not alter the pattern of his life. In October the family took a late holiday at Blackpool:

for the benefit of the sea air. We were, however, very unfortunate in our selection of time. The weather was just breaking up and with that and extreme exposure we returned with bad colds & c. My sister was very ill for some time but now recovered to her usual state of health, not much to boast of at the best, still I think she has on the whole been gaining ground. Alice was very poorly on her return but is now getting round again nicely.[105]

There was also the Lit & Phil to claim his attention. He had been a Vice-President since 1850, his friend Edward Schunck, the organic chemist, being the Honorary Secretary. He was also the editor of the *Memoirs* and in this capacity he, with the strong support of Edward Binney, continued Dalton's policy of excluding non-scientific papers. He arranged for copies of the *Memoirs* to be sent to the numerous Honorary Members and he began the independent publication of the *Proceedings* of the Society. These gave much fuller accounts of the activities of the members and the diversity of their interests. Between 1857 and 1887 twenty-six volumes of the *Proceedings* were published. Although independent publication ceased two years before Joule's death the practice of reporting the proceedings continued in the *Memoirs and Proceedings* of the Society. It is notable that the 'Proceedings' section for 1912 included Rutherford's first announcement of the nuclear atom.

Towards the end of 1857 *The Times* had published an ill-advised article enthusing over the possibilities of electromagnetism as a source of power.[106] Plainly, they had not had a correspondent at the meeting of the Institution of Civil Engineers on 21 April 1857, when 'Electro-magnetism as a motive power' had been thoroughly discussed and effectively discredited.[107] Joule therefore wrote to the newspaper pointing out the fallacies

---

*I.e. The present standard gauge of 4ft 8½in. in contrast to Brunel's 7 ft. gauge that was finally abandoned as late as 1892.

in the articles; fallacies that he had exposed in his researches from 1841 onwards.[108]

This was not his only venture into public affairs at that time. His trips to London to attend the meetings of the Council of the Royal Society gave him the opportunity to inspect the machinery to be used to launch the *Great Eastern;* his guide was John Scott Russell. He was unimpressed, as he explained to Thomson:

> It seems to me that Mr Scott Russell has been ill used by the public who now mention no name but Brunel in connexion with the ship. The fact is that the entire merit of the ship as a piece of naval architecture belongs exclusively to Mr Russell while the merit or demerit of the launch is as exclusively Brunel's. I have made a calculation of what her speed would be when fully laden and find it somewhat less than that of the *Persia*. I think some limit should be placed on the enormous consumption of coal by steamships which is rapidly exhausting our coal mines.[109]

To the engineers and men of science of Glasgow and of Manchester I. K. Brunel would be an outsider and a southerner; John Scott Russell, FRS, was, assuredly, an insider and a northerner. But the main interest in the paragraph lies in the last sentence. Wildly exaggerated as his fear now seems, it foreshadowed – and may very well have contributed to – the publication of an influential book eight years later. As for the difficulties in launching the great iron ship Joule felt impelled to write a letter about it to the *Manchester Courier*, the Tory paper that had published his St Ann's lecture in 1847. The letter was grossly unfair, if not libellous. 'The fact', Joule wrote, 'appears to be that although Mr Russell designed and built the ship, the company had the wisdom to entrust the launching to Mr Brunel – a man who, although he had gained some notoriety as a railway engineer, knew nothing of either ship building or ship launching'. This assessment of the man who built the magnificent Great Western Railway and had been responsible for the revolutionary ships *Great Western* (1837), and *Great Britain* (1843), condemns itself.

A public event of even wider interest than the launching of the *Great Eastern* was the annular eclipse of the sun that would be visible near Peterborough on 15 March 1858. Joule decided to photograph the eclipse. He described his experience to Thomson.

> My brother and I started at 8½ yesterday amid fog and cloud in the hope that the sky would clear before we arrived at Peterboro. We saw the sun, partially eclipsed as we were travelling at 65 miles per hour on the Gt. Northern; the lamps on the train being lit in anticipation of obscure darkness. On arriving at the junction (4 miles north of Peterborough) we got out and found 1,000 persons assembled among whom I was glad to see Mr Stokes. The sky was quite

obscured with clouds and I despaired of getting any chance of taking a photo-graphic image of the annulus for which I was prepared. I therefore, four minutes before the time of the central eclipse, used the camera to obtain a picture of the country, pointing it in a particular direction as respects the sun. Although to most eyes the darkness was hardly visible [*sic!*] I could by my experience of photography at once perceive that minutes instead of seconds would be required to produce a picture. At the end of four minutes the darkness increased almost fourfold and remained so about 20″ when it suddenly became lighter again . . . I am glad to say that although disappointed of a view of the complete annulus our party got a glimpse of the sun as a very thin crescent soon afterwards, and we returned after seeing the Cathedral at Peterboro much pleased with our excursion.[110]

Travelling by train in mid-Victorian England had its hazards, as Joule discovered two months later, on 10 May 1858, when returning from London by the 9 a.m. 'Scotch Express'. At Attleborough, near Nuneaton, the locomotive hit a cow that had strayed on to the track. The locomotive stayed on the rails but the leading coaches were derailed and three of the hundred passengers were killed. Joule was shocked to see the engine crew casually eating their sandwiches as if nothing had happened. He himself was unhurt, but the accident made him even more reluctant to travel by train and for this reason, according to Osborne Reynolds, he declined to be renominated for the Council of the Royal Society.

Pleasure at the publication of his letters to the press and concern about the depletion of the coal reserves may have combined to encourage him to express his views publicly on a topic very different from anything he had spoken or written about before. He went so far as to trespass into the fields of applied biology and what would now be called ecology. On 30 November 1858, he read a paper to the Lit & Phil entitled 'On the utilization of the sewage of London and other large towns'.[11] The problem had been a scandal for many years; now there was a firm proposal to discharge water-carried sewage into the Thames at Barking Creek and Crossness Point. This, argued Joule, meant polluting the lower river and shifting the problem from one part of the populace to another. Furthermore, and no less harmfully, it would deprive the land of vital fertilisers, the natural ingredients without which the yield could not be kept up (it must be remembered that in those days, horses contributed greatly to the sewage of major cities). Joule could quote Liebig in support of his argument. The country was importing guano from Peru but that could continue for only a limited number of years. The importation of corn, cattle and bone manure helped to make up the loss of our natural fertilisers but this could go on for only as long as foreign countries accepted the impoverishment of their own soils. His solution was a system of public cesspits, regularly emptied, and the sewage carried back to the country, by rail, to restore the land. The cesspits could be cleansed after each emptying by means of McDougall* and Smith's 'disinfecting powder' (carbolic acid).

As Joule explained to Stokes, the obligation to read his paper to the Lit & Phil prevented his attendance at the meeting of the Royal Society Council: this had happened at a previous meeting of the Council.[112] 'I fear', he wrote, 'I shall be considered to have been a very indifferent member. The subject of sewage which has occupied my attention is one I dare say it will be thought I have no business with; but it is one which sooner or later will force itself on every intelligent member of the community.' Joule, it appears, felt himself more committed to the Lit & Phil than to the Council of the Royal Society. Moreover, he did not have to travel by the 'Scotch Express' to attend meetings of the Lit & Phil.

Joule's fears may appear exaggerated, but he was speaking at a time when the revolution in ocean transport was only just beginning and before the opening up of the rich wheatlands of mid-western USA and Canada; before, too, the importation of frozen meat from Australasia and Argentina was possible. Domestic food resources were limited while the population of the British Isles was still rapidly increasing. Finally, there was the memory of the appalling Irish famine and the hungry forties. There were good reasons for concern and every reason for the conservation of fertile land. Joule's own researches had taught him that the life and work of the nation depended on its fuel, or energy, resources. The draught horse, the steam-engine, the air-engine, the voltaic cell all 'burn' fuel to do work. And the amount of available fuel was finite. A sense of insecurity is not the unique privilege, or misfortune, of the present age.

Joule was no propagandist. Having delivered his message to what was an influential body in one of the most important cities in the world he turned back to science. He was not a publicist; he was a man of science. Honoured by the Royal Society with its highest awards, he never delivered a Bakerian Lecture. In the course of his life he gave no more than a handful of public lectures and these were to small, local gatherings. The one exception was the lecture he gave at a meeting in Greenock, to commemorate the anniversary of James Watt's birth on 19 January 1736.[113] He was never able to accept the Presidency of the British Association and he refused academic appointments. It could be argued that for a man who did not have to earn a living as a professional scientist his researches were of the nature of a hobby, an entertainment event. There may be an element of truth in

---

*Alexander McDougall, a Manchester chemist, is best known for his invention of self-raising flour.

this; but his rarely dormant scientific curiosity coupled with his anxious concern that his researches should not over-tax his health or his brain indicate a deep personal commitment rather than a relaxing hobby. Joule was a private man who lived for science, not by it.

Of course he was fortunate to have a private income so that he could pursue his researches in whatever direction he chose; fortunate, too, in his tutor, John Dalton, and in his long association with the Lit & Phil among whose members were some very able engineers and men of science. He was fortunate that the engineer's measure of work, or force times distance, central to the affairs of Manchester, indispensable for the design, construction and operation of engines and mills, was so readily at hand and, at the same time, was to prove the key to the energy concept. And he was particularly fortunate in finding such a good friend as William Thomson whose gifts, personal and scientific, so aptly complemented his own.

Joule, then, was lucky. But luck, in one form or another, is essential for success in life. Unlike the tragic J. R. Mayer, who met with indifference or downright hostility, Joule found influential friends in Manchester, Cambridge and Glasgow; his opponents, such as they were, exercised no power over him. Apart from these advantages he was lucky in that his upbringing in Manchester insulated him from certain scientific doctrines – such as the positivism of Fourier – that could easily have inhibited the dynamical theory of heat and the conservation of energy. And this upbringing combined with his philosophy of science – his suspicion of speculation uncontrolled by experiment – made him unreceptive of such fashions as *Naturphilosophie*, a creed to which Westermarck's acid words could be applied: it gave the impression of depth because it was so muddy. On the other hand the Manchester, or more particularly the Lit & Phil environment, seems to have stifled any doubts Joule may have had about the existential status of Daltonian atoms. Elsewhere this was a matter of dispute. Faraday was sceptical; Herschel, Whewell and lesser pundits were doubtful or hostile. Generally, the chemists were indifferent, being concerned only with the quantitative application of the atomic theory. And yet it was the realist atomic theory, inherited from Dalton himself, that gave plausibility to the dynamical theory of heat and the conservation of energy. In its absence in what sense could work be considered convertible into – or from – heat? Work and heat belong to radically different realms of experience. Dalton's atom was the bridge between them.

10

Years of change

The end of the 1850s found Britain fearful of a French invasion. Disasters in the Crimea and the Indian 'Mutiny' combined with the adventures of Napoleon III to alarm the British public deeply. An official poem by Tennyson, the Poet Laureate, printed in *The Times*,* helped to expedite the Volunteer Rifle Corps movement. In a short time a small, neglected force was tripled in numbers to 200,000 men and forts were built round the southern coast of Britain. It is a paradox and an implicit comment on political judgement that these forts will endure, monuments to a war that was never fought, when the military buildings of the Napoleonic wars, the Crimea, the South African War and the two world wars have long disappeared.

Joule had some interesting strategic and political ideas to express:

> I have not yet 'formed' as a rifleman. With regard to national defences my own opinion is that government ought long ago to have encouraged railways round the coasts . . . They would thus have been constructed at comparatively little public cost, and afforded the means of throwing large bodies of artillery on the beach which nearly always affords a commanding position, before an enemy could effect a landing. In addition we ought to have very heavy cannon, says 200 pounders, all round the coast nowhere less frequent than one per mile . . . in time of invasion any one of them might save the nation. I have sometimes speculated however, whether a much more fatal calamity than invasion will not soon overtake us if nothing is done to check the reform mania. The election of members of the H of Commons is to be in the hands of the rabble† and the constitution in the hands of the H of C. If Bonaparte came he would probably leave us our constitution in Church and State, and perhaps reduce the H of C to its legitimate position.[1]

*The stanzas end with the euphonious, if banal, line: 'Riflemen, Riflemen, Riflemen form!' The poem finds a place in Wyndham Lewis and Charles Lee's anthology, *The Stuffed Owl*.
†The reference is to Lord John Russell's abortive reform bill that would have extended the franchise.

A little later he expressed the view that

In itself I believe an invasion by L Nap^n would be a frightful calamity. But would it be worse than what Bright & others are endeavouring to bring us by Americanising our constitution? However I am extremely glad that the present Government is going on with our defensive arrangements for I must say I had rather personally have a republic here to the degradation of a French invasion. Manchester is very backward with its rifle club, but there is no convenient place for practice.[2]

From several points of view the Britain of Joule's day, when the idea of progress was hardly to be questioned, appears to have been a country of increasing social stability, reform and prosperity. For western Europe these were years of unparalleled creativity in the arts and sciences; the contrast with the 1960s is instructive.

A great triumph was celebrated, a little prematurely as it happened, when the Atlantic telegraph link was completed on 5 August 1858, and greetings were exchanged between President Buchanan and Queen Victoria. Because of a damaged cable and incompetent working the line began to fail, becoming finally inoperable on 20 October 1858. Thomson had been fascinated by the whole project and was still devoting much time and effort to it.[3] 'I do hope,' wrote Joule, 'ere long we shall again be working on the "thermal effects of fluids in motion". Still I trust you will endeavour to *finish* off the necessary part of your Atlantic work so as to be able to know the time you have at your disposal.'[4] Joule himself had not lost interest in the Atlantic cable. He tried, without success, to persuade the Lit & Phil formally to identify itself with the project, clearly with a view to publicising Thomson's part in the enterprise.[5]

A short paragraph at the end of a letter of 10 December 1858, gave some sad domestic news: 'We have all had very bad colds but otherwise are pretty well. We have been unfortunate in losing our cook, who died very suddenly having been with us about twenty years. There is quite a blank in consequence.'[6] And, on 30 December 1858, the head of the family died:

The event long anticipated occurred on Thursday night when my father died suddenly and without pain or struggle. He had an attack of sickness about 10 days before from the effects of which he appeared to have recovered. His medical attendant said he was still better on the day he died. Having been nearly helpless for nearly ten years this is to him a most happy release.[7]

Benjamin Joule's death at the age of seventy-four meant the end of the old commercial family. Sooner or later 'Oak Field' would have to be sold and the daughter and three sons left to dispose of their patrimonies as they thought fit. Benjamin stayed on for a few years before moving to Southport;

John had already married and moved away (his eldest child was five); James and Mary remained together in Manchester. James was a man of science of independent means with a circle of acquaintances and scientific colleagues. His career resembled, in many ways, that of a typical Victorian engineer and entrepreneur who, having made his pile, retired to a life of leisurely science. W. H. Perkin, the pioneer of the synthetic dyestuffs industry, did this, as did David Edward Hughes, inventor of the microphone and of numerous improvements in telegraphy. James Nasmyth, engineer, inventor of the steam hammer and friend of the Gaskells, later turned to the study of astronomy while Henry Wilde, who made a fortune from numerous inventions, turned to more abstract science in his later years. Something else, however, had changed in James Joule's life; he had fallen in love with his cousin, Frances Charlotte Tappenden, the daughter of his mother's half-sister and his old tutor, Frederick Tappenden. She was at this time a young woman of twenty-one, while he was just forty.

Early in 1859 Joule paid a visit to Thomson, travelling by sea, of course. He was persuaded to write a short article for Nichol's encyclopaedia, but his main efforts were directed towards the completion of the experiments for the joint paper with Thomson on the changes of temperature of bodies moving through the air – the 'whirling' experiments – to be published in the following year together with further studies on the surface condensation of steam,[8] using the organ bellows.[9] He was only mildly irritated by Liebig's ascription of the mechanical equivalent of heat entirely to Mayer.[10] And he was delighted when he found that his surface condenser seemed to be far more efficient than he thought possible.[11] He considered patenting it before he realised that his experimental results were deceptive and he was unable to repeat them.[12] Nevertheless, he thought it worthwhile to patent his idea of inserting a wire spiral in the water tube that surrounded the inner tube carrying the steam. This, he had found, improved the refrigerating effect of the cold water. As for patents,

> I have read up a good deal on the subject and am much annoyed with finding that none but complete specifications are published so that a patentee goes quite in the dark for at least 6 months. I am almost induced to have no part in patents because it is such a swindling system on the part of Government. It is a trap for poor men with mechanical genius and many such are annually ruined thereby. My work with the condensation you will think has been long enough but it is now near a close and I will then be able to go on with our air experiments without delay.

That summer the family took a modest one-week holiday at Seascale, on the Cumbrian coast. Joule himself enjoyed what could well have been a second holiday when he went up to Aberdeen for the meeting of the British

Association. The Prince Consort was President that year and made a memorable speech, holding out hopes that the government would, in the future, increasingly recognise the claims of science. Two hundred delegates went by train to Balmoral where they were entertained to lunch in the ballroom. They watched the highland games, in which the Farquharson, Duff and Forbes clans competed, and in the evening Professor Owen, Sir Roderick Murchison and Mr Secretary Philips were entertained to dinner by the Queen. But beyond that, the *Manchester Courier* reported, no formal notice was taken of the visitors. This caused offence, as Joule observed:

> I had an opportunity to speak to Lord Brougham* not long ago. He had evidently heard a very bad account of the Balmoral visit from Sir D. Brewster. Sir D was incensed and I think justly with the way in which the thing was managed. I would have felt the same if I had occupied so prominent a position. I told Lord B that I individually was not disappointed because I had expected no better but on the contrary was much gratified. I found no fault with anything but the arrangements which were very bad and could only have been made by a very ignorant or a very ill-conditioned person. Feeling sure that Her Majesty did all she could to please I am amused, and I am sure the majority of the visitors are, that so much has been badly said about the trip, in the Papers & *Punch*.[13]

Perhaps as a result of his visit to Balmoral Joule felt obliged to express his views on military and political matters to Thomson and Rankine, part-time soldiers in the Volunteer force:

> So we are to have a Capt Prof Dr T as well as R. All honour to the Riflemen. But I think they ought to let Government know they will not be 'sold'. What has the administration been doing but making the rifle a pretext for not drilling the volunteers and snubbing the militia and thus saving a million or so to be made away with by Mr Cobden and the Chancellor of X. Now my notion is that the rifles ought to supplement not to substitute for the regular force and I suppose this is the opinion of all who have volunteered. You know I have not a sanguine temperament but even if I had I know not how I could forsee anything but disaster from the 'treaty', the 'budget' and the so-called Reform Bill of Bright and Russell. Lord John and the Goverment are I believe so thoroughly convinced of the mischievous tendency of their own measure that they would feel relieved if it were thrown out. You will see I am still a 'tory' and do not think the government is quite as perfect as H gas.[14]

The cryptic simile in the last sentence is explained by the preceding paragraph of the same letter that dealt with quite a different matter. Joule had resumed experiments with the heating effects of fluids in motion and, in particular, was tackling the difficult problem of the behaviour of

---

*Lord Brougham (1778–1868) would have been eighty-one at this time.

hydrogen. As he could obtain only limited quantities of hydrogen he had to adapt the apparatus and make a new, small 'nozle' (Figure 5(4)). The letter gave a particularly clear account of the difficulties and even dangers of the experiments:

> I was perhaps in too great a hurry to give you figures for the hydrogen [*sic*]. I found afterwards that the gas was only 83 per cent pure. I have since experimented with another quantity 95 per cent H, the rest air and the result, so far as I am able to decipher it, is that there is *a heating effect* not a cooling one. This would confirm one of Regnault's results showing that hydrogen was better than a perfect gas. I will not let hydrogen alone until I get the real truth undeniably established. You will understand the difficulties. The variations that troubled us at first almost overwhelm the small thermal effects of hydrogen. And my gas holder with 40 cubic feet is pretty well exhausted before an hour however tight the joints are kept for H has small shoulders. Then there is the necessity of keeping up the steam well, for the engine has to work efficiently at 4 horse power. I make my gas in the morning, experiment in the afternoon and analyse the gas in the evening. I have worked with explosive mixtures when the pump was too hot to be touched from condensation of the gas, but I hope no destruction will take place before we have done with the engine and until we have had a few more discoveries out of it.

A degree of urgency had entered the research programme, since 'Oak Field' was up for sale. With his next letter Joule reported that he was working hard with hydrogen.[15] He had to use up about a third of the gas merely to clear the pipes of air. It was difficult to get hydrogen of greater purity than 95% so he thought it best to experiment with different mixtures of air and hydrogen; from the observed thermal effects he hoped to deduce the effect with pure hydrogen. Unfortunately, hydrogen appeared to have a disproportionate influence, particularly when forming a smaller part of the mixture. Failing a supply of pure hydrogen a consistently satisfactory figure for its effect could not be obtained. Two things, however, were clear. Hydrogen, streaming through a porous plug, was, unlike other gases, heated. And the heating effect at about 90° was twice that at low temperatures.[16] This compared instructively with the behaviour of carbon dioxide in which case the *cooling* effect at 90° was half that at lower temperatures.

Joule was anxious that Thomson should join him in his experiments; and no less anxious that Thomson should avoid the 'dangerous "Limited Scotch Express" '. It was now May, and 'I have been endeavouring to make time square with work and as it is very desirable to take my sister and children to the sea air soon (my sister not having been very well lately), I think we will go to the Isle of Man on Thursday, the 10th.'[17] He was 'very disappointed that we cannot see you for a chat before you go to London . . .

My sister has been very anxious to get to the Isle of Man before the cheap trips begin of which she has a horror. Do endeavour to arrange that we can have at least a fortnight's work together in June.'[18] With or without Thomson's help Joule was now working on oxygen and nitrogen. He found to his surprise that different mixtures of these two gases (including common air) were 'more perfect', or showed less cooling effect, than either one, taken individually.[19]

The results of these experiments were published in 1862 in what was to be the fourth major and virtually the last of the twelve joint papers on the thermal effects of fluids in motion.[20] The enterprise had begun with Thomson's desire to test, and, he hoped, refute Mayer's hypothesis together with Joule's wish to settle the issue of the 'gas of springs' (as Mendoza has put it ('The kinetic theory of matter' – see Ch. 5, n. 1)). Thereafter it had broadened out into a comprehensive, authoritative, and in more ways than one, revolutionary research. Many years later Joule summarised the course of their work very clearly.

> You will recollect that the very first experiments we made were using a piece of leather and the results were very good, even on a small scale, for the heating of hydrogen came out very distinctly.* There would be a number of capillary tubes which would, of course, be enormously better than a simple capillary tube. You recollect the trouble we had with rapids and that with a single orifice we could get anything almost, either hot or cold, through a range of hundreds of degrees. I burned my fingers frequently in the stream. If you put the needful cotton wool & c to mix up the currents you get the conduction to the sides. Just as in the plug we used. By the way we must, if time holds out, make experiments on high temperatures with an asbestos plug. There is a quantity of apparatus for this by me which might be put to use ultimately.[21]

but the experiments with an asbestos plug were never published.

Their researches confirmed Mayer's hypothesis, at least approximately, and indicated that saturated steam diverged from the gas laws. In their Bakerian Lecture of 1860 William Fairbairn and Thomas Tate reported direct experiments confirming that the density of saturated steam was invariably greater than predicted by the gas laws.[22] But Thomson had already been persuaded, as a result of their researches, to accept Joule's suggestion of December 1848 and had reconstructed his absolute scale of temperature, showing that it accorded with the ideal gas scale. Their extended researches showed that all gases, with the exception of hydrogen, were cooled when they expanded without doing external work, that the

---

*They did not publish this at the time. Presumably they were uncertain about the reliability of the experiment using the calfskin leather 'plug'.

cooling effect was greater as the temperature was lower and that it was most marked as the gas approached 'the condition of a vapour at saturation'. Carbon dioxide, the gas nearest the state of a vapour (it liquefies at $-57°C$), showed the greatest cooling effect. Hydrogen was furthest from the state of a vapour; only at $-80°$ does hydrogen cease to heat up on streaming through a porous plug. Experiments at such a low temperature were quite impossible for Joule and Thomson; accordingly, they never found the inversion temperature of hydrogen below which it, too, would be cooled, streaming through a porous plug. Nearly forty years later, in 1898, (Sir) James Dewar succeeded in liquefying hydrogen using von Linde's method, based on the Joule–Thomson effect. Ten years later Kammerlingh Onnes liquefied helium using the same process. But helium was undiscovered in 1860. More in keeping with the mid-nineteenth century was an experience that Joule described: 'On Saturday last our little ones had a famous treat on seeing a balloon come exactly over the house where in consequence of there being little or no wind it remained for 2 to 3 minutes at about 300 yards high without the least apparent change of position.'[23]

And yet there was a symbolic connection between this example of Victorian aviation and the joint researches of Joule and Thomson. Although the theoretical and practical importance of what was to become known as the Joule–Thomson effect were soon appreciated, the extension of their researches to include the study of the heating of a body moving rapidly through the air was only of the remotest academic interest, and was properly ignored by their first biographers for whom it was a minor piece of research of little theoretical and no practical value. Even Joule's awareness of the complex nature of the apparently simple process whereby meteorites are raised to incandescence was not regarded as particularly important. It is only in the age of supersonic flight and space travel that this part of the joint research could be fully appreciated.

Physics, earlier in the nineteenth century, included those branches of physical science, together with certain technologies, that were capable of mathematical interpretation. What were lacking were concepts and theories that could unite the different branches. The mid-century doctrine of energy was such a theory. Joule's researches brought heat, electricity and magnetism within the scope of mechanics and suggested that light and sound must be subject to the same set of principles. Following the establishment of the comprehensive energy principle, the joint researches with Thomson form as good and as complete an example of the pursuit and practice of physics as can be found. They marked a new departure in physics; a collaboration, sustained over a long period, by an experimentalist and a theoretician. This is the reason why the Joule–Thomson partnership has been discussed in some detail. It is a testimony to their collaboration that the fruit of their researches has been summed up in the designation of the Joule–Thomson *effect*.[24] Thereafter, earlier discoveries of Faraday, Seebeck, and Peltier, as well as later ones of Hall, Stark, Zeeman, Compton, etc., have all been described as *effects*.

In April 1860, while Joule was studying the heating effect of streaming hydrogen, Roscoe, professor of chemistry at Owens College, was writing to Stokes for advice about new appointments at the College.[25] He had already made tentative enquiries about a professorship of physics;[26] now it was proposed to establish a Chair of natural philosophy, separate from the Chair of mathematics, as well. He wanted Stokes's advice:

> Is it advisable to have two courses of lectures, one an experimental course & one a course in which the subject is treated more mathematically & for which the student should be required to show a certain amount of previous mathematical training? What degree of mathematical training should be considered necessary?
>
> Then I should be glad to hear what sum of money you think would be required to purchase a tolerably complete physical cabinet containing such apparatus as is required for illustrating a course of lectures. Do you think that with an endowment of £200 per annum with the addition of fees to the amount of £60 to £100 we could secure the services of a good man? Is there any way by which a man holding such an office might supplement his income in a place like Manchester?
>
> I understand fully what you said about the difficulty of obtaining a man great in both experiment & in mathematics.
>
> We, in England, have, as you say, no school for physicists & I fear that a mere mathematician* who has only book knowledge of the subject would answer but badly for us. Do you know of any young Cambridge men who might possibly be suitable for the post? I have accidentally heard that a fellow of St John's, Clifton by name, takes a great interest in such pursuits – are you acquainted with him?
>
> Of course one's first idea in Manchester was respecting Joule – but I doubt if he would accept the office.
>
> At any rate the selection will be an open one.

Roscoe was familiar with Joule's achievements before he joined the Lit & Phil in 1858 when Joule was Vice-President. In 1860 Joule became President for the first time. It will be recalled that Joule had advised Stokes on the design of a heat laboratory for Cambridge. From these facts it would be reasonable to infer that Joule and Thomson played a key role, possibly the key role, in the establishment of physics as an autonomous discipline in England.[27] In Scotland natural philosophy was widened to include the new

---

*This does not seem very tactful in view of Stokes's distinguished position as Lucasian Professor of Mathematics.

branches and the old name retained for what was physics in all but name. Roscoe was right about Joule, who wrote to Thomson to explain that

> I have not had the courage to apply for the Owens professorship. The fact is that I do not feel it would do for me to overtask my brain. A few years ago I felt a very small mental effort too much for me, and I in consequence spared myself from thought as much as possible. I have felt a gradual improvement, but I do not think it would be well for me to build too much on it. I shall do a great deal more in the long run by taking things easily. It was a great difficulty for me to forego the place because it is one I would have much liked if I could have fulfilled it.[28]

A fortnight later, on 20 August, Thomson wrote to Roscoe to say that he had been much obliged for the notification about the vacancy at Owens, adding that he had written immediately to Joule to persuade him to come forward but, 'as you have probably learned, he has decided not to'.

R. B. Clifton was duly elected to the Chair.* 'We are fortunate to get so good a man', wrote Roscoe, 'and I shall be very glad to have a physicist near me.'[29] Clifton turned out to be an excellent and successful teacher but he did little research, and after six years moved to Oxford.[30] He was succeeded by William Jack, who stayed for four years before going off to edit a Glasgow newspaper ('I hope a tory one', Joule was to remark). It was the successors, Balfour Stewart and Sir Arthur Schuster, who put Manchester University physics firmly on the path to glory.

While the Owens professorship was being decided Joule was in Northern Ireland. Benjamin, with family affairs settled, had decided to become a landed gentleman and was contemplating buying an estate in County Donegal. Joule was not very impressed:

> A fortnight ago I was within fifty miles of Invercloy, viz, at the Giant's Causeway. I took a rapid survey of Donegal with my brother and Mr Sowler. We were very much more pleased with the country than with the inhabitants. However they might improve on further acquaintance. I did not like to see so many police stations. The weather was fortunately calm enough to allow our taking a boat to look at the waves and headland near the G. Causeway which surpassed anything I had seen before. I was sorry I had not a chance to call on your brother in Belfast, but we had no alternative but to drive straight to the boat for Fleetwood.[31]

On 22 December, Thomson had a serious accident when he fell heavily on the ice while indulging in the sport of curling. In very great pain, he was sedated and chloroformed as the doctors tried to find out whether or not he had fractured his thigh bone. Joule wrote to send his condolences and also

---

*The name 'natural philosophy' was retained. The first professor of physics was Thomas Core, appointed in 1870.

to tell of their impending move to another house, for they had to be out of 'Oak Field' by 25 March:

> Doctors are very fallible as I know to my own cost, but it is happy that nature and a strong constitution frequently defeats their 'exhibitions' and 'diagnoses'. However, we are civilised creatures and can only be allowed to recover 'en régle'. I almost passed through the same myself (in imagination most vividly) when I read in your letter of the Doctors putting you under choloroform in order to find by hearing the bones grate against one another whether there was a fracture. You are all right now but it is most certain that you ought to have been treated for fracture forthwith.[32]

As for finding a new home, they had run into some difficulties: 'It is a remarkable fact that there is scarcely any decent house to be got in the neighbourhood of Manchester. All are occupied. This may make it needful to go where there will not be much room for apparatus.' and he was having problems with Newall and Company:

> I have had a little correspondence with the Newalls, not very pleasant. Knowing that they were merely actuated by a mercenary spirit, I thought it would be well to send them an account of what I had done. After some dispute I got one half what I demanded. You may depend I will have nothing more to do with the Newalls unless I receive a distinct understanding. I think their conduct about the Rangoon cable simply abominable.

A month later his wrath was unappeased. He described the conduct of Newall and Company as 'abominable villainy'. More agreeably, the Joule family had found a new home:

> To turn from this disagreeable subject I may say at length we have got a comfortable home at Old Trafford, near where the exhibition for destroying works of art was placed. I shall be able to put up the air apparatus which is a great comfort as we have a very great deal yet to do with it. I have tried an asbestos plug which serves perfectly well and therefore feel almost sure we can get on with high temperatures. I have been trying oil to find out whether it would do.*[33]

In the previous autumn Joule had given one of his rare public lectures. It had been to the Birkenhead Literary and Scientific Society and the subject was 'The plurality of inhabited worlds'[34] He could neither prove nor disprove the existence of life on other planets; what he could do was to specify carefully the conditions for life to exist. The requirements with respect to temperature range, atmosphere, gravity, and water were as familiar then as they are now. What was, perhaps, novel, was his insistence that the capacity to form communities was essential for higher forms of life

---

*Lubrication would be a serious problem at high temperatures.

for without communities learning was impossible. On the whole he thought Mars the most likely of all the planets to be able to support life, and he accepted that the stars in the galaxy might well have planets capable of sustaining life. The lecture was printed, at the request of his friends in Birkenhead, and a copy sent to Thomson was read in Glasgow.

Joule had particularly enjoyed hearing Nasmyth's paper, read to the Lit & Phil, describing his discovery of a supposed 'leaf' pattern on the surface of the sun.[35] This pattern, Joule thought, might be related in some way to the immense energy radiated by the sun. It was, he believed, the most wonderful thing we had learned in physical science for a long time. But all was not light at the Lit & Phil; there was some heat too. 'Ignorant persons' had tried to hold up reforms proposed by Council,[36] and a proposal that the subscription be raised from £1 5s to £2 2s was opposed by a faction led by the Mayor of Manchester. But the new policy of publishing the *Proceedings* in a separate volume, dear to Joule's heart, coupled with the expense of developing the fine library, 'soon . . . not inferior to any scientific library in the Kingdom',[37] meant that the Society was living beyond its means. However, the increased subscription was approved and the Society remained solvent.

The last letter from 'Oak Field' was at once sad and ominous.[38] Mr Crum, Joule had just learned, had committed suicide. No one, he wrote, should be judged more harshly in such an event than if they had fallen victim of any other mental disease.

> I know from my own feelings that I might do just the same thing myself. That I have not done so is not owing to any strength of mind or superiority of religious feeling but simply that the Almighty has not so willed that my life should terminate. I think most of us would say the same thing of ourselves if we were to accurately scrutinize our feelings.

This second letter of condolence in as many months had to be written amid the turmoil of moving house, made worse by the knowledge that he was 'opposed by our next neighbours in bringing our engine. You may depend that I shall do my best to get it to our new quarters, but I cannot be sure what I can do in the face of legal covenants & c.'

Their new house was called 'Thorncliff', on the Stretford Road, to the south-west of Manchester.* Benjamin, James, Mary and the children moved there with a staff of four servants. Joule could not begin to understand the opposition of the neighbours to the introduction of his

---

*Dodie Smith, the well-known playwright, spent part of her childhood at 'Thorncliff' before the First World War. She recalls that the house stood in a pleasant suburb and that it had a big lawn with a fine willow tree (Dodie Smith, *Look Back with Gratitude* (Muller, London, 1985)).

steam-engine. He was a man of science and the engine was an essential tool in his researches, supported as they were by the Royal Society. With great bitterness he wrote that 'a Mr Bowker, an Alderman of Manchester & Chairman of the nuisances committee, a very important man in his own estimation like most people who have risen from the dregs of society', was the principal opponent.[39] Sir H. de Trafford, the leaseholder, had washed his hands of the affair and referred the protesting Joule to his agent, a Mr Ayres. 'I have half a mind to set them at defiance and put it up', he wrote, 'for I think my opponents dare not enter a court of justice.'[40] He then added, with startling inconsistency:

> But I have a horror of *law* which may almost be considered synonymous with *injustice*. If the experiment yielded me a couple of pounds a day in cash I would certainly feel advised to fight it out. However I think I shall yet beat them another way. I think that they will find that they are incurring an immense amount of odium. The chief thing I have to contend with is the profound ignorance of the rich class in Manchester. They are literally 'know nothings' and worse than that they cannot imagine anyone doing a thing from any but a sordid nature. I am sorry to say it but I am quite certain that during the last 80 years Manchester has declined in every art which is calculated to elevate human nature. This is the natural consequence of the love of money, the root of all evil. It is certainly enough to make me continue a protectionist to find that science suffers in consequence of the increase of the trading spirit and the wealth of the community. I believe the safety of our existence at the head of nations is imperilled in like manner.

These passages, with their sweeping generalisations and collective denunciation, could have been written by any ranting radical. In particular, the comparison with the Manchester of 1781, the year in which the Lit & Phil was founded, was absurd. Joule must have known that the Owens College was beginning to grow in student numbers and in scientific repute. By the beginning of the next century it was to be the best endowed – financially and intellectually – of all the English provincial colleges and superior to any one of those in London. But the invective continued:

> As for the olefiant gas experiment I will try it as soon as I can get rid of the effect of a most villainous attack on me in the neighbourhood and convince the people that the report that my experiments will burn up the vegetation & c & c is an infamous & malicious falsehood. My chief and most unscrupulous opponent is an *Alderman* and a Chairman of a town committee. Two or three of my friends proposed to make a deputation to conciliate him but I declined to be party to any step calculated to increase his self-importance. I shall, I feel confident, gain the day without his help.

Alderman Bowker had a case, although Joule could never have accepted it. Whoever, he might have asked, quite reasonably, heard of a steam-engine being used in a scientific experiment? And even if he could have been reassured on that point he could have argued, plausibly, that if a man of science may have a steam engine why should not an inventive engineer, experimenting with a new design? And thereafter, what would prevent the appearance of vast, smoking mills and factories in what had been a select residential area? As for Joule, the intense frustration of finding himself stopped after nine years of intensive research at the frontiers of knowledge was more than enough to account for his grief and the violence of his language. One thing is perfectly clear: Joule was neither diplomat nor politician. What, his friends must have asked themselves, was to be lost by conciliating Bowker? What was to be gained by refusing to do so?

Sandwiched between the passages denouncing Alderman Bowker, Manchester and the commercial spirit was, in contrast, a temperate paragraph dealing with Thomson's argument with the biologists:*

> I am glad you feel disposed to expose some of the rubbish which has been thrust on the public lately. Not that Darwin is so much to blame because I believe he had no intention of publishing any finished theory but rather to indicate difficulties to be solved and indications to be followed to their consequences. It appears that nowadays the public cares for nothing unless it be of a startling nature. Nothing pleases them more than parsons who find a link between mankind and the monkey in the gorilla – certainly a most pleasing example of what muscular Christianity may lead us to.

A month later he had to admit that he had not got the better of his adversaries.[41] 'Ignorant men', he wrote, 'are generally obstinate likewise.' 'Do you believe', he continued, 'that such a state of affairs existed 100 years ago?' And he came to the rather surprising conclusion that 'science is less thought of now than it has been for some hundreds of years before'; which begged the question how science was to be defined. Even more surprising, in view of his own work, was his belief that one of the causes was that science was more practically useful than it had ever been before. Finally, by 16 August, he accepted defeat: the engine could not be put up.[42] Sir H. de Trafford had convened a meeting to which he and only two others accepted the invitation. The other two had claimed that the mere rumour that a steam-engine was to be in the neighbourhood would depreciate the price of houses by 50%. As he was not a master of rumour he had withdrawn his proposal.

---

*Biologists and palaeontologists had inferred that the earth must be many millions of years old to accommodate the evolution of living species. Darwin estimated that the Weald of Kent, between the North and South Downs, had taken 300 million years to erode. Thomson, arguing on the basis of Fourier's theory and the known thermal properties of the earth, had argued that this was impossibly long. Joule naturally sided with Thomson.

The engine, wrapped in tallow to prevent rust, was in store at the works. He had designed a pump that was to be worked by hand and he gave details of the new asbestos plug (Figure 5 (5)).[43] Joule's plan was that the apparatus was to be run at a very high temperature, for 'I think it would be very desirable for us to get hold of the neutral points for carbonic acid and air.' 'Neutral point' is clearly Joule's expression for the inversion temperature.* He had inferred that as the cooling effects of air and of carbon dioxide steadily diminish with rise in temperature there must come points at which the cooling stops, to be replaced at still higher temperatures by heating effects. The neutral point for hydrogen was inaccessible for Joule and Thomson but the points for air and carbon dioxide were considered to be within experimental range. There was no difficulty in keeping the pipes very hot. The asbestos plug and the new pump could stand high temperatures. And he contemplated using thermocouples in place of mercury-in-glass thermometers. Thomson was therefore asked if he could suggest suitable wires for use in thermocouples at temperatures between 600°F and 700°F.

There were diversions. The 1861 meeting of the British Association was to be in Manchester and, for Joule, attendance was no problem. As it happened this particular meeting turned out to be one of the most fruitful that the Association had ever held. Two telegraph engineers, Sir Charles Bright (knighted after the laying of the first, temporarily successful, Atlantic cable), and Mr Latimer Clark submitted a paper urging the establishment of a universally acceptable standard of electrical resistance. In retrospect it is surprising that a major international project like the Atlantic cable could be undertaken in the absence of a simple, basic unit like the ohm. But such was the case. The entire project was, in engineering terms, empirical in the extreme. Werner Siemens commented that, with characteristic perseverance, the English (*sic*) launched into the new project before the scientific and technological problems had been solved.[44] He was quite right. He knew what he was talking about for his firm had supplied equipment to the cable-makers Newall & Co.

Further discussion showed that it would be necessary to establish (1) a unit of electromotive force, or tension, or potential; (2) a unit of absolute electrical quantity, or of static electricity; (3) a unit of electrical current, formed by the combination of the unit of quantity with the unit of time; and (4) a unit of electrical resistance which would be the same unit as that of current and defined by a wire that would carry a unit of quantity of

---

*Thomson's inversion temperature (33° on the old theory) was necessarily the same for all gases.

electricity in a unit time.[45] In addition a nomenclature was needed to adapt the system to the requirements of practical telegraphists. They therefore suggested that the unit of resistance might be called the 'ohmad'. (4) seems, at first sight, absurd. But, as Lynch points out Bright and Clark were concerned not with absolute units but with standards analogous to the standard yard and the standard pound weight.[46] Therefore the standard length of wire would have unit resistance and would define the unit emf that would send a unit current through it. The General Committee of the Association responded by co-opting A. W. Williamson, Charles Wheatstone, William Thomson, W. H. Miller, A. Mathiessen and Fleeming Jenkin on to a committee to report on electrical standards; £50 was put at their disposal to cover expenses.

There had been previous suggestions for the establishment of electrical standards. Given lengths of specified wire had been proposed for standards of resistance; Werner Siemens, more reasonably, had favoured a spiral glass tube of agreed diameter and length, filled with mercury, which was more easily obtainable in the pure state than any other metal. Joule had proposed that the unit quantity of electricity would be that which would dissociate nine grains, or the electrochemical equivalent of water, while the unit current would be that quantity flowing in one hour. This was a fundamental unit in that it related electrical measurement to the laws of electrolysis. Published in the failing *Annals of Electricity*, however, the idea was soon forgotten. The best basis for a set of units, one that could certainly be called absolute, was put forward by Wilhelm Weber in 1851. Following Gauss's seminal contribution to the magnetic crusade,[47] Weber saw how current, resistance and electromotive force could be expressed in units of length, mass and time; or, in other words, based on the principles of mechanics. Thomson took the point. Arbitrary units were unavoidable in the measurement of length, mass and time, but once these had been agreed electrical units expressed in these three dimensions could fairly be considered absolute for they would have no reference to arbitrary measures such as the emf of a Daniell cell. In his paper of December 1851, Thomson had expressed electrical measures in Weber's absolute units and related them to Joule's laws of electrical energy.

The committee decided that the main requirements were that the unit of resistance should, together with the other units, form a complete system of electrical measures; all the units in the system should bear a definite relation to the unit of work, 'the great connecting link between all physical measurements' (*sic*); the unit of resistance must be quite definite and not require correction from time to time; it must be easily and exactly reproducible, and it should be based on the metric system.[48]

In this way the ideas of Weber and of Joule were, through Thomson's understanding, united to form the basis for a rational system of electrical units that, with progressive modifications, was to lead to the SI system and to provide the rationale for every electricity bill in the world. But much work had to be done before the system could be satisfactorily completed. What is quite clear is that Thomson and his fellow committee members were about 100 years ahead of their compatriots in seeing the advantages of the French metric system.

The British Association meeting over, Joule travelled up to Scotland to stay with Thomson on the Isle of Arran. He had hoped to travel up with Mathiessen, whom he had met at the meeting, but 'he hates the sea which I love'.[49] After this Joule went over to Northern Ireland with his brother Benjamin who, earlier in the year, had paid £6,500 for a stretch of country-side and coastline of County Donegal together with Tory island, ten miles out in the wild Atlantic. At the end of September Roscoe received a letter from Joule, written from Dunlewy, in Donegal, making some suggestions about the organisation of the Lit & Phil Council following Fairbairn's sudden resignation and explaining that he was to have his love of the sea put to the test for he had 'to go over to Tory island, 10 miles from the mainland in a small boat and it is a matter of uncertainty, when the weather may permit our return'.[50] Nine days later he gave fuller details of his trip to his beloved Frances Charlotte:

My dearest Fanny   Thorncliff,
                                                    October 5, 1861

I am afraid you will think me negligent in writing but I have been where it was almost impossible to post a letter under any circumstances and besides you gave me absolution in such circumstances. I have just arrived after our expedition, safe and sound I am thankful to say. Benjamin and I sailed on last Sunday but one to Belfast & thence by train to L'derry, thence to L'kenny [Letterkenny] by car in a deluge of rain to Dunlewy House (You can't think how pleasant it is to ride in an open carriage for 4 hours with the rain pouring down all the while). Dr Brady's house is really splendidly situated – the view on every side most magnificent with lake, mountain, wood and waterfall. There are sundry little inconveniences notwithstanding, for instance you must go 10 miles to buy a loaf of bread. However he had furnished a table in the wilderness & we had capital cheer, besides there were some wild Irish girls (now you need not be jealous) and we had a good deal of merriment in the evening when there. We had to wait for the weather to get to Tory island and thus had an opportunity of ascending Errigal, 2,600 feet above the sea. On the summit I heard the roar of the sea quite distinctly (10 miles off). There was a very splendid view of a great part of Donegal. The top of the mountain is quite sharp, a precipice on each side. The next day we tried to get to Tory, got up at 5, got to the strand at 10 and engaged a boat. But the wind having got up to a hurricane, though in a favourable direction, the boatmen would not venture to take us. So we returned, sitting in a cart with some straw in it, jolting over 4 hours in heavy rain and wind. This was however better than being food for fishes! We waited till last Tuesday before we got a chance of good weather. On that day we got off and had a splendid passage. 1½ hours to the island, the wind being favourable though there was a considerable swell on the ocean. Tory had not been visited by any strangers since Benjamin was there last. People are not very fond of venturing 10 miles in the Atlantic in an open boat. We walked to our house at the end of the island carrying with us bread, tea, meat & c from the mainland. The natives got us beds to put on the floor. The people were assembled in a room each day and business was transacted with them as far as it could be done by an interpreter.[51]

The rest of the letter is, unfortunately, missing. On the same day Joule wrote, rather more scientifically but hardly less graphically, to Thomson. He began with a rather strange acknowledgement:

I have only just received your letter enclosing the half of a £5 note for which I thank you. There was no possibility of forwarding the post to my variable locality in Donegal. When I wrote to you from Dunlewy we were waiting for the weather to get to Tory. We went once to the beach, a 2 hour drive (*sic*), but the weather was such that the boatmen would not venture and we returned in a cart, a 4 hour journey in rain & wind. The next time we were more fortunate and got to the island in 1 hour 25′, no bad sailing for a small boat. Tory island is a remarkable place and no one can be said to have been through Ireland without having trod its shores, consisting of perpendicular rocks of felspar and granite 300 feet high. It is however a very possible contingency that when once there one may be detained for 5 weeks for if there is a N wind the sea is too high, if a S the boatmen cannot contend against it. We luckily got a medium sea in a S.W. gale on Thursday and got on mainland again after enduring some risk for 5 hours. The boat was a model of symmetry, 22 feet long, six broad and 2:6 deep at midships, 3 in 6 at ends,* pointed at both ends. Two low masts. We shipped no water to speak of. Waves 4 to 600 feet from crest to crest and 20 feet high. Dr Brady who was with us and had yachted in the ocean for 25 years said he never was in a more dangerous sea. However the magnificence of it took away the disagreeable sense of danger which might have prevailed. We saw a seal and landed just when landing had become practicable by the rise of the tide and the consequent absence of breakers which before had been over the channel . . . and all along the coast.[52]

It is doubtful if Joule ever visited Tory island again. It did not prove a satisfactory investment for Benjamin. The islanders were a canny lot as

---

*It is not clear what the last two figures mean. They could be interpreted as 3 in. 6 lines, or 3½ in.

well as remarkably inaccessible. Benjamin, or rather his agent, had great difficulty in collecting rents and it seems that after 1872 no more rents were forthcoming.[53] In 1883 Benjamin reproduced, in a short pamphlet, the exchange of letters, originally printed in the *Liverpool Daily Post*, between himself and the priest on Tory island, Father James J. O'Donnell, CC.[54] Exaggeration was a feature on both sides. Benjamin accused the Catholic Bishops of being Communists (!), while the Father asserted that the islanders had been reduced to eating seaweed. On the whole, writes an evidently fair-minded scholar, Benjamin got the better of the argument, if not of the rents.[55]

While Benjamin was settling, as he hoped, his Irish estate, Joule was busy completing the last joint paper on the heating effects of fluids in motion, to be published in the *Philosophical Transactions* in 1862. From Joule's extensive and reliable data Thomson derived an empirical law, that the cooling effect per unit pressure difference varied as the inverse square of the absolute temperature. Joule wrote:

> I am most pleased with your success in getting a law for the air experiments. It will, however, if true to high temperatures, defeat my expectation of finding a point where the thermal effect vanishes. However we must try the higher temperatures which will at any rate enable you to verify the law of the thermal effect more decisively.[56]

He seems to have had second thoughts about this law, for a week later he wrote to say that he had found a markedly better agreement in the case of carbon dioxide on the 'I suppose inadmissible' hypothesis that the effect varied as the temperature measured from $-200°$ and not $-273°C$.[57] Obviously it was inadmissible, for nothing further was heard of the hypothesis although it appears that they were contemplating further work on the problem.

In Manchester the Lit & Phil was flourishing. Joule was particularly proud of the library. It was, he claimed, the most cheerful thing about the relative state of science in Manchester that he could report,[58] and he was not particularly cheerful about the state of affairs in London, referring as he did to 'our friend Tyndall's moonshine' at the Royal Institution.* He himself was working over some old results of experiments on the formation of amalgams of iron, copper, silver, platinum and zinc; the resulting paper was read before a meeting of the Lit & Phil.[59]

World affairs, in particular the outbreak of the Civil War in the United States, impinged briefly on his interest. Imagination fades with distance.

---

*This was a punning reference to Tyndall's ideas about the temperature of the surface of the moon.

Joule wrote, coldly, 'I think the best possible state of things is for the States to fight one another till they are all separate like the legs of a starfish. Therefore I hope we wont go to war with them. Messrs Cobden and Bright ought now to go and take their sides with their chosen friends.'[60] In holding this view he was very much at odds with Manchester opinion which strongly supported the Northern States, despite the suffering caused in the textile areas by the cotton famine that resulted from the Northern blockade of Southern ports. Four months later he expressed a more magnanimous, and surprisingly modern, point of view:

> What a hubbub about iron plated ships! It seems to me quite clear that if our navy is reconstructed with 5 inch plates it will have to be reconstructed in a year or two with 10 inch plates and so on. It is a pitiful thing to see going on in the year of grace 1862 and although I am no disciple of Bright I would much prefer the enormous outlay to be diverted to the purposes of constructing huge telescopes or gigantic voltaic batteries.[61]

Early in 1862 Thomson submitted a short paper to the Lit & Phil. It was read by Joule on 21 January, under the title, 'On the convective equilibrium of temperature in the atmosphere'.[62] If, the argument ran, the radiation and conduction of heat in the atmosphere are ignored (and the latter is known to be extremely small), then any movement of air upwards or downwards will be accompanied by an appropriate change in temperature due to the expansion or compression of the air. Erasmus Darwin, it was noted, had used this phenomenon to account for climatic stability at different heights of the Great Andes of the equator. The explanation, however, was incomplete; cold descending air, heated by compression, would soon tend to expand and so stop in its descent; hot rising air, cooled by expansion, would soon stop in its ascent. Furthermore, actual measurements of the fall in temperature with altitude (about 530 ft for a drop of 1°C) were far less than predicted by this theory (329 ft for 1°C). There must therefore be a hidden source of heat to fuel the continued ascent of rising air. Joule suggested that it came from the condensation of vapour in the ascending air.[63] As warm, moist air rises and the temperature begins to fall, due to the expansion of the air, so the moisture tends to condense and in doing so releases latent heat that counters the cooling effect and maintains the temperature of the air. This was an extension of Dalton's idea that clouds were due to condensation caused by the cooling of rising air. Thomson adopted Joule's suggestion and added a calculation to his paper showing that such a mechanism would, indeed, produce enough heat to account for the reduced rate of cooling and the continued ascent of warm, moist air.

Although it is a well-established fact that some of the greatest advances
in science and technology have been due to 'outsiders' there can be no
guarantee that the outsider will bring wholly novel ideas to the field into
which he ventures. He will not, usually, know much of the background, of
the literature, and he may end up by announcing a discovery or an invention
that has already been made. This was the case with Joule's theory of the
continued ascent of warm, moist air. The same idea had been proposed
some twenty years earlier by the American meteorologist James P. Espy in
his *Philosophy of Storms* (1842). Espy also explained the formation of
hailstones in rapidly ascending currents of air in thunderstorms. Joule
should have known – and possibly did know – of Espy's work: it was
reviewed in Sturgeon's *Annals* (vol. 5, n.d., p. 442). And Joule and Thomson are open to criticism for their failure to acknowledge Tyndall's important work on the radiation and absoroption of heat by gases. Relations
between Thomson and Tyndall had, as we saw, been cool for some years;
soon they were to become as icy as Erasmus Darwin's Andean peaks.

With or without knowledge of Espy's earlier work, Joule went on to
speculate about the mechanism of thunderstorms. As warm air ascends its
moisture condenses and, as the process continues, the moisture will freeze.
The frozen moisture will fall, either as snow or as hail. Joule considered
that 'The fall of hail is mysterious. I never knew an instance in which it was
not accompanied by lightning; and I think the reverse may be stated – that
in thunderstorms hail either falls to the ground or exists in the upper
regions (evidenced by the largeness and coldness of the drops of rain).'[64]
He had, in fact, a plausible theory of the mechanism of thunderstorms.[65]
Considering a region about a hundred miles across, he envisaged air
descending on the left and ascending on the right to generate the thunderstorms. The air, drawn over the warm land towards the thunderstorm,
picks up moisture as it goes along. As it rises in the storm it gives out the
latent heat of its moisture which condenses and freezes. The air is now dry
and the water is in the form of ice particles. Friction between the particles
and the dry air generates electricity. The particles are thrown out from the
most rapid uprush of air, continuing the electrification process as they fall;
many of them will be carried up again and in this way a massive charge is
built up until, at last, a lightning flash takes place, lowering the charge to
earth. Where, and in what manner, the charge is located is not clear; nor, as
Joule admitted, are various other details. But the outline picture Joule drew
for Thomson bears a resemblance to the diagram in a modern standard
work.

Unless it is true that the Victorians worked much harder than we do
today (which is not difficult to believe), it is probable that Thomson was

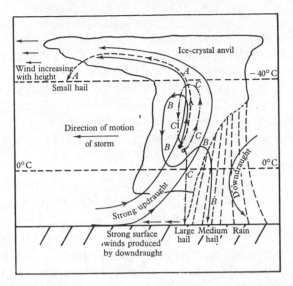

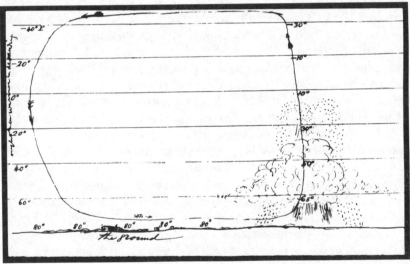

Fig. 7 (Below) Joule's idea of the mechanism of a thunderstorm, from a letter to Thomson in 1862 (Cambridge University Library), compared with (*above*) a modern interpretation (reproduced by kind permission from Sir John Mason's *Clouds, Rain and Rainmaking*, 1962 edn, Cambridge University Press). Joule's temperatures are, of course, in degrees Fahrenheit

unusually industrious, which is easy to believe. Apart from his teaching and other academic obligations at the University, he had been involved from the beginning in the work of the British Association Committee on Electrical Units. It was his rotating coil that the Committee members were to use in their experiments, carried out at King's College, London, and he was to design a current balance for them.[66] Furthermore, the Atlantic Telegraph Company was bestirring itself; the government had advanced money and given certain guarantees. As if this were not enough Thomson was acting as a juryman for the Great Exhibition that was to be held in London in the summer of 1862. '

Thomson tried to persuade Joule to participate in the Exhibition by acting as an associate juryman, but Joule declined. Had he known Thomson was to be a juryman he might have agreed, even though he had disagreeable memories of the 1851 Exhibition. He thought his solid piston might be worth exhibiting and he was quite sure that Mr Dancer's instruments were well worth putting on display: 'There are few instrument makers to whom science is more deeply indebted than to Mr Dancer and I am sure what he has sent is the best of its kind. I myself would have been frequently at a dead loss but for him.'[67] But as for acting as a juryman, associate or otherwise, it was now too late. In any case he had personal problems. His brother Arthur, living on the Isle of Man, was ill and although he had rallied and was much better it was difficult to know how long the improvement would last. A personal problem of a different nature involved his relations with his fellow men of science. Over the years he had, in his letters to Thomson, been critical of, sometimes clearly hostile towards, Tyndall while, at the same time, keeping on friendly terms with him. Joule can be fairly accused of duplicity or hypocrisy. But effective human relations are hardly possible without at least a modicum of hypocrisy. And, moreover, he was doing no more than giving support to his friend and valued ally, Thomson. The roots of Thomson's hostility to Tyndall went back to the quarrel between Tyndall and Forbes about the cause of glacier motion, and perhaps further. There was no sign that the breach had healed.

Providence has been kind to Scotland. The country is beautiful and the Scots are a highly gifted people. Among their many gifts are military virtues that are necessarily associated with pugnacity and it was this quality that was to become conspicuous in the following few years. On the other side Tyndall was an Irishman and the Irish are, proverbially, always happy to join in a fight, unless it is a strictly private one. The immediate occasion was Tyndall's lecture on energy, delivered at the Royal Institution. At the end of the lecture he ascribed the energy doctrine to the labours of 'a German physician named Mayer'.[68] He praised Joule's contribution but he stressed Mayer's work because, he believed, Mayer had been unfairly neglected; personal misfortune and academic persecution had led to a mental breakdown; now he was isolated, a cultivator of his vineyard in Heilbronn. Joule, on reading an account of Tyndall's lecture, wrote to Thomson to say that although he was sorry to hear of Mayer's misfortune he felt constrained to write a few lines to the *Philosophical Magazine*, as temperately as he could, to set the record straight.[69] He added:

> I think the walls of the Royal Institution might be almost expected to cry out against the neglect by the present professor of Davy and of Thomas Young. To the former, the ablest man who ever belonged to the Inst[n], the merit surely belongs of making an experiment decisively in favour of the dynamical theory.

This was a revealing comment. The reference can only be to Davy's famous ice-cube experiment; an experiment that Joule would surely have dismissed as wholly inconclusive had it been quoted by, say, Mayer. Davy was important for his authority as a man of science, not for the value of this particular experiment. And it is notworthy that Joule, by implication, dismisses Faraday as less able than Davy; an opinion that few men of science, even then, would have supported.

Daub has shown that Tyndall's target was not Joule, but Thomson. Tyndall had succeeded Faraday in the Chair at the Royal Institution, the most exalted appointment in physical science at that time; Faraday had made it so. But according to Daub, everywhere Tyndall went, in the UK, in France, in Germany, the acknowledged authority to whom everyone deferred was Thomson. It is not difficult to imagine how galling this may have been to a man who was a distinguished physicist in a most distinguished position. We may even guess that Thomson may have been a little difficult to live with, scientifically speaking. From his youth onward Thomson's record was one of unbroken success to the days when he could take the other leader of world physics, Hermann von Helmholtz, cruising to the Western Isles in his yacht, the *Lallah Rookh* (for which Thomson had headed notepaper printed: a certain indicator of success) and beyond that to the time when he became Baron Kelvin of Largs, the first man ever to be raised to the peerage purely for his scientific attainments; and, finally, to the day when he received the Order of Merit, one of the first small group to be so honoured. All things considered, William Thomson was one of the most successful men of the Victorian age.[70] Such a man would be a challenge to the naturally competitive like Tyndall, particularly if there was the added provocation of a quarrel of long standing.

Speculation about personalities apart, the evidence supports the Daub thesis, and further confirmation comes from a letter Joule wrote to Tyndall only twelve days after the lecture:

> I thank you for your kindness in sending me the second part of your admirable researches on radiation and absorption of heat by gases and vapours. It is almost impossible to exaggerate their interest as setting forth original facts of most extensive application to the phenomena of nature. I thank you also for your Royal Inst[n] lecture on the subject of which you will see I have made one or two remarks in the Phil. Mag[ne]. I think that in a case like that of the Equivalent of Heat the experimental worker rather than the mere logical reasoner (however valuable the latter) must be held as the establisher of a theory. I have determined the mechanical equivalent in nearly a dozen ways, and the figure I arrived at in 1849 has not yet been altered or corrected. Mr Dyer of this town was, I believe, the first man who noticed the rise in temp[e] in shaking water,* but he applied it to nothing – in fact explained away what he saw.
>   Believe me, Dear Tyndall,
>   Yours always truly,
>   J. P. Joule.[71]

He had suited his style to his correspondent and it is impossible to gauge where his true feelings lay. He reserved his judgement, merely reporting to Thomson what he had heard from Tyndall and adding that he did not think he would write again, whatever Tyndall might say.[72] Verdet had just sent him his book in which there were many things 'that are fair and just' concerning the dynamical theory. Later in the year the elderly Marc Séguin wrote to thank him for the way in which, in his reply to Tyndall, he had justly acknowledged the work that others – including Marc Séguin himself and his great uncle Joseph Montgolfier – had done in trying to establish the dynamical theory of heat.[73] At the Cambridge meeting of the British Association that autumn Tyndall had, according to Joule, given 'a discourse which would have done well for the Polytechnic'.[74] There the matter rested.

Apart from some work on boiler-testing, 1862 was a fallow year.[75] There had been a fire at the works, the floor had been badly burned and the engine in store had fallen through to the ground floor.[76] There had been a squabble at the Lit & Phil involving Binney.[77] Arthur had been ill again and both Joule and Benjamin had had to go over to the Isle of Man. But more interesting than these little incidents was P. G. Tait's request to Joule for an autobiographical note. Tait, professor of natural philosophy in Edinburgh University and a most combative gentleman, was to play an active part in the dispute that was brewing up between Tyndall and Thomson. Joule

---

*Once again Dr Reade had been forgotten.

expressed the opinion to Thomson that he did not 'like the fashion but it is becoming very usual to write accounts of living people'.[78] Nevertheless, he expressed his gratitude to Tait and added: 'Lives of scientific men are generally uneventful and mine you will find particularly so, and uninteresting. One is born, writes a few papers, experiences a succession of cares and disappointments and pleasures common to all, and then is no more found.'[79] He was grateful to the Lit & Phil: 'My intercourse with its members and the very excellent and able men whom the institution of Owens College has brought into the City has been a source of much advantage and gratification to me. I am a Conservative and a member of the Church of England.' Perhaps the most revealing sentence was the last. Is there a slight note of defiance about it? One should not assume that everyone in Manchester votes Liberal, attends a Nonconformist chapel and carries two umbrellas.

Running through Joule's active life was a continuing counterpoint of scientific observations, suggestions, innovations, and improvements. Some of these were published in *Manchester Memoirs* and republished in the collected *Scientific papers*; others never went further than private letters to friends. This is a pity for they show, in personal terms, what it was like to be a man of science; and, perhaps, what every young would-be scientist should try to be like today. He read a short account of his new air-pump to a meeting of the Lit & Phil and, to another meeting, described a mirage, seen from Douglas in the Isle of Man, where he had been visiting his ailing brother. In February 1863 he told the Society of a simple, yet extremely sensitive barometer he had invented.[80] It could be made of materials to be found in any home or school. But perhaps the most intriguing of his inventions at this time was one that he used to challenge Tyndall. In March 1863 Joule wrote to Thomson to say that he had been amply revenged on Tyndall for 'I find that the moon is *hot*, not *cold* as he pretended[81] and', he added, 'If you find space you and Tait must add something to your book* on the *wind* produced by the action of our satellite.' He had made a simple, but highly effective thermoscope that registered a 5° swing as a shaft of moonlight passed over it. (But this included reflected heat.)

Less than three weeks later Joule wrote a very friendly letter to Tyndall to thank him for his kindness in sending him copies of his papers.[82] Joule was sorry he had nothing important to send in return. He did, however, enclose the latest number of the *Proceedings* of the Lit & Phil: 'in which I profess to have detected the heat radiated by the moon by means of a sort of wind

---

*This was the *Treatise of Natural Philosophy* (1867), that Thomson and Tait had, in 1862, decided to write. It is discussed below.

thermometer. Our Secretary, Mr Baxendall, says that M . . . had observed the same thing but I have not yet been able to refer to his paper.' This was hardly ample revenge! He commented on the

> lucubrations of one of our local luminaries, Mr Dyer . . . I have disputed (with Mr Dyer) on these matters for a good share of 20 years but now he seems to be attacking higher game. I daresay you will not think it worthwhile to write or reply to his observations.[83] I once invited him to go with me to Niagara and offered to pay our joint expenses if a higher temperature was not found at the bottom than at the top of the falls.

Was it, perhaps, a slight feeling of guilt, or of unease, that caused him to transfer his criticisms from Tyndall to the scientifically insignificant J. C. Dyer?

It was in character for Joule to take refuge in a very minor dispute when the great national debate, soon to degenerate into a row, with Tyndall on the one side and Thomson and Tait on the other, was raging. The article by Thomson and Tait in *Good Words*, a popular journal of the time, ensured that the arguments would be heard – and shared in – by a much wider public than the members of the Royal Institution, the Lit & Phil and the senior common rooms of Edinburgh and Glasgow universities. Whatever the tensions, however deep the hostilities of the time, Joule became very silent. Perhaps it was because of his dislike of public controversies;[84] perhaps it was a consequence of private personal troubles. Whatever the cause he published notably fewer papers and the number of letters he wrote to Thomson and other friends fell sharply over the period 1863–6.

Thomson invited him up to stay in the new year of 1864.[85] There were some new things Thomson wanted to show him, notably 'electric clocks controlled from the Observatory, of which one is this moment being set up in my lecture room. Our College Tower clock has been so for three weeks now, and the first stroke of every hour is correct to within a small fraction of a second to true Greenwich mean time.'* But some weeks later, writing to Margaret Thomson to thank her for her kind letter, Joule added:

> We were prepared for a long time for our loss which nevertheless, as is always the case, came as a shock. My poor brother had suffered a long time from some hidden mischief in the brain which although it did not produce the distressing symptoms of mental aberration made fatal inroads on his strength. I had a letter on the Sunday when I was with you which made me uneasy although it merely said he was not so well again. However, had I left you then I could not by any

---

*Apart from the technical achievement of setting up a system of accurate master and slave clocks, this remark is interesting in that Thomson refers not to 'railway time', but to Greenwich mean time.

possibility have reached the island before the fatal scene. John has left a family of four children, three girls and a boy aged from 5 to 11.[86]

He then gave Mrs Thomson some useful advice on the best way of making small deflecting magnets.

Since 1863 Joule had been a member of the British Association Committee on electrical units. It was on behalf of this Committee that, from 1865, he worked on the electrical determination of the mechanical equivalent of heat. The idea was simple and straightforward. The heat generated by a current flowing through a resistance should, expressed in mechanical units, *equal* i^2r, where both i and r are measured in the same units; the first by means of a tangent galvanometer, the second by comparison with the standard BA ohm, determined by the experiments at King's College.[87] All Joule had to do was to divide the heat generated by an electric current by i^2r, expressed in mechanical units. The result should be equal to his classic determination of the mechanical equivalent of heat (1849). This would confirm the accuracy of the BA ohm and bring the new system of electrical units into harmony with the dynamical theory of heat and the energy doctrine.

Joule's experiments to confirm the accuracy of the BA ohm had, of necessity, to be carried out as accurately and carefully as those conducted by Maxwell and his colleagues at King's College. They took him the greater part of two years to complete. Daniell cells provided the current that flowed through a coil of wire whose resistance had been carefully measured in terms of the standard unit sent him by the British Association. The coil of wire was immersed in a gallon of distilled water in a copper calorimeter and elaborate precautions were taken to prevent heat losses. Having calculated the energy (i^2r) and measured the heat produced in the calorimeter he divided the former by the latter. The result came out to within 1/200th of the value he got in 1849, which was considered very satisfactory. The measurements were reported to the 1866 meeting of the British Association at Nottingham, but they were not published.[88] Unfortunately he had relied on the Kew measurement of the earth's magnetic field (H), which was, he found, smaller than in his locality; and the higher Manchester value made the mechanical equivalent come out at 792 foot.pounds.[89] He suggested to Fleeming Jenkin that perhaps the resistance, as measured by Maxwell and his colleagues, was higher than it should have been due to the inductive effect of the alternating current.[90] But Jenkin had Thomson's assurance that there could be no error from this source. Joule therefore went back to his apparatus to improve it as far as possible. The water in the calorimeter was now stirred by clockwork, the lagging was improved and the strength of the earth's magnetic field measured systematically, for it had been found to vary from day to day as well as from place to place. The new determination of the mechanical equivalent was 782 foot.pounds, closer to the 1849 figure, derived from experiments on fluid friction, but still not entirely satisfactory.[91] The published report of the Committee nevertheless accepted the figure of 783 (*sic*) foot.pounds and quoted Joule as saying that the electrical method 'has been carried out with greater accuracy than the frictional method, assuming the B.A. standard to be an exact decimal multiple of the absolute unit'. The report added that 'Dr Joule expresses himself willing to make a new determination by friction.'[92] With great candour Joule suggested to Thomson that someone else should carry out the required experiments in order to eliminate any bias on his part. But, he added: 'I don't think anything will be found more simple than the friction of water.'[93] This was not inconsistent with his statement to the British Association.

Joule was always willing to change his mind in the light of scientific evidence, and sometimes in the light of scientific authority; but on one issue he was quite unwilling to change. The Committee had insisted, from the beginning, that the absolute units must be expressed in metric measures. Joule would have none of it; in the matter of units he remained a stubborn conservative. With some zeal he mustered arguments in favour of Imperial measures. He noted that the 'Imperial cubic foot' of water weighed, at maximum density, 999.32 British Imperial ounces avoirdupois.[94] This had been fixed in 1823,

> But if Sir George Schuckburgh's grains had been adhered to the weight would have been 999.73 ounces. Could anything possibly be more convenient than to make one cubic foot contain exactly 1,000 ounces of water? And if we made 10 inches to the foot we should have an ounce to the cubic inch. Surely this is as good as the French system. I know you will think me a heretic, but I am firmly convinced that it will be impossible to make ¾ of the globe adopt the metre which is now only very particularly adopted in continental Europe. Surely so exact an approximation to an exact number cannot be fortuitous.

A little later he wrote to Cromwell Varley, a member of the Committee, deprecating any new words (such as 'ohm') and railing against the metric system.[95] And he found further support for the Imperial measures when he worked out that the diameter of the earth's orbit was nearly a billion feet.* What more could one ask?

A few days later his conservatism showed itself in quite a different context:

---

*He did not say whether the diameter in question was the major or the minor axis of the earth's elliptic orbit or whether it was the average diameter.

If you [Thomson] read Bright's speech at Rochdale you will see that he says that in England corporations are elected almost by universal suffrage while in Scotland they are elected only by those who can vote for MPs. But, says Bright, 'I never knew that corporations in England are a bit less efficient than similar bodies in Scotland.' Blind, violently prejudiced man! Is it not notorious that nearly every corporation of the larger towns of England is the object of the derision and contempt of all intelligent and respectable inhabitants! As for our own I am sure that it has almost destroyed public spirit. This must always be the case when the lowest of the community are placed in a domineering position. The lowering of the franchise with which we are threatened will inevitably do the same for the empire that it has done, in municipal bodies, for the towns.[96]

And he added, with some inconsistency, 'Our Owens College is about to apply for means to extend its usefulness and to build a new house. I hope they may get the money. Certainly they ought to do, for Manchester is considered to be richer than Glasgow.'

Joule could no more resist the tide of municipal and parliamentary enfranchisement than he could resist the acceptance of the metric system by the Committee which had taken care to consult continental colleagues. Weber was involved in the project from the beginning as was Werner Siemens whose engineer, Esselbach, had, like Joule, joined the Committee in 1863. From its inception the Committee took the advice of four German professors, in addition to Siemens and Weber, one Swede, one American, one Frenchman and one Italian. With the probable exception of Dr Henry, of Washington, it was virtually certain that the overwhelming weight of overseas opinion would favour the metric system.

Joule showed a more liberal side of his nature when he wrote:

We have had very much fever in Manchester and of a malignant kind. How can it be otherwise when the poor are thrust from the houses to be pulled down for improvements to crowd into already overcrowded houses. Instead of lowering the franchise to £7 would it not be better to put the people into £10 houses. I fear that this remark may be applied to many of our agitators & legislators: 'not that he cared for the poor'.[97]

In Joule's opinion, then, the lowest of the community were not the poorest.

A few months later he was concerned about Margaret Thomson's health. She was now Lady Thomson for her husband had been knighted in October 1866, on the successful completion of the Atlantic telegraph. His solicitude also revealed his parochialism:

I think it most fortunate she did not try Mentone. What could possess a medical man to send his patients to a place where the winds may alternate between the deserts of Sahara and the Alpine snows I cannot imagine. The climate of Devon or Cornwall must be infinitely preferable.[98]

He had been invited to act as a juryman at the Paris Exhibition of 1867, 'which would have been very pleasant', but he had to decline as he was too busy. Nevertheless, he accepted an invitation to stay with the Thomsons over Easter. Before he went he had a confession to make:

> Besides other things which weigh on me an affection has sprung up between me and my cousin you saw when last here. There are hindrances in the way so that nothing may come of it. But I cannot allow anything which occupied so much of my thoughts to be unknown to my dearest friend, in confidence I need not say.[99]

This was written five years after that affectionate letter to dearest Fanny. Joule was nothing if not discreet in his personal affairs.

11

Syntheses

The work of the British Association Committee on Standards of Electrical Resistance was immensely valuable to the whole of physical science and to much else as well. The world's energy business is now carried out in the currency the Committee devised. Of course there were progressive refinements as the Committee met, year after year, up to 1914, and, no doubt, the process of correction and improvement will continue into the future. But in addition to this the Committee – which attracted to its service some of the best talents of a highly gifted age – helped to bring about radical changes in physical science and its procedures. Maxwell, in a contribution to the Committee, wrote a lucid paper on units and dimensions. No longer were measurements to be expressed in arbitrary units, or relationships in terms of proportions; furthermore, equations must be dimensionally homogeneous.[1] Following the naming of the ohm, the ampère, the volt, and the watt were established, although not always as we accept them today. *Pace* Joule, before the end of the century the joule was named by the Committee; it is now the internationally accepted name for the unit of energy. Even in a relatively minor matter, the Committee helped to establish and popularise the familiar circuit diagram with its straight lines representing wires and symbols for batteries, capacitors, resistances, inductances, transformers, etc., in place of the old quasi-realistic illustrations of complete voltaic cells, coils of wires, galvanometers, and so on, often with a severed hand holding, or pointing to, an appropriate component. Finally, it should be noted that in 1865 Maxwell, a most active member of the Committee, published his classic paper on the dynamical theory of the electromagnetic field, the keystone of which was the relationship between electromagnetic and electrostatic units. The ratio of these units involved a factor having the dimensions of a velocity and the same numerical value as the velocity of light. It would be no great exaggeration to say that physics, as we know it, began at this time. All this, however, belongs to the general history of physics and electrical engineering as well as to the philosophy of science and to economic history. It is enough to say that it originated with the practical requirement of two telegraph engineers and that Joule's first major contribution to the Committee had been made twenty years before it was set up when he demonstrated the connection between electricity and magnetism on the one hand and mechanical energy and heat on the other. The connection with Manchester was fortuitous: the Committee could as well have been set up at Oxford (1860) or at Cambridge (1862).

On the other hand a work that unquestionably bears the hallmark of Manchester was the book that W. Stanley Jevons published in 1865. Jevons (1835–82), like his cousin H. E. Roscoe, studied chemistry at University College, London. After a spell in Australia, working as an assayer, he returned to England and, in 1862, took an M.A. in logic, moral philosophy and political economy at University College. This led to his appointment as tutor and later professor at Owens College. His book had the comprehensive title: *The Coal Question: An Inquiry Concerning the Progress of the Nation and the Probable Exhaustion of Our Coal Mines.* The work amounted to the first recognition of a potential – and according to Jevons an inevitable – energy crisis. It could not have been written before Joule's work had been generally accepted. The last five words of the title echo Joule's words to Thomson seven years earlier when he was expressing alarm about the heavy consumption of coal by steamships. There can be no reasonable doubt that Jevons was, through Roscoe if from no other source, acquainted with Joule's experiments and ideas.[2]

And, to be fair, the book could not have been written before the geological survey had been carried out and before the Mining Records Office had been established. The former, together with the progress of geology, made possible a reasonable estimate of the economically recoverable coal reserves of the country; the latter's records, going back over twenty years, showed that every year Britain mined $3\frac{1}{2}\%$ more coal than in the previous year. By very simple arithmetic Jevons proved that by 1965 Britain should be mining more coal annually than lay under the ground. This was impossible; long before 1965 the rate of extraction would be bound to fall. And even if the annual rate of increase dropped to $2\frac{1}{2}\%$, the crossover point at which a decline in the rate of extraction began would be deferred by only a few years. The awful problem was that, by 1865, Britain's prosperity had become coal-dependent. The rapidly growing, and now vital, railways depended on cheap coal as did more and more cotton and woollen mills, foundries and forges, metal works and manufactures generally, flour mills, breweries and even such services as canals, gasworks and waterworks.

What alternatives were there? The indestructible atom* represented the limit of chemistry; above the level of the atom we knew enough about chemical reactions to know that there was no alternative to the simple process of combustion. Electricity, dominant physical science of the mid-nineteenth century, on which great hopes had been built, offered no hope of an alternative energy source (as Joule had so clearly proved). As for the rest – tidal power, water power, wind power – Jevons had no difficulty in showing that they could not possibly make up the energy deficit that must accompany falling coal extraction. Of course, no one supposed that the mines would become, quite literally, exhausted. Coal would become more and more expensive as the best seams were worked out. And suppose that an alternative fuel could be found. Why should it be present in Britain in any quantity? It could just as well be found anywhere else in the world: in the United States, for example. And the United States had abundant coal reserves in such states as Pennsylvania and Ohio. The Yankees were as ingenious, as industrious, and as inventive as the British. Obviously it would be far cheaper to use American coal to drive American factories than to ship it across the Atlantic to drive British factories.

At first sight stringent fuel economy was called for. But this, Jevons pointed out, would be counter-productive. The more efficient use of fuel meant that profits would increase; accordingly capital investment would increase, leading, inevitably, to a greader demand for fuel. The cure would make the disease worse! It was not surprising that W. E. Gladstone was perturbed when he read Jevon's book. Britain, it appeared, was boxed in between the established laws of science, the simple facts of geography, the findings of geology and the relentless operation of the iron laws of economics. The only choice for the country was between a short life and a gay one or a protracted decline into mediocrity. A Royal Commission was therefore appointed to look into the coal question.

Jevon's book was clearly written with a minimum of technical terms to puzzle the layman. A modern reaction to the work would be to accept it at face value. Jevons apparently foresaw what was to happen to Britain over the following hundred years; his prognosis was correct. But his diagnosis was flawed. How could he possibly have explained the subsequent rise to prosperity of Japan, a country with little indigenous coal; or of Hong Kong,

---

*Ironically, Robert Angus Smith, in his *Memoir of the Life of John Dalton* (Manchester Lit & Phil, 1856), had already suggested that a sub-atomic chemistry might be possible; a chemistry in which entirely new reactions might take place. But this was a heterodox view. Jevons was properly scornful of those who hoped science could find a substitute for coal.

Singapore, and Taiwan with little or no coal at all; or of Holland, a country with negative energy resources? Jevons did not foresee the consequences of the immense improvement in the marine steam-engine that was to take place over the remainder of the century and that was beginning even as he wrote. Nevertheless, whatever its faults, Jevon's book initiated a debate that, with varying degrees of urgency, has continued up to the present and will, no doubt, continue in the future.

Another consequence of the establishment of the principle of the conservation of energy, and one that is widely misunderstood at the present time, was the invention of the dynamo, or, more correctly, the dynamo-electric machine. The invention of the magneto-electric machine was based on Faraday's discovery of electromagnetic induction in 1831. It was understood to work by using permanent magnetism to generate electricity, the limit of its capacity to do so being set by the strength of the permanent magnet. It was not until the 1860s that anyone thought of substituting electromagnets for permanent magnets.[3] The first to do so, or at least to publish his ideas, was the remarkable Henry Wilde (1833–1919). A self-made man, born in Manchester of working-class parents, Wilde was an enthusiastic member of the Lit & Phil, which he joined in 1859 and of which he was President from 1894 to 1896. He was a generous supporter of the Society and endowed its first named lecture: the Wilde Memorial Lecture. Wilde also endowed a prize, to be awarded annually by the Académie des Sciences in Paris, made a generous gift to the Institution of Electrical Engineers' Benevolent Fund and endowed, in succession, a Readership, a Scholarship, a Lectureship and an annual lecture at Oxford University. He bequeathed the residue of his fortune to Oxford.[4]

On 26 April, 1866, a paper by Wilde, communicated by Faraday, was read before the Royal Society. The title was non-committal but the subject-matter was explicit and straightforward.[5] Following a simple statement of the principle of the conservation of energy, he claimed to have discovered a 'means of producing dynamic electricity in quantities unattainable by any apparatus hitherto constructed'. He postulated that 'an indefinitely small amount of dynamic electricity, or of magnetism, is capable of evolving an indefinitely large amount of dynamic electricity'. This was a concise statement of the principle of the dynamo. Wilde then described the machine he had made. It consisted of a relatively small magneto-electric machine supplying current that energised a large stationary electromagnet, or stator. The armature was shuttle-wound, on the prinple introduced by Werner Siemens. Both machines were driven from the same shaft. Wilde reported some sensational results. The current from a large machine, weighing 4½ tons, was enough to melt a rod of iron 15 in long and ¼ in diameter.

The basis for his invention was his realisation that, according to the principle of the conservation of energy, it should be possible to convert dynamical energy into the equivalent of electrical energy. There need be no limit: massive machines were conceivable that could convert the energy of powerful steam-engines into electrical energy. The connection with Joule's work on electrical energy was obvious at this point – had not Joule already said that the magneto-electric machine converted mechanical force (not magnetism) into electrical force? At this time, though, Wilde was careful not to mention Joule.

Eight months later, at the beginning of 1867, an improvement in the new technique was announced independently and almost simultaneously by Werner Siemens, Charles Wheatstone and C. F. Varley. Siemens gave his account to the Berlin Academy of Sciences on 17 January, 1867; Wheatstone gave his to the Royal Society on 14 February, and Varley followed suit nine days later.[6] The improvement in question was that of self-excitation. It was not necessary, they realised, to employ a small magneto-electric machine. As soon as the armature began to rotate, the very small residual magnetism of the big electromagnet would induce a small current that could be fed back into the electromagnet to induce, in turn, a larger current; this would continue, cumulatively, until the mechanical energy, supplied by the steam-engine, was all being converted into electrical energy. The principle was explained in a short paper sent to the Royal Society by William Siemens on 4 February, 1867. It bore the indicative title: 'On the conversion of dynamical into electrical force without the aid of permanent magnetism'.[7]

It is natural to wonder if the dynamo,* or dynamo-electric machine, could have been invented empirically, and also to ask who should have the credit for the invention. Surely there was no great difficulty in conceiving of an electrical generator, in which an electromagnet was substituted for a permanent one? Such a machine would have the outward form of the familiar electromagnetic engine. There was, indeed, a demand for a mechanical or a steam driven means of supplying heavy electric currents, particularly for metallurgical and electroplating works.[8] But the stumbling block was the close association in men's minds of induction with permanent magnetism. William Siemens put it very clearly when he wrote: 'the

---

*Werner Siemens claimed that he invented the word 'dynamo'; according to Wilde, Golding Bird was the first to use it, while Charles Brooke certainly used it in March 1867. But the issue is trivial: the word could easily be inferred from Wilde's expression 'dynamic electricity'.

power of the magneto-electrical machine seems to depend in equal measure on the *force expended* on the one hand, and upon *permanent magnetism* on the other' (his italics). The general acceptance of the conservation of energy, or more explicitly, of the transformability of energy, broke the inhibiting connection with magnetism and asserted the direct linkage between mechanical and electrical energy. The comprehensive theory allowed the inventors to see over the hill and to realise the possibilities that were entailed.[9] One thing is perfectly clear: Faraday did not invent the dynamo; and it is seriously misleading to suggest, as is often done, that once he had discovered electromagnetic induction in 1831 little stood in the way of the development of an electrical supply industry. This by no means uncommon, simplistic distortion of history ignores the importance of the energy principle and does great injustice to the essential contributions of Sturgeon, Joule, Thomson, Wilde, the Siemens brothers and others down to and including Edison, Swan, Hopkins and Tesla.

Werner and William Siemens did not mention Wilde; Wheatstone and Varley mentioned only his machine. This was perhaps understandable, as they were all in the business of inventions and patents. But it was hardly magnanimous, as they must all have been aware of his paper and its fundamental insight as well as the dramatic experiments he claimed to have made. This neglect – that continues to the present day – left Wilde with a bitter sense of grievance. And it was doubly unfortunate, for Wilde was disputatious. He relished being the plaintiff in law cases as other men enjoy mountaineering, sailing, and gardening. And he had ample money to indulge in his hobby.[10] He harried Silvanus P. Thompson through the courts, charging that Thompson's authoritative textbook, *Dynamo-Electric Machinery,* libelled him by implicitly denying that he was the sole inventor of the dynamo. And when the Society of Arts wanted to give him their highest awared, the Albert Medal, for his contribution (*sic*) to the invention of the dynamo he responded with a solicitor's letter asserting his proprietorial right to the title of the only and complete inventor of the dynamo.[11] It is sad that a man who had made many valuable inventions and who was a generous supporter of education and science should have made such an unhappy impression on his contemporaries.

The third quarter of the nineteenth century, a richly creative epoch, saw the publication of a number of authoritative books as well as many scientific papers. If there has been no mention of Darwin, Huxley, the Bishops and the *Origins of Species* (1859), that is because the engineers and physicists did not seem particularly interested. Most of them (Tyndall was an exception) were religious men. Stokes was particularly devout; Joule, Thomson and Maxwell were believers. For these men Rankine's *Steam Engine and Other*

Prime Movers (1859) was more significant than Darwin's famous, if controversial, book.[12] They had a case. Rankine's work went through seventeen editions and was the first book of its kind in the English language. From it descended modern works dealing with the power technologies. It divided the old engineering books – descriptive works – from modern, highly technical treatises. Rankine presented the theory behind the engines he described and worked out his own thermodynamics. His 'thermodynamic function' was formally the same as Clausius's entropy. Rankine followed this seminal textbook with three others dealing with civil engineering, millwork and naval architecture. These books formed the basis for engineering education up to degree standard in British universities and technical colleges.

The publication, in 1867, of the *Treatise of Natural Philosophy* by Thomson and Tait performed a similar, if rather less obvious service, for physics. Peter Guthrie Tait (1831–1901) was a Cambridge graduate who, in 1860, succeeded Forbes in the Chair of natural philosophy at Edinburgh University. By about that time he had become a convert to Joule's views; by 1862 he was a 'fully indoctrinated disciple'.[13] It was the enthusiasm of the convert allied to a naturally pugnacious nature that made him such a zealous defender of Joule's claims against those of Mayer, espoused by Tyndall. He and Thomson, sympathetic allies, resolved to present the new approach to physical science through the medium of a textbook. Mechanics, heat, light, sound, electricity and magnetism were to be embraced in one system, the co-ordinating principle of which was the conservation of energy. The new and efficient terminology devised (or reintroduced) by Rankine was used although, to suit the scheme of the work, the adjective 'kinetic' was substituted for 'actual' and the world has, since then, become accustomed to the expressions 'kinetic' and 'potential energy'. Although the *Treatise* was never completed in the two-volume form originally planned, the work published amounted to the Declaration of Independence of British physics.

The third major work relating to energy published at this time was the *Théorie Mécanique de la Chaleur* (1862).[14] The author, Gustave-Adolphe Hirn (1815–90), lived at Logelbach, near Colmar, about 40 km from Mulhouse, the centre of a large textile industry. Hirn's career and personality, as well as his environment, were remarkably similar to those of Joule. One of a family of three brothers and two sisters, he was educated at home by private tutors. He did not suffer the restraints of a formal discipline; he passed no examinations, which may well have been to his advantage as far as his later, scientific, work was concerned. Like Joule he had a slight physical deformity – he was blind in one eye – and this may have helped to make him a shy, retiring child. His character does not seem to have changed as he grew up. He and his wife used to take their holidays at Lucerne, or Interlaken, not very far away, rather as Joule used to take his family to north Wales, or Blackpool, the Lake District, or the Isle of Man. Hirn made relatively few visits to Paris to attend scientific meetings. His local society was the Société Industrielle de Mulhouse, a body that was not so much an association of like-minded gentlemen, similar to the Manchester Lit & Phil, as a professional association of engineers and industrialists.[15]

When he was nineteen Hirn entered the family firm, working first as a colour chemist and then as an engineer. In the second capacity he was concerned with improving the efficiency of the Boulton and Watt steam-engine, installed in 1824, and in reducing frictional losses in the textile machines.[16] This led him to make a long series of experiments on friction, using a form of Prony brake, or friction balance. He concluded that the accepted laws of friction were only approximately correct and needed to be modified. His paper was rejected by the Académie des Sciences as 'incompatible with the principles of mechanics':[17] shades of Joule and the Royal Society!

It was said of Hirn that he did not stop with the solution of technical problems but went on to study the scientific laws that underlay them. This he had in common with Joule, and, for that matter, with James Watt. His systematic researches on friction involved experiments with different lubricating oils and in some cases necessitated the use of water to cool the apparatus. He was able to find a law relating the applied load to the steady-state temperature that the water would reach when the apparatus was in thermal equilibrium and the heat loss equalled that generated by friction. 'A natural question,' he wrote, 'but of the greatest interest from the point of view of physics, here presented itself.'[18] The natural question was, of course, whether of not mechanical work could be converted into heat. This was the position he had reached, independently, by about 1847. Significantly, in the manuscript of his rejected paper of 1848,[19] he had deleted the expression 'la force absorbée' and pencilled in 'la force dépensé'. Convinced that heat and work were interchangeable, Hirn set to work to find the exchange rate, using a variety of techniques including hammering metals in addition to frictional experiments. He concluded that the mechanical equivalent was 370 kilogramme. metres per 'grand calorie' (or the heat required to raise 1 kg water by 1°C). He knew that his result might not have been very accurate and he described a new apparatus for making the same measurement. A cylindrical calorimeter, full of water, was fitted with a paddle to be driven by a steam-engine. Instead of being fixed, as in Joule's experiments, the calorimeter was free to rotate but was held motionless by two weights, acting over pulleys. The balance was arranged so that the weights exactly countered the frictional drag of the paddle against the water. By this method he obviated the tedious business of winding up the weights to let them fall again. This apparatus of Hirn's was a development from the original Prony brake.

It would be interesting to know more about Hirn's beliefs at this particular time. The conversion of what may be regarded as the abstract concept of work into tangible heat was unacceptable to many critically-minded men of science. Hirn, we know, was later to be critical of materialist interpretations of nature and of the status of unobservable entitles.[20] But his position may have been simpler than this suggests. As an engineer and industrialist of great experience and skill he knew that there was nothing mysterious about 'work'. So much work corresponded to, or produced, so many metres of spun thread, so much sawn wood, so much ground corn. It may be that Hirn's intellectual progress ran on the same lines as that of Rankine who, in a short paper praised by Duhem, distinguished between abstractive science and hypothetical science. The latter, the primary stage, was concerned with the postulation of the mechanisms that, obeying the laws of mechanics, could explain and predict phenomena. When, tested and tried, they were found to work satisfactorily (cf. Rankine's theory of atomic vortices), they could be dispensed with and science could move on to the more mature plane of abstraction, in which fictions like vortices and atoms played no part at all. It may be that, as a class, engineers were, and are, more prone to positivist interpretations than men of science. After all, it is the efficiency of the final product or process that matters, not the exact status of unobservable entities that might have been useful in getting there.

In the meantime Hirn had learned from Léon Foucault of Joule's and Mayer's works. Without questioning their priority in any way he demonstrated his own originality by starting work on a problem that, in its solution, was to give him a place as one of the founders of thermodynamics: the difficult but most important problem of demonstrating the converse operation: the conversion of heat into work. Joule had believed that he had solved this problem when he had shown, in 1844, that heat was lost when compressed air did work in expanding and when he had demonstrated that the work done by an electric motor had been at the expense of the heat that the current could otherwise have generated. But Joule's experiments had been on a very limited scale and his demonstration was not general. With steam-engines at work all over the world it was plainly a desideratum of thermodynamics to prove that they did so by converting heat into work. Hirn has the credit for doing this.

He had certain advantages. He had experience of steam-engines and the family firm now had two Woolf compound engines in addition to the original Boulton and Watt engine. On the other hand it was extremely difficult to demonstrate and then to measure the actual conversion of heat energy into mechanical energy. Allowance had to be made for frictional losses, for the loss of heat by conduction, convection and radiation after every precaution had been taken to minimise such losses. And then it was necessary to measure the work done by the engine, the heat input and the heat rejected to the condenser. Finally, to clinch the argument, it was vital to show that the mechanical work done divided by the difference between the heat input and the heat rejected was, within acceptable limits of error, equal to the mechanical equivalent of heat as determined by Joule and by Hirn himself. The mere detection of a difference between heat input and heat rejected would not have been enough; any such difference could – and would – have been ascribed to experimental error. And indeed Hirn's first experiments gave contradictory results. They indicated that the heat that disappeared was not proportional to the work done. When the engine worked non-expansively there seemed to be no loss of heat – as in George Lee's experiments some sixty years earlier[21] – while if the engine worked expansively there was a loss of heat. The results, ranging between 100 and 200 kilogramme.metres per grand calorie, led Hirn to doubt the exactitude of the principle of equivalence. But, gradually, more and more experiments of increasing accuracy confirmed the principle: however an engine worked, whether expansively or not, there was always a proportionality between the heat that disappeared and the work done and this proportionality was equal to the mechanical equivalent of heat.

In January 1855, the Physical Society of Berlin announced a prize for the best determination of the mechanical equivalent of heat. Hirn submitted a paper that won a prize of 250 gold thalers although it missed the accolade of 'crowning', the divergence of his results being considered too wide. Nevertheless, the judge of Hirn's paper, Clausius – and who was better qualified? – wrote, in his report dated 22 March, 1857, that

> The set of results seem to me to be a most beautiful confirmation of Joule's researches and, at the same time, the essential complement of all observations up to the present; because this determination of the mechanical equivalent of heat is the first obtained by a process that involves, not the generation of heat through work (*Wärme durch Arbeit*), but of work through heat and in which the body measured is returned to its original state.[22]

The superiority of Hirn's experiments to those of George Rennie (see above, p. 170). need not be stressed.

Hirn's book of 1862 has been claimed, probably correctly, to be the first comprehensive textbook on the dynamical theory of heat. He had carried out highly original researches in this field and he had established himself as a leading authority – perhaps the leading authority – on the steam-engine.[23] He pointed out that there could be no comprehensive theory of this machine. This was a rebuttal of what had been eagerly sought in the first half of the century. Whether or not Carnot had considered the possibility of a theory of the *steam*-engine is irrelevant; what is to the point is that there were those who believed that one was possible and that it would be based on steam-pressure considerations alone;[24] but, as Hirn saw, thermodynamics ruled this out. The negative specific heat capacity of saturated steam and the role of the cylinder as a source of heat or a cause of condensation were important parameters governing the performance of engines. In other words the steam-engine was a far more complex machine that it had seemed in the days of Watt and his immediate successors and in those heady years when the great railway boom was beginning. By the end of the nineteenth century D. K. Clark, in his four-volume treatise on the steam-engine,[25] asserted that Mulhouse was the most advanced centre for the study and development of the steam-engine. That it was a leading centre is indisputable and much of the credit for this was due to Hirn.

Hirn and Joule were both outsiders from the points of view of national academies and universities; each was strongly associated with a provincial, industrial culture; both made fundamental contributions to the doctrine of energy and the work of one complemented that of the other. Unquestionably Hirn arrived at the dynamical theory of heat quite independently and yet he is not usually bracketed with those who, with varying degrees of plausibility, are credited with formulating the idea: Rumford, Davy, Marc Séguin, F. Mohr, Colding, Grove, Mayer and Joule. This is illogical. The explanation must lie with his retiring personality and with the relative isolation of a provincial city. Hirn, like Joule and unlike the most of the other claimants, was led to the dynamical theory through the logic of his own researches and not as a result of speculation or some prior metaphysic. He was undoubtedly fortunate in possessing both the apparatus and the facilities for his researches, fortunate in living in the right cultural milieu and fortunate in possessing the financial independence that enabled him to carry out his researches. With great fairness he gave the credit for formulating the 'magnificent idea of the equivalence of all the forces of nature' to Colding, Joule and Mayer.[26] But he pointed out that Dr Mayer believed that movement, whether continuous or vibratory, ceased to be movement when heat appeared in its place, while Colding went further and considered 'force in general as a *specific essence* susceptible of *transformations* and of successive *perfections*'. Joule, on the other hand, held the contrary idea that 'imponderables' (such as heat) were no more than modes of motion of matter. Most analysts, and in particular Clausius and Rankine, followed Joule's interpretation.[27]

Three years after the publication of Hirn's book Clausius published a memoir, his ninth, on thermodynamics. It had had a very long gestation. The imbalance in nature, revealed by thermodynamics, had long been recognised: there was no restriction on the conversion of work into heat – implicitly acknowledged by primitive man when he generated fire by friction – but the converse operation, the transformation of heat into work, was far more difficult and only became possible on a substantial scale with the invention of the steam-engine in the technologically advanced eighteenth century. The steam-engine, like all heat-engines, operated by transforming heat into work, as Joule had insisted and as Hirn had proved, but it can only do so if, as Carnot recognised, heat at the same time flows from the hot body, or furnace, to the cold body, or condenser. The acceptance of the two laws of thermodynamics and the recognition that, in the real world, a perfect engine cannot be made and that, therefore, complete recovery of the initial situation is impossible led Thomson to posit in 1852 that there is universal tendency in nature to the dissipation of mechanical energy.[28] Energy, in all other forms, tends to end up as heat, and heat tends to move to the body at the lowest temperature.

There was, Clausius reasoned, a need for a simple measure that could express this bias in nature and that would be universally applicable. He began with his doctrine of the equivalence of transformations.[29] According to this the transformation of a certain amount of work into heat energy has the equivalence value of the flow of a quantity of heat energy from a hot body to a cold body. These equivalent transformations were given a positive sign to indicate that they were in the direction favoured by, or the bias of, nature. Transformations in the opposite sense were given a negative sign.

Thomson had already shown that the second law of thermodynamics could be expressed by a simple algebraic equation.*[30] Clausius borrowed this expression, adapted it to express equivalence values and used it show that a perfect engine, working on a Carnot cycle, must be such that the equivalence value of the transformations of heat energy into work must be equal, and of opposite sign, to the equivalence value of the transformations

---

*Thomson's expression for the second law was $\dfrac{Q_1}{T_1} + \dfrac{Q_2}{T_2} + \dfrac{Q_3}{T_3} \ldots \dfrac{Q_n}{T_n} = 0$

or $\displaystyle\sum \frac{Q}{T} = 0$

of high-temperature heat into low-temperature heat (or, in simple language, the flow of heat from hot to cold). In a real and imperfect engine, or in any thermomechanical process, no matter how complex, the latter must be the greater and the net result must be equivalent to a flow of heat from hot to cold, or what is equivalent, the transformation of work into heat. 'The whole mechanical theory of heat', wrote Clausius, 'rests on two fundamental theorems – that of the equivalence of heat and work and that of the equivalence of transformations.' But so far the theory was too general to be of immediate and particular application, and Clausius therefore sought to extend his argument to the transformations that can take place in individual bodies.

Generally speaking, when heat enters a body its heat energy content is increased and the arrangement of its molecules is changed. Clausius calls the latter the 'disgregation', a word whose meaning is practically self-evident. These two transformations have equivalence values and are, in principle, independent. For example, a gas can be heated at constant pressure or at constant volume. In the latter cases the disgregation is zero. Again, if a gas expands into a vacuum, as in Joule's experiments of 1844, no heat enters or leaves the gas. But there has been a thermodynamic change, for if we try to restore the gas to its original volume by compressing it we find that heat is generated, to the equivalence value of the disgregation, which *had* changed. The sum of transformation values, the transformation content of the body, Clausius calls the 'entropy'. The same simple algebraic equation is used and the rule of signs is that heat entering the body is designated positive; leaving it, negative. In the second case no heat entered the gas but the entropy increased by the equivalance value of the increased disgregation.[31] It is familiar knowledge that in all technological and natural processes in the real world the net entropy of the bodies involved must increase. In this way Clausius gave an analytical expression to Thomson's realisation that energy always tends to dissipate.[32] Clausius summed it up in a memorable statement:

> The energy of the universe is constant,
> The entropy of the universe tends always to a maximum.

The formulation of the entropy concept in 1865 was not the last of the advances in physics during this remarkable decade. There was also Maxwell's enunciation of his electromagnetic field theory and the development of the kinetic theory of gases, revived by Herapath and Joule and carried forward by Clausius, Maxwell and their successors, Gibbs and Boltzmann.[33] It is enough to recall that in all these advances Joule, directly or indirectly, participated and in some of them he played the leading part.

12

Some friends

The subject of Thomson's Rede Lecture, delivered at Cambridge on 26 May 1866, was the dissipation of energy. He paid generous tribute to Joule:

> The genius to plan, the courge to undertake, the marvellous ability to execute and the keen perseverance to carry through to the end the great series of experimental investigations by which Joule discovered and proved the conservation of energy in electric, electromagnetic and electrochemical actions, and in the friction and impact of solids, and measured accurately, by means of the friction of fluids, the mechanical equivalent of heat, cannot be generally and thoroughly understood at present. Indeed, it is all the scientific world can do just now in this subject to learn gradually the new knowledge gained.[1]

Their scientific paths were, however, diverging. Thomson's dispute with the geologists over the age of the earth was warming up nicely. Furthermore, he was actively developing his ideas on vortex rings. In 1867 Tait translated an elegant paper by Helmholtz on vortex motion in fluids. A closed-ring vortex in a friction-free fluid would be permanent and elastic. This, Thomson thought, provided a model for the structure of the atom; a model, moreover, that would make it possible to combine the ether, regarded as friction-free and essential for the undulatory theory of light, with atomism and the structure of matter. This new Cartesianism held the promise of a grand theory unifying physics in terms of a basic substance, plenum or ether, and motion, or energy. Thomson devoted a great deal of thought and effort to these theories in the decades that followed. It puzzled Joule, who commented to Roscoe: 'Thomson is now at work on atoms and has no end of enormously involuted wires to show what they are like. It is a most curious subject I will tell you of when we meet.'[2] But the theory of the 'smoke-ring' atom (the most obvious analogy) and the theories of the ether were to fall out of favour with the rise of relativity, the discovery of the electron and the nuclear atom at the beginning of the twentieth century.

Joule was devoting himself to far more mundane affairs. He had begun to work out the details of the new measurement of the mechanical equivalent of heat in order to settle the doubt raised by the small differences between his original measurement and that made electrically on the basis of the standard BA ohm. Thomson suggested that if the paddle-wheel were to be driven by a suitable power source it would cut out the waste of time, with consequent errors of observation, involved in having to rewind the weights.[3] After all, Thomson had applied continuous power in order to demonstrate the transformation of work into heat; and so, for that matter, had von Rumford nearly seventy years earlier. But Joule had other commitments and it was some years before he could actually carry out the work. He was making a current balance on the lines proposed by Thomson and he had plans to study the viscosity of liquids and gases up to pressures of the order of 1,000 lb psi.[4]

In 1868 Joule was elected President of the Lit & Phil for the second time. It was during this second presidency that Tyndall was elected an Honorary Member of the Society. Any ill-will due to the row that had broken out in 1862 had been forgotten and, notably, sour remarks about Tyndall disappear from his correspondence with Thomson. Another change that year was the sale of the house, 'Thorncliff', where he had been frustrated in his researches, and the purchase of a new home, 5 Cliff Point, Higher Broughton, which he had to buy in a hurry as 'Thorncliff' had been sold rather more quickly than he had expected. Cliff Point was on the other side of the twin cities; it was in Salford and due north of Acton Square, overlooking a meander in the Irwell. The house was not so convenient for scientific work but Higher Broughton was, he hoped, a healthy area. As he explained,

> It is a very curious fact that the average mortality per 1,000 in Broughton during ten years was only 13.9 whilst in neighbouring districts it amounted to 30 or more. I proposed that the Corporation ought to solicit our Society's help to improve the sanitary conditions giving us the requisite funds for a searching inquiry. But alas they don't really care whether the poor die off or not.[5]

It would be pleasant if this just indignation, this manifestation of social conscience, could be shown to be personal and strictly spontaneous. But the probability is that he was repeating views commonly held at that time by members of the class to which he belonged. The late 1860s were, Pickstone has remarked, 'a particularly suitable time for philanthropic gestures'.[6] In fact, in the previous decade schemes for sewerage and water supply were well under way and in 1868 Manchester appointed its first Medical Officer of Health, John Leigh.[7]

Having moved to Higher Broughton Joule found that his own health had not improved:

> I ought to have written before . . . I would have done had I not been taken with a
> bleeding from the nose which made me very weak and confined me to my bed
> for several days. I am now able to stay up for 8 hours a day and hope to progress
> to health although I fear it will be some time before I am strong again. You may
> be sure I was low enough when I tell you that I could not go out to vote for the
> Tory candidates.
>
> This place is not made for scientific work, but I have a long room, two cellars
> and one or two places outside. I think I shall have to get a room in town with
> power, ie. a vertical shaft running at a uniform speed.* This would be a great
> convenience for the equivalent experiments for which you see the grant is
> renewed. Arthur is now going to Owens College. I had great difficulty in
> deciding whether he should go to Laird's at Birkenhead. But in the end decided
> he would do better even for that, for a well grounded knowledge of mechanics
> &c. He is doing the usual 1st year course. Arts or Sciences is the same for the
> first year. He is I think doing well and is very assiduous having attended every
> lecture since he began in October.[8]

The bleeding from the nose was the first serious symptom of a
breakdown in his health; it was to be followed by a much more serious
attack some years later. At least he did not have to worry about Arthur. One
might have supposed that Arthur, as the only son, would have been sent to
Cambridge. Joule himself had thought of going there in those distressing
days just after his wife died. Perhaps Arthur, while industrious, was not
very academic; perhaps local patriotism was then very much in the
ascendant; perhaps an apprenticeship to a first-class local engineering
firm, like Laird's, was as attractive as Oxford or Cambridge? We know that,
in those days, a premium apprenticeship could cost up to £400 or £500,
more than enough to send a son to a university.[9] On the other hand,
perhaps the family finances were modest?

Over Christmas and the New Year (1869), Joule took the trouble to
present Thomson with his brass calorimeter and paddle-wheel (he had lost
the spindle, but that could easily be remedied).[10] And he very willingly took
Thomson's advice, and that of his friend and physician, Dr Samuel
Crompton (grandson of the inventor of the spinning mule), to take things
more easily.[11] But misfortunes often multiply. His sister was taken ill (when
was she not?), and Arthur and Alice went down with measles. This was too
much and he had another attack. Then things began to improve. He looked

---

*A number of small masters, each employing a journeyman and a boy, might have their
separate workshops in one building. Power would be supplied by vertical and line shafting
from a communal steam-engine in the basement. This practice continued, particularly in the
small metal trades, such as cutlery, until very recently.

forward to going to the seaside; he was sure it would do them all good. And he thought he had found the cause of his illness: 'an untrapped grid in the cellar. The evil is now remedied and I am attacking the hidden enemy with Calvert's carbolic acid.* I think the cellar system in England is bad, as in most cases a great part of the air of what is called the entertaining rooms &c is derived from them.'

That spring he was unwell again and, dreading a return of 'my disagreeable visitor', he feared to go far from home lest he was taken ill again.[12] He could, at least, indulge in his hobby of devising and making extremely accurate scientific instruments. And he could try to do something in support of Owens College in its campaign to secure the status of a public corporation, no longer to be governed by private trustees: the first step on the road to becoming a university.[13] He had hoped, if well enough, to go up to London with the deputation of the Executive Committee. But he was suspicious of any government aid. In the event of the Irish Church Bill (disestablishment) being passed there would be a precedent for disendowing the College. His fears ran even deeper:

> I have no doubt but that the security of property will be most fatally affected by Mr Gladstone's policy and I feel happy that we in Lancashire have voted against it in a proportion of 2:1 . . . No one can say that the British Empire will not be R. Catholic in 5 years . . . But enough of this. Gladstone certainly has the merit of stirring up political life a little.

The move to Higher Broughton had proved a disappointment. In spite of Joule's sanitary engineering Arthur had gone down with scarlet fever and his sister Mary was 'taken with severe illness at the same time'.[14] He had had to do something in the nursing line. Alice had been packed off to Southport and he hoped that before long he, with Arthur (who was recovering) and Mary, could join her there. These troubles meant that work on the new measurement of the mechanical equivalent of heat had had to be put aside. In letter to George Griffith at Oxford he explained the reason for the delay and hoped that the BA Committee would be reappointed and the £50 grant renewed.[15] He trusted he would soon be able to resume his researches. In the meantime he was working on his dip-circle, which he regarded as important, and less demanding. By then the family had joined Alice at Southport where they were to stay for more than two months. By the early autumn Joule felt much better.[16] Southport, with its miles of sandhills and, out to sea, miles of sandbanks, was attractive. An experience there prompted him to philosophy and almost to poetry. As

*Crace Calvert had collaborated with R. A. Smith and A. McDougall in the manufacture of their disinfectant.

he explained to Thomson,

> I had the good fortune to see a beautiful display of 'phosphorescence' on Friday week. It was the commencement of the spring tides when the sea comes over a large area of sand which is uncovered at low tides and in doing so liberates a large quantity of air. I went down at dusk to look at the incoming tide and found it at the edge brilliant with a bluish white light. When the water ran down the narrow furrows of sand it seemed exactly like melted silver poured into a mould. I had never seen anything so brilliant before although I have frequently seen the more ordinary forms of the phenomenon which seems occasioned by a multitude of sparks, each spark occasioned by a small insect. I recollect seeing some of the insects in sea water I had collected in a bottle to examine. It is really a very wonderful phenomenon and you may depend a most important one to be studied. It may seem strange that in what we are pleased to call the 'lower forms' of animal life there seem to be at least equally elaborate contrivances to those in the so-called higher organisms. I suppose Huxley will settle all this with a stroke of his pen but really as you say, Natural Historians are remarkable for incredulity themselves while they insist upon credulity in others.

Southport set them all up for the winter. But Joule was almost ashamed of the little he had been able to do in science.

The Owens College, assured of its Charter (1870, 1871), was looking for new and more suitable premises, its original accommodation in Cobden's old house in Quay Street being cramped and in an increasingly grimy neighbourhood. The new site was on Oxford Road, about a mile to the south of the city centre and not far from the Gaskells' house on Plymouth Grove. They money had to be raised by local donations as Gladstonian economy was now the rule. And Owens had another, if minor, problem. The departure of William Jack to edit the *Glasgow Herald* was, to Joule, a kind of apostasy.[17] To Thomson it looked like a good opportunity for his nephew, the son of his late sister Anna, James Thomson Bottomley, who had assisted him at Glasgow University. Joule naturally agreed to support his friend's candidate.[18] But there was a stronger applicant in the field. Roscoe, the most influential man in Owens, was supporting an application from Balfour Stewart, at that time kicking his heels in Kew, doing routine work while wanting to carry out original research.[19] Balfour Stewart was duly elected. And to judge by the careers of the two men, although Balfour Stewart was to die prematurely, the right choice was made.

If 1870 was a year of reduced scientific effort by Joule, a year in a period when he devoted himself to scientific instruments, it was also a time with its own rewards.[20] He was soon to be nominated by the Duke of Richmond, Lord President of the Privy Council, to sit as a Governor on the Court of the new Owens College.* Tyndall gave him a present in the form of his collected works on diamagnetism and he was invited to join Roscoe, Balfour Stewart and others in an effort to make the public more aware of the importance of science.[21] It was widely believed that the Paris International Exhibition of 1867 had shown that in some areas, particularly those relating to modern 'science-based' industries, Britain was outclassed by foreign rivals. A movement to remedy this was initiated by the Society of Arts. This gave rise to the Society for the Promotion of Technical Education whose activities led, in turn, to the Royal Commission on Technical Instruction (1882–84), of which Roscoe and the Mancunian Sir William Mather were active members. Following the Report of the Commission, the Acts of 1889 and 1890 authorised the establishment of local, rate-supported technical colleges. Another Royal Commission, of a somewhat different, although related, origin was that on Scientific Instruction and the Advancement of Science. Chaired by the seventh Duke of Devonshire its reports, with those of the Commission on Technical Instruction, lent strong support to the movement to found the provincial university colleges that were to become autonomous universities in the following century.[22] But all this lay in the future. For Joule the great event of 1870 was the award by the Royal Society of the Copley Medal, the final and complete accolade. One other person must share in it. He wrote:

My dearest Fanny,

I know nothing with certainty about my medal but I do not propose to deny myself the pleasure of seeing you. So if all be well I will come out at the Willesden Junction at 5 on Tuesday and so be with you at about 6. I shall expect to see you quite well & hearty. If you should chance to be in the neighbourhood of Willesden as you are such a traveller you must meet me at the station. Otherwise dont mind for I will only see you an hour later. I should go on to the Royal Society on Monday and we can then sit in judgement upon it. Only I ought not to count my chickens before they are hatched. You will laugh if I am sold.

With best love to you all,
Yours with a kiss,
James P. Joule.[23]

According to Osborne Reynolds, Joule was dining with W. C. Williamson, professor of natural history at Owens, when he first heard the news about the Copley Medal. His pleasure was obvious, Reynolds added, but he regarded it as an award for the truth that he had discovered rather than

*He was duly disqualified for failing to attend a single meeting of Council in eighteen months. This did not prevent the Lord President nominating him again, or Owens disqualifying him again. Presumably he found some committee work uncongenial.

for himself; a distinction by no means easy to comprehend.

Recurrent bouts of ill-health had compelled Joule to occupy himself with lighter tasks than his intended research. These tasks were by no means trivial. Two series of observations he reported were novel and of great interest. The two thermometers he had acquired in 1844 were, he claimed, the first accurately-calibrated thermometers in Britain (he did not give the reasons for this claim).[24] One, made by J. B. Dancer, was particularly sensitive, thirteen divisions corresponding to 1°F; the other thermometer was made in Paris. In April 1844, Joule had marked the freezing point as zero. Thereafter he re-determined the freezing point seven times up to 1867 and noted that it rose steadily, until by the last year it had risen by 11.8 divisions, or 0.91°F. The other, rather less sensitive, thermometer showed a rise of 0.6°F. He continued to determine the freezing points until December 1882, by which time the Dancer thermometer showed a rise of 1.1°F. After Joule's death Schuster determined the freezing points in 1894. The final determination was made on 15 August 1930, in the room at the Lit & Phil where the thermometers had stood undisturbed in a vertical case for thirty-six years. J. R. Ashworth found that the rise on the Dancer thermometer was 1.2°F.[25] The rate of rise had initially been comparatively rapid; it was slowing down and, it could be inferred, would ultimately become inappreciable. Alas, further determinations are impossible as the thermometers were destroyed with the Society's House in an air-raid in 1940.

A parallel series of observations was begun in 1864. This was a study of the permanency of 'permanent' magnets and it continued until 1882.[26] Joule magnetised small steel needles to saturation, mounted them in a cardboard frame to form a compound magnet and noted its strength from August 1864 onwards. The strength fell rapidly. This he thought, might have been due to the diurnal variation in temperature, so he tried systematically heating and cooling the magnet. This reduced the magnetism. He then placed two compound magnets in bottles and buried them in the ground. Three years later, in 1868, and twelve years later in 1877, the strength of the magnets was found to have progressively fallen, although much less markedly over the longer period.* As the earth's magnetic field had not changed significantly over this period Joule concluded that the cause of the decline, rapid at first and then slow, was yet to be discovered. He completed his paper with accounts of more extended experiments on the effects on magnetism of heating, cooling and mechanical shock.

*As Joule had changed houses over this period the magnets were, presumably, buried on land belonging to the Lit & Phil.

These two extended series of experiments, or observations, show that however persuasive authority and convention might be, Joule understood that no measurement in science can ever be treated as permanent, fixed or unalterable.

The winter of 1870–71 was unusually severe and a number of railway accidents were caused, according to the railway companies, by the effect of cold in making the iron or steel tyres of carriage wheels brittle. Joule was a nervous railway traveller, particularly after the accident of 1857. He was scornful of this excuse and suggested that the real cause was the hardening of the ground, due to the cold, resulting in the wheels suffering greater shocks. To confirm his point he tested large numbers of conveniently small garden nails and iron needles. He subjected samples of the same weight to sudden shocks when cold (2°F or 3°F) and when warm. His results showed that cold nails were no more likely to fracture than warm ones. As he was tending to do more and more, Joule communicated his findings to the Lit & Phil, publishing three short papers in the *Proceedings*.[27] This brought about some heated discussions; practical men did not take kindly to the idea that experiments on garden nails could throw light on the behaviour of railway-carriage wheels. Osborne Reynolds, who had joined the Lit & Phil, was present. The discussions, he wrote,

> gave those present opportunities of seeing Joule under circumstances such as had not happened within the memory of many, if any, of the members. He was much excited by the opposition and entered warmly into the discussion, hitting out straight and with spirit, but at the same time with dignity, courtesy and kindness which took the sting out of the hard things he said, and was very gratifying to witness.[28]

Joule did not exercise quite the domination over the Lit & Phil that Dalton had enjoyed in his time.[29] And he had to face more persistent criticism from a polite but determined clergyman, the Rev. H. Highton, who sought to overthrow the science of electrodynamics, to refute thermo-dynamics and to falsify the doctrine of the equivalance of heat and work.[30] Highton grounded his attack on the paper that Joule and Scoresby had published in 1845. Although not a member of the Lit & Phil he was allowed to publish his criticisms in the Society's *Proceedings*. However, as John Hopkinson* pointed out, Highton had confused the maximum of work

---

*John Hopkinson, an Owens graduate and subsequently a Cambridge Wrangler, collaborated with his brother Edward in designing the highly efficient Edison–Hopkinson, or 'Manchester', dynamo. Edward Hopkinson (the father of Katherine, Lady Chorley) was managing director of Sir William Mather's firm, Mather & Platt, who made the dynamo. A third brother, Sir Alfred Hopkinson, was the first Vice-Chancellor of Manchester University.

with most economical duty and had made other mistakes.[31] Highton replied, unabashed and at length.[32] This time Joule felt that he ought to make his position clear. Characteristically, he did not attack, or even comment on, Highton's arguments; instead he described and interpreted a new series of experiments illustrating the performance of an electric motor under different loads.[33] He claimed that he had arrived at the theory of electric motors in 1840. This was plausible. He did not have the mechanical equivalent of heat in 1840, but it is reasonable to assume that he knew that the power of a motor reached a maximum when the current had fallen to half its value when it was held stationary. By 1843 he explained this in terms of the relationship between the heat and work. Unwisely, Highton returned to the attack; one short, opening sentence revealed his continuing mis-understanding: 'The whole basis of Dr Joule's new reasoning is, that when a magnetic engine works rapidly, less heat is evolved and more absorbed by it.'[34] Joule responded briefly to this,[35] but he need not have bothered; for besides Hopkinson his old Dublin ally, Dr Apjohn, had come to his defence as did, most effectively, an anonymous reviewer in the new journal, *Nature.* For all that, Highton was no ignoramus. At the 1861 British Association meeting he exhibited two scientific instruments he had invented. His misunderstandings were an indication of the difficulties men of science of moderate ability had in comprehending and accepting the new theory. Thomson, in his Rede Lecture, had pointed out that this would be the case.

Apart from the disputes with Highton and over the strength of iron, 1871 was a fallow year. The following year, 1872, opened with Joule writing to Tyndall to express his gratitude for the kind references Tyndall had made to him in articles in *Nature,*[36] and to admit that he was working more slowly than he once did. But he hoped before long to make an even more accurate measurement of the mechanical equivalent of heat. Apart from this he was unwilling to take on additional obligations. When Roscoe tried to persuade him to accept the Presidency of the British Association, he declined: 'if anything could have helped me into the office it would have been such kind encouragement. But it cannot be, I am not strong enough and must be content to go on my present quiet way'.[37] He was, however, willing to suggest alternatives; he particularly favoured prominent members of the nobility. It was, he believed, most desirable to gain the sympathy of the 'upper ten'. Eminently well qualified were Lord Derby and the Duke of Devonshire. Joule disliked and feared the rise of popular democracy which explains why he could write: 'we are losing rather than gaining in parlia-mentary and political influence and every opportunity should be seized to keep at any rate what is already held'. He need not have worried; however widely the franchise was extended Britain remained, as Matthew Arnold noted, a country with an aristocratic form of government. The future of British science would, in Joule's view, be best assured under the protection of the nobility. This could fairly be described as the feudal theory of science.

Joule had the opportunity, six weeks later, to explain his views on the needs of science when he was called as a witness before the Royal Commission on Scientific Instruction.[38] He must have been flattered when the Duke of Devonshire commented that he had paid considerable attention to the advancement of science. When asked to identify areas in which government should aid, or increase its aid to science he suggested, first, the establishment and maintenance of observatories for solar physics, geophysics and meteorology. Second on his shopping list for government aid came science museums –

> extremely useful institutions and it seems very desirable to have them both numerous and very accessible . . . The things which I think would be desirable in museums are specimens in natural history, specimens in chemistry, specimens in geology and minerology, manufactured products, machines, tools &c, scientific instruments, patented inventions and historical instruments.

Manchester museums had collections in natural history and geology but nothing in the other fields. Science libraries, too, should benefit from government help, particularly in small towns and cities. Scientific research was supported by grants from the British Association and the Royal Society (government grant) but these did not cover personal expenses, which could be considerable. It would be a notable advance if local societies could have laboratories, or at least laboratory space, that their members could use. With bitterness he recalled that the landlord of the Trafford estate had threatened legal proceedings if he 'used a one horse-power steam-engine . . . so that [he] was compelled to discontinue the experiments because [he] was unable to go to the expense of purchasing another plot of ground and re-erecting the requisite building'.

Joule envisaged a nation-wide network of laboratories, supervised by local societies, supported to some extent by government and open to all responsible researchers and men of science. He conceded that such a system would, like everything else in this world, be open to abuses, but men of science might be credited with sufficiently high principles to ensure that any abuses were very exceptional. Problems of a scientific nature concerning defence, the mining industries, and public health should be the responsibilities of scientific men and must be supported by government. All these different proposals implied that a new department of state – a Board of

Science – was required. This Board should also be responsible, on the advice of the Royal Society, for persons and financial rewards for scientific men. On this last point he took the opportunity to let the Commissioners know his opinion of a contemporary man of science. Did he know, asked Dr William Sharpey, one of the Commissioners, that Sir William Snow Harris had been rewarded for his improvements to lightning conductors for ships? 'Yes,' Joule replied, 'Sir W. Harris was rewarded for introducing Mr Henley's ship conductors.'*

The view of the desirable relationship between science and government taken by Joule together with the majority of his scientific contemporaries was in direct opposition to the economic doctrines of the Chancellor of the Exchequer, Robert Lowe, and those who thought like him. The idea that the State should intervene to support science, even on the most modest scale, was repugnant to radical individualists.[39] Joule and most of his scientific colleagues were Conservative in their political sympathies. Their opinions, expressed to the Devonshire Commission, indicated the progress, since the days when the British Association had been established, towards a common political attitude among men of science. Joule's own suggestion of nationally-supported laboratories associated with local societies was, on his own evidence, impracticable. The Lit & Phil, he said, depended on the goodwill of its members; it had to be run as frugally as possible and had no endowments apart from its house, 36 George Street. And the Manchester Lit & Phil was the most distinguished of all local societies. The age of the devotee man of science was coming to an end; that of the professional scientist was beginning. The nationally-supported laboratories of the future were to be those in universities and university colleges. But for these laboratories, too, Joule's plea was equally valid: 'I think none of us would wish extravagance. What we want is the means of work, and useful work too.'[40]

Joule was by no means the first to urge the establishment of a science museum concerned with the physical sciences and related technologies. As far back as 1795 the Revd Thomas Barnes made a similar proposal in a paper he read to the Lit & Phil, and thereafter the same proposal was repeated in every generation until 1964, when the late Sir Maurice Pariser initiated a scheme that was to develop into the very successful Greater Manchester Museum of Science and Industry.

It is entirely appropriate that Manchester should have a science museum. Over the past 200 years Manchester's record of scientific achievement can bear comparison with any other city or town in Britain;

*Snow Harris had been granted a civil list pension of £300 per annum.

and if we take science and technology together – is it reasonable to separate them? – then Manchester's record is unrivalled. Why, then, did it take 180 years or more to open a science museum?

Elements of the old Manchester, the pleasant country town with orchards and trout streams, survived when Joule was born. At the end of his life Manchester was rapidly changing into the major component of a vast conurbation in which one could travel from Bolton in the north to Altrincham in the south, a distance of about twenty miles, without seeing a field or hedgerow. A traveller would, however, pass through a number of different towns, each with its own local authority. There was no overall civil authority for what was, in all other respects, one huge city. A share of the wealth that had been generated by the cotton industry and its ancillary industries, including banking and insurance, went towards the funding of Owens College, the Whitworth Art Gallery, the Free Trade Hall and the Hallé Orchestra. All this was to the credit of the (often much abused) people of the towns concerned. But a museum that must display the achievements of outsiders and foreigners as well as locals could not have the same immediate and obvious appeal of a college, a concert hall, or an art gallery. This political and financial vicious circle could be broken only by the State itself or by the establishment of a comprehensive authority. The institution of the Greater Manchester Council at last enabled the creation of a science museum on a scale appropriate to Manchester's achievements.

The economic forces associated with industrialisation that were transforming Manchester and its sister towns had relatively little effect on the affairs of the Lit & Phil. Membership exceeded 200 in the early 1860s but sank to 140 in 1882, possibly as a consequence of the 'cotton famine', a depression in trade and the increase of the subscription from £1 5s to £2 2s.[41] The rise in subscriptions had enabled the Society to continue its policy, dear to Joule's heart, of building up its library which numbered 12,000 volumes with complete sets of periodicals.[42] In 1857 the Society had established a Microscopical and Natural History Section. This was followed by a Physical and Mathematical Section and a Photographical Section. Joule was an active member of both the last Sections; in the second his fellow enthusiasts included John Benjamin Dancer, Alfred Brothers, James Mudd and Joseph Sidebotham. These were the men who, for a decade or two helped to make Manchester the photographic capital of the world. The main Society met once a fortnight, with a President or Vice-President in the Chair. Meetings began with a general invitation to members to raise any problems that they thought would be of interest to the Society; thereafter a paper would be read and subsequently discussed. If the paper was approved it might be published in the *Memoirs*, or at least summarised for the *Proceedings*.

The Lit & Phil remained throughout the nineteenth century what it had been in Dalton's day, an association of men interested in and, very often, actively contributing to science. It had no rivals in Manchester. As a society it had far more in common with the Royal Society than with the Royal Institution. The Lit & Phil included among its members engineers, industrial chemists and inventors as well as physicians and surgeons. And among those who belonged to the liberal professions there were men like the Revd Thomas Kirkman, FRS,[43] and Edward Binney, FRS, who had strong commitments to science. In the modern world such men would have every opportunity and every incentive to become professional scientists; in those days their scientific interests found expression and encouragement in the Society. In this respect the Lit & Phil was a true scientific society. For Joule it was at once his club, his university, his inspiration.

As the opportunities for scientific careers increased in the later part of the nineteenth century so the Lit & Phil began to lose its scientific pre-eminence. The development of Owens College, first into an institution with a charter, then into the senior partner of the federal Victoria University (1880), and then into the autonomous Victoria University of Manchester (1905), meant more salaried posts for men of science.* So too did the transformation of the old Mechanics' Institution into the Municipal School of Technology, and then into the Manchester College of Technology, housing and incorporating the Faculty of Technology of the University (1905). These changes were paralled by the foundation of the Royal College of Science and Technology, Salford, and of local technical colleges in Openshaw, Stretford and elsewhere. All these bodies were funded, at least in part, from the public purse.

Like all institutions the Lit & Phil has passed through prosperous and through difficult times. As the Manchester Royal Institution and the Athenaeum faded away so, too, the Lit & Phil went into decline. The centre of scientific and intellectual life moved decisively to Owens College. By the end of its centenary (1881) it was, according to Robert Angus Smith, in the doldrums:

> It is certainly marvellous how much the usual authorities of the city have been influenced in early times by the Society; we cannot say the same now . . . many people look on the members as . . . amusing themselves with harmless

---

*Subsequent affiliated colleges of the Victoria University were the Yorkshire College of Science (now the University of Leeds) and University College, Liverpool (now the University of Liverpool).

speculations. One account is: 'we went to the Society and saw a number of old men sitting round a table talking about the moon'.[44]

The Society had abandoned the few public lectures it had once offered and, Smith complained, members preferred to send their scientific papers to other journals than the *Memoirs*, favoured by Dalton and Joule. He hoped (too late!) that the Society could acquire funds to spend on scientific and literary research and he recommended that the Society should move to new premises, as the area round George Street was now dominated by warehouses and commercial buildings, the physicians and surgeons having long since moved out to Fallowfield and Didsbury, far from the smoky heart of Manchester. 'We begin a new century', wrote Smith – 'it would be well to begin it with hope'.

Thirty years later it might have seemed that things had not improved. The young H. G. J. Moseley, who could have been one of the leading physicists of the twentieth century (he was killed in action in the Gallipoli campaign) gave, with all the intolerance of youth, his opinion of the Lit & Phil in 1912:

On Tuesday I had to read two papers to the grey-haired fogeys who make up the Manchester Literary and Philosophical Society, a very old fashioned and serious minded little society, founded by Dalton (*sic*), the chemist, just over a century ago. I had to explain everything in words of one syllable and yet try to appear very technical, lest they should be offended. It is surprising what a lively interest in science is taken by these old merchants and city men.[45]

Moseley was at that time working at Manchester University under the direction of Ernest Rutherford, Langworthy Professor of Physics. It was ironic, and at the same time symptomatic, that the meeting of the Council of Owens College on 17 April 1874 should have resolved to disqualify Dr Joule under the eighteen months rule and, under a different item, to acknowledge gratefully the bequest of £10,000 under the will of Mr Edward Ryley Langworthy to endow a 'Chair of Experimental Physics'. Whatever the opinions of able young men, members of staff of the University, the 'Tech' and other colleges continued to join the Lit & Phil, often becoming enthusiastic and dedicated members.

As the fortunes of the Lit & Phil seemed to wane so, apparently, did those of its most distinguished member. Joule had told the Devonshire Commission that he could not afford to continue experiments with his little steam-engine when it was banned from Old Trafford. A decline in his fortunes was noticed by his friends. Roscoe, successful, influential, and wealthy, took the lead in an effort to gain national recognition and recompense for Joule. Early in 1872 he wrote to Tyndall and others:

We feel that the pre-eminent scientific merits of our friend, Dr Joule, have not been sufficiently appreciated by the prominent men in this district and it seems to us that a proper recognition of his great services ought if possible to take place during his life time.

We have in contemplation a scheme for achieving this in a way agreeable to his own feelings, but before taking any steps it would be desirable to obtain an expression of the opinion entertained by a few prominent scientific men respecting the great value of his researches and the position they have gained for him in the world of science.

We shall therefore be obliged by a short statement which can be shown to our Manchester friends.[46]

The effort was unsuccessful.[47] Joule was not a familiar national figure. He was no Faraday, able to enthral large and distinguished audiences; he was no Huxley, prominent in the public controversies of the day. And even if he had had those gifts a government headed by Gladstone and with Robert Lowe as Chancellor of the Exchequer would not have dreamed of giving him public money.

Joule's own attitude to public obligations and policies was revealed when he told Roscoe that he had 'been captured for the uncongenial duties of a Common Juror at the Assizes'.[48] He disliked this for he believed that 'all the worst criminals are invariably *outside* the walls of a jail'. Inconsequentially he added that Robert Lowe had been sailing with Thomson in the *Lallah Rookh*. Thomson had praised the previous administration for giving money to Glasgow University and added that it should be a precedent for the present government to assist the Owens College. But Lowe had stuck to 'his old text – "bad precedent". The real meaning being "inconvenient".' Joule added: 'There is a great work before some administration and it is natural for those who pursue statesmanship as a trade to work it as easily as they can. I should not be surprised however if they did some good thing on a sudden at the last moment,'*

During 1873 Joule's health continued to deteriorate. On 6 April 1873, he had a renewed attack of bleeding from the nose. It was so serious that Dr Crompton came at 5 a.m. 'and remained, with two short intervals, till 11 p.m. He inserted a plug.'[49] On 4 June 1873 Joule wrote to Stokes, Secretary to the Royal Society, to apologise for being unable to undertake a detailed assessment of a paper submitted by Lord Rosse. He had, he said, been very unwell.[50] And, later in the year, he was, he claimed, too ill to carry out what would have been the most important public engagement of

---

*Joule, and perhaps Thomson, apparently misunderstood Lowe who had a rooted, ideological objection to all grants, subsidies, etc. For Lowe a good government was one that appropriated and spent as little as possible of the people's money.

his life. Since he had told Roscoe in March 1872 that he was not strong enough to be President of the British Association, he had been persuaded to change his mind and had been duly elected President for the 1873 meeting in Bradford. But just two months before the meeting he had, on the advice of his physicians, felt compelled to resign, even though he had prepared his Presidential address. In the circumstances W. C. Williamson accepted the office and paid generous tribute to Joule in his address.[51] A residual doubt remains. Perhaps Joule's evident dislike of public occasions and public lectures was an additional factor in his withdrawal from the Presidency.

In February 1874 Joule had a further attack while staying with his brother at Southport. This time he emphatically refused to have another plug inserted; he would, he said, rather have died. But Benjamin produced a rather more persuasive physician, a Dr Daniel Elias, who was successful in his immediate treatment. Benjamin wrote in his diary: 'It was most providential that this second attack occurred when James was with us, where he was kept quiet and properly attended to.'[52] Dr Elias was zealous in attendances on his patient. On 21 February, 'Dr Elias called to see James. Arthur [son], called same evening.' Dr Elias called every day for the next three days; four days later he came at 5 a.m.: 'He called twice this day and so on up to the 19th of March.' On 20 March, 'Dr Elias called. I accompanied James and Arthur to Manchester (this was by far the worst attack he ever had).' On 4 May, 'James had a return of the bleeding. He was hesitating which of his medical friends, members of the Literary and Philosophical Society he should call in, but I spoke strongly in favour of Dr Dixon Mann and I received permission to call Dr Mann, of which I at once availed myself by calling upon him.' Many years later Benjamin recalled: 'I never had occasion to regret my advice, Dr Mann soon obtained my brother's confidence, and proved a most attentive and judicious friend as well as medical adviser. I think I may fairly say that I had the privilege of saving my brother's life for a quarter of a century.'[53] Although Benjamin's estimate of a quarter of a century was an exaggeration, his claim concerning Dixon Mann was entirely fair. Mann was not only a leading Manchester physician but he was also a talented musician, and it was through music that he became a close friend of Benjamin Joule.

On his recovery from his long illness Joule took a six-week holiday with his family on the Isle of Man. In the following year he made some improvements in the mercury pump he had invented earlier.[54] By this time he was sufficiently recovered to resume work on the definitive measurement of the mechanical equivalent of heat. The Royal Society awarded him a grant of £200 to cover the costs, at least in part, of what was to be a long and demanding research.

The method he adopted was, in principle, that of the 1849 and earlier experiments.[55] A cylindrical calorimeter was fitted with baffles and, within it, a paddle-wheel carried blades that passed neatly between the baffles. The calorimeter was filled with pure, distilled water. But there was one notable refinement. Joule used Hirn's method in which the calorimeter was not fixed, but was held in balance against the frictional drag of the water as the paddle-wheel rotated. Two fine silk threads passed over two pulleys, each being joined at one end to a weight and at the other end to a groove in the calorimeter. The speed of the paddle-wheel was such that the drag of the water was just balanced by the weights and the calorimeter did not move. Drive came from two cranks worked energetically by Joule's son, Arthur.

The whole apparatus, mounted in the cellar of his house at Cliff Point, was exceptionally robust and rigid. He took elaborate precautions to minimise and to compensate for heat losses, and for friction losses in the pulleys and he measured the heat capacities of the calorimeter and associated equipment with exemplary accuracy. He recalibrated his thermometers. In order to minimise frictional losses due to the pressure on the bearing between the top of the calorimeter and the spindle driving the paddle-wheel he mounted the calorimeter on three supports that rested on a small floating drum in a concentric vessel. Water was carefully added to this outer vessel until the calorimeter had been raised on its three supports sufficiently to ease the friction on the bearing, or to 'relieve its weight on the axis'. The whole magnificent project was the work of a master experimentalist; the more remarkable as it was carried out by a man of nearly sixty who had been seriously ill during the previous year. His final figure for the mechanical equivalent of heat was 772.55 foot.pounds per British thermal unit, the pound weight being reduced to its value *in vacuo* at sea level (Higher Broughton being 120 ft above sea level), at the latitude of Greenwich (Higher Broughton being 53° 28½" N).

This result was in close agreement with the figure he had obtained from the friction of water in 1849, which was 772.692. On that occasion he had concluded, after taking all factors into consideration, that the true figure was 772 foot.pounds. This, however, was significantly different from the measurement he made in 1867 by the electrical method which assumed the correctness of the British Association standard of resistance. Although this standard had been determined by experimenters of great skill – Fleeming Jenkin, Maxwell and Balfour Stewart – Joule was understandably reluctant to accept that his measurement of the mechanical equivalent of heat, made with such skill and confirmed over a long period of time, could be at fault.

And his experiments provided the only quite independent check on the value of the BA standard of resistance. A matter of such importance for science, as well as for the developing electrical supply industry, could not be left undecided for long.

This last great research occupied him between 1875 and 1877. His paper was read to the Royal Society on 28 January 1878 and easily passed the scrutiny of the referees, who included Clifton and Thomson. Just before the paper was read Joule wrote to Stokes to explain that he had expressed the weighings in air 'because this was the authorised British use',[56] but it would have been more convenient and proper to express the result in measures independent of the medium. Weighing *in vacuo* reduced the result to 772.55 and this, multiplied by 'g', gave 24,867 as the absolute mechanical equivalent of the unit of heat. When the paper came to be printed the first amendment was made but the second was not.*

After he had completed his last research Joule signed a petition in support of a proposal, made by the Devonshire Commission, that an astrophysics laboratory be established.[57] And he moved house yet again, and for the last time, to 12 Wardle Road, Sale, in Cheshire. Sale, about five miles to the south-west of Manchester city centre, was a rapidly-growing suburb on the railway to Chester and on the line of the Bridgewater canal. Wardle Road was an avenue of large villas, many of which have now been demolished to make way for modern apartment blocks. Joule wrote to Frances Charlotte to describe the move.[58] His style is that of a normal letter between relatives on friendly terms with each other. It was no love letter, for Frances Charlotte had married Francis Nathanael Dancer, of Chiswick.[59] According to Joule,

> We are now comfortably settled with only a few of the grumblings which seem to be the essential quality of life. Of course the house is rather cold – they very often are, in winter. But we have some essential requirements, viz, a handy post, a good road and a clear sky through which to look at the stars. I saw one, the evening star, a few days ago, at 3 oc in the afternoon. I had Sir William Thomson here on the last day of the old year. He had been at Lord Derby's and consequently had a little of the air of a Statesman. He has much too favourable a notion of the Russians than I had, and I think he will see by present events that I am right. Mr Gladstone is to blame for the present state of things just as Mr Bright is responsible for the Crimean War.

It was appropriate that the completion of Joule's last great research should have coincided with the marked improvement in his fortunes. He

---

*The comparable figure for the mechanical equivalent by the electrical method of 1867 was 25,187.

was, as his comments made clear, far from wealthy although certainly not poverty-stricken. Osborne Reynolds commented tactfully that 'owing to unfortunate investments' his income was 'much diminished'. There are two slight clues as to what these investments might have been. Among the copies of the *Philosophical Magazine* that formed part of his library and are now in the Joule Collection at UMIST is a slip of paper used as a bookmark. On it is printed: 'The Santa Cruz Sulphur and Copper Company. Form of Application for Shares (to be retained by Banker).' And among the Joule letters in Cambridge University Library is a printed note: 'The Atlantic and Pacific Junction Company (For a Panama Canal without Locks). Chairman, Lord Wharncliffe; Deputy Chairman, J. P. Heywood. With a Form of Application for Shares' (letter dated 1 March 1853). Thin evidence indeed; but these were hardly the sort of enterprises that would have commended themselves to a family solicitor, bank manager or responsible trustee.

Fortunately the endeavour of some of his friends to secure suitable recognition of his achievements had never lapsed; now it took on renewed vigour. It is not known who was responsible for fanning the embers; it is, in any case, immaterial. On 16 April 1878 Sir Joseph Dalton Hooker, President of the Royal Society and Director of the Royal Botanic Gardens, Kew, sent to M. W. Lowry Corry (later Lord Rowton), Private Secretary to Lord Beaconsfield, Prime Minister and First Lord of the Treasury, a petition on Joule's behalf signed by virtually every notable man of science in Britain (see Appendix 3). The covering letter was brief, but informative:

> Kindly place the enclosed before Lord Beaconsfield & assure his Lordship that a higher claim of the kind never came under the cognisance of a Prime Minister.
> The doctrine of the 'conservation of energy' is, as the framer of the memorial (Dr Tyndall) puts it, co-ordinate in importance with gravitation & with the discoveries of Faraday & we venture to hope that Dr Joule may meet with the same recognition as did Dr Faraday, namely a pension of £300.[60]

A month later Sir Francis Sandford wrote to Algernon Turner, of Lord Beaconsfield's office, to give the senior civil servant's view:

> I heard a good deal about Dr Joule when we were looking for a 'man of science' to put upon the Council of Owens College in Manchester. The Lord President appointed him on ascertaining that his reputation at home and abroad – where the great value of his work has been fully acknowledged – stands very high.
> In addition to the irrefragable position he built up, on the part alluded to in your note, he discovered the 'Mechanical Equivalent of Heat' – which you will be glad to hear is 'an experimental foundation of one of the most important generalisations of modern science'.
> What can I say now except that I believe him to be one of our greatest men, in

his special line – & in every way deserving.

We made official acquaintance with him through Cowie (Dean of Manchester – Senior Wrangler & etc & etc)* on whose special recommendation the Lord President acted – But I have heard of him through other savants.[61]

On the same day Hooker was keeping up the pressure by writing to Corry to ask for an interview with the Prime Minister. Five days later a senior clerk at the Foreign Office wrote to Algernon Turner to express Lord Salisbury's view that Joule's services to science were of the greatest value and 'would fully entitle him to the recognition of the Queen'.[62] Tyndall had already been in touch with Lord Salisbury:

You may count on the entire sympathy of Lord Salisbury. In the letter in which he mentioned you as the proper medium he said that although official etiquette prevented him from presenting the memorial himself, he would support it and speak to Lord Beaconsfield about it; adding these emphatic words – a claim of greater strength to that of Dr Joule has not been submitted to the Prime Minister for many a year.

If you think it . . . necessary . . . I could come to you by the 12.15 train. The great point to be dwelt upon is the great merit of Joule which will make it an honour to the Country to recognise him. He is not in absolute want and there is no doubt that sooner than accept anything which savours of almsgiving he would live on half his present crust. But presented in the delicate, generous way which nobody understands better than Lord Beaconsfield, the pension will smooth the declining years of a noble life. Joule was a Manchester brewer, but his heart was not very much in his business and the little which he extracted from it has, I believe, been seriously lessened by losses of various kinds. At the present hour he is engaged in adding to our knowledge.

You may say to Lord Beaconsfield, that had it been an object to multiply names, not only would every scientific man in the United Kingdom, not officially disqualified, attach his name to the memorial, but every scientific man in Europe and America would do the same . . . if you decide to telegraph please address the telegram to me,
Bates Hotel,
Folkestone.[63]

Tyndall went off to Folkestone the following day en route for Switzerland where he was to stay for the next four months at his chalet on the Bel Alp, above the Aletsch Glacier and the Rhône valley. No one could have written of Joule in more understanding and fundamentally generous terms than Tyndall did in this letter. The recriminations of the past had been

---

*Benjamin Morgan Cowie was not popular as Dean of Manchester. A High Churchman, he quarrelled with the Protestant League and was translated to Exeter in 1884. He was not a member of the Lit & Phil and is nowhere mentioned in Joule's correspondence. His opinion would, therefore, have been entirely impartial – or else based on hearsay.

completely forgotten. Some years ago I wrote that Tyndall's championship of Mayer indicated that he had a generous temperament.[64] It has subsequently been shown that Tyndall's main target was Thomson, not Joule. I submit that Tyndall's letter, and his whole conduct in the affair of Joule's pension, confirms my judgement; and, futhermore, that the whole dispute can now be consigned to a minor footnote in the history of nineteenth-century physical science.

Hooker had his interview with the Prime Minister and as a result wrote to Roscoe for information:

> I have had a long interview this day at Downing Street on the subject of Joule's pension.
>
> It will not be easy to get £300 but I do no despair. Not a shilling is to be had from any other source but the £1,200 granted annually* and to get ⅓ of that [*sic*] for one applicant will require a strong push.
>
> Faraday's pension of £300 is in one sense no precedent. When he got this the Govt, under Peel, granted pensions of that sum to various distinguished men, more as a recognition of merit than anything else. In many years past the practice has been abandoned & Parliament has voted £1,200 to meet all claims scientific, literary, military, artistic and civil service.
>
> For many years no one has had more than £200 & *only one that sum.* The rest goes in sums of £50 to £100 & in a few of £150.
>
> Lord Beaconsfield will gladly do what he can, but he must make the case as strong as possible in all points of view. He asks me to ascertain privately & let him know.
>
> 1) What was Joule's parentage and education? particularly the last.
> 2) Is he married?
> 3) If so has he a family?
> 4) What are his actual circumstances?
> Can you, without publicity, get me these questions answered?
> I shall now get Lord Salisbury to speak to Lord Beaconsfield tonight.[65]

Roscoe replied, without delay, in a letter that while part truthful was, in other parts, somewhat more than the truth:

> In reply to your letter I have to say that his father was in trade in Manchester; that he is a widower with a family of two or three children; that he is almost entirely self-educated. In his early days there were no facilities such as at present exist for young men obtaining [*sic*] scientific education in the provinces – the only instruction he ever received in science were some private lessons from the illustrious Dalton. Hence the nation owes his important discoveries solely to Joule's own original genius & ability.
>
> As regards Joule's actual circumstances I may say that although he was left

---

*This was, of course, cumulative. The annual cost of civil list pensions at this time was of the order of £20,000.

with income sufficient to keep his family respectably this has been altogether insufficient to enable him to carry out successfully the researches which as a scientific man he felt it his duty to the world to continue. Indeed his friends have good reason to know that this want of means has rendered him personally uneasy & this greatly retarded the progress of science. In addition to these arguments there remains the powerful one of thus marking the material recognition of his life-long services. Would it be too much to ask for such a soldier of science a special pension to be voted in Parliament? Military pensions have been given by the hundreds with peerages and every other honour. A modest £300 per annum as a reward for his peaceful Victories would surely meet with ministerial approval if proposed by the Premier.[66]

The first paragraph could equally well have applied to Sturgeon. It would, of course, hardly have done to have mentioned that the Joule household had six indoor servants; that Benjamin Joule, sen., employed a coachman; that Joule's education went far beyond a few lessons from the illustrious Dalton. But then Roscoe was a worldly man as well as an able chemist.

While Roscoe was doing his best for Joule, Hooker was writing two letters to Turner, as remarkable in their way as Roscoe's:

At the risk of boring you I would call attention to an important distinction between Faraday's and Joule's claims on public recognition; namely that the former earned his country's recognition as much by the genius and disinterestedness with which he devoted so many years of his life to instructing the public of all classes and all ages as by his discoveries and researches.

Joule has not earned this position, and this justified your observation that Faraday became recognised by the public in a way that Joule has not been. As Lord Beaconsfield has done me the honour of consulting me it is my duty to ask you to lay the above consideration before him – At the same time; while in the abstract Dr Joule's work deserves £300 I think his friends should be content with £200.[67]

The first paragraph of this letter could be taken to imply that had Faraday not been a brilliant lecturer and teacher his researches would not have merited recognition by the State; which would have been preposterous. But the observation that Faraday's role as a teacher made his outstanding scientific merits much more readily and widely appreciated than those of Joule is plainly correct. As for Hooker's concluding suggestion, it would seem that his ethical reasoning was defective. The second letter, written on the same day, continued his argument:

I enclose a letter from Professor Roscoe of Owens College, Manchester, relative to Mr [*sic*] Joule's parentage, education and circumstances. I am not prepared to recommend such a course as that suggested in the last paragraph of the letter. Any system of special pensions would be liable to great abuse.

> After very careful consideration of all the circumstances of Mr Joule's case; especially in reference to the source from which the pension must come I think that £200 should be considered a very *sufficient & satisfactory recognition on the part* of the Government, for services which, after all, cannot be appraised in cash! & that the manner in which Lord Beaconsfield is sure to convey the intimation of this recognition to the recipient, or to his friends for him, will be regarded as the best evidence of the Nation's appreciation of the services rendered.
>
> Dr Tyndall has not yet paraphrased the crabbed sentence which I copied out and sent to him for the purpose.

Why did Hooker change his mind about the amount of the pension, why did he take it upon himself to interpret Treasury policy? Was it perhaps because his interview with Lord Beaconsfield led him to believe that they could not hope to get more than £200? Or was it because he was anxious to assure the deeply-entrenched utilitarian radicals of the administration that he, too, was an entirely responsible and most frugal dispenser of public funds?[68] In any case the correspondence illustrates the ambiguity at the heart of the pensions scheme in the last quarter of the nineteenth century. Were they intended as rewards for work done or as marks of national recognition? If Joule's work could not 'be appraised in cash' a decoration or medal awarded by the Queen or Prime Minister would have been appropriate; if his financial circumstances were to be weighed against the value of his scientific work then £200 per annum – the basic salary of a new professor at Owens – was grossly inadequate.

On 15 June 1878 Lord Beaconsfield recommended the list of pensions payable from the civil list for the year 1877–78. One of about half a dozen went to 'Dr James Prescott Joule, F.R.S. (5, Cliff Point, Higher Broughton, Manchester). In recognition of his eminent scientific achievements and valuable discoveries including the application of the principle of the 'mechanical equivalent of heat' . . . £200.'[69]

A month later Tyndall wrote to Roscoe from his chalet above the Aletsch Glacier: 'It is deeply gratifying to me to know the spirit in which Joule has accepted the pension. The only misgiving that haunted my mind related to this point – and now that shadow is happily removed. I hope each one of us did his duty'.[70] Tyndall's hope was amply fulfilled.

13

Last labours

Joule's last paper in the *Philosophical Transactions* was received with acclaim and for generations to come was to form a staple ingredient of basic physics courses. The award of a civil list pension gave pleasure to the scientific community in Britain. But as far as Joule was concerned there remained the worrying problem of the divergence between the measurements derived from experiments on fluid friction and those from the electrical experiments based on the assumption that the value of the BA standard resistance was correct. However, a new figure had emerged. This was the young American physicist, H. A. Rowland (1848–1901), who had originally trained as an engineer at Rensselaer. Rowland was fortunate in that, besides his gifts as an experimenter and a theoretician, he had just been appointed to the Chair of physics at the new Johns Hopkins University with ample funds to initiate a research programme. A first fruit of this was his classic confirmation of a deduction from Maxwell's electromagnetic field theory. He showed that a changing electric field generated a magnetic field.[1] Another investigation he undertook was the measurement of the mechanical equivalent of heat, which he found to be 778 foot.pounds.[2] In fact he did more; he showed that the value of the equivalent fell as the temperature of the water in the calorimeter was increased, reaching a minimum at about 30°C (later increased to about 37°C). In other words, the specific heat capacity of water, as measured by the mechanical equivalent of heat, fell over this temperature range. This meant that the universally accepted measure of the quantity of heat, as understood since Joseph Black's day, had been displaced in favour of the dynamical measure. As Poynting later put it, the real superiority of the work measure of specific heat capacity lies in the fact that it is independent of any particular substance and there is nothing hypothetical about it.[3] The concept of energy had, therefore, replaced the concept of heat.

Rowland sent a draft of his paper to Joule who was evidently slightly

Fig. 8 Joule in later life (photo Lady Roscoe, n.d., Schuster Collection, Wellcome Institute, by courtesy of the Wellcome Trustees)

disturbed by it. He observed to Thomson:

> I dont think my result can be wrong by 1/400 but you can judge as well as I . . .
> You will see by the enclosed that Rowland came to within 1/400 of my result. I
> have received his thermometer and shall as soon as possible compare it with
> mine. I do not suppose I shall find it graduated in the unexceptionable manner
> mine is . . . the fineness of the markings is much inferior to mine.[4]

Two features of this letter are puzzling. In the first place the difference
between Joule's and Rowland's results was nearer 1/140 than 1/400. And,
in the second place, subsequent letters show that he had not received
Rowland's letter at the date on this letter (25 May 1879), from which it
appears that the letter was wrongly dated.

In June of that year, Joule wrote to Rowland enclosing an offprint of his
Philosophical Transactions paper and adding:

> I feel very much interested in the results which you have arrived at and I trust
> that the two will corroborate each other. I did not try to ascertain the specific
> heats of water with my apparatus because I thought they would be more readily
> got by the method of mixtures. If you will send me the thermometer I shall be
> very glad to compare it with mine.[5]

Joule clearly saw that the final corroboration would depend on an exact
accordance between his and Rowland's thermometers. It is not known
whether or not Joule had given any thought to the variation of the specific
heat capacity of water before he received Rowland's letter.

Rowland, at that time in Munich, was grateful to hear from Joule.[6] He
had been surprised to learn that Joule's method was the same as his (or
Hirn's), having read only second-hand accounts of it. He commented:
'Correcting for the mercurial thermometer as nearly as I can we agree at the
temperature you have used within about 1/400, but the comparison of
thermometers may make it easier. I will order the thermometer sent at
once.' Rowland had been careful to check and correct his thermometers
against an air thermometer. He had found that some thermometers made
an error of more than 1% in the equivalent 'in the very direction in which
yours differ from mine. Geissler thermometers are the worst and Fastré's
or Kew thermometers best,* the latter only differ about 1/10°C at the 40°C
point.' Rowland ended his letter by thanking Joule for his 'great kindness to
so young and unknown a physicist'.†

---

*Joule used both Fastré and Kew thermometers besides those made by Dancer.
†Joule was ever a courteous correspondent. An industrious enthusiast, S. Tolver Preston,
author of *Physics of the Ether* (London, 1875), wrote several times to Joule for advice and
assistance. Although Joule was unwell at that time it seems that he wrote kind and helpful
letters to Mr Preston (book in Joule Collection, UMIST Library).

Rowland's careful work brought Joule sharply up against the inherent defects of all mercury-in-glass thermometers, as distinct from the defects of one particular thermometer compared with another. Joule had recorded the secular change of the freezing points of his thermometers over the years. He had hoped to find the 'true' fixed points by exposing his thermometers alternately to 0°C and to 100°C, initially for short intervals of time, say ten minutes, and then for longer periods ending with very long exposures. By drawing a graph he hoped to find the points that would not change over an indefinitely long time: the 'true' fixed points.[7] There were, Joule recognised, many problems with the mercury thermometer. Sometimes the mercury, seen under a magnifying glass, appeared to move in jerks; another problem was the large and variable expansion of glass. Perhaps a thermometer with an iron bulb could be made? And he had the idea that if a thick coating of copper could be deposited on the bulb of a mercury thermometer at 100°C it would exercise pressure on the bulb at lower temperatures and so counteract the expansion of the glass.[8] He even toyed with the idea of an elaborate, and most certainly expensive, nitrogen thermometer in which platinum weights were needed to submerge a vessel containing nitrogen in a bath of mercury.[9] The difficulty with air thermometers was, he considered, the corrosive effect that oxygen had on mercury, which was the ideal pointer.

Another problem for Joule was the selection of a place where the force of gravity could be used as the standard for all measurements of the mechanical equivalent of heat. Greenwich had two advantages; it was not a national capital and was therefore unlikely to arouse opposition on that score; and it had the oldest observatory.[10] But Joule could not resist dragging in his political views:

> It was once said that when Mr Gladstone took refuge in the town of Greenwich he represented the most contemptible community which ever had the franchise, but it was rejoined that we agreed nevertheless in taking our longitude from it. That was wrong for in speaking of Greenwich no one thinks of its Arrys [*sic*], or its member but of the grand old observatory. There will always be jealousies about localities, but we cannot afford to give up our milestones ... Now the latitude of the observatory of Greenwich is impartial in just skirting the south of Ireland and the north of France and also the north of Austria; or at least it used to do so before the Devil with his wars displaced the countries and I dont buy fresh maps every year. I will say one other word which is more likely to weigh with you than any other argument I could bring – our Observatory is on the same parallel as Göttingen!
>
> I am examining Rowland's thermometer. It seems a very good one – divisions about 1/30th inch to about 1/10°C. I find no jerking at present.[11]

A preliminary study of Rowland's thermometer with its calibration table and a comparison with Joule's own thermometer showed that it would have raised Joule's figure by 2.8 and made their results more accordant.[12] A second and more careful comparison made six weeks later showed that of 6.1, the difference between Rowland's and Joule's figures (778.6 and 772.5 respectively), 3.8 could be accounted for by the difference in the thermometers, 0.87 by the difference in latitudes and hence in 'g' between Baltimore and Manchester; and further, if Rowland had not reduced his value to *in vacuo*, 0.94 should have been added which have made the results nearly identical.[13] It seems that in these experiments Rowland and Joule pushed the mercury thermometer to the very limit of its accuracy at that time. Rowland, having reduced his temperature measurements to those of the air thermometer, must have applied the same corrections to Joule's temperature readings to justify his conclusion that their final results agreed to within 1/400. Joule was doubtful about the use of air thermometers. They were cumbersome; they had to incorporate a liquid as a pointer, but all liquids except mercury tended to stick to the glass and mercury, he argued, was liable to corrosion.[14] If subsequent research, with greatly improved thermometry, has vindicated Rowland's figure against Joule's, the latter had no reason for disappointment. He was to write to Rowland:

> I hope some day to resume my own experiments with an air thermometer I have had constructed many years. Although I have not yet studied your paper as closely as I intend to do I can with the utmost sincerity congratulate you on the achievement of a most valuable contribution to science and I feel much gratification at the close correspondence of our several results.[15]

While Joule was comparing notes with Rowland a tragic event was to make possible a vindication of his work from an unexpected quarter. On 5 November 1879, Maxwell died, prematurely. Joule was greatly upset. 'I was talking to Dr Joule on Tuesday night', wrote Osborne Reynolds to Stokes, 'when he was almost cross with me for saying that there appeared to be no hope.'[16] And, after learning of the death, Joule wrote to Thomson: 'I was deeply grieved and shocked by the death of Maxwell. It seems only a short while since you mentioned him to me as a "very clever boy" I would see when I came to Glasgow.'[17]

The sad death of Maxwell meant that the Cavendish Chair was vacant. Lord Rayleigh was elected to fill the vacancy. On taking up his appointment Rayleigh decided to associate the Cavendish Laboratory with a substantial research programme; one in which several people could profitably be involved.[18] The re-determination of the absolute electrical units was Rayleigh's choice for a beginning. After this there was the problem of the unresolved difference between Joule's measurement of the mechanical equivalent of heat by fluid friction and his measurement by the electrical heating method, which assumed the correctness of the value of the BA standard resistance. Other experimenters had differed over the correctness of the BA ohm: Kohlrausch had found it to be 2% too big while Rowland, in 1878, had found it 1% too small.

Rayleigh's work at the Cavendish Laboratory, carried out with the assistance of Mrs Sidgwick (Eleanor Balfour, sister of the politician A. J. Balfour) and Arthur Schuster, was published towards the end of 1881 and it supported Joule's suggestion that the BA ohm was incorrect. Rayleigh diagnosed the error in the work of Fleeming Jenkin, Maxwell and Balfour Stewart (1863) as compound. There had been confusion over the depth and breadth of the rotating coil. The original BA ohm was, Rayleigh showed, 1.3% too small. Joule was vindicated and the last scintilla of doubt about the dynamical theory and its application to electrical energy was removed.

On 6 January 1882 Joule wrote to Lord Rayleigh to congratulate him on the result.[19] They were not to meet until nearly four years later when Schuster, by then professor of applied mathematics (he became professor of physics in 1888) at Owens College, invited Joule to meet Rayleigh who was visiting Manchester.[20] Rayleigh had long wanted to meet Joule but when the opportunity came it was almost too late, for Joule's powers were fading.[21]

During the 1880s the pace of innovation hardly slackened.[22] When the decade began Joule was debating with himself whether to accede to the request of the Physical Society that his scientific papers be collected and published in one volume.[23] He feared that they would be a hotchpotch and would require a great deal of scissor-work to cut down tables of figures and other repetitive details. But the request from the newly-formed Society was flattering. So, too, was the award of the Albert Medal of the Society of Arts, which he received from the President, the Prince of Wales.[24] Another event in which he professed an interest, although he could not attend, was the granting of a Charter, much to Robert Lowe's disapproval, to the federal Victoria University.[25] A minor matter concerning the Charter aroused some local jealousies. It had been intended that the seal should bear the title 'Victoria University, Manchester', but there were objections. 'We', remarked Joule, 'gave way': 'wasn't it mean. For myself I think it certain that Liverpool and all the great towns will ultimately have their own universities. And then it would be objected if Manchester were *not* named in our seal as showing a degree of cosmopolitan arrogance.' He concluded his letter to Thomson by adding:

After I left you in London I thought I must have made some mistake in supposing we had seen all the pictures in the National Gallery. So I went there next morning and stayed 3 hours and had I the time to do so I should have stayed much longer. There are 28 rooms in all and the largest contains the best pictures of Turner – most magnificient works which I am sure will delight you when you have time to visit the Gallery again.

Joule was now busily occupied in preparing his papers for publication in book form. He took time off, briefly, to add his signature (and incidentally confirm his deep conservatism) to a petition protesting about the scheme to build a Channel tunnel. Other men of science signed the petition together with numerous bishops, admirals and generals.[26] In February 1882 he had an attack of bronchitis and Dixon Mann insisted that he took great care to avoid a recurrence.[27] This did not prevent him going to London four weeks later to sit for his portrait by the Hon. John Collier; it had been commissioned by and for the Royal Society.[28] After that he took a short holiday on the Isle of Wight. He was additionally busy now for it had been decided to publish a second volume of his papers: those he had written jointly with Scoresby, Playfair and Thomson.

In a cryptic note, penned at the top of a letter to Thomson, he remarked that he was 'glad of your success in using Swan's light but dont sympathise as tremendously as I would if I had no gas shares!'[29] The reference was to the invention of the incandescent electric light bulb, made simultaneously and independently by Joseph Swan and Thomas A. Edison in 1879. W. G. Armstrong was the first in Britain to install the new form of electric lighting in his mansion, 'Cragside', and Thomson was the second, the power in both cases being provided by a small turbine driven by a nearby stream. The arc lamp had been in use for some years to illuminate important public squares, streets, railway stations, etc., but it was unsuitable for private and domestic use. The new electric light bulb received wide publicity when it was triumphantly displayed at the Paris Exhibition of 1881. The proprietors of the Grosvenor Gallery, in New Bond Street, were sufficiently impressed to install electric light; its advantages were obvious where expensive works of art were on display. So successful was their installation that before long they were supplying current to neighbouring premises who wanted to switch to electric light; and shortly after that, guided by their young engineer Sebastian Ziani de Ferranti, they found themselves in the electricity supply business.

It was recognised that, with its evident advantages, the electric light bulb could displace the ubiquitous gas light. But it was also clearly understood that it could not do so until the cost of generation and supply was brought down to a level that was competitive with the well-established gas industry.

If that could be done there were millions of private homes, an enormous market, ready to be equipped for electric light. To reduce the cost of generation, much larger power stations with the most efficient steam-engines would be required. Large power stations, supplying current necessarily over a wide area, predicated the most efficient method of transmission. And here Joule had already supplied the basis for the answer in his discovery of the electrical heating law in 1840–41. In 1879 the engineer W. E. Ayrton had proposed that electric power should be distributed at low current and high voltage, thereby minimising the heat energy lost in transmission.[30] Of course the voltage would have to be transformed down, for safety's sake, at the consumer's end.[31]

The general problem of the transmission of energy was dealt with in impressive fashion by Joule's friend and biographer, Osborne Reynolds, in his Cantor Lectures, delivered before the Society of Arts in the spring of 1883.[32] The treatment was broad in scope but scholarly in rigour. He began by pointing out that over the previous ten to fifteen years mechanics had been radically changed by the general acceptance of the concept of energy. And he observed public concern about energy resources: the coal question was still alive in people's minds. Much enthusiasm had been aroused by the arrival in Britain of Faure's improved Planté battery, the first of the modern accumulators or storage batteries.[33] This, it was hoped, would banish the fear of exhausted coal-mines; for every stream or brook, every hillock over which the wind blew, could be a source of energy to generate storable electricity to be used as and when wanted. Reynolds was severely critical of this and other versions of what are now called 'renewable' energy schemes – tidal power, water power, and so on. A fundamental limitation on energy was that imposed by transmission.

The radical improvement in the steamship meant that it was cheap to import wheat and corn from the mid-western States of the USA and the prairie provinces of Canada. The two basic sources of energy in Britain were horses and steam-engines, the amount derived from each being, *in toto*, approximately equal. Remarkably, by that time most of the corn (maize) fed to horses in Britain came from across the Atlantic. It followed that all alternative forms of the transmission of energy had to compete with steam-engines for bulk transmission, and horses for smaller quantities. In other words, you had to take your fuel to where you needed it and there use it in steam-engines for big power, or horses for little power.

Every mode or means of transmission of energy requires a material medium and has this characteristic: energy is necessarily consumed in its transmission. This is most obvious in the two basic forms of 'packaged' energy: a coal train burns coal in the firebox of the locomotive; a horse can only pull a load of hay or corn if it has been fed on hay or corn. Inevitably, therefore, energy is lost in transmission. Of the two main means of transmission the horse is, weight for weight of fuel, the more efficient converter of heat into mechanical energy. There is, therefore, scope for research into the direct conversion of organic matter. This had been hinted at by Joule and Scoresby.

The same basic rule applies to every conceivable means for the direct transmission of energy; that is, to belting, shafting, compressed air or hydraulic mains. The limitations are twofold: the physical strength of the materials used and the frictional resistances that have to be overcome and that therefore consume energy. Reynolds had no difficulty in showing that the limits of transmission by all these means were of the order of twenty miles. By that distance energy losses reduced the output to a small fraction of the input, most of the energy having been used up in transmission.

When it came to the electrical transmission of energy, along wires, Reynolds was dismissive. He referred to experiments and quoted them as showing that much more energy would be lost, using a 1/16 in. telegraph wire, over a given distance than would be the case if belting were used: 'electric transmission is far inferior to the flying rope'. On the other hand, coal-gas pumped along ordinary gas mains could be used most efficiently by gas-engines, then rapidly coming into vogue and for which a great future was predicted.[34] Reynolds's lecture ended on a note of optimism. If Britain's prosperity had been built up on her coalfields there was no need to fear the foreseeable need to import coal, such had been the enormous advance in bulk transport, particularly by sea. But continued prosperity depended on Britain's willingness to look boldly forward and 'foster every means, political, social and mechanical, which may render this a favourite spot to live upon'.

Reynolds's Cantor Lectures amounted to a complete refutation of the thesis that Jevons had propounded in *The Coal Question*. What was also notable about the lectures was the almost contemptous rejection of the possibilities inherent in the electrical transmission of energy. This is particularly striking in view of the fact that Sir William Siemens and Sir William Thomson had, only a few years before, spoken favourably about the possibilities of the electrical transmission of energy,[35] that Ayrton had clearly specified the optimum conditions for efficient transmission and that Engels – a layman in such matters – had, in the previous year, commented on the 'recent discovery, that electrical currents of very high voltage, propagate with relatively small loss of energy through a simple telegraph wire over distances undreamed of until now and at the end can be converted [into a more convenient voltage]'. The matter was still embryonic but it meant, according to Engels, that industry would be definitely freed from 'all local restraints'.[36]

It is possible that Reynolds considered the dangers of high-voltage transmission to be unacceptable. On the other hand he had been greatly impressed by the dramatic improvements in transportation by steamship and railroad, the all-important methods of transmitting packaged energy. No doubt he expected the improvements to continue, if not accelerate, in the future. And he may not have realised that the creation of an electrical supply network to meet the increasing demand for domestic electric lighting would lower the price of electrical energy to such an extent that the electric motor would become increasingly competitive with local power sources. Or, more simply, that one massive and efficient steam-engine in a central power station could, using electricity to transmit and distribute its power, replace hundreds of little local steam-engines. If, *pace* Reynolds, the way was now open for the electrical supply industry, it was additionally fortunate that the BA Committee had successfully standardised the electrical units and, through Joule's work, related them to mechanical energy. Now electricity could be sold to the consumer and charged for in exact measures of work.

While the fruits of so much devoted work by small groups of men were being harvested, Joule's active career was coming to an end. In 1881 his friend and Lit & Phil colleague, Edward Binney, died. Binney's loyalty to and work for the Lit & Phil had equalled that of Joule. They had joined the Society on the same day, 25 January 1842 and they had both been Vice-Presidents and Presidents, each for a total of ten years. Binney was an abrasive and, some said, quarrelsome man, by no means popular with all the members. Nevertheless he and Joule were close friends. He had, fittingly, a strong sense of justice. He was a leader of the successful appeal to win a civil list pension for William Sturgeon and he led a movement to help the famous Peterloo veteran and radical Sam Bamford in his old age.

Joule was diminished by Binney's death. How he felt about Thomson's imaginative gloss on the account of their meeting in the Alps in 1847 – if he ever read of it – is not known.[37] What he cannot possibly have known is that since 1882 other writers have improved the tale still further. Joule is now to be found actually measuring the temperature of the water while his bride waits in the carriage. Towards the end of 1882 he told Thomson that his health was not good:

> My position is like that of Jacob, xxxiii, end of v 13 (. . . and the flocks and herd with young *are* with me: and if men should overdrive them one day all the flock will die). I am going on with the reprint of my papers but not so quickly as I should. Still it is quite pleasing as bringing to mind things so old as to make one

almost an antiquarian. That is certainly the most delightful science because all things are getting older and therefore more precious whereas in new discoveries everything is getting older and more common. All the world here is mad about a ship canal so it is probable that in 10 years we shall have in our midst 100 acres of evil smelling water, in the shape of a dock, which will drive all men who have not a deficiency in the seven senses out of the district. I would like them to have made a straight canal to bring up the sea. It would have been pretty to see the 'bore'.[38]

Towards the end of the following year he learned with regret of the death of Sir William Siemens whom he had not met very often but who was always friendly and helpful.[39] He remained anxious about health matters, but now vicariously, for he was convinced that the British sanitary system was so superior to that on the Continent that it was hazardous to go abroad:

We find an increasing quantity [*sic*] of travellers who return with enfeebled health. Thanks for your enquiries after mine. I have been recovering steadily and am now nearly quite well again. This has been much promoted by the re-establishment of my daughter's health. I have been much struck with the beautiful sunrise & sunset for the last 3 weeks. The most brilliant colors were half an hour before sunrise and ½ hour after sunset. The brilliant blue seemed to me the most remarkable and also the pink was very beautiful. I am inclined to think that the phenomenon is due to volcanic dust from Java as appears to be also the general opinion and is confirmed by a writer in the 'English Mechanic' who says that he had observed similar skies in Italy after the eruption of Vesuvius.

This reference to the atmospheric consequences of the eruption of Krakatoa was his last known meteorological observation. His scientific career was on the point of being brought to a formal conclusion by the publication of the first volume of his scientific papers in 1884; the second volume, that of his joint papers, appeared in 1887. Osborne Reynolds considered that the publication of these papers gave the scientific world

the opportunity of becoming acquainted not only with the full scope and completeness of Joule's research, but, what was more important, with the extent to which Joule himself had anticipated those who followed him in generalising from his own results. Up to that time Joule's work was mostly known as second hand, or by reference to the paper containing the final determination [*sic*] of the Mechanical Equivalent of Heat, in the *Phil. Trans.*, 1850.[40]

In other words, the full range of Joule's researches, from the beginning up to the last measurement of the equivalent published in 1878, was now displayed – the early, key, papers as well as the two familiar, later ones. But Reynolds's expectation was only partly realised. Such has been the pressure on syllabuses, examinations, and textbooks that, as a rule, space was available only for the papers of 1850 or 1878. In consequence Joule has been known, to generations of students, only as the man who measured the mechanical equivalent of heat with unrivalled accuracy. Unfortunately, the papers of 1850 or 1878 could be beautifully honed into examination questions: 'Give an account of Joule's measurement of the mechanical equivalent of heat. What precautions did he take to ensure an accurate result?' Such treatment, combined with some bad histories, have distorted the impression of Joule that has been left to posterity.

Joule had occasion to thank Roscoe for his congratulations on the publication of the first volume of the collected papers: 'Your approval is very pleasing to me inasmuch as the too constant attention to one's own work is liable to produce in one's mind a feeling of weariness and almost disgust with a consciousness of a multitude of imperfections.'[41] A short time later it was Joule's turn to congratulate Roscoe on the award of a knighthood.[42] Nevertheless it was nothing like a 'sufficient reward for your exertions for the national prosperity'. He added a disrespectful postscript: 'On being presented to the Queen wont she be a little confused as from what you tell me I suppose Her Majesty is still under the impression that you are Dr Dalton.'

If he was somewhat disrespectful towards the Queen he was positively abusive about the increasingly venerable Gladstone. He made his views very clear when writing to Tyndall:

> Some time ago I had the pleasure of reading your letter to Mr Grant on Party Politics and I wished at the time to thank you for your able denunciation of dishonesty in high places. The fact is that Mr Gladstone was fashioning a neat machine of 'representation' with the object of keeping himself in power when he ought to have used his whole endeavours to save Gordon and to reverse his previous policy generally. Posterity will judge him as the worst 'statesman' that England ever had and the verdict with regard to that Parliament will be ditto, ditto. The whole of politics is considered by him with a view to aggrandise himself and to gratify his personal hatred against Lord Beaconsfield, an infinitely wiser and far better man than himself. In all his conduct there is a heartlessness and total disregard for the welfare and even the safety of the Empire.[45]

It could be objected that he was an interested party, having been rewarded by a government led by Lord Beaconsfield. But there is no doubt that, irrespective of other considerations, Gladstone was at that time his particular *bête noire*. He told his cousin, Frederick Tappenden, jun. (Frances Charlotte's brother), that 'I do not know of anyone who does not rejoice at the overthrow of Gladstone's mischievous legislation and the deep disgrace of having a minister like Dilke wiped away'.[44]

Joule's dislike of Liberal politicians like Bright and Gladstone was unrelenting. It is easy to appreciate that the propertied classes felt menaced by the apparently irresistible advance of democracy. Matthew Arnold summed up the feeling: 'At the present time, almost everyone believes in the growth of democracy, almost everyone talks of it, almost everyone laments it.' Joule may well have feared that his own small property could be expropriated by a government elected by newly enfranchised working men. Even Bagehot's faith in the Royal Family as a kind of social lightning-rod, diverting and mollifying the wrath of the multitude, would have been cold comfort. As for Mr Gladstone, what reliance could be put on a man who, according to the current story, if caught out with a fifth ace up his sleeve would protest that the Almighty must have put it there; or, of whom it was said that, in his later democratic days, if a committee of working men decided that black was white would at once agree with them and put forward half a dozen excellent reasons, which none of them could have thought of, why it must be so.

Joule was outwardly a mild and diffident man. The violence of his denunciations of Gladstone, a man who in no way challenged or obstructed his scientific work, is puzzling. One possible explanation lies in the totally different temperaments and abilities of the two men. It is hardly necessary to stress that Gladstone was an able politician and, by all accounts a brilliant orator. In his later years he advocated policies that were repugnant to Joule and he did so with eloquence and conviction. This can only have been intensely frustrating and Joule, who lacked Gladstone's gifts, responded in the only way he could, with violent denunciations addressed to friends who more or less shared his opinions.

Whatever the defects of Gladstone's Home Rule Bill, rejected by the House of Commons on 7 June 1886, few would now dispute that Gladstone was, in principle, right, and his opponents wrong. Coercion was the only alternative to home rule. However, in his failure to see this Joule had good company; both Thomson and Tyndall strongly opposed Gladstone's Irish policy. But then Joule's record of political comment hardly reveals unerring prescience. His comments on the American Civil War lacked magnanimity, and he was, like many of his fellow countrymen, unnecessarily fearful of the French and the Russians at different times. In remarkable contrast with the great care he took in his researches to avoid speculations and to be as accurate as possible, his socio-political observations were mainly sweeping and unsupported generalisations. He, in fact, provides further evidence to confirm the common view that the political opinions of scientists have no greater value than those of the man in the street.

He had, he told Frederick Tappenden, jun., not been to London for two or three years. By the time the second volume of his papers appeared he was seriously unwell, especially during the winter and spring.[45] Towards the end of 1887 he began to recover. He had attended a meeting of the Council of the Lit & Phil for the last time on 9 March 1886; and he signed the library book of the Society on 9 October of that year. His last contributions to science had been printed in the *Proceedings* for 1882–83.[46] They were on the best form of hull for ships – he advocated a fish-shape – and on a simple device to damp out the oscillations of a telescope.

In 1886 he was again invited to be President of the British Association, due to meet in Manchester in 1887. But his health would not permit it. According to Osborne Reynolds his brother, by then living in Rothesay, persuaded him to avoid unnecessary excitement by staying at Seaforth with his daughter who had married her cousin (John's son), an oil merchant in Liverpool. But he must have paid at least one visit to Manchester during the British Association meeting. He was a Vice-President of the Association and represented the Lit & Phil on the Local General Committee.[47] There is also a photograph showing Roscoe together with D. I. Mendeleev and a group of five, mostly German, men of science. An eighth figure, standing to the right and steadying himself against a small table, can only be Joule. The coat he is wearing is similar to, if not the same as, the one he wears in Lady Roscoe's photograph (Fig. 9).

His last letter to Thomson explains that over the winter and spring he has been so unwell that he has been unable to do anything.[48] During these last two years of his life he rarely left his house and spent his time reading. He died at 12 Wardle Road, Sale, on the evening of Friday 11 October 1889, having been in a coma for most of the time during the last days.[49] Clausius and Hirn died within a few months while Dancer, the instrument-maker, had died in 1887. According to Dixon Mann, who certified the cause of death, Joule died of 'atheroma of the cerebral vessels. Degeneration of the brain. Two years.' The funeral on the following Wednesday was essentially private, in sharp contrast with Dalton's civil funeral. The mourners were Joule's son, daughter and son-in-law, brother Benjamin, John's three daughters and a few other relatives. The Lit & Phil was represented by its officers: Osborne Reynolds, Henry Wilde, Arthur Schuster, Edward Schunck and Dixon Mann. The officiating clergy were the Vicar of Brooklands, the Revd H. B. Jones, and the Vicar of Broughton, the Revd C. T. Watson.

The grave is at the north end of Brooklands cemetery which is by the west bank of the Bridgewater Canal. On the other side of the canal are moored the pleasure craft of the Sale Cruising Club, while beyond them is the busy railway that carries heavy commuter traffic between Manchester and the prosperous southern suburbs of Altrincham, Bowdon, Hale and

Fig. 9 Group at the British Association meeting in Manchester, 1887: *(left to right, standing)* J. Wislicenus, G. Quincke, E. Schunck, C. Schorlemmer, J. P. Joule: *(seated, in front)* Lothar Meyer, D. I. Mendeleev, H. E. Roscoe

Timperley. The tombstone is modest and no more conspicuous than the others. One has to cross the turf to read the inscription which includes the memorable number 772. The text is from St John 9:4: 'I must work the works of him that sent me, while it is day: the night cometh when no man can work.' Also buried there are Mary, who died in Chiswick in 1893, and Benjamin Arthur, who died in Ealing in 1922. Although Wardle Road is a street of well-kept houses, number 12 is now sadly dilapidated.

The tributes that were paid on the news of Joule's death confirmed what the course of his life had demonstrated. Even before he died the *Manchester Guardian* had published a eulogy by Hirn.[50] According to Hirn, Joule was 'not only the eminent savant whose magnificent works have been recognised by the scientific world but he has been the most honest, faithful and good, always ready to render justice to all who appeared to merit it'. 'He was not a man who courted fame', wrote one obituarist. 'He died as he had lived, a fervant Christian', wrote another.[51] Williamson's tribute at the British Association was remembered: 'Dr Joule . . . a modest and unobstrusive man, well contented to work quietly at science for its own sake without making any stir in the world by lecturing or book writing, so that his voice has rarely come before the public.' But of all the many tributes paid perhaps the most perceptive was in a letter that Clerk Maxwell had written to Balfour Stewart many years earlier:

> There are only very few men who have stood in a similar position and who have been urged by the love of some truth which they were confident was to be found though its form was as yet undefined to devote themselves to minute observations and patient manual and mental toil to bring their thoughts into exact accordance with things as they are.[52]

Soon after the funeral a delegation of the Lit & Phil led by the President, Osborne Reynolds, called on the Lord Mayor, Alderman Marsh, to urge that there should be a suitable memorial to Joule.[53] Among the long list of signatories were those of officials of various local trade unions as well as the Secretary of the Manchester and Salford Trades Council. Contributions to the memorial fund came from local leaders and from large and small firms.[54] The Chairman of the administering committee was the Lord Mayor, the Treasurer was Oliver Heywood, of the famous banking family, and Reynolds was the Convenor.[55] It was decided to commission a statue by Alfred Gilbert, RA. This now stands in the main entrance to Manchester Town Hall, opposite the statue of Dalton. It was unveiled on 8 December 1893, by William Thomson, Baron Kelvin of Largs, who could not resist repeating the anecdote about Joule on his honeymoon; it raised the expected laugh. Manchester is unique among British cities and towns in that its fine town hall has two statues at the entrance commemorating its two most distinguished men of science. The national memorial is a tablet in Westminster Abbey. The inscription reads:

> This tablet is placed near the graves of Newton, Herschel and Darwin by those who, in many lands, have united to perpetuate the memory of James Prescott Joule, F.R.S., of Manchester, in recognition of services rendered to science in establishing the law of the Conservation of Energy and determining the Mechanical Equivalent of Heat.

The probate of Joule's will revealed a respectable, if modest, fortune of £12,765 (say, £400,00 in today's money), two-thirds of which was to be put into a trust fund to provide Alice Amelia with an independent income. Household effects were left to Mary; his books and apparatus went to his son.[56] Benjamin St John Baptist Joule, the first-born, outlived the rest of the family to die at his home in Rothesay on 21 May 1895. He had married again but his second wife had died in 1884. And although he made a point of visiting Wardle Road regularly his closing years must have been lonely. A brief newspaper item of 18 November 1892 reported an action, heard before the Vice-Chancellor, by the three daughters of John Arthur Joule, against their uncle, Benjamin Joule, for maladministration of his trusteeship under the terms of their father's will.[57] He had, it was alleged, refused to give the ladies an account of his trusteeship after they had attained the age of twenty-one. The case was settled between counsels. But a month later Benjamin made his will. The three sisters were not mentioned. Apart from modest bequests to two servants, one of whom was given his 'faithful dog Carlos', virtually everything went to Alice Amelia and her husband in equal shares. The only other item of interest was some silverware bequeathed to 'my friend John Dixon Mann in recognition of his friendship' and of 'his unremitting attention to my late brother Doctor James Prescott Joule'. It was a very modest estate that Benjamin left; the net valuation was £744 15s 1d in England and Scotland.[58] He had an annuity of £240 a year and, presumably, the rents from his (mainland) estate in Ireland. It would be reasonable to conclude that his failure as a trustee indicated that he, and perhaps his brother James, lacked the business acumen of his father and grandfather.

Besides the statue in Manchester Town Hall there is a bust of Joule in Sale Park. A crater on the moon has been named after him, and a French submarine was named *Joule*; sadly, she was lost with her crew in the Dardenelles in 1915.[59] Although it has never been recognised as such, perhaps that most significant tangible memorial to Joule was Deptford Power Station that, by coincidence, went on stream in the month that Joule died. The creation of the young Sebastian de Ferranti, following his success at the Grosvenor Gallery, Deptford Power Station was conveniently situated on the Thames to receive coal from Newcastle coal-ships. The other characteristic feature was that it generated alternating current (at 86 Hz) for convenience of transformation up to an unprecedentedly high 10,000 volts for transmission by cable to substations in London, eight miles away. The use of high-voltage transmission meant that the heating loss in the long cable was small, consistent with Joule's i^2r heating law of 1840–41. All subsequent power and transmission systems have followed the Deptford lead and may therefore be said to exemplify Joule's heating law and his fine insight of 1843: 'Electricity may be regarded as the grand agent for carrying, arranging and converting chemical heat.'

14

In retrospect

Osborne Reynolds described Joule at the age of fifty-one as rather under medium height and somewhat stout and rounded in figure. His dress, though neat, was 'commonplace in the extreme' and his 'attitudes and movements were possessed of no natural grace', while his manner was somewhat nervous and he possessed no great facility of speech. However, he conveyed an impression of the simplicity and utter absence of all affectation that had characterised his life; while 'his fine head and the reflective intelligence of his grave face accorded with the possession and long exercise of the highest philosophical powers'. This last impression of Reynolds is supported by surviving photographs, the portrait and, particularly, the Alfred Gilbert statue. Others who knew him confirmed that he was shy and reserved in company but much more forthcoming when with a group of friends. A recurrent theme in his correspondence was an anxious concern about his health and, consistent with this, a distaste for foreign travel; his holidays were taken on the west coast or on the Isle of Wight. Although he was not more xenophobic than the majority of his fellow countrymen it is remarkable that very few foreigners were elected to Honorary Membership of the Lit & Phil during the period when he was its most influential member. Over the years 1886 (when he effectively with-drew from the Society) to 1889 no fewer than forty-one Honorary Members were elected, among them Clausius, Hirn and Helmholtz. The Council was making up for lost time.* Despite his strong political views Joule was, according to Reynolds, tolerant of those from whom he differed (except perhaps in correspondence!). He had a strong sense of humour and was particularly fond of that Victorian invention: entertaining nonsense. His son stated that he a deep love of nature and was a talented

*There was a similar barren period over the years 1918–50. Surprisingly, neither Einstein nor Planck were made Honorary Members.

draughtsman; his drawings in his letters and notebooks confirm this.

These assessments do not, however, help us to understand the sources of his characteristic scientific skills and ideas, his motivations, his assumptions and expectations. There is no reason to doubt that, as he stated, Dalton was a most powerful influence. It was Dalton who impressed on him the importance of mathematics and the need to direct his researches towards the discovery of simple mathematical laws. Through Dalton he learned to accept the atomic theory together with the related concepts of *vis viva* and 'attraction through space' that made possible the performance of work. These 'measures of moving force' had been advocated strongly by Dalton's friend Peter Ewart and were accordant with the measures and practices of Manchester manufacturing industry.

When and how he acquired his practical skills are questions about which we can only speculate. It may be that Porter, Tappenden and, later, John Davies were able to teach him some practical skills and to stress their importance, but it is unlikely; and it is unlikely that Dalton was the source for he was not a notably exact experimenter. The only other sources were casual or informal contacts, experience in the brewery and inborn genius. But we should not overlook the fact that experimental skills develop with use and practice. There is no doubt that Joule's early published researches showed a rather casual attitude to precision and accuracy. He was criticised – sometimes fairly – for drawing sweeping conclusions from inadequate data. It is probable that he took these criticisms to heart, for his experimental precision, and with it his awareness of errors to guard against or allow for, increased to reach their peak with experiments between 1845 and 1878. He seems to have trained himself to be able to read thermometers with the utmost accuracy and at one point talks of the possibility of training himself to judge very short intervals of time. His early observations on the complex nature of the lightning-stroke prompt the suggesion that leading experimental scientists may have sharper senses than most people.

With experimental precision went a reluctance to speculate beyond the limits of reasonable experimental evidence (as he himself might have put it). This, of course, is a matter of personal judgement. One man's speculation is another man's evident truth and a third man's wild fantasy. Joule remarked that premature speculation retards the advance of science; but this is true only if everyone pays attention to the speculation. Furthermore, if a man does not speculate he is not a scientist; he is a technician; and Joule was patently much more than a technician, practically skilled though he was. Quite apart from the grand speculation concerning the energy doctrine – for which he amassed such impressive evidence – he was willing to speculate about the kinetic theory of gases, following Herapath's hypothesis, and about the true nature of meteors. But caution saved him – as it did not save Mayer, Thomson and Waterston – from suggesting that the heat of the sun was due to the collision of meteorites. And caution stopped him from straying into speculations about the true nature of atoms, of electricity and magnetism, and from attempting to solve the atom–ether dualism. There were many temptations by the way.

It may be that a growing emphasis on precision coupled with a naturally cautious disposition inhibited his later researches. His papers after about 1862 do not show the flair of, for example, those inspired researches into the heat of electrolysis that were to lay the foundations for the conservation of energy. He had, of course, suffered the trauma of his wife's death – its effect was noticed by his contemporaries – he had had recurrent bouts of ill-health, and there was his association with the masterful Thomson. In addition, radical revolutionary though he was (more, probably, than he himself realised), Joule was in some ways as conservative in science as he was in politics and in the affairs of the Lit & Phil. He was averse to the metric system and appears to have been reluctant to use graphs, preferring to express his results in tablular form. Had he been willing to use graphs more readily he might have gained new insights and saved himself trouble; he might not, for example, have spent so much time trying, unsuccessfully, to find simple laws of magnetisation.

A lifetime of laborious, and sometimes unfruitful, work for so slight a financial reward requires some explanation. It would be no more than a tautology to say that he was motivated by the love of truth. It may be that as a shy, retiring man he hoped to achieve status through recognition as a natural philosopher and a leading member of the Lit & Phil. This would have been reasonable when Dalton was at the height of his fame. Benjamin enjoyed a certain social cachet through his association with St Peter's and other churches and through his composition of hymns and chants. John Arthur, on the other hand, was quite content to be a gentleman of leisure, living first in Victoria Park before going to the Isle of Man. Joule was, despite his custom of sleeping through sermons, a sincere Christian.[1] He and Mary had their pew at St Peter's and, later, at St Paul's Church, Sale. But there is no evidence of a religious motivation for his researches. The occasional references to the Almighty to be found in his papers and very occasionally in his correspondence are no more than conventional expressions, shorthand for the principle of the uniformity of nature, and therefore acceptable in Victorian Britain.

There is no doubt that an economic motivation was present when he was, like others, swept along by the electrical euphoria in his very first researches. But after his initial disappointment in 1841 there is only sporadic evidence of economic motivation. He took out two patents, devised and made ingenious instruments and carried out researches with a severely practical purpose (on, for example, the surface condensation of steam). Like Maxwell, Thomson, Wheatstone and the majority of British physicists Joule carried out researches in what, today, would be called technology. In those days they would be considered a part of science, a part of experimental philosophy. When Joule gave up his work on electric motors to study the generation of heat by an electric current he was not making a radical change; he was not abandoning one discipline for another. It would therefore be pointless to enquire what led him to stop being an inventor, or an engineer, and to become, instead, a 'pure' scientist. He himself would not have understood the question. The idea of a division between 'pure' science and applied science, or whatever the other sort is called, is an imported notion. It reflected the division between the tradi-tional universities of Germany and the *Technische Hochschulen,* later the technical universities. The idea was brought back to Britain and the United States by enthusiastic students who had attended German universities and who returned home rightly impressed by the excellent educational and scientific achievements of that country. Among the early apostles of pure science was Lyon Playfair, and, consistent with the excellence of German chemistry in the nineteenth century, it was mainly the chemists who spread the gospel abroad.

This is not, of course, to deny the autonomy of physical science. The example of Newton himself refutes any such suggestion. It is, however, insisted that the history of physical science cannot be understood without reference to the technological factors that, at different times, have helped to decide, or even decided, the course of progress. A history of pure physics would be a very one-sided affair.

Many of those who contributed to or supported the dynamical theory of heat were engineers – Marc Séguin, Montgolfier, Carnot, Rankine, Waterston, Hirn – and most of them, together with Joule and Mayer, were outsiders; that is, they had little or no connection with universities or other academic institutions. The hope or expectation of official advancement cannot have been a motive for Joule's dedication to his researches. We are left, therefore, with the only remaining hypothesis, that though his natural capacity for research in the particular field that he found for himself he achieved deep personal satisfaction and fulfilment. What we can never know, important though it was, was the part played by those debates, discussions, and private conversations that occurred during his faithful attendances at the Lit & Phil. These were never recorded and have been lost for good.

The leading parts taken by outsiders in the development of the energy doctrine and of thermodynamics and the indifference or hostility of men such as Herschel, Potter, Kelland and Whewell, the representatives and defenders of orthodoxy, suggest that here was, in Kuhn's sense, a scientific revolution. The crisis occurred not in established natural philosophy but in experimental philosophy.[2] Specifically, the crisis could be identified as occurring in connection with the study of the electric motor and with the problem of the flow of heat without the performance of work. Simple as the basis concepts now seem they were by no means easy to understand at the time, particularly for those whose education and experiences had not equipped them to learn the language of the new physics. The Revd Mr Highton was by no means alone. It was to meet the need of such people that Balfour Stewart wrote his simple textbook on the conservation of energy.[3] In place of the austerely simple Newtonian picture of attractive or repulsive forces acting through space there was now a complex system of energy relationships explained in terms of the new concepts of kinetic and potential energy. Joule, like Tyndall and others, can be criticised for using the blessed word 'force' to denote, indifferently, *vis viva*, work, attraction. But old words often have to serve when new ideas are being introduced; and in Joule's case, the context almost always made clear the sense in which the word was being used.

The conservation of energy and the application of the energy principle generally were launched at a time when science was about to begin the rapid expansion that continues to the present day. With expansion went proliferation. New autonomous and semi-autonomous subjects were recognised. In addition to physics, organic chemistry, physical chemistry, astrophysics, solar physics, physiology, bacteriology, mechanical engineering,* electrical engineering and, finally chemical engineering, were all added to the list of specialisms. Such was its general importance that, after the 1860s, thermodynamics was divided between physics, chemistry, mechanical engineering and eventually other disciplines as well, each one drawing from the common pool what it required and developing the subject on its own lines. Many, perhaps most, of nineteenth-century advances did not undergo this process of division.

In 1872 Walter Bagehot, one of the best informed of nineteenth-century commentators, published his *Physics and Politics*, which was an attempt to

---

*The Institution of Mechanical Engineers was founded in 1847. Up to and for some years after that time the Institution of Civil Engineers included mechanical engineering within its province.

apply Darwinian natural selection to politics.[4] Nevertheless, whatever the highly intelligent man in the street thought, physics by that time was a fairly clearly defined discipline in which energy and field theory had greatly advanced the unification demanded by Whewell and others. In fact, so complete was the success that the science was considered to be completed much as Whewell had believed that Newtonian mechanics had been completed.[5] However, the physics of the nineteenth century was, despite the lip service paid to him, non-Newtonian in important respects. And it was from these non-Newtonian aspects – energy and field theory – that the twentieth-century revolutions of quantum theory and relativity sprang.

At the same time that the new disciplines were being recognised, the agencies of the State were beginning to intervene in the organisation of science. Increasingly, science was included in school education, and to supply the demand for teachers, universities expanded their science (in Germany, philosophy) faculties and recruited more staff. Syllabuses were drawn up and refined in the light of experience and the progress of science. Standard textbooks were written, improved, sometimes copied, and published in successive editions. Science became an affair of separate disciplines and the man of science was imperceptibly replaced by the professional scientist, first as teacher in school, college and university and then as worker in government or industrial laboratory. The devotee man of science has now disappeared except in a few marginal areas and Joule's hope that entirely voluntary organisations, like the Lit & Phil, would continue to carry the main burden of scientific research has been falsified. It is not difficult to see how this happened. For many years science courses to suit all interests have been available. Colleges and universities offer the would-be scientist libraries, laboratories, facilities on a scale no voluntary organisation could match; and, moreover, grants, fellowships, jobs for life in scientific research. Ironically, in the same year that the Lit & Phil celebrated its centenary (1881), the Victoria University instituted its Bishop Berkeley fellowships for research in science, engineering and the arts.

This development has not been without its dangers. No one would wish to go back to the days of the Lancashire geometers, the working men who, when the rungs of the academic ladder were far apart and very fragile, still managed to exercise their talents and interests to a remarkable extent. But 'big science', however defined, is not without its conservative elements, potentially as restrictive as they were in Joule's early days but more difficult to deal with now that fair provision has, seemingly, been made for everyone. Joule, and men like him, enjoyed complete freedom. No one told them what to do; they did not have to muster paper qualifications and go through the routines of application and interview before being admitted to a laboratory. They rarely had to render account to official bodies. And they had to live within their means, a requirement whose benefits are sometimes overlooked.

Joule's scientific career was as satisfactorily complete as it was eminently successful. It was rounded off by the confirmation of the accuracy of his measurement of the mechanical value of the unit of heat by the master experimentalist Rowland and, from the opposite direction, by Lord Rayleigh and his group at Cambridge. With Rowland's demonstration that the specific heat capacity of water, measured in mechanical and therefore absolute units, varies with the temperature, the science of heat *per se* was formally brought to an end. There is no entity called heat. Joule, although he often used the expression 'mechanical equivalent of heat', was aware from the beginning that heat was basically mechanical in nature. And 'heat' has now dropped from the elementary textbooks. In one sense this is a pity for heat is a universal human experience and essential for life. It earned a place in science for it was through the study of heat that modern thermophysics and thermochemistry evolved, and if the tyro understands this by so much will his knowledge be better grounded.

In retrospect Joule's researches seem to fall into a pattern of inevitability. His thoughts were, as several informed commentators have pointed out, quite remarkably clear and, it should be added, economical. There was little that was superfluous about his papers and, apart from the early ones, every precaution was taken to eliminate or account for errors. Reading them gives the same impression as reading Faraday's papers; one feels that this was the way things must go. And what becomes clear after a study of the whole sequence is the single-mindedness with which he pursued his researches right up to the recognition and establishment of the energy principle. It cannot be stressed too much, however, that at any time he could have been deflected from what we now know to have been the correct and fruitful direction. Others had, at different times, come close to his position and had expressed views that could be interpreted as similar to his. But it was not simply a question of being right; it was essential to show why and how he was right and what were the implications of his discoveries. None worked as consistently as he did; none had shown the same understanding or the same discipline of mind. To borrow Pocock's useful expression, Joule set the standard by which all the others must be judged.[6]

In one respect only Joule disappoints the student. His correspondence and his papers give no indication whatsoever of any philosophical doubts or interests of any kind. There is no sign that he was influenced by Boscovitch, Kant, Hegel, Hamilton or any other philosopher in the way that, according to some historians, certain of his contemporaries and immediate pre-decessors were. Nor is there any discernible connection between his religious faith and his scientific beliefs. His refusal to speculate extended beyond his scientific theories and hypotheses. He would never, one feels, have proposed such a sweeping generalisation as Thomson's assertion that there is a universal tendency to the dissipation of energy, or Clausius's statement that the energy of the universe is constant, and the entropy tends always to a maximum. Joule, unlike the celebrated lady from New England, did not feel it necessary to say that he accepted the universe, or indeed, to say anything at all about it. His attitude was strictly scientific. The conser-vation of energy is either a scientific principle, or a cosmological principle, or a combination of the two. For Joule, the quintessential physicist, it was the first of these; for many, perhaps most, it is probably the last.

Perhaps Manchester's single most remarkable achievement is its unique scientific record. As we have seen, science and learning had previously been associated with ancient universities, capital cities and national academies. Now, for the first time, a parvenu industrial city established a scientific tradition of its own. Industry was the engine of Manchester science; but it offered no guarantees. For 100 years the Cornish mining industry had led the world in steam-engine technology. The names of Cornish engineers like Hornblower, Woolf, Trevithick, and Harvey were, and are, world famous. There were Cornish men of science too. But the technology was too narrowly based and when the terms of trade changed the engineers and the men of science left. Manchester also went through rough times, but Manchester science went from strength to strength. For this Dalton, Joule and the Lit & Phil must have a major share of the credit. Joule was no orator on behalf of science, he had no political or administra-tive skills and, like Faraday, he had no pupils, no eager disciples. But, as Tyndall wrote, he enjoyed immense international prestige. It was obvious, even to those with limited scientific knowledge, that what he had achieved was worth doing, worth developing, worth supporting. He must have some credit for the fact that, by 1900, the Owens College was the best endowed of all English provincial colleges.

Joule's political predictions were substantially incorrect; his political sociology was little more than a display of prejudices. True to his nature, he offered no predictions about the future course of science. But one predic-tion he offered was remarkably accurate, as were the judgements that accompanied it. Among his archives is a short paper that Crowther believes, probably correctly, was a draft for the Presidential address to the British Association that, in the event, he never delivered. After a eulogy of the spiritual and moral benefits of science and an account of its proper aims and purposes he concluded with a prophecy:

It is deeply to be regretted that another and most unworthy object has been introduced and has gradually and alarmingly increased in prominence. This is the improvement of the art of war and the implements of mutual destruction. I know there arc those who think that these improvements will tend to put an end to war by making it more destructive. I cannot think that such an opinion is based on common sense. I believe war will not only be more destructive but be carried on with greater ferocity. Individual campaigns will doubtless be short as well as decisive, but this will necessarily cause the rapid rise and fall of states and unsettling of boundaries and constitutions which must eventually deteriorate civilisation itself and render peace impossible. And thus by applying itself to an improper object science may eventually fall by its own hand. In reference to this subject we must also deplore the prostitution of science for the aggrandisement of individuals and nations, the result being that the weaker is destroyed and the stronger race is established on its ruins. In making the above remarks, I intend no disparagement of the efforts being made to secure the integrity and liberties of Great Britain. These have been forced upon us and it is a matter of congratulation that we are not responsible for the present military attitude of Europe.

The final paragraph shows the influence of the Bible on Joule's prose style; in particular Corinthians 1, 13:

Such being the characteristics of the spirit fostered by the cultivation of natural science, and such being the great objects which are in view, it is almost incredible that anyone should be bold enough to deny its importance, nay its absolute necessity in education. Suppose a student to be thoroughly acquainted with every event which has occurred in the history of the world, suppose him to have a perfect knowledge of every language that has been spoken by man, suppose him to have an accurate perception of the most subtle questions of metaphysics, suppose him to be acquainted with the practice of the fine and industrial arts, yet however important and essential all of these and much more may be he cannot be considered more than half educated if he does not know something of the objects of the material world, their history, their forces and the laws which keep in order what would otherwise be chaos.[7]

Appendix 1

The maximum density experiment

Most of the experiments, or measurements, carried out by Joule and Playfair in their joint researches are of little interest in themselves. Their determination of the temperature at which water reaches its maximum density is, however, an exception. Although their technique was based on the same principle as T. C. Hope's experiment they improved it to such an extent that it became, in effect, a wholly new method.

Two metal cylinders, 4½ft high and 6in. in diameter, stood side by side. They were joined at the bottom by a brass pipe 1in. in diameter, 6in. long and fitted with a stopcock. At the top they were joined by a metal trough of 1in. square section. A slide, or barrier, was fitted in the middle of the trough.

Previous experimenters had shown that water reached its maximum density at about 40°F. Joule and Playfair therefore poured distilled water at 37°F into both cylinders, closed the stopcock and the barrier and added enough hot distilled water to one cylinder to raise the temperature to about 41½°F. After the water in the two cylinders had been stirred and the temperatures taken, the stopcock was opened and the barrier raised. A small glass sphere, ⅜in. in diameter and of such a weight that it would only just float, was placed in the trough and its velocity of drift from one cylinder towards the other noted. The small glass sphere had to be of minimal positive buoyancy in order to reduce surface tension effects which would have pulled it to the side of the trough.

This experiment was repeated five times as the temperatures of the water in the two cylinders tended towards equality. In each case the water was stirred and the temperatures taken before and after the experiment. The velocity of drift of the sphere was recorded and the mean of the temperatures of the water taken as the temperature of the experiment. The two mean temperatures between which the direction of drift of the sphere reversed were plainly on either side of the temperature of maximum density. By plotting a graph of mean temperatures against velocity of drift in inches per hour they were able to find the exact temperature of maximum density. In all they carried out four series of experiments. Their conclusion was that water reached its maximum density at 39.1°F.

Appendix 2

Helmholtz and Joule

Apart from the misrepresentation already mentioned, Helmholtz is open to criticism on the following grounds:

1   He stated that Joule had endeavoured [*sic*] to prove experimentally ('durch das Experiment Joule zu beweisen gesucht') that a magneto current develops heat and no compensating cold can be detected. One would not think that this was the key experiment of Joule's 1843 paper (wrongly dated at 1844), and the statement is put *after* Helmholtz has made the same observation. Joule is, implicitly, denied originality (Tyndall, p. 133).

2   Writing of Joule's experiments on compressed air he mentions an experiment by Joule which seems [*sic*] to have been carefully done ('einen versuch von Joule anfuhren, der ziemlich zuverlasssig zu seinscheint'). This suggests that Joule's other experiments may not have been carefully done! (Tyndall, p. 135).

3   He states that when a gas expands without doing work there is no change of temperature. This appears [*sic*] to follow from the above experiments of Joule. In this case the cart is put before the horse and the 'appears to follow' obscures the purpose of Joule's experiments (Tyndall, p. 137).

4   He notes that Joule determined from his own experiments the force equivalent which Holtzmann from the experiments of others reckons at 374, to be 481, 464, 479. But Holtzmann did not accept the dynamical theory of heat (Tyndall, p. 137).

5   Helmholtz ascribes the discovery of the i^2r law to Lenz and implies that Joule followed up Lenz's work by showing that it extended to liquid conductors ('wie es Joule gefunden hat'). This, of course, is a travesty of the truth. Joule published the i^2r law two years before Lenz confirmed it. The same paper by Joule extended the law to cover liquid conductors, as Helmholtz *must* have known if he had read the paper! The conclusion is that he never actually saw Joule's paper (Tyndall, p. 146).

6 This is confirmed by Helmholtz's statement that the only measurements of conduction through electrolytes that he has been able to find were those made by Lenz and Poggendorff. It is certain, therefore, that he cannot have seen Joule's 1841 paper; nor can he have seen any of the subsequent papers on electrolysis (Tyndall, p. 149).

7 Dealing with Joule's work on chemical and electrical heat Helmholtz says that his method is open to many objections ('doch ist gegen seine Messungsmethoden mancherlei einzuenden'). Rather lamely he adds that E. Becquerel was said to have corroborated Joule's results (Tyndall, p. 151).

The errors and omissions that characterise Helmholtz's references to Joule confirm that he himself never read Joule's papers but must have relied, unwisely, on the opinions of others. Helmholtz was a young man at the time, with only two papers to his name. The men he depended on were presumably established academics. Who they were is not relevant to this work; nor are they of interest to the writer.

Appendix 3

Petition to the Prime Minister

Petition drawn up by Tyndall requesting the award of a civil list pension for Dr Joule. This petition was signed by practically every distinguished man of science alive at the time. The two notable exceptions, Grove and Playfair, probably considered that they were disqualified by virtue of public office.

Joule did not hold an honorary degree of Cambridge University. His honorary degrees were from the Universities of Dublin, Edinburgh, Oxford, and Leiden. He was an honorary member of the Cambridge Philosophical Society and of many other learned societies in Britain and abroad.

To the Right Honourable the Earl of Beaconsfield
First Lord of the Treasury, &c. &c.

My Lord,

We, the undersigned, cultivators of Science in the United Kingdom, beg respectfully to submit to your Lordship's attention the following facts and considerations.

By the achievements of individuals, rather than by the contributions of any large class of the community, the scientific reputation of this country among the nations of Europe has been hitherto maintained. Such achievements, moreover, have been in part the work of men whose motive power was the love of research, rather than professional duty. Neither Cavendish nor Darwin ever filled a Professor's chair, and a similar remark applies to the illustrious investigator whose scientific claims form the subject of this memorial.

For forty years, without official appointment or pecuniary reward, Dr. James Prescott Joule has devoted himself to the cultivation of science. Whether we regard the magnitude of the problems on which he has been engaged, or the success and completeness with which he has solved them, he is almost without a rival. Not only in this country, but in the scientific world generally, he occupies, by common consent, a position accorded only to the greatest names. Thirty-five years ago, he began researches on the great principle of the conservation of energy, and from that time to the present he has been for the most part engaged in strengthening and illustrating this principle. No law or theory ever enunciated in science transcends this one in importance, and its vast expansion and varied application at the present moment are in great part to be traced directly to the initiative of Dr. Joule. He it was who, with a sagacity far in advance of the average insight of his time, with an originality and skill of conception and device worthy of all admiration, and with a resolute patience in the face of difficulties which might well have been deemed insurmountable, placed the doctrine of the conservation of energy on the irrefragable basis of experiment. It is the claims of a philosopher who stands in this relation to a principle, which in point of importance ranks with that of gravitation, as enunciated by Newton, that we respectfully submit to your Lordship's consideration.

The labours rather than the lives of those who have added to the material resources of the country, or to its intellectual renown, form the data which the English statesman has to take into account. Still it may not be out of place to mention that the private life of Dr. Joule has been marked by the modesty and simplicity characteristic of the true philosopher. These very qualities, indeed, have rendered his labours less conspicuous to the general public than they otherwise might have been.

Many of the highest distinctions of continental Academies have been bestowed upon Dr. Joule. Nor, so far as such marks of honorary recognition go, has England been unmindful of the merits of one of the worthiest of her sons. In 1870, the Royal Society emphasised a previous honour by conferring upon Dr. Joule the highest reward which is in its power to bestow, while the Universities of Oxford and Cambridge long ago conferred upon him their honorary degrees.

On these facts and considerations, we respectfully base the following request. We ask your Lordship to ratify the universal esteem in which the labours and character of Dr. Joule are held, by placing him, as regards the fund set apart for the recognition of eminent services, in the position occupied by Faraday and other illustrious men, in honouring whom your Lordship's predecessors have at the same time shown friendliness to science and done honour to themselves.

Wise as the selections for this distinction have hitherto been, there is not one of them more worthy of a nation's approval, or of a statesman's regard, than the one which we now respectfully press upon your Lordship's favourable consideration.

We have the honour to be,

My Lord,

Your Lordship's most obedient servants,

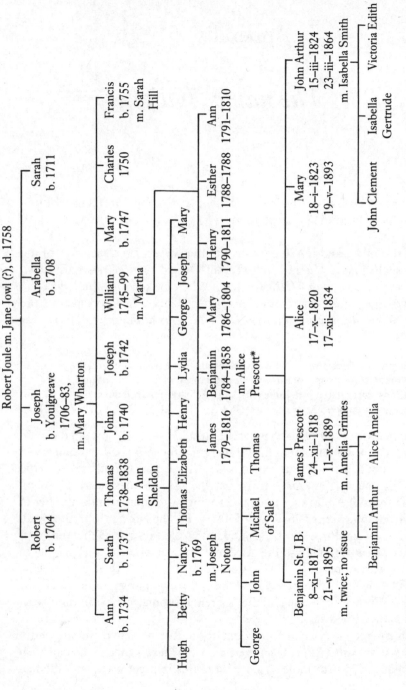

Robert Joule m. Jane Jowl (?), d. 1758

*Elder daughter of Thomas Prescott of Wigan and his wife Grace Bradshaw. Thomas Prescott married twice; his second wife's sister, Caroline Turner, became the mother of Dean Farrar, author of *Eric, or Litte by Little*. She was therefore the great grandmother of Field-Marshal Montgomery.

Appendix 5

The name 'Joule'

The pronunciation of the name 'Joule': a note by Mr Henry Button (reproduced by kind permission).

I was recently asked if I could ascertain the correct pronunciation of the word spelt 'joule'. I found that the big Oxford dictionaries gave 'jowl' whereas the new *Concise OD* gave 'jool'. When I asked Dr John Sykes, the editor of the *Concise*, what caused this change of heart, he referred me to the entry in the *Supplement* to the *OED* (H-N, 1976). This runs, in part, as follows:

> The pronunciation 'jool' is now usual for the name of the unit and the physicist. Although some people of this name call themselves 'Jowl' and others 'Jool' . . . it is almost certain that J. P. Joule (and some at least of his relatives) used Jool. For evidence on this point, see *Nature* (1945), vol CLII, pp. 354, 418, 479, 602.

The articles in *Nature* will repay careful study. Here I will pick out the main points. The argument about the correct pronunciation had arisen in 1943 because it was just a century since Joule had read his famous paper to the Brit. Ass. meeting at Cork on August 16, 1843. Professor H. S. Allen, writing from St Andrews, set the ball rolling by quoting from a number of authorities in favour of 'jool' – Sir D'Arcy Thompson, Sir John Stopford, Lord Kelvin and Professor G. W. O. Howe. Allen suggested that the 'jowl' version was attributable to the 'sardonic humour of local workpeople' in Salford who referred to Jowl's brewery by analogy with the expression 'cheek by jowl'. He thanked W. D. Oliphant for pointing out that 'jool' was better in French (cf *boule*) and that a French submarine lost in the Dardenelles was named *Joule*.

A fortnight later a correspondent from Rugby School mentioned a conversation with a Manchester man who had known a man who had been well acquainted with Joule. According to this indirect witness, Joule had pronounced his name 'Jole' as in 'Joe'.

On October 23 another correspondent referred to a survey carried out by Professor Lloyd James and reported in the *Radio Times* in February 1933. This showed that 12 near relatives and friends of the man himself had pronounced 'Joule' to rhyme with *cool*, six more distant relatives and friends rhymed it with *coal* and nine other friends rhymed it with *cowl*. On the other hand, among living bearers or friends of bearers of the name, the frequency was ten for *cool*, twenty-six for *coal* and thirteen for *cowl*. The writer went on to suggest that in Joule's time the name rhymed with cool but that 'the present tendency is towards *coal*'.

In the same issue, J. B. S. Haldane, writing from Rothamsted Experimental Station, contributed a poem by T. C. Porter of Eton College in support of 'jool':

Old Dr Joule he made this rule:
   The self-same energee
Which lifts a gram of matter to
   42640 c. (centimetres)
Will heat a gram of water through
   one centigrade degree.

In the same issue was a letter from the publishers of Chamber's Dictionary hoping that the confusion could soon be cleared up and explaining why they had given 'Jowl' for the man but 'jool' for the unit.

More support for the pronunciation 'jool' appeared on November 20. One of the contributors to this issue was K. R. Webb from Southampton, who drew attention to a work by A. Schuster and A. E. Shipley (*Britain's Heritage of Science*, 1920), in which the name Joule was derived from the Derbyshire village of Youlgreave where the family orginally resided. Joule's son was also reported to have said that 'Jool' was the right pronunciation.

Reviewing all the evidence in *Nature*, it looks as if 'jool' has it both for the man and for the unit. But one is reminded of the Duke of Wellington's comment on the battle of Waterloo: 'It has been a damned nice thing – the nearest run thing you ever saw in your life'.

The brewery of John Joule and Sons at Stone in Staffordshire was once described, probably in error, as 'the oldest brewery in England' (see the *Guinness Book of the Business World*, by Henry Button and Andrew Lampert, page 15).

H.G.B.
26 March 1981.

One point may be added to this judicious summary of the evidence.

Benjamin St J. B. Joule was an amateur genealogist who devoted considerable effort to tracing the history of the family. He considered it possible that they had 'come over with the Conqueror', but the evidence was not forthcoming. It seems likely that a man who described himself in census returns as 'J.P. and landowner' would prefer 'Jool', with the suggested French connection, to the somewhat plebeian 'Jowl'.

Notes and references

I am grateful to the Libraries of the Institution of Electrical Engineers, the National Library of Wales, the Royal Institution, the Royal Society, the universities of Glasgow and St Andrews and to the Syndics of Cambridge University Library for permission to quote from correspondence in their collections.

Chapter 1

1 For a full account of the invention and development of early textile machinery see R. L. Hills, *Power in the Industrial Revolution* (MUP, 1970).
2 For steam power and engineering over this period see A. E. Musson and E. Robinson, *Science and Technology in the Industrial Revolution*, (MUP, 1969), pp. 393–426, 427–58.
3 W. V. Farrar, K. R. Farrar and L. Scott, 'The Henrys of Manchester. Part 6. William Charles Henry; the magnesia factory', *Ambix*, vol. 24, pt 1 (Mar. 1977), pp. 1–26.
4 Alexis de Tocqueville, *Journeys in England and Ireland*, trans. G. Lawrence and K. P. Mayer (Faber & Faber, London, 1958), pp. 107–8.
5 Farrar *et al.*, 'The Henrys of Manchester', pt 3, pp. 208–28.
6 D. S. L. Cardwell and J. Mottram, 'Fresh light on John Dalton', *Notes and Records of the Royal Society of London*, vol. 39, no. 1 (1984), pp. 29–40.
7 R. Steven Turner, 'The growth of professorial research in Prussia, 1818–1848 – causes and context', *Historical Studies in the Physical Sciences*, vol. 3 (1971), pp. 137–82. Liebig had much the same opinion as Jacobi.
8 See the *Declaration and Protest* (942.730731 P86), in Local History Library, Manchester Central Reference Library.
9 Typewritten transcript of some notes by James Galloway, written about 1890, in Manchester Central Reference Library. Galloway founded one of the best known engine-building firms in Manchester. See also J. B. Morrell, 'Science in Manchester and the University of Edinburgh', in D. S. L. Cardwell (ed.), *Artisan to Graduate*, (MUP, 1974), pp. 39–54.
10 Elizabeth Raffald published the first Manchester and Salford Directory in 1772. She published further editions. Subsequent directories were published by Edward Holme, Wardle & Wilkinson, Pigot & Dean, Slater, Scholes, Bancks, R. & W. Dean, and W. Holden.
11 C. W. Bardsley, *Memorials of St Ann's Church, Manchester in the Last Century* (Manchester, 1877), p. 157.
12 Joule family records in the Archives Department, Manchester Central Reference Library, MS 080 J1.
13 *Ibid.*
14 According to *Manchester Faces and Places*, vol. 1 (Manchester, 1881), p. 81, he was born at Elton in Derbyshire. F. S. Stancliffe repeats this in his *John Shaws, 1738–1938* (Sherratt

& Hughes, Manchester, 1938), p. 308.

15 According to Scholes's *Directory* (1797), his house was 14 New Bailey Street; the brewery was at no. 13.

George Lee wrote to James Watt, jun., on 9 November 1798: 'A neighbour, Mr Joule a brewer who has one of Sherat's [*sic*] engines wishes to pay the premium (ab' 8 horse) and have an air pump made by you or him – . . . he is stimulated by the Magistrates who threatens an Indictment for a pestiferous smoke upon their Sanctuary the New Bayley.' Quoted in Jennifer Tann, *The Selected Papers of Boulton & Watt*, vol. 1 (MIT Press, Cambridge, Mass., 1981), p. 68.

16 Peter Mathias, *The Brewing Industry in England, 1700–1839* (CUP, 1959), p. 81.

17 J. T. Slugg, *Reminiscences of Manchester Fifty Years Ago* (Manchester, 1881), p. 99.

18 It is possible that Hugh or Henry, sons of William's older brother Joseph, came to help. Their names occur in the Directories from 1794 to 1829. Henry had the house next door in New Bailey Street and was described as a brewer; so was Hugh's widow, Helen (Manchester and Salford Directories; see note 10).

19 Samuel Greg, who in 1784, established Quarry Bank Mill at Styal in Cheshire, lived next door to the mill. It is now a museum of the early textile industry and is open to the public.

20 W. Gordon Robinson, 'William Roby, 1760–1830, and the Revival of Independency in Lancashire and the North' (Ph.D. thesis, Manchester University, 1951).

21 B. Love, *Manchester As It Is* (Manchester, 1839), p. 97. According to Love, Leonard Horner, the Factory Inspector, reported that thirty-one boys and twenty-one girls attended classes in reading, writing, arithmetic, geography, sewing and knitting. The classes had been running for two years and were free. This, reported Horner, was the best scheme.

22 Richard Roberts eventually moved south, whereupon he was made an Honorary Member of the Lit & Phil; R. A. Smith, *A Centenary of Science in Manchester* (Manchester Lit & Phil, 1883). The appendix shows that Roberts joined the Society in 1823 and was made an Honorary Member in 1861.

23 *Manchester Faces and Places*, vol. 5 (1894), p. 92 and Mathias, *Brewing Industry*, p. 98.

24 W. Browning, 'John Benjamin Dancer, F.R.A.S., 1812–1887', *Memoirs and Proceedings of the Manchester Literary and Philosophical Society* [hereafter *Manchester Memoirs*], vol. 107 (1964–1965), pp. 115–42. Also H. Milligan, 'New light on J. B. Dancer', *Manchester Memoirs*, vol. 115 (1972–1973), pp. 80–8.

25 Robinson, 'William Roby', p. 43.

26 *Ibid*, p. 37.

27 Anon., 'A week in Manchester', *Blackwood's Magazine*, vol. 45 (1839), p. 481 *et seq.*

28 R. H. Kargon, *Science in Victorian Manchester: Enterprise and Expertise* (Johns Hopkins UP and MUP, 1977) offers a valuable and reliable guide to the development of science in Manchester.

As Morrell has pointed out, the Scottish universities, and particularly Edinburgh, supplied much of the intellectual capital for early nineteenth-century Manchester. It has been claimed that Dalton, among others, was influenced by the Scottish 'commonsense philosophy'. While there may be some truth in this suggestion, it is hardly enough to explain the comprehensive and sustained growth of Manchester science. For this we must invoke other cultural traditions: those of the practical man and the engineer, so much at home in Manchester and its sister towns.

Chapter 2

1 'Fragment of autobiography', in J. R. Ashworth, 'List of apparatus now in Manchester which belonged to Dr J. P. Joule, F.R.S.; with remarks on his MSS, letters and autobiography', *Manchester Memoirs*, vol. 75 (1930–1931), pp. 105–17.

2 J. L. West, *The Taylors of Lancashire; Bonesetters and Doctors, 1750–1890* (H. Duffy, Manchester, 1977). See also the review by W. Brockbank in *Manchester Memoirs*, vol. 120

(1977–1980), pp. 110–11.

3 Ashworth, 'List of apparatus'.

4 O. Reynolds, *Memoir of James Prescott Joule* (Manchester Lit & Phil, 1892), p. 26.

5 *Ibid.*

6 W. C. Henry wrote the first biography of Dalton. Eaton Hodgkinson became professor of civil engineering at University College, London. Two of Dalton's other pupils became politicians: J. A. Yates, MP and B. Gaskell, MP.

7 Reynolds, *Memoir*, p. 27.

8 Gough, who had been blind from childhood, is mentioned in Wordsworth's poem, 'The Excursion'.

9 T. T. Wilkinson, 'The Lancashire geometers and their writings', *Manchester Memoirs*, vol. 11 (1854), p. 123.

10 *Ibid.*

11 D. S. L. Cardwell, *The Organisation of Science in England* (Heinemann, London, 2nd edn, 1972), pp. 53–5.

12 Ashworth, 'List of apparatus'.

13 Probably Tiberius Cavallo's *The Elements of Natural and Experimental Philosophy* (London, 1803). John Dalton's *New System of Chemical Philosophy* appeared in two volumes (1808 and 1827). See the *Manchester Courier*, 17 Oct. 1889.

14 Reynolds, *Memoir*, p. 3.

15 From a Joule notebook in the Department of Physics, UMIST. The 'servant girl' was quite possibly Caroline Molyneux.

16 K. R. Farrar in D. S. L. Cardwell (ed.), *John Dalton and the Progress of Science* (MUP, 1968), pp. xx–xxi.

17 M. Crosland and C. Smith, 'The transmission of physics from France to Britain, 1800–1840', *Historical Studies in the Physical Sciences* (1978), pp. 1–61. This authoritative paper examines the influence of French mathematical physics on the development of the mathematical schools of Cambridge, Dublin and Edinburgh universities. They rightly discount any possibility that *Naturphilosophie* could have influenced the development of physics in Britain. For the development of French physics over this period see R. Fox, *The Caloric Theory of Gases* (OUP, 1971); 'The rise and fall of Laplacian physics', *Historical Studies in the Physical Sciences* (1975), pp. 89–135; and, with G. Weisz, the Introduction to *The Organization of Science and Technology in France, 1808–1914* (Maisons des Sciences de l'Homme and CUP, 1980), pp. 1–28.

18 Crosland and Smith, 'Transmission of physics'. Whewell was well aware of the lack of conceptual and theoretical unity and was doubtful about the scope of physics. He included botany, chemistry and mineralogy in physics; presumably in the hope that they would eventually prove amenable to mathematical treatment.

19 Galileo's principles were enunciated in his work, 'On machines'; they are also implicit in his general mechanics. For the progressive clarification of the concepts of work and of potential and actual 'forces vives' (Mgh and $\frac{1}{2}mv^2$) by French mathematicians and engineers, see D. S. L. Cardwell, 'Some factors in the early development of the concepts of power, work and energy', *B.J.H.S.* vol. 3 (1967) pp. 209–24. See also I. Grattan-Guinness, 'Work for the workers: advances in engineering mechanics and instruction in France, 1800–1830', *Annals of Science*, vol. 41 (1984), pp. 1–33.

20 The standard work on Carnot is R. Fox's *Reflexions on the Motive Power of Fire* (MUP, 1986).

21 E. Daub, 'The regenerator principle in the Stirling and Ericsson hot air-engines', *B.J.H.S.*, vol. 7 (1974), pp. 259–77.

22 Biographical details of Peter Ewart are to be found in two articles by W. C. Henry and Eaton Hodgkinson in *Manchester Memoirs*, vol. 7 (1846), pp. 113–34, 137–56. It was through his brother's friendship with another Liverpool merchant and fellow Scot that the latter christened his son William Ewart Gladstone. Peter Ewart's nephew, William Ewart, also became a Liberal politician and a determined opponent of the death penalty.

23 P. Ewart, 'On the measure of moving force', *Manchester Memoirs*, vol. 2 (1813), pp. 105–258.
24 D. S. L. Cardwell, *From Watt to Clausius* (Heinemann, London, 1970), pp. 162–3.
25 W. W. Haldane Gee, 'John Dalton's lectures and lecture illustrations parts I and II', *Manchester Memoirs*, vol. 59 (1914–1915), pp. 24–5.
26 The standard work is L. Pearce-Williams's *Michael Faraday: A Biography* (Chapman & Hall, London, 1965).
27 Jacobi's paper, 'On the application of electromagnetism to the moving of machines', was translated and printed in Sturgeon's *Annals of Electricity*, vol. 1 (Oct. 1836–Oct. 1837), pp. 408, 419, 444.
28 Cardwell, *From Watt to Clausius*, p. 75.
29 For further details of the 'electrical euphoria' see D. S. L. Cardwell, 'Science and technology: the work of James Prescott Joule', *Technology and Culture*, vol. 17 (1976), pp. 674–87.
30 Revd N. J. Callan, 'Description of an electromagnetic repeater', *Annals of Electricity*, vol. 1 (Oct. 1836–Oct. 1837), p. 229.
31 G. H. Bachhoffner, *Annals of Electricity*, vol. 1 (Oct. 1836–Oct. 1837), pp. 496–7; and vol. 2 (Jan.–Jun. 1838), p. 207. See also G. Bird, *Philosophical Magazine*, vol. 12 (1838), p. 18.
32 W. Sturgeon, 'On electro-pulsations and electro-momentum', *Annals of Electricity*, vol. 1 (Oct. 1836–Oct. 1837), p. 40 and *Phil. Mag.*, vol. 2 (1836), p. 202.
33 W. Sturgeon, 'On the theory of magnetic electricity', *Annals of Electricity*, vol. 1 (Oct. 1836–Oct. 1837), pp. 251–65. The theory is clearly discussed by T. M. Brown, 'The electric current in early nineteenty-century French physics', *Historical Studies in the Physical Sciences*, vol. 1 (1969), pp. 61–103.
34 *Annals of Electricity*, vol. 2 (Jan.–Jun. 1838), pp. 149–52.
35 Kargon, *Science in Victorian Manchester: Enterprise and Expertise* (Johns Hopkins UP and MUP, 1977), pp. 36–41 and *passim*.
36 D. S. L. Cardwell, 'Castlefield: past and present', *Manchester Memoirs*, vol. 3 (1982–1984), pp. 84–101.
37 My dear Sir,
     Accept this volume as a humble token of the high regard that is due to your valuable scientific labours.
     May you long enjoy health and continue to cultivate science.
     I am, dear sir,
     With great esteem,
     Yours very truly,
     W. Sturgeon.

Chapter 3

1 J. R. Ashworth, 'Fragment of autobiography', in 'List of apparatus now in Manchester which belonged to Dr J. P. Joule, F.R.S.; with remarks on his MSS, letters and autobiography', *Manchester Memoirs*, vol. 75 (1930–1931).
2 Osborne Reynolds, *Memoir of James Prescott Joule* (Manchester Lit & Phil, 1892), pp. 26, 44. Repeated by W. W. Haldane Gee (newspaper cutting, Archives Department, Manchester Central Reference Library).
3 The Joules were prominent in Manchester life at this time; *Anon.*, 'A week in Manchester', *Blackwood's Magazine*, vol. 45 (1839), p. 481 *et seq.*
4 Census return for 1841.
5 Comment by Alexis de Tocqueville, *Journeys in England and Ireland*, trans. G. Lawrence and K. P. Mayer (Faber & Faber, London, 1958).
6 *The Scientific Papers of James Prescott Joule*, 2 vols. (The Physical Society, Taylor & Francis, London, 1884, 1887; reprinted by Dawsons, London, 1965) (hereafter *JSP* (i)

and (ii)), vol. 1, pp. 1–3.

7 W. Sturgeon, 'Historical sketch of the rise and progress of electromagnetic engines for propelling machinery', *Annals of Electricity*, vol. 3 (1838–1839), p. 429.

8 *Annals of Electricity*, vol. 3 (1838–1839), p. 508, letter dated 17 Sept. See D. S. L. Cardwell, 'The origins and consequences of certain of J. P. Joule's scientific ideas', in *The Springs of Scientific Creativity*, ed. R. Aris, H. T. Davis and R. H. Stuewer (University of Minnesota Press, 1983), pp. 44–70.

9 Faraday argued that the effect was due to distant flashes illuminating the edges of clouds. *Annals of Electricity*, vol. 7 (1841), p. 226; *Phil. Mag.*, vol. 19 (1841). Faraday returned to the subject later: 'On the persistent appearance of a lightning flash', *Phil. Mag.*, vol. 13 (1857), p. 506.

10 The words 'of the many things which prevent an infinite velocity', used in his original paper in the *Annals of Electricity*, become 'of the many things which limit the velocity' in *JSP* (i), p. 4; a more modest claim.

11 *JSP* (i), pp. 6–18.

12 *Phil. Mag.*, vol. 2 (1851), pp. 306, 447.

13 P. M. Roget, 'Magnetism', *Natural philosophy*, vol. 2 (SDUK, Robert Baldwin, London, 1831), p. 11, §42. N. Callan, 'On the best method of making an electromagnet', *Annals of Electricity*, vol. 1 (1836–1837), pp. 259–302.

14 E. Lenz and M. H. Jacobi, 'Über die Anziehung der Electromagnete', Poggendorff, *Annalen der Physik*, vol. 47 (1839), pp. 401–17.

15 *JSP* (i), p. 14.

16 J. Farey, *A Treatise on the Steam Engine*, vol. 2 (page proofs in Patent Office Library, London). Sadi Carnot, *Reflections on the Motive Power of Fire*, ed. R. Fox (MUP, 1986).

17 *JSP* (i), pp. 16–18.

18 *JSP* (i), pp. 19–26. He did not, of course, use the expressions, 'shunt wound' and 'series wound'. In the paper as printed in *Annals of Electricity* the words 'Duty' and 'economical duty' were used; in *JSP* (i) they become 'work' and 'duty'.

19 *JSP* (i), pp. 27–39, 40–2; *Annals of Electricity*, vol. 6 (1841), pp. 187–98.

20 The line integral, or magneto-motive force, round a complete magnetic circuit is directly proportional to the number of ampere-turns.

21 *JSP* (i), pp. 42–6; *Annals of Electricity*, vol. 6 (1841), pp. 431–3.

22 N. Rosenberg and W. Vincenti, *The Britannia Bridge, the Generation and Diffusion of Technological Knowledge* (MIT Press, Cambridge, Mass., 1978). This is an excellent monograph on a most important technological achievement.

23 Joule may well have learned of Ohm's law from the statement of it in the translation of Jacobi's paper in vol. 1 of *Annals of Electricity*. W. Snow Harris argued that the heating effect of an electric charge was proportional to the charge; Brooke, Cuthbertson and others stated that it was proportional to the square of the charge. Joule showed, unambiguously, that the heat due to a *current* was proportional to the square of the current.

24 *JSP* (i), pp. 46–53; *Annals of Electricity*, vol. 8 (1842), p. 219.

25 F. M. X. de Pambour, *A Practical Treatise on Locomotive Engines upon Railways* (John Weale, London, 1836), pp. vii, 161 *et seq.*, 172–3. De Pambour drew heavily on information from the Liverpool and Manchester Railway.

26 Antoine Parent, *Histoire de l'Académie Royale des Sciences*, Année 1704 (2nd edn, 1722), pp. 116, 323. For the importance of this paper, see D. S. L. Cardwell, *From Watt to Clausius* (Heinemann, London, 1970), p. 68 *et seq.*

27 *Annals of Electricity*, vol. 7 (1841), p. 509. The prize was for his papers on electromagnets in vol. 6 of the *Annals*.

28 According to Slater's *Directory*, G. Arstall was a wheelwright of Ashton Old Road.

29 A. M. Pattu supposed that the 'irresistible' force of metal expanded by heat could replace the steam-engine. See Cardwell, *From Watt to Clausius*, pp. 305–6.

30 R. Fox, 'James Prescott Joule, 1818–1889', in J. North (ed.), *Mid-Nineteenth Century*

Scientists (Pergamon Press, Oxford, 1969), pp. 72–103.

31 He was by no means alone in retaining ideas of subtle or aetherial fluids as a universal substratum of light, heat, electricity and magnetism. See, for example, A. C. Becquerel, 'Précis de nouvelles recherches sur le dégagement de la chaleur dans le frottement', *Comptes Rendus*, vol. 7 (1838), pp. 365–8.

32 *JSP* (i), pp. 60–81 and *Phil. Mag.*, vol. 19 (1841), pp. 260–77. It has been suggested that Roget may have advised Joule to extend his researches to cover batteries and electrolytes, thus making it more general. E. Becquerel seems to have been ignorant of this second and longer paper. He wrote: 'we know very little about the rise in temperature caused by the passage of electricity in liquids. The only experiments published are those of Davy and Oersted'; *Comptes Rendus*, vol. 16 (1843), pp. 724–8; *Annals de Chimie et de Physique*, vol. 9 (1843), pp. 21–70.

33 A. Crawford, *Animal heat* (2nd edn, London, 1788), p. 256 *et seq.*

34 M. Faraday, *Experimental Researches* (Dover edn, 1965), para. 870, p. 256.

35 Y. Elkana, *The Discovery of the Concept of Energy* (Hutchinson, London, 1974), ascribes the i^2r law to Lenz. But it is clear that this author is unfamiliar with Joule's papers.

36 Sir A. Schuster, *Biographical Fragments* (Macmillan, London, 1932), pp. 201–6. Schuster pointed out that Joule was open to criticism on the grounds that he gave inadequate experimental data and made too few references to other workers in the field. It is possible that his work was uncongenial to Snow Harris who may have been a referee and his mathematical style was not acceptable to Faraday who may also have been a referee. A possible explanation is that Joule may have referred the second, extensive paper to Roget for guidance before a formal submission. Roget may then have recommended publication in *Phil. Mag.*

37 *JSP* (i), pp. 81–102; *Phil. Mag.*, vol. 20 (1842), pp. 98–113.

38 By the method of proportions, 1.32:1 can be made proportional to 1.93:1 by adding 1:9 to each term so that 1.32:1 :: (1.93 + 1.9):(1 + 1.9). 1.9 is therefore the expression of the added emf required to turn oxygen into the gaseous form. He remarked, in a footnote added later, that this was 'much too high'.

39 He measured the current i (in his absolute units), that a single Smee cell could send through a given resistance and also the heat, H, generated. But 3.7 Smee cells were needed to electrolyse zinc oxide and this is the measure of the affinity of zinc for oxygen. The heat that 3.7i would generate in the given resistance is $[(3.7i)/i^2]$.H. But 3.7i, being in absolute measure, would electrolyse 3.7i equivalents of zinc, so that the heat generated by the combustion of one equivalent of zinc would be $[(3.7i)/i^2]$.H. This is independent of the given resistance, since the only effect of a change of resistance would be a change in the time taken for electrolysis or combustion. The argument depended on Joule's realisation that H was proportional to emf times current. See *JSP* (i), pp. 100–1.

40 *JSP* (i), pp. 102–7; *Phil. Mag.*, vol. 22 (1843), pp. 204–8.

41 *JSP* (i), pp. 109–23; *Manchester Memoirs*, vol. 7 (1846), pp. 87–106, 109–12. The paper, for all its importance and profound insights, was badly written. One sentence contains 143 words with only one semi-colon.

42 Joule measured the heat generated by a unit of electricity from a Daniell cell flowing through a long copper wire immersed in water. It was equivalent to raising 1 lb of water by 6.129°. One simplified result from his paper will illustrate his argument:

Elet rdes (1)	Cur rent (2)	Rest elec (3)	Rest cond (4)	Heat evld (5)	Heat i^2r (6)	Diff 5–6* (7)	Rest elec† (8)	Col 3 less 8 (9)	New R con (10)	New heat (12)
Pt/Pt	3.66	2.47	1.05	11.43	7.27	6.82	1.11	1.36	1.63	11.33

11.33 was, within the limits of experimental error, close enough to 11.43. The 'new resistance to conduction' was calculated by a simple formula given in the paper and by using the derived resistance to electrolysis (column 8).

*Expressed in units of electrolysis. †Expressed in units of one Daniell cell and derived from column 8; i.e., 6.82/6.129.

43 *JSP* (i), pp. 159–71, esp 170–1; *Phil. Mag.*, vol. 24 (1844), pp. 106–15. Joule pointed out that if the resistance of different voltaic circuits were to be the same the currents, by Ohm's law, must be proportional to the electromotive forces. If, therefore, the resistance of a galvanometer were to be very large compared with the other resistances in the circuits, it could be used to measure the relative emfs of the voltaic cells. It would, in effect, be a voltmeter, but it cannot be called that as the 'volt' had been neither standardised nor even named.

44 This was not quite correct. See p. 131, p. 306 note 44.

45 Von Rumford's association of heat with 'motion' gave no information about the nature of heat. It was not so much a refutation of the caloric doctrine as an operational statement that heat appeared as long as motion continued.

46 J. G. Crowther, *British Scientists of the Nineteenth Century* (Kegan Paul, London, 1935), pp. 129–97.

47 Becquerel, 'Précis des nouvelles recherches'.

48 M. Faraday, *Experimental Researches*, paras. 918,916, 1031.

49 There is little evidence of correspondence between the two men.

50 J. Dalton, *New System of Chemical Philosophy*, vol. 1 (1808), pp. 49–50, 54, 61–3, 74, 75–82.

51 Joule's copy is in UMIST Library.

52 J. D. Forbes, 'On the refraction and polarization of heat', *Phil. Mag.*, vol. 6 (1835), p. 210.

53 W. V. Farrar, K. R. Farrar and L. Scott, 'The Henrys of Manchester. Part 6. William Charles Henry; the magnesia factory', *Ambix*, vol. 24, pt 1 (Mar. 1977), pp. 208, 228. Also W. V. Farrar and L. Scott, 'The Henrys of Manchester, Sixth Grove Lecture, *R.I.C. Review*, vol. 4 (1971), pp. 35–47.

Chapter 4

1 W. Reid, *Memoirs and Correspondence of Lyon Playfair* (London, 1899).

2 Letters from Playfair to his cousin, A. C. Ramsay, the geologist, in the National Library of Wales, Aberystwyth.

3 His interests were in agricultural chemistry and mining. As a first step he was anxious to get on the staff of the newly created Museum of Economic Geology.

4 J. F. La T. Bateman, civil engineer, was responsible for the creation of the great Manchester waterworks system, one of the major achievements of nineteenth-century civil engineering. Bennet Woodcroft, a Manchester engineer, became Director of the Patents Office and founder of the national Science Museum in South Kensington; R. H. Kargon, *Science in Victorian Manchester: enterprise and expertise* (Johns Hopkins UP and MUP, 1977), pp. 27–33, 60–6.

5 This was the considered opinion of the late Dr W. V. Farrar.

6 A complete account of the early years of the British Association is given by J. B. Morrell and A. Thackray, *Gentlemen of Science* (OUP, 1981).

7 T. and C. Stamp, *William Scoresby, Arctic Scientist* (Whitby Press, 1975).

8 T. C. Hope, professor of medicine in Edinburgh University where he had succeeded Joseph Black in the Chair, was a most successful lecturer. John Playfair was professor of natural philosophy.

9 Stamp, *William Scoresby*.

10 J. Cawood, 'Terrestrial magnetism and the development of international collaboration in the early nineteenth century', *Annals of Science*, vol. 34 (1977), pp. 551–87; and 'The magnetic crusade: science and politics in early Victorian Britain', *Isis*, vol. 70 (1979), pp. 493–518.

11 Joule to Scoresby, 20 July 1942, Whitby Lit & Phil Society.

12 Whitby Lit & Phil Society.

13 *Ibid.*

14 *JSP* (i), pp. 123–50; *Phil. Mag.*, vol. 23 (1843), pp. 263, 347, 435.

15 It is paradoxical that a continuous current should generate less heat than a regularly interrupted current of the same (apparent) magnitude. Joule remarked that the explanation was 'obvious', which it surely was not.

16 His assumption that the galvanometer would indicate $3/4$i was gratuitous. In any case the wave form of the pulses of current would be anything but smooth and rectangular! See R. Westfall, 'Newton and the fudge factor', *Science*, vol. 179 (Feb. 1973), pp. 751–3.

17 From J. Scott Russell's article, 'The steam engine', *Encyclopaedia Britannica* (7th edn, 1842).

18 The engine at Wheal Towan – Joule used the Breton spelling, 'Huel Towan' – achieved fame when it recorded a great improvement in duty thanks to the use of thermal insulation to cut down heat losses. This was due to 'Captain' Samuel Grose.

19 Joule to Thomson, 21 July 1863, Glasgow University Library.

20 Personal communication from Professor Eric Mendoza.

21 This has been pointed out by J. Forrester, 'Chemistry and the conservation of energy', *Studies in the History and Philosophy of Science*, vol. 6 (1975), pp. 273–313.

22 'Fragment of autobiography', in J. R. Ashworth, 'List of apparatus now in Manchester which belonged to Dr J. P. Joule, F.R.S.; with remarks on his MSS, letters and autobiography', *Manchester Memoirs*, vol. 74 (1930–1931), pp. 105–17.

23 For brief details of the rapid development of the Cambridge mathematics school over this period, see D. S. L. Cardwell, *The Organisation of Science in England* (Heinemann, London, 2nd edn, 1972).

24 J. G. O'Hara, 'Humphrey Lloyd (1800–1881) and the Dublin Mathematical School in the nineteenth century' (Ph.D. thesis, Manchester University, 1979).

25 Hermann Boerhaave's seminal textbook, *Elementa Chemiae* (1732; English translation 1735), put heat at the centre of chemistry. Joseph Black's lectures on heat were world famous.

26 Dr Apjohn was a Dublin chemist. Lord Rosse's telescope on his estate at Birr was publicised as an attraction to those attending the BA meeting. One of Lord Rosse's sons was (Sir) Charles Parsons, who developed the successful steam turbine.

27 *The Athenaeum*, 9 Sept. 1843.

28 *The Literary Gazette*, 2 Sept. 1843.

29 For accounts of Montgolfier and Séguin, see C. C. Gillispie, *The Montgolfier Brothers and the Invention of Aviation* (Princeton Unversity Press, 1983).

30 J. J. Waterston, 10 July 1846 and Sir J. F. W. Herschel, 22 July 1846; Royal Society. Herschel's a reply was not sent; Waterston had given no address.
    J. Agassi remarks that Herschel 'tried to return to the old view that all errors are culpable and hence that all speculation is dangerous and to be avoided'. J. Agassi, 'Sir John Herschel's philosophy of science', *Historical Studies in the Physical Sciences*, vol. 1 (1969), pp. 1–26.

31 M. Séguin, 'Observations on the effects of heat and of motion', letter to Sir J. F. W. Herschel, 12 Sept. 1822; *Edinburgh Philosophical Journal*, vol. 10 (1824), pp. 280–3; *Edinburgh Journal of Science*, vol. 3 (1825), pp. 276–81.

32 It was customary to teach the theory of heat on the assumption that it was always conserved and then to admit that it was not conserved. Joule's mechanical equivalent of heat experiments were supposed to effect the transformation from one theory to the other.

33 Osborne Reynolds, *Memoir of James Prescott Joule* (Manchester Lit & Phil, 1892), pp. 77–8.

34 Erasmus Darwin, 'Frigorific experiments on the mechanical expansion of air', *Philosophical Transactions* (1788), p. 43. Darwin argued that cold air blowing downhill would be heated by compression, and hot air blowing uphill would be cooled by expansion. And so equilibrium was preserved.

35 J. Dalton, 'Experiments and observations on the heat and cold produced by the mechanical condensation and rarefaction of air', *Manchester Memoirs*, vol. 5 (1798), p. 515; 'On the

expansion of gases by heat', *Nicholson's Journal*, vol. 6 (1803), p. 257; also in *Manchester Memoirs*. J-L. Gay-Lussac, 'Researches on the expansion of gases and vapours', *Annales de Chimie*, vol. 45 (Year 10, 1802), p. 137. Dalton's expression of the law was complex and inaccurate; Gay-Lussac expressed it correctly.

36 J. P. Joule, 'On the changes of temperature produced by the rarefaction and condensation of air', *Phil. Mag.*, vol. 26 (1845), pp. 369–83; *JSP* (i), pp. 172–89. He made allowance for the heat generated by the friction of the air-pump, the cooling due to the atmosphere and the difference in friction when the pump was not under pressure and when it was. Boyle's law should not be used when air changes in temperature.

A. P. Hatton and L. Rosenfeld have demonstrated, using data from Joule's laboratory notebook, 1843–58, the accuracy of the conclusions he drew from his experiments; 'An analysis of Joule's experiments on the expansion of air', *Centaurus*, vol. 4 (1955–1956), pp. 311–18.

H. J. Steffens has suggested that Mayer's paper of 1842 may have led Joule to use this method to measure the mechanical equivalent of heat: *James Prescott Joule and the Concept of Energy* (Science History Publications, New York, 1979). But Joule did not know of Mayer's work until 1848. Furthermore, recent evidence refutes this hypothesis: E. Mendoza and D. S. L. Cardwell, 'Note on a suggestion concerning the work of J. P. Joule', *B.J.H.S.*, vol. 14 (1981), pp. 177–80.

37 See W. Browning, John Benjamin Dancer, F.R.A.S., 1812–1887', in *Manchester Memoirs*, vol. 107 (1964–1965), pp. 115–42; and H. Milligan, 'New light on J. B. Dancer', in *Manchester Memoirs*, vol. 115 (1972–1973), pp. 80–8. Dancer made instruments for Whitworth, W. G. Armstrong, Brewster, Tyndall, W. B. Carpenter, Joule and many others. He was a prolific inventor, his best known invention being microphotography, now essential in commerce, academic work, industry and espionage.

38 This was the furthest deviation in these experiments from the accepted figure (778 foot.pounds). It confirms the accuracy of his experiments.

39 Described much later in 'Some thermodynamic properties of solids', *JSP* (i), pp. 413–73; *Phil. Trans.*, vol. 149 (1859), p. 91.

40 J-L. Gay-Lussac had already carried out an experiment that, outwardly, was the same as Joule's. But Gay-Lussac was comparing the specific heats of different gases. He was not considering the dynamical theory of heat. See D. S. L. Cardwell, *From Watt to Clausius* (Heinemann, London, 1970); M. P. Crosland, *Gay-Lussac, Scientist and Bourgeois* (CUP, 1978), pp. 27–8.

41 Joule, 'On the changes of temperature'; *JSP* (i), pp. 188–9; Y. Elkana, *The Discovery of the Concept of Energy* (Hutchinson, London, 1974), asserts that Joule had not heard of Carnot until told about him by Thomson. This is plainly refuted by Joule's paper, written three years and published more than two years before he met Thomson.

42 It is not clear what opinions of Roget or Faraday Joule had in mind. In 1829 Roget published an article in the 'Library of Useful Knowledge' (SDUK), arguing cogently that the contact theory of electricity implied a source of perpetual motion (or energy). Faraday repeated the argument ten years later and acknowledged Roget's priority.

43 Faraday did not understand the principle of the conservation of energy as his articles 'On the conservation of force', *Phil. Mag.*, vol. 13 (1857), p. 225 and vol. 17 (1859), p. 162, indicate. For him the conservation of force meant the conservation of the causes of things and was equally valid whether, for example, heat was due to motion or to caloric. Lord Rayleigh later expressed doubts about Faraday's abilities as a philosopher in such matters; R. J. Strutt, *John William Strutt, Third Baron Rayleigh* (Edward Arnold, London, 1924), p. 369.

44 Peter Mark Roget (1778–1859) was a Swiss physician who settled in Britain. When in Manchester he was a member of the Lit & Phil, and in London he became Secretary of the Royal Society. He was also the author of the famous *Thesaurus*.

45 Joule to Roget, 7 June 1844, RS., Misc. Corr.

46 Playfair to Dewar, in Reid, *Memoirs*, pp. 73–5.

47 Joule to Playfair, 22 May 1847, Lit & Phil. In 1847 F. W. L. Fischer was elected professor of natural philosophy at St Andrews University. He held the Chair until 1859 when he became professor of mathematics, a post he retained until 1877. He does not appear to have published any papers.

Major (later Sir) Hugh Lyon Playfair was elected Provost of St Andrews in 1842 and held office until his death. He was instrumental in obtaining government grants for the improvement of the University. He also put the famous golf course on a sound basis. Joule's colleague was his nephew.

48 Reid, *Memoirs*, p. 92.

49 The elderly Dalton had announced, in 1840, that when hydrated salts were dissolved in water the only increase in volume was that due to the water of crystallisation; anhydrous salts, he claimed, dissolved without causing an increase in volume. It is an intriguing, if idle, speculation what Dalton would have thought of the Playfair–Joule experiments. He was dismissive of Gay-Lussac's law and there is no evidence that he ever changed his mind about it.

50 *JSP* (ii), p. 11 *et seq.*

51 Joule to Playfair, 17 April 1845, Lit & Phil.

52 Joule to Playfair, 2 May 1845, Lit & Phil.

53 Joule & Playfair, 15 Jan. 1846, Lit & Phil.

54 Joule to Playfair, 24 Feb. 1846, Lit & Phil.

55 Joule to Playfair, 1 Apr. 1846, Lit & Phil.

56 Their reasoning implied that the dimensions of the hydrogen and the oxygen atoms must be the same. See *JSP* (ii), p. 124. A letter from Joule to Playfair of 26 May 1846 (Lit & Phil), contains a reference to Avogadro, but to the end water remained HO for them.

57 *Memoirs of the Geological Survey of Great Britain and of the Museum of Practical Geology in London*, vol. 2, Part 2 (London, 1848), p. 554.

58 J. P. Joule and W. Scoresby, 'Experiments and observations on the mechanical powers of electromagnetism, steam and horses', *JSP* (ii), pp. 1–11; *Phil. Mag.*, vol. 28 (1846), p. 448.

59 Up to 1847, J. C. Adams and J. Challis published 2 joint papers; Humphrey Lloyd, 3; Charles Babbage and J. F. W. Herschel, 2; D. Brewster, 4 (out of a total of 303); Faraday, 4 (all on practical chemistry); J. F. W. Herschel and J. South, 1; and W. Whewell, 1. Dalton, Davy, Forbes, Barlow, Christie, Grove, Ivory, etc., wrote none. A history of joint research and the joint paper would be of some interest.

60 *JSP* (i), pp. 189–92, 192–200; *Phil. Mag.*, vol. 25 (1844), p. 334 and *Manchester Memoirs*, vol. 7 (1846), p. 559.

61 *JSP* (i), pp. 202–5; BA Report (1845); *Phil. Mag.*, vol. 27 (1845) p. 202.

62 George Rennie, 'On the friction and resistance of fluids', *Philosophical Transactions* (1831), pp. 423–42.

63 Paul Ermann, BA *Report* (1845), p. 102. Goodman's writings are to be found in *Phil. Mag.*, *Manchester Memoirs*, and BA *Reports* of the period.

64 Joule to Faraday, 28 May 1845, Institution of Electrical Engineers.

65 Joule to Herschel, 29 Oct. 1846, Cambridge University Library, (hereafter CU).

66 John Gough, Dalton's blind tutor, had been the first to detect the adiabatic heating of expanded rubber. He did this by rapidly stretching a rubber band between his lips; *Manchester Memoirs*, vol. 1, 2nd ser. (1805), pp. 288–95.

67 *JSP* (i), pp. 235–65; *Phil. Mag.*, vol. 30 (1847), pp. 76, 225. He showed that increase in length is compensated by diminution in area of cross-section so that the volume is unchanged. He also derived a simple law: elongation was proportional to magnetic intensity. With very thin wires the slight tension needed to keep the wire straight resulted in a shortening. Later, there was a minor dispute as to priority: see J. Tyndall, *Phil. Mag.*, vol. 1 (1851), p. 194, and J. P. Joule, *Phil. Mag.*, vol. 2 (1851), pp. 306 and 447.

68 J. P. Joule, 'On matter, living force and heat', *Manchester Courier*, 5 und 12 May (1847); *JSP* (i), pp. 265–76. I am grateful to the Revd Canon Eric Saxon, formerly Rector of St

Anns, and Mr David Taylor, Local History Library, Manchester Central Reference Library, for identifying the School Library (see the Ordnance Survey map for 1848).

69 The representation of *vis viva* either in the traditional form of mv^2 or in the 'new' form of $\frac{1}{2}mv^2$ was no great problem for Joule. His researches were almost all concerned with work, or potential energy, Mgh.

70 The material nature of meteorites was proved by E. F. Chladni (1794); D. Olmsted and A. Twining showed that meteor swarms orbit round the sun.

71 Binney to Joule, 10 May 1847, Physics Department, UMIST.

72 *Phil. Mag.*, vol. 31 (1847), p. 236.

73 E. Mendoza, 'The kinetic theory of matter, 1845–1855', *Archives Internationales d'Histoire des Sciences*, vol. 32 (1982), pp. 184–220.

74 Joule's description of the meeting is in *JSP* (ii), p. 215; Thomson's is in a letter to J. T. Bottomley, published in *Nature*, vol. 26 (1882), p. 618 and in O. Reynolds, *Memoirs of James Prescott Joule* (Manchester Lit & Phil, 1892). Thomson's account seems more plausible; he was a young man of twenty-three and the audience included some formidably distinguished men. William Bottomley had married Thomson's sister, Anna, and J. T. Bottomley was their son.

75 *The Athenaeum*, 3 Jul. 1847, p. 709 *et seq.*

76 E. Clapeyron, 'On the motive power of heat', *Journal de l'Ecole Polytechnique*, vol. 14 (1834), p. 153. Translated and published in Richard Taylor's *Scientific Memoirs* (London, 1847), p. 347.

It is curious that Clapeyron, having understood the importance of Carnot's ideas and having put them in a clear, analytical form, did nothing further about them. Possibly:
(a) he might have abandoned the caloric theory of heat and therefore assumed that Carnot's theory must be fatally flawed. Or:
(b) he might have been converted to de Pambour's highly regarded theory of the steam-engine. De Pambour's approach, quite different from Carnot's, was based on extensive practical experience of steam-engines. As R. L. Hills has pointed out, the steam-engine was regarded as essentially a pressure engine, and this was the approach that de Pambour took. See D. S. L. Cardwell and R. L. Hills, 'Thermodynamics and practical engineering in the nineteenth century', *History of Technology*, vol. 1 (1976), pp. 1–20; D. S. L. Cardwell, 'Science and the steam engine reconsidered', *Transactions of the Newcomen Society*, vol. 49 (1977–1978), pp. 111–20. Or:
(c) he might have failed to recognise the 'growth point' seen by Thomson, which was, in the first instance, that Carnot's theory made an absolute scale of temperature possible. Or:
(d) there may have been other, including personal, reasons.

77 Carnot assumed, with the majority of men of science, that the specific heats of gases increased with their volumes; a belief consistent with the caloric or conservationist theory of heat. From this error of fact he deduced a correct conclusion (Cardwell, *From Watt to Clausius*, pp. 204–6). The basic formula, in classical thermodynamics, $W = J.Q(T_1 - T_2)/T_1$, indicates that the work done by a unit of input heat must decrease with the temperature T_1. But, of course, in this case the heat does not 'fall' unchanged through $T_1 - T_2$. Some, determined by the fraction, is converted into work.

78 *JSP* (i), pp. 282–3; *Phil. Mag.*, vol. 31 (1847), p. 114.

79 Tappenden used a testimonial from Dalton as publicity for his school.

80 Joule to Thomson, 29 Jun. 1847, CU, J59.

81 Thomson to J. Thomson, sen., 1 Jul. 1847, CU, Add.MS.

82 Thomson to Forbes, 1 Mar. 1847, St Andrews University Library. Thomson lost no time in restoring the engine and, on 21 April, demonstrated it before a meeting of the Glasgow Philosophical Society (*Proceedings*, vol. 2 (1844–1848), p. 169). He pointed out that, as the engine could work over a far bigger temperature range than the best steam-engine, it was capable of great improvement, in accordance with Carnot's theory. He noted, too, that if the engine was driven in reverse the lower end of the cylinder was cooled to such an

300 *Notes and references*

extent that when immersed in cold water ice formed round it. In effect, the engine became a refrigerator.

83 Joule to Thomson, 7 Jul. 1847, CU, J60.
84 Joule to Stokes, 10 Jul. 1847, CU, Add.MS, J73.
85 Thomson to J. Thomson, jun., 12 Jul. 1847, CU, Add.MS, T 429.
86 J. Thomson, jun., to Thomson, 25 Jul. 1847, CU, T 433.
87 (Marc) Séguin, Ainé, *De l'influence des chemins de fer* (Paris, 1839), p. 378 *et seq.*, especially 382–3.
88 Thomson to J. Thomson, sen., 5 Sep. 1847, CU, T 373.
89 Letter to J. T. Bottomley (see n. 74, this chapter).
90 Thomson to Stokes, 20 Oct. 1847, CU, K 21.
91 Forbes to Thomson, 7 Oct. 1847, CU, F 183. It should be noted that Thomson did not mention Joule in his letters to Forbes and Stokes at this time.

According to Arnold Lunn, Forbes 'opened up' the Chamonix area to mountaineers and tourists.

Chapter 5

1 E. Mendoza, 'The kinetic theory of matter, 1845–1855', *Archives Internationales d'Histoire des Sciences*, vol. 32, December 1982, pp. 184–220, and 'The surprising history of the kinetic theory of gases', *Manchester Memoirs*, vol. 105 (1962–1963), pp. 15–28. G. R. Talbot and A. J. Pacey, 'Some early kinetic theories of gases: Herapath and this predecessors', *B.J.H.S.*, vol. 3 (1966), pp. 133–49.

The comprehensive history is by S. G. Brush, *The Kind of Motion we Call Heat: a History of the Kinetic Theory of Gases in the Nineteenth Century* (North–Holland, 1976), 2 vols., (1) *Physics and the Atomists* (2) *Statistical Physics and Irreversible Processes*.

2 They were, however, published in *Annals of Philosophy*.
3 John Herapath, *Mathematical Physics, or the Mathematical Principles of Natural Philosophy*, 2 vols. (London, 1847). Copy in Joule Collection, UMIST Library.
4 *Ibid.*, vol. 1, p. 183; vol. 2, pp. 107–42.
5 *Ibid.*, vol. 2, pp. 131–2.
6 *Ibid.*, vol. 1, pp. 217–18.
7 Joule to Playfair, 12 Mar. 1846, Lit & Phil. Joule referred to Herapath's paper of 1824 in *Phil. Mag.* He did not mention atomic volumes in this context.
8 Article, 'Steam', in *Encyclopaedia Britannica* (3rd edn, 1797).
9 Herapath, *Mathematical Physics*, Introduction, vol. 1, p. xi.
10 Ostwald's *Klassiker*, trans. John Tyndall and published in *Scientific Memoirs*, ed. J. Tyndall and W. Francis (London, 1853).
11 A. J. Pacey and S. J. Fisher, 'Daniell Bernoulli and the *vis viva* of compressed air', *B.J.H.S.*, vol. 3 (1967), pp. 382–92. They point out that potential energy was called 'potential *vis viva*' by Bernoulli and 'latent *vis viva*' by Lazare Carnot. This was the tradition to which, in effect, Helmholtz appealed.
12 This must have been the famous experiment reported by Davy.
13 W. Thomson, 'On an absolute thermometric scale founded on Carnot's theory of the motive power of heat and calculated from Regnault's results' (June 1848), *Mathematical and physical papers* (hereafter MPP), vol. 1 (CUP, 1882), pp. 100–6.
14 *Comptes Rendus*, vol. 25 (23 Aug. 1847), pp. 309–11. Joule quoted the values in metric measures: 428.8, 429.1 and 432.1 gms.metre per calorie, (1 gm of water raised 1°C). Joule was helped in making translations by his former language tutor, J. L. Mordacque, a Frenchman long resident in Manchester and a member of the Lit & Phil.
15 Menabrea, a military engineer, was one of the few people who understood and appreciated Babbage's work on computers.
16 Joule to Playfair, 14 Jan. 1848, Lit & Phil.

17 Sir J. Lubbock discussed these hypotheses in *Phil. Mag.*, vol. 32 (1848), pp. 81, 170. Joule replied without delay (*ibid.*, p. 349) with a calculation showing that a cube of stone, of six inches' side, travelling at the inferred speed for twenty miles through an atmosphere of one hundredth of the density at sea level, would raise the air temperature enough to vaporise it. He considered that the main effect would be the immense compression of the air in front of the meteorite. Lubbock's paper in *Phil. Mag.*, vol. 35 (1849), p. 356, did not mention Joule's hypothesis.
    Sir John Lubbock, a mathematician, was the father of Lord Avebury.
18 *JSP* (i), pp. 288–90, 290–7.
19 BA *Report* (1848). Thomson used Joule's i^2r law to show that Neumann's theorem for the strength of an induced current can be simply expressed by the rate of change of Ampère's 'force function', or $i = 1/k.dU/dt$, where U is the force function and k a constant depending on the resistance of the wire.
20 Joule to Thomson, 6 Oct. 1848, CU, J 61.
21 D. S. L. Cardwell, 'The origins and consequences of certain of J. P. Joule's scientific ideas', in *The Springs of Scientific Creativity*, ed. R. Aris, H. T. Davis and R. H. Stuewer (University of Minnesota Press, 1983), pp. 44–70.
22 (Marc) Séguin, Ainé, *De l'influence des chemins de fer* (Paris, 1839), p. 403.
23 Thomson to Joule, 27 Oct. 1848, CU, J 62.
24 W. Thomson, 'An account of Carnot's theory of the motive power of heat; with numerical results deduced from Regnault's experiments on steam', *MPP* (i), pp. 133–55. In this paper Thomson coined the word 'thermodynamics'.
25 The formula given in Thomson to Joule, 27 Oct. 1848, CU J 62, and subsequently Thomson, 'An account' is $W/Q = \mu(1+Et)/E$, where μ was Carnot's function and E the coefficient of thermal expansion of a gas; t was the temperature.
26 Thomson to Joule, 27 Oct. 1848, CU, J 62. He added: 'agreeing with you as I do when you say you coincide with Faraday and Roget'.
27 Joule to Thomson, 6 Nov. 1848, CU, J 63.
28 Joule to Thomson, 9 Dec. 1848, CU, J 64.
29 J. Thomson in W. Thomson, *MPP* (i), pp. 156–64 and W. Thomson, *MPP* (i), pp. 165–9.
30 The majority of steam-engines in Britain and France were located away from the capital cities and the centres of learning.
31 Carnot's function was, according to the analysis of the steam-engine, equal to $(1 - \delta)dp/kdt$, where δ was the ratio of the density of steam to that of water, dp the change in pressure, dt the change in temperature and k the latent heat per unit *volume* of steam. To calculate k, Thomson assumed that saturated steam obeyed the gas laws; *MPP* (i), p. 136. For an air-engine Carnot's function was given by $Ep_0v_0/v.dq/dv$, a much less convenient formula.
32 Many years later such engines – the steam–diesel combination, for example – were designed and made.
33 See, for example, Robert Stephenson's comments at the end of the protracted discussion following Robert Hunt's paper, 'Electromagnetism as a source of power', in *Minutes of Proceedings of the Institution of Civil Engineers*, vol. 16 (1856–1857), p. 327. Stephenson was President of the Institution and an engineer of wide experience.
34 Joule, 'On the mechanical equivalent of heat', *Philosophical Transactions* (1850); *JSP* (i), pp. 298–328. He headed the paper with a quotation from Locke on the mechanical nature of heat and a quotation from Leibniz asserting that 'force' is measured by the square of the velocity of a body or the height to which it can rise against gravity.
35 *Comptes Rendus*, vol. 25 (1847), pp. 420–2.
36 It is clear that von Rumford had no idea of the numerical equivalence of work (which he had not measured), and the quantity of heat (which he had not measured). Obviously, Joule was anxious to find respectable precedents and acceptable authorities for his ideas (cf. Thomas Young and the dispute over the undulatory theory of light).
37 C. W. Smith, 'Faraday as a referee of Joule's Royal Society paper: on the mechanical

equivalent of heat', *Isis*, vol. 67 (1976), pp. 444–9.
38 Joule to Thomson, 8 Mar. 1849, CU, J 66.
39 Joule to Thomson, 14 Jul. 1849, CU, J 67.
40 Joule to Thomson, 26 Mar. 1850, CU, J 68.
41 Joule to Stokes, 3 Jul. 1850, CU, J 75. He added that an accurate measurement of the velocity of sound was desirable and suggested a method based on his experience of the notes emitted by resonating railings in Claughton Park, Birkenhead!
42 D. S. L. Cardwell, *From Watt to Clausius* (Heinemann, London, 1970), pp. 244–5.
43 *Ibid.*, pp. 247–50.
44 That a kettle of water placed on a block of ice will not boil is certainly an illustration of the second law of thermodynamics, albeit a very simple one. But the application is far wider than this elementary example suggests; it extends to physical, chemical, biological and technological processes in which it is by no means obvious that heat cannot flow from cold to hot without compensation.

Chapter 6

1 There is a plaque commemorating Sturgeon in Kirkby Lonsdale church.
2 D. S. L. Cardwell and J. Mottram, 'Fresh light on John Dalton', *Notes and Records of the Royal Society of London*, vol. 39, no. 1 (1984), pp. 29–40.
3 The definitive study of the development of public health in Manchester is by J. V. Pickstone, *Medicine and Industrial Society* (MUP, 1985).
4 Details are from H. B. Charlton, *Portrait of a University, 1851–1951* (MUP, 1951), and particularly, Kargon, *Science in Victorian Manchester: Enterprise and Expertise* (Johns Hopkins UP and MUP, 1977), p. 153 *et seq.*
5 Joule of Thomson, 26 Mar. 1853, CU, J 68.
6 All that he published in the remainder of 1850 were a brief note on the appearance of lightning and a note on amalgams; *JSP* (i), pp. 329–31.
7 Lubbock letters, Royal Society.
8 Joule to Thomson, 30 Aug. 1850, CU, J 69.
9 Joule volunteered to do this through the Exhibition Committee set up by the Manchester Royal Institution. S. V. F. Butler, 'The universal agents of power: James Prescott Joule, electricity and the equivalents of heat' (in press).
10 W. J. M. Rankine, *Miscellaneous Scientific Papers* (London, 1881), esp. Pt II. Rankine's mechanical theory of heat assumed that heat phenomena were due, not to the projectile motion of atoms but to the rapid rotation of vortices in the 'atmospheres' round the atoms. The higher the temperature the more rapidly they rotated, the greater centrifugal forces causing them to expand upwards. The dynamics of the model were sound and the results therefore reasonable. It may be that Rankine's vortices influenced Maxwell in his original formulation of the dynamical theory of the electromagnetic field. For authoritative studies of Rankine's thermodynamics, see K. Hutchison, 'Der Ursprung der Entropiefunktion bei Rankine und Clausius', *Annals of Science*, vol. 30 (1973), pp. 341–64; 'W. J. M. Rankine and the rise of thermodynamics', *B.J.H.S.*, vol. 15 (1981), pp. 1–26.
11 This was why Watt opposed the use of high-pressure steam. D. S. L. Cardwell, *From Watt to Clausius* (Heinemann, London, 1970), pp. 44–7.
12 Joule to Thomson, 30 Aug. 1850, CU, J 69.
13 Thomson, *MPP* (i), pp. 170–3.
14 Joule to Thomson, 6 Nov. 1850, CU, J 72.
15 Cardwell, *From Watt to Clausius*, pp. 162–3. Experiments were made with engines using liquids with lower latent heats of vaporisation than water; but no advantage was found, and in all cases the liquids were more expensive and less convenient; pp. 176–7. Holtzmann, in 1845, commented on the loss due to the high latent heat of vaporisation of water; p. 227. It should be noted that in the Newcomen engine the high latent heat of vaporisation was not a disadvantage; the source of inefficiency was the alternate heating

and cooling of the cylinder; pp. 49–51.

16 'I feel confident you will find the theory of the convertibility of heat into force capable of explaining a greater number of natural phenomena than Carnot's view'; Joule to Thomson, 19 Dec. 1850, CU, J 73.

17 *Ibid.*

18 Thomson to Joule, 15 Jan. 1851, quoted in *JSP* (i), 'On the air engine', *Philosophical Transactions* (1852), p. 65. The formulae are:

$$\frac{T}{T}^1 = (\frac{V}{V_1})^{k-1} \quad \text{and} \frac{P}{P}^1 = (\frac{V}{V_1})^{k}$$

– due to Poisson, where k is the ratio of the two principal specific heats.

$$\text{And} \quad W = P.V. \frac{1}{k-1}[(\frac{V}{V_1})^{k-1} - 1]$$

– due to Thomson, who does not refer to absolute temperature or absolute zero whereas Joule does. Joule confided to Thomson that he had misapplied the simple formula in that he took the lower temperature as that of the atmosphere, not that of the exhaust air as it left the engine.

19 Joule to Thomson, 17 Jun. 1851, CU, J 75.

20 Cardwell, *From Watt to Clausius*, Ch. 6.

21 Statement by John Farey to Select Committee of House of Commons on Laws of Patents, *Phil. Mag.*, vol. 7 (1830), p. 152; vol. 8 (1830), p. 305. It was stated that an 1813 engine working in 1829 would require all the profits to pay for the additional coal needed.

22 W. S. Jevons, *The Coal Question* (2nd edn, London, 1866), p. 128.

23 The British Association granted £100 to a committee of three to design and develop a dynamometer suitable for use on a steam-engine where the load and power output varied. The members of the committee were the Revd Henry Moseley, Eaton Hodgkinson and J. Enys. Moseley developed an ingenious version of Poncelet and Morin's dynamometer, for horse-drawn vehicles, that incorporated a mechanical integrator. See British Association *Reports* (1841), p. 307; (1842), p. 98; (1843), p. 104; (1844), p. 90.

24 The disastrous boiler explosion on the Yarmouth packet in 1819 led a Parliamentary Committee to examine the desirability of high-pressure steam-engines. The Committee was impressed by the evidence in favour of high-pressure engines.

25 BA *Reports* (1858), p. 211; (1859), p. 231; (1860), p. 204. In the last year Elder was elected a member of the BA Committee on Steamship Performance, set up in 1859. The engines were compound; that is they had a small, high-pressure cylinder followed by a large, low-pressure cylinder. The steam expanded in the high-pressure cylinder before being admitted to the low-pressure cylinder where it expanded again down towards the pressure of the condenser.

26 F. C. Marshall, 'On the progress and development of the marine engine', *Proceedings of the Institution of Mechanical Engineers* (1881), p. 449. In the following decade ships with steel hulls and with triple or quadruple expansion engines had reduced the time taken to cross the Atlantic to less than a week. They became known popularly as 'ocean greyhounds'.

27 E. Daub, 'The regenerator principle in the Stirling and Ericsson hot air-engines', *B.J.H.S.*, vol. 7 (1974), pp. 259–77.

28 W. W. Poingdestre, 'Description of Sir George Cayley's air-engine', *Minutes of Proceedings of the Institution of Civil Enginers*, vol. 9 (1850), p. 194.

29 B. Cheverton, 'On the use of hot air as a motive power', *M. P. Inst. Civ. Eng.*, vol. 12 (1852–1853), p. 312. 'Both parties', wrote Cheverton, 'rest the efficiences of their engines on the repeated use of caloric . . . it is made to operate over and over again.' According to Ericsson, 'the production of mechanical force by heat is unaccompanied by loss of heat' (in practice some will be lost by unavoidable waste). Cheverton was, however, rather unfair. Stirling made no claim to have invented a perpetual motion machine and

Ericsson was, at worst, ambiguous; at best very doubtful. As is usually the case, the extreme claims were made by eager disciples and journalists.

30 I am indebted to Dr Keith Hutchinson for further details about Cheverton. A description of Cheverton's 'gas power engine', invented in 1826, is in Elijah Galloway's *History and Progress of the Steam-Engine* (London, 1835), p. 659.

31 C. W. Siemens, 'On the conversion of heat into mechanical effect', *M. P. Inst. Civ. Eng.*, vol. 12 (1852–1853), p. 659.

32 M. Duffy, 'Commemorating Einstein', essay review, *Annals of Science*, vol. 39 (1982), pp. 593–603.
    Aesthetic physics, in which the highest importance is attached to mathematical elegance and experimental facts disregarded, is a product of the academic snobberies of European universities of the present and recent past. It would not have appealed to Thomson and his contemporaries.

33 W. Pole, *A Treatise on the Cornish Pumping Engine* (London, 1844), Preface. For some details of Cornish engines see the papers by W. J. Henwood, J. Taylor, and J. Farey in the *Phil. Mag.* during the 1830s. The Cornish engine was brought to London by T. Wicksteed. An authoritative and clear account was given by C. Combes, 'Memoire sur l'exploitation des mines des comtes de Cornwall et de Devon', *Annales des Mines*, 3^{ieme} Sér., tome 5 (1834), pp. 109, 345, 593.

34 For example, J. C. Dyer in *Proceedings*, Lit & Phil, vol. 1, p. 91; vol. 2, p. 43; vol. 3, p. 77; vol. 6, p. 52; vol. 7, p. 165; J. Goodman, BA *Report* (1844), p. 11 (section); *Phil. Mag.*, vol. 24 (1844), p. 174; *Manchester Memoirs*, vol. 8, p. 276; vol. 9, p. 80; vol. 10, p. 155.

35 He was convinced that only established science should be taught to undergraduates. Nothing progressive or remotely speculative was to be allowed. In practice this meant that Newton should be taught to undergraduates, reading for the Mathematics Tripos, only in the strict geometrical canon that he employed in the *Principia*. His ideas are well – and convincingly – set out in his *Of a Liberal Education* (1839). His attitude was very similar to that of his contemporary, Sir J. F. W. Herschel. See J. Agassi, 'Sir John Herschel's philosophy of science', *Historical Studies in the Physical Sciences*, vol. 1 (1969), pp. 1–26.

Chapter 7

1 T. S. Kuhn, 'Energy conservation as an example of simultaneous discovery', in M. Clagett (ed.), *Critical Problems in the History of Science* (Madison, Wis. 1959), pp. 321–56. Some instances of simultaneous discovery, such as that of the reversing layer by Janssen and by Lockyer, are clear and unambiguous; others are far less sharply defined and lead, inevitably, to disputes.

2 His observations of the difference in colour of venous blood in the tropics and in high latitudes led him to speculate on the roles of oxygen and metabolism in the physical work done. This, in turn, gave him his initial insight into energy transformation; *ibid.*

3 R. B. Lindsay, *Julius Robert Mayer: Prophet of Energy* (Pergamon Press, London, 1973). This gives a fair account of Mayer's work and ideas and includes a reprint of his papers. P. M. Heimann (Harman), 'Mayer's concept of "force": The "axis" of a new science of physics', gives a clear and fair summary of Mayer's position. R. S. Turner, 'J. R. Mayer', in *DSB*, vol. 9 (Scribners, New York, 1974), pp. 235–40.

4 J. Smeaton showed how a spring, fitted with a ratchet, offered an analogy with the loss of *vis viva* in inelastic collision. He did not, however, suggest how, in such cases, the *vis viva* could be recovered, as it can be from a spring, or whether it could take other forms.

5 Lindsay, *Julius Robert Mayer*.

6 Private communication.

7 Joule notebook, in Physics Department, UMIST.

8 E. L. Scott, 'W. R. Grove', *D.S.B.*, vol. 5 (1972), pp. 559–60.

9 Stokes to Roscoe, 19 Mar. 1890, CU. Harman is, in my view rightly, dismissive of Grove's claim.

10 A. Colding, 'An examination of steam-engines and the power of steam', (Copenhagen, 1851), presented to Joule. See also his 'On the history of the principle of the conservation to energy', *Phil. Mag.*, vol. 27 (1864), p. 56. His first publication was his treatise *Theses on Force* (1843, in which he determined the mechanical equivalent of heat by various frictional methods.

11 Joule to Thomson, 6 Feb. 1851, CU, J 76.

12 Potter thought that a vibrating object compressed all the air on one side as it rarefied it on the other. The velocity of sound should, therefore, be different on different sides if Laplace was correct! *Phil. Mag.*, vol. 1 (1851), pp. 101–4.

13 W. J. M. Rankine, the Revd S. Haughton, G. G. Stokes, and G. B. Airy all refuted Potter in the same volume of *Phil. Mag.* The unkind comment was repeated in H. H. Bellott, *The History of University College, London: 1826–1926* (London, 1928). But it was unfair: Potter, as a former pupil of Dalton, did accept the atomic theory.

14 W. Thomson, 'On the dynamical theory of heat, with numerical results Deduced from Mr Joule's equivalent of a thermal unit and M. Regnault's observations on steam', *MPP* (i), pp. 174–210 and *passim*.

15 Joule to Thomson, 11 Mar. 1851, CU, J 77.

16 M. P. Crosland, *Gay-Lussac, Scientist and Bourgeois* (CUP, 1978).

17 Thomson to Stokes, 10 Apr. 1851, CU, K 47.

18 Thomson to Joule, 25 Apr. 1851, CU, J 78.

19 Joule to Thomson, 28 Apr. 1851, CU, J 80.

20 Thomson, 'On the dynamical theory of heat', p. 188.

21 Joule to Thomson, 28 Apr. 1851, CU, J 80.

22 Joule to Thomson, 10 May 1851, CI, J 83.

23 W. Hopkins to Joule, 8 Apr. 1851. In Physics Department, UMIST. See also *The Life of Sir William Fairbairn*, rev. and ed. E. A. Musson (David & Charles, Newton Abbot, 1970), Ch. 17, p. 287.

24 Joule to Thomson, 28 Apr. 1851, CU, J 80.

25 William Edward Staite was the pioneer of the electric arc lamp. He was the first to use the current to control the carbon rods so that the arc remained struck. He made a number of other inventions concerning the arc lamp, some of which were of considerable importance. The committee on which Joule sat was instituted by Manchester corporation. I am indebted to Mr J. O. Marsh for information about Staite.

26 Thomson to Forbes, 8 May 1851, St Andrews University Library. Thomson wrote from Acton Square.

27 Joule to Thomson, 10 May 1851, CU, J 83.

28 He thought it was due to the heat gained, or the 'cold lost', in the passage of the air from the cylinder to the stopcock.

29 R. Clausius, 'On the deportment of vapour during its expansion under different circumstances', *Phil. Mag.*, vol. 1 (1851), pp. 398–405. Clausius considered three cases: (1) when the steam in a cylinder expands against a piston, imparting all its energy to the piston; (2) when the steam expands against atmospheric pressure only, doing far less work; here Clausius referred to Joule's experiment of 1844, and (3), when it escapes into the atmosphere through a narrow orifice, the steam having to do work against the drag of the atmosphere, this work becoming heat.

30 *Ibid.*, p. 474. Thomson merely said Clausius was wrong.

31 R. Clausius, 'Reply to a note from Mr Thomson', *Phil. Mag.*, vol. 2 (1851), pp. 139–42; and W. Thomson, 'Second note on the effect of fluid friction', *ibid.*, pp. 273–4 (written in September on his return from Italy).

32 Thomson to Stokes, 9 May 1851, CU, J 50. Why 'the insult'?

33 A. S. Ede and C. H. Creasey, *The Life and Work of John Tyndall* (MacMillan, London, 1945), p. 34.

34 *Phil. Mag.*, vol. 1 (1851), p. 194.

35 *Phil. Mag.*, vol. 2 (1851), pp. 301, 449.

36 Joule to Tyndall, 4 Sept. 1851, Royal Institution.
37 W. Weber, 'Messungen galvanischer Leitungswiderstande nach einem absoluten Maasse', *Annalen der Physik*, vol. 82 (1851), pp. 337–69.
38 Joule to Thomson, 20 Jun. 1851, CU, J 85.
39 *Ibid.* The voltmeter may have been intended for use in connection with the application of the Gauss-Weber system to electrolysis.
40 *Ibid.*; Joule to Thomson, 10 Sep. 1851, CU, J 89. Grove had concluded that 'in water there is no conductibility without decomposition'. See also Joule to Thomson, 22 Sep. 1851, CU, J 91; and Thomson to Joule, 27 Sep. 1851, CU, J 92. The conductibility of pure water was established by Kohlrausch and others.
41 W. Thomson, 'On the mechanical theory of electrolysis', *Phil. Mag.*, vol. 2 (1851), p. 429; and W. Thomson, 'Applications of the principle of mechanical effect to the measurement of electro-motive forces and to galvanic resistances in absolute units', *Ibid.*, p. 551.
42 A. Thackray, 'Quantified chemistry – the Newtonian dream', in D. S. L. Cardwell, (ed.), *John Dalton and the Progress of Science* MUP, 1968). Thackray points out how the eighteenth-century hope of a quantified chemistry based on the Newtonian concept of force was superseded by the basically simple but operationally powerful concept of Daltonian atomic weight. The energy concept enabled chemistry to advance further, again without reference to Newtonian force.
43 The emf across the disc is $\frac{1}{2}r^2Hw$, where r is the radius of the disc, H is the strength of the earth's magnetic field and w the angular velocity. The emf of the cell is $J\theta\xi$, where θ is the heat of combination of a unit weight of zinc; ε is the electrochemical equivalent, the weight of metal electrolysed or combined in unit time by a unit current. When no current flows these two are equal and $J\theta\xi$ is the emf of a fully-charged cell.

Thomson used the analysis of the rotating disc to show that the earth's magnetic field cut by the flowing water of the River Thames, as discussed by Faraday in his Bakerian lecture, would induce only one-hundredth of the emf needed to electrolyse water; the current through the associated resistances (Thames plus return wire) would be far too small to detect.
44 Helmholtz showed that the emf of a cell is given by

$$e = Q + T\frac{de}{dT} \quad \text{where Q is the heat and T the absolute temperature.}$$

$$\text{For a Daniell cell, } \frac{de}{dT} = 0$$

The law was subsequently confirmed experimentally.
Ironically, Joule followed Daniell in believing that the emf of a Daniell cell varied with the temperature; *JSP* (2), p. 7.
45 Joule to Thomson, 3 Dec. 1851, CU, J 96.

Chapter 8

1 Robert's genius was recognised in his lifetime. Charles Babbage and Andrew Ure acknowledged him as the leading production engineer of the Industrial Revolution (see *Economy of Machines and Manufactures* (1833), and *Philosophy of Manufactures* (1835). C. F. Beyer, a disciple and employee of Roberts, later founded, in partnership with R. Peacock, the famous locomotive building firm of Beyer Peacock. Beyer and Peacock were two of the seven founder-members of the Institution of Mechanical Engineers. Beyer was also a notable benefactor of Owens College.
2 Joule to Thomson, 16 Mar. 1852, CU, J 110.
3 *JSP* (i), pp. 342–7. Joule's letter to Thomson, 28 Jan. 1852, CU, J 105, shows that Miller was insistent on this point.
4 Miller calculated, from Moll's measurement of the velocity of sound, that k, the ratio of

the specific heats of air, was 1.41. From this and from his figure for the mechanical equivalent of heat Joule deduced that the specific heat of air at constant pressure must be 0.238944 (!), which was reasonably close to his experimental measurement of 'nearly 0.23'. This confirmed Miller's criticism. *JSP* (i), p. 347.

5 Thomson, *MPP* (i), pp. 215–22.
6 Clausius's formula for the excess, or loss, of heat as steam is forced through a narrow orifice is

$$Q = \int_{t_1}^{t_2} h.dt - \frac{1}{J} \int_{v_1}^{v_2} p.dv + \frac{1}{J}(p_2 v_2 - p_1 v_1)$$

where the first team represents the heat required to maintain steam in a state of saturation as it does work, expanding slowly against a piston. Thomson's formula for the heat, assumed to be an excess, is

$$Q = \frac{1}{J} \int_{v_1}^{v_2} p.dv + \frac{1}{J}(p_1 v_1 - p_2 v_2) - \frac{1}{\mu} \int_{v_1}^{v_2} \frac{dp}{dt}.dv$$

(R. Clausius, 'On the deportment of vapour during its expansion under different circumstances', *Phil. Mag.*, vol. 1 (1851), pp. 398–405; Thomson, *MPP* (i), p. 219.) The above formulae have been changed only to the extent of using the same symbols where the original authors differed. For example, Clausius wrote 'A' – the 'equivalent of heat for a unit of work' – where 1/J has been substituted above. μ in Thomson's formula is, of course, Carnot's function.

7 Joule to Thomson, 21 Feb. 1852, CU, J 109.
8 Joule to Thomson, 26 Mar. 1852, CU, J 111. Shortly after this Joule read a short paper to the Lit & Phil (*JSP* (i), pp. 363–8) pointing out the analogy but he was unable to take the argument any further. He concluded that the air-engine must be more efficient than the steam-engine. Rankine read this paper later and wrote an open letter to Joule about it; 'On the mechanical effect of heat and of chemical forces', *Phil. Mag.*, vol. 5 (1853), p. 6.
9 Joule to Thomson, 26 Mar. 1852, CU, J 111.
10 Joule to Thomson, 28 Jan. 1852, CU, J 105. An additional justification for such a research was Joule's discovery of the change in dimensions of iron on magnetisation.
11 Thomson to Forbes, 8 May 1852, St Andrews University Library.
12 Joule to Thomson, 1 May 1852, CU, J 112.
13 Thomson to Forbes, 31 May 1852, St Andrews University Library.
14 Joule to Thomson, 31 May 1852, CU, J 114.
15 Joule to Thomson, 14 Jun. 1852, CU, J 115.
16 Joule to Thomson, 24 Jun. 1852, CU, J 116.
17 Joule to Thomson, 10 Jul. 1852, CU, J 117.
18 Thomson to J. Thomson, jun., 21 Jul. 1852, CU.
19 Joule to Thomson, 13 Aug. 1852, CU, J 119.
20 Thomson, *MPP* (i), pp. 219, 232.
21 *JSP* (ii), pp. 216–30; *MPP* (i), pp. 333–45.
22 Joule to Thomson, 20 Aug. 1852, CU, J 120.
23 Joule to Thomson, 9 Sept. 1852, CU, J 124.
24 *Ibid.*
25 Joule to Thomson, 22 Sept. 1852, CU, J 125. The letter was forwarded to Aberystwyth.
26 Joule to Thomson, 4 Oct. 1852, CU, J 126; 25 Nov. 1852, CU, J 129.
27 J. Tyndall to S. H. Christie, 15 Nov. 1852, Royal Institution.
28 Joule to Thomson, 6 Dec. 1852, CU, J 130. Joule included a sketch of the ball, or drop valves that made choking impossible. See *JSP* (ii), p. 235; *MPP* (i), p. 349.
29 Joule to Thomson, 20 Dec. 1852, CU, J 131.
30 Joule to Thomson, 22 Jan. 1853, CU, J 134.

31 Joule to Thomson, 3 Feb. 1853, CU, J 135.
32 W. J. M. Rankine, *Miscellaneous Scientific Papers* (London, 1881). Rankine later said that he did not know of Bernoulli's actual and potential *vis viva* at the time when he coined his terms. He was, however, aware, as Bernoulli cannot have been, of the wide application of the concepts outside the realm of mechanics.
33 Joule to Thomson, 15 Feb. 1853, CU, J 136.
34 Joule to Thomson, 1 Mar. 1853, CU, J 137.
35 Joule to Thomson, 15 Mar. 1853, CU, J 139.
36 Joule to Thomson, 19 Mar. 1853, CU, J 141 (*sic*) and 24 Mar. 1853, CU, J 140. See also *JSP* (ii), pp. 231–45, esp. 238.
37 Joule to Stokes, 12 Apr. 1853, CU, J 78.
38 Joule to Thomson, 2 Apr. 1853, CU, J 142.
39 *Proceedings of the Royal Society*, vol. 6 (1850–1854), pp. 298–300, 307. Joule's lowest figure was 0.226; the one he used was 0.2389. Regnault's figure was 0.237.
40 *JSP* (ii), pp. 231–45; *MPP* (i), pp. 346–56.
41 In 'Dynamical theory of heat', *MPP* (i), pp. 219, 221.
42 Joule to Thomson, 8 Sept. 1853, CU, J 148.
43 Joule to Thomson, 29 Aug. 1853, CU, J 147.
44 Joule to Thomson, 17 Sept. 1853, CU, J 149.
45 Joule to Thomson, 11 Oct. 1853, CU, J 150.
46 Joule to Thomson, 22 Oct. 1853, CU, J 152.
47 Joule to Thomson, – Nov. 1853, CU, J 153.
48 Joule to Thomson, 8 Nov. 1853, CU, J 154.
49 Joule to Thomson, 10 Nov. 1853, GUL.
50 Joule to Thomson, 19 Nov. 1853, CU, J 157.
51 Joule to Thomson, 25 Nov. 1853, CU, J 159.
52 Joule to Thomson, 22 Nov. 1853, CU, J 158.
53 Joule to Thomson, 6 Dec. 1853, CU, J 162.
54 Joule to Thomson, 7 Feb. 1854, CU, J 169 (*sic*); 13 Feb. 1854, CU, J 168.
55 S. P. Thompson, *The Life of William Thomson, Baron Kelvin of Largs* (London, 1910), vol. 1, pp 238, 305.
56 Joule to Thomson, 9 Dec. 1853, CU, J 163.
57 Joule to Thomson, 19 Jan. 1854, CU, J 167. Assuming that the *volumetric* specific heats of air and carbon dioxide are the same, and v is the volume of air, c, its cooling effect, v′ the volume of gas, x its cooling effect and c′ the cooling effect of the mixture, we have

$$x = \frac{(v + v')c' - v.c}{v'}$$

58 Joule to Thomson, 30 Mar. 1854, CU, J 179; 20 Mar. 1854, CU, J 177; 14 Jun. 1854, GUL. It had been assumed that the properties of individual gases were unchanged when they mixed (Dalton's axiom). These experiments were made to test that assumption.
59 Joule to Thomson, 4 Mar. 1854, CU, J 172. He found that damping the plug with alcohol caused a sharp fall in the temperature of the air; 13 Mar. 1854, CU, J 174. He found that air passed more readily through a stopcock than did carbon dioxide; 18 Mar. 1854, CU, J 176. He showed that heating the metal tube below the 'nozle' by steam or hot water caused a slow rise in temperature of the air passing through.
60 Joule to Thomson, 13 Feb. 1854, CU, J 168.
61 Joule to Thomson, 14 Feb. 1854, CU, J 170.
62 Joule to Thomson, 6 Mar. 1854, CU, J 173.
63 Clausius, *Phil. Mag.*, vol. 7 (1854), p. 297; Thomson, *ibid.*, p. 347. The squabble dragged on for some time, caused, apparently, by a confusion as to the distinction between a static charge and a current. Clausius also took issue with Thomson over the exact form of Carnot's function and accused Thomson of having ignored his assertion, independent of that of Joule, that it was as the reciprocal of the absolute temperature.

64 Joule to Thomson, 15 Mar. 1854, CU, J 175; 28 Mar. 1854, CU, J 177; 8 Apr. 1854, CU, J 180.

65 Joule to Thomson, 20 Apr. 1854, CU, J 181.

66 Joule to Thomson, 'On the thermal effects of fluids in motion – part II', *Philosophical Transactions*, vol. 144 (1854), p. 321; and in *JSP* (ii) and *MPP* (i).

67 Joule to Thomson, 28 Jan. 1854, GUL.

68 The work done on the gas up to the plug being P.V and the work done by it against atmospheric pressure after it has passed the plug being P'V', then $w - (P'V' - PV)$, where w is the whole work done, will be the work spent overcoming 'friction' and turbulence and converted into heat. It will fall short of compensating the cold of expansion by $1/J[Km.(P'-P)/\pi]$, where $(P'-P)$ is the pressure drop across the plug, π is the atmospheric pressure, K the specific heat capacity and m is a constant, different for each gas.

69 The law is

$$H = \frac{w}{J} + \frac{PV}{J} \wedge \frac{P-P'}{n}$$

where $\wedge$ is a (positive) constant and H the amount of heat that would exactly compensate the cold of expansion. The law shows that work w, expended by the gas on expansion, generates less heat than H; work w, expended on the gas by compression, generates more heat than its thermal equivalent w/J, P' being greater than P.

70 Thomson, *MPP* (i), p. 147. The argument is valid on the dynamical theory.

Chapter 9

1 Hodgkinson had a close relationship with Dalton. He married Catherine Johns, of the family with whom Dalton lodged for many years. Dalton was a witness at their wedding. Other scientific partnerships of the time were those of Joule with Scoresby, Fairbairn with Hopkins and Fairbairn with Tate (1862).

2 'Physics' in the eighteenth century and earlier included biological sciences. The interpretation was Aristotelean.

3 E. Patterson, 'Mary Somerville', *B.J.H.S.*, vol. 4 (1969), pp. 331–9. See also Dr Patterson's D.Phil. thesis on Mary Somerville in Oxford University, E. E. C. Patterson, 'Mary Somerville and the Cultivation of Science: 1815–1840', 1980.

4 D. S. L. Cardwell, *The Organisation of Science in England* (2nd edn, Heinemann, London, 1972). Most of those reading for the Natural Sciences Tripos intended to study medicine. The Oxford Honours School in Natural Sciences attracted few students.

5 Joule to Stokes, 12 Nov. 1853, CU, J 79; and in *Memoirs and Scientific Correspondence of the Late Sir George Gabriel Stokes* (CUP, 1907), 2 vols., pp. 48–9.

6 Stokes to Joule, 16 Nov. 1853, Physics Department, UMIST.

7 Perhaps Whewell was responsible for blocking the project. See J. G. Crowther, *The Cavendish Laboratory, 1874–197* (MacMillan, London, 1974), pp. 8–9.

8 Joule to Thomson, 20 Jun. 1854, GUL.

9 Joule to Thomson, 6 Jul. 1854, GUL.

10 Joule to Thomson, 22 Jul. 1854, GUL.

11 Joule to Thomson, 10 Aug. 1854, GUL.

12 Joule to Thomson, 25 Aug. 1854, GUL.

13 Joule to Thomson, 8 Sept. 1854, GUL.

14 Joule to Thomson, 16 Oct. 1854, GUL.

15 Joule to Thomson, 14 Nov. 1854, GUL.

16 Joule to Thomson, 1 Jan. 1855, GUL.

17 Thomson, 'On the mechanical, antecedents of motion, heat and light', BA *Report* (1854), pt 2, pp. 59–63. S. P. Thompson, *The Life of William Thomson, Baron Kelvin of*

Largs (London, 1910), vol. 1, p. 306.

18 Pesumably the Trent and Mersey and the Grand Junction canals.

19 Joule to Thomson, 22 Feb. 1855, CU, J 192.

20 Joule to Thomson, 29 Mar. 1855, CU, J 193.

21 Thomson to Joule, 15 Feb. 1855, GUL.

22 Thomson, *MPP* (i), pp. 213–315. Subsequently written up for the 1860 edition of Nichol's *Cyclopaedia of the Physical Sciences.*

23 Joule to Thomson, 17 Apr. 1855, CU, J 194.

24 Joule to Thomson, 5 Jun. 1855, CU, J 197.

25 Joule, 'Introductory researches on the induction of magnetism by electric currents', *Philosophical Transactions* (1856), p. 287; *JSP* (i), pp. 369–81, esp. 379. He made a mistake in the thickness of the wire, confusing one eighth with one sixth of an inch. He commented to Thomson: 'I dont know how so glaring a mistake occurred and I think I was never before so careless' (24 Dec. 1855).
    Presumably Joule was guided by an analogy with Hooke's law of elasticity. Had he displayed his results graphically he might have gained a better insight than by scanning tables of figures.

26 Royal Society, Referee's Report, 23 Jul. 1855. Joule had apparently assumed that the length of wire in an electromagnet was proportional to the number of turns. The inadequate results are apparent from Joule, 'Introductory researches', e.g., *JSP* (i), p. 372.

27 Royal Society, Referee's Report, 4 Jan. 1856.

28 Joule to Thomson, 11 Sept. 1855, CU, J 200, and in *JSP* (i), pp. 368–9.

29 Joule to Thomson, 4 Oct. 1855, CU, J 202.

30 Joule to Thomson, 23 May 1855, CU, J 196.

31 Joule to Thomson, 5 Jun. 1855, CU, J 197.

32 Joule to Thomson, 4 Oct. 1855, CU, J 202.

33 Cylindrical electromagnets were used. There were made by cutting iron tubes in half, laterally, so that one half formed the electromagnet, the other half the armature. They are now in Greater Manchester Museum of Science and Industry.

34 Joule to Thomson, 23 Oct. 1855, CU, J 203.

35 Joule to Thomson, 7 Nov. 1855, CU, J 204; 1 Jan. 1856, CU, J 208.

36 Joule to Thomson, 3 Jan. 1856, CU, J 209; 26 Jan. 1856, CU, J 211.

37 Joule to Thomson, 8 Feb. 1856, CU, J 212.

38 Joule to Thomson, 21 Feb. 1856, CU, J 213.

39 The relative abundance of fresh water near mills and factories made such condensers unnecessary. Textile mills usually had large ponds – called 'lodges' – beside them in which condensing water could cool down.

40 Joule to Thomson, 21 Feb. 1856, CU, J 213; 19 Mar. 1856, CU, J 216. He envisaged using a blast of cold air, instead of a stream of water, to condense the stream, and he suggested that by keeping the condenser wet, the cooling effect of evaporation would greatly increase the efficiency of the air-blast condenser.

41 'Certain improvements in steam-engines', *British Patents*, no. 486, 1856. Application dated 26 Feb. 1856, p. 2.

42 Joule to Thomson, 11 Sept. 1855, CU, J 200.

43 'On the fusion of metals by voltaic electricity', *JSP* (i), pp. 381–4.

44 Wilde was a remarkably prolific inventor, mainly in the field of applied electricity. He was the first to notice that two alternators, coupled to the same circuit, would pull themselves into phase.

45 B. S. Finn, article, 'Elihu Thomson', *DSB*, vol. 13 (1976).

46 Joule to Margaret Thomson, 28 Mar. 1856, CU, J 218.

47 Joule to Thomson, 8 Apr. 1856, CU, J 220.

48 *JSP* (ii), pp. 304–12; *MPP* (i), pp. 437–44. The velocity of the air could not, of course, be directly measured. The 'reduced velocity' was calculated from the known pressure

and the mass flowing in unit time. There were, therefore, two 'reduced velocities' according to the densities on the high pressure and on the low-pressure sides. It was apparent that the actual velocity was greater than either of these.

49 Joule to Thomson, 26 Jun. 1856, CU, J 223. The deduced velocity of 550 feet per second was sufficiently close to the predicted velocity of 644 (or 0.578 the velocity of sound at 13°C and normal atmospheric pressure) to confirm the theory.

50 W. Giedt, *Thermophysics* (Van Nostrand, New York, 1971), p. 109.

51 E. R. G. Eckert, 'Experiments on energy separation in fluid streams', *Mechanical Engineering* (Oct. 1984), pp. 58–65.

52 T. Woods and J. P. Joule: letters, 21 Feb. 1856, *Proc. Roy. Soc* (1856–1857), p. 62; *Phil. Mag.*, vol. 12 (1856), pp. 155–6 and pp. 321–2. Joule complained to Francis, of Taylor & Francis, publishers of *Phil. Mag.*, about Woods's accusations.

53 Joule to Thomson, 20 Oct. 1856, CU, J 231.

54 *Ibid.* See also *Phil. Mag.*, vol. 12 (1856), pp. 385–6.

55 Clausius was not elected an Honorary Member of the Lit & Phil until 1886.

56 G. Rennie, 'On the quantity of heat developed by water when violently agitated', BA *Report* (1856), p. 156. Rennie said that he had 'long entertained the idea that steam, as applied to the movement of engines, lost a large portion of its heat in the act of transmission'. But this did not mean that he had satisfied the desideratum of the dynamical theory of heat – the disappearance of heat when work was performed by an engine. The loss he ascribed to the steam and he hoped to find a more economical medium. The BA committee awarded him £20 to cover the cost of further research.

57 'On the quantity of heat developed by water when rapidly agitated', BA *Report* (1857), p. 196. A deal box of 8 cubic feet held 50 gallons of water agitated by a paddle. After many hours the maximum temperature rise was about 75°. No reading was more accurate than to within half a degree. After one series of experiments the quantity of water was found to be reduced to 42.5 gallons (!). He believed, without giving evidence, that beyond a certain point the rise in temperature would level off.

58 E. G. Brown, "The History of Metallic Magnesium from 1808 to 1890' (M.Sc. thesis, Salford University, 1972).

59 Joule, 'Description of a new camera', *Photographic Notes*, vol. 1 (1 Sept. 1856), pp. 155–7.

60 This was about the time that Dora Potter, who later married H. E. Roscoe, began to be interested in photography, in which she subsequently became very skilled.

61 'On a surface condenser', *Proc. Inst. Mech. Eng.* (1856), pp. 185–95. He advocated the use of rubber jointing for condenser tubes.

62 'A short account of the life and writings of the late Mr William Sturgeon', *Manchester Memoirs*, vol. 14 (1857), pp. 53–83.

63 The most recent account of Sturgeon is by G. Hodgkinson, 'William Sturgeon, 1783–1850: his life and work to 1840' (M.Sc. thesis, Manchester University, 1979).

64 *JSP* (i), p. 414. A small spring immersed in a can of water was compressed and then released. Repeated experiments showed that practically no heat was generated while appreciable work had been done (and recovered).

65 Joule to Thomson, 10 Oct. 1856, CU, J 228.

66 Joule to Thomson, 11 Oct. 1856, CU, J 229; 13 Oct. 1856, CU, J 230.

67 Joule to Thomson, 30 Oct. 1856, J 232.

68 *JSP* (i), pp. 405–7. The inclusion of an iron wire to separate the copper lead to the galvanometer from the wire under strain (supposedly to obviate possible strain effects at the support end) meant, in effect, the introduction of a new thermocouple. Joule to Thomson, 30 Oct. 1856, J 232; 18 Nov. 1856, CU, J 233.

69 *JSP* (i), p. 406. He claimed an accuracy to within 1/8000°C(!).

70 Joule to Thomson, 8 Jan. 1857, CU, J 239; and *JSP* (i), pp. 409–12. The formula was derived by a straightforward application of the Carnot cycle. The parameters were temperature, load (or pressure), coefficient of expansion, specific heat and 'J'. H, the

heat, was given by H = t/J.P.e; P being the weight applied, e the coefficient of expansion, t the absolute temperature.

71 Joule to Thomson, 18 Jan. 1857, CU, J 240.
72 Joule to Thomson, 22 Jan. 1857, CU, J 241; and *JSP* (i), pp. 406–7.
73 Joule to Thomson, 27 Jan. 1857, GUL.
74 Thomson to Forbes, 8 Feb. 1857, St Andrews University Library.
75 *Ibid.*
76 *Ibid.*
77 Joule to Tyndall, 2 May 1857, Royal Institution.
78 Joule to Thomson, 6 May 1859, GUL.
79 Joule to Thomson, 11 Feb. 1857, CU, J 242.
80 Joule to Thomson, 22 Feb. 1857, CU, J 243.
81 Joule to Thomson, 14 Mar. 1857, CU, J —. He was careful to carry out the experiment when the sky was overcast.
82 Joule to Thomson, 30 Mar. 1857, CU, J 245.
83 Joule to Thomson, 8 Apr. 1857, GUL.
84 Joule to Thomson, 15 Sept. 1857, GUL. It is not clear what this work involved. Lewis Gordon, formerly Regius Professor of Civil Engineering in Glasgow University, preceded Rankine in that Chair. Anne Gordon, his sister, married William Siemens. According to a letter of 17 July 1857 (GUL), Joule contemplated joining Thomson on the *U.S.S. Niagara*, one of the two ships engaged on the initial attempt to lay the cable.
85 *JSP* (i), pp. 422–3.
86 Joule to Thomson, 23 Apr. 1857, CU, J 246.
87 Joule to Thomson, 5 May 1857, GUL.
88 G. S. Messinger, *Manchester in the Victorian Age: the Half Known City* (MUP, 1985), p. 126.
89 Joule to Thomson, 5 May 1857, GUL. See also Joule to Thomson 17 Jul. 1857, GUL.
90 The assumption was that e was measured when the solid was not under tension and was therefore smaller than it would be under the experimental conditions. Shortly afterwards Joule found that e for cast iron was less under tension; Joule to Thomson, 3 May 1857, GUL.
91 *JSP* (i), pp. 409–12.
92 The table of heating effects for water at different temperatures from 0° to 100°, given in *JSP* (i), p. 412, does not accord with the numbers calculated when Thomson's 'rough estimate' formula for e is used:

$$e = \frac{t - 278}{46} \cdot \frac{1}{2200}$$

Joule's letter to Thomson setting out the table is dated 10 Aug. 1857, GUL, but according to *JSP* (i), p. 412, the table was added on 1 Aug. 1857.

A letter from Joule to Thomson, 18 Jun. 1857, CU, J 247, shows that Joule did not use Thomson's 'rough estimate' formula for e but relied on Despretz's table of the expansion of water at different temperatures.
93 *JSP* (i), pp. 474–9.
94 *JSP* (i), pp. 413–75, 'On some thermodynamic properties of solids', *Philosophical Transactions*, vol. 149, (1859), p. 91.
95 *JSP* (ii), pp. 312–21; *MPP* (i), pp. 445–53.
96 Joule to Thomson, 4 Jun. 1857, GUL.
97 Joule to Thomson, 6 Jun. 1857, GUL.
98 Joule and Thomson, *Philosophical Transactions* (1860), p. 325; *JSP* (ii), pp. 322–41; *MPP* (i), pp. 400–14.
99 Joule to Thomson, 14 Jun. 1859, GUL.
100 Joule to Thomson, 7 Jul. 1859, GUL.
101 Joule to Thomson, 19 Jul. 1859, GUL.

102 Joule to Margaret Thomson, 21 Sept. 1858, CU, J 257; and Joule to Thomson, 1 Oct. 1858, CU, J 259.
103 Joule to Thomson, 24 Jul. 1857, GUL.
104 Joule to Thomson, 7 Dec. 1857, GUL.
105 Joule to Thomson, 25 Oct. 1857, GUL.
106 *The Times.*
107 R. Hunt, 'Electromagnetism as a source of power', in *Minutes of Proceedings of the Institution of Civil Engineers,* vol. 16 (1856–1857), p. 327. At this meeting Tyndall suggested that it might be possible to utilise the back emf from a motor. Tyndall appreciated the relationship between work and heat but had evidently not fully grasped the implications of the energy doctrine. This was an interesting example of the effect of specialisation on a man of science of the highest ability; it also indicates the wide, revolutionary nature of the new doctrine. Hunt wrote to Joule, 22 Apr. 1857, GMMSI, asking for a contribution to which request Joule acceded. Thomson, too, sent a letter. Others present at the meeting included Grove, Smee, Petrie and Stephenson.
108 *The Times,* 31 Dec. 1857.
109 Joule to Thomson, 23 Jan. 1858, GUL; 1 Jan. 1858, CU, J 248.
110 Joule to Thomson, 16 Mar. 1858, CU, J 253.
111 *JSP* (1), pp. 399–412. A number of fellow members of the Lit & Phil, among them Crace Calvert, R. A. Smith and, up to August 1857, Frankland, were very interested in problems of sanitation and sewerage.
112 Joule to Stokes, 29 Nov. 1858, CU, J 78.
113 J. P. Joule, 'On some facts in the science of heat developed since the time of Watt', a lecture to the Greenock Philosophical Society, 19 Jan. 1865. Published by the Greenock Philosophical Society.

Joule's work on the surface condensation of steam culminated in a paper in the *Philosophical Transactions,* vol. 151 (1861), pp. 133–60; *JSP* (i), pp. 502–31. He presented a wealth of data on the transmission of heat from steam in a pipe to cold water flowing outside. The diameter of the pipe was varied, as was the rate and direction of flow of the water. He found that heat transfer was most impeded by films of hot water on the inside and outside of the pipe. These could be reduced by increasing the rate of flow of the water and by breaking it up by means of a wire spiral round the pipe. Condensation by cold air blast was, contrary to his hopes, much less effective and would only be useful in special circumstances.

Chapter 10

1 Joule to Thomson, 22 Jul. 1859, GUL.
2 Joule to Thomson, 20 Aug. 1859, GUL.
3 'Telegraphic work', wrote Thomson to Joule (25 Sept. 1858), 'done through 2,400 miles of submarine wire . . . when its effects are instantaneous exchange of ideas between the old and new worlds, possesses a combination of physical and (I mean in the original sense of the word) *metaphysical* interest which I have never found in any other scientific pursuit'. Quoted by S. P. Thompson, *The Life of William Thomson, Baron Kelvin of Largs* (London, 1910), vol. 1. The whole passage is of great interest.
4 Joule to Thomson, 31 Oct. 1858, CU, J 260.
5 Joule to Thomson, 10 Dec. 1858, CU, J 261.
6 *Ibid.* The cook was probably Elizabeth Rigby, recorded in the Censuses of 1841 and 1851.
7 Joule to Thomson, 1 Jan. 1859, GUL. Benjamim Joule made his will in 1822, by which time he had three surviving children. A succession of codicils took account of the deaths of his wife and of his daughter Alice and made his sons executors as they reached maturity. Under the terms of his will his real estate was to be disposed of by 'public auction', 'private contract', or a combination of the two. His signature to his last codicil

(1850) was witnessed by Robert Isherwood, 'coachman to Mr Joule'. When probate was granted on 13 April 1859 the value of his estate was put at under £10,000. Presumably in his final years he had bestowed the bulk of his fortune on his heirs at law.

8   Joule to Thomson, 14 Feb., 2, 9 and 30 Mar. 1859, GUL.
9   Joule to Thomson, 29 Apr. 1859.
10 *Ibid.*, and 2 Apr. 1859, GUL.
11 Joule to Thomson, 5 Sept. 1859, GUL. 'It is possible', wrote Joule, 'to use a surface condenser so that the water returned to the boiler is hotter than the excellence of the vacuum warrants'.
12 Joule to Thomson, 16 Dec. 1859, GUL.
13 *Ibid.*
14 Joule to Thomson, 26 Mar. 1860, GUL.
15 Joule to Thomson, 6 Apr. 1860, GUL.
16 Joule to Thomson, 17 Apr. 1860, GUL.
17 Joule to Thomson, 1 May 1860, GUL.
18 Joule to Thomson, 2 May 1860, GUL.
19 Joule to Thomson, 4 May 1860, GUL.
20 J. P. Joule and W. Thomson, 'On the thermal effects of fluids in motion, Part 4', *Philosophical Transactions* (1862), p. 579; *JSP* (ii), pp. 342–61; *MPP* (i), pp. 415–32. Their general expression for the cooling effect was

$$\frac{d\theta}{dp} = -\frac{1}{JK}\left(t.\frac{dv}{dt} - v\right) \quad \text{now usually written as}$$

$$\Delta T = \frac{T\left(\frac{dv}{dT}\right)_p - v}{C_p}.\,\Delta p$$

21 Joule to Thomson, 2 Sept. 1879, CU, J 295.
22 W. Fairbairn and T. Tate, 'Experimental researches to determine the density of steam at different temperatures, and to determine the laws of expansion of superheated steam', the Bakerian Lecture, *Philosophical Transactions*, vol. 50 (1860), pp. 185–222.
23 Joule to Thomson, 12 Jul. 1860, GUL. The same letter contains an account of an ingenious method of raising a tall mast. A number of concentric tubes stand vertically on the ground. From the base of the innermost tube ropes pass up over pulleys at the top of the next outermost to the base of which other ropes are attached to pass over pulleys at the top of the third tube; and so on. When these ropes are pulled from outside the tubes will rise telescopically. When the mast is fully erected, or extended, the ropes would act as stays.
24 An 'effect' might be described as deviation from a general law.
25 Roscoe to Stokes, 2 Apr. 1860, Add.MS, CU.
26 Roscoe to Stokes, 19 Mar. 1860, Add.MS, CU.
27 This is not, of course, to deny the individual contributions of, for example, Tyndall in London, Forbes in Edinburgh, Stokes and Hopkins in Cambridge, Hamilton and Lloyd in Dublin or the contributions of Regnault, Helmholtz, Clausius and many others outside the United Kingdom.
28 Joule to Thomson, 6 Aug. 1860, GUL. His friend Binney was critical of the Owens College at this time. Science and industry in Manchester had been created by private individuals, he argued, not by college men (R. A. Smith, *A Centenary of Science in Manchester* (Manchester Lit & Phil, 1883)).
29 Roscoe to Thomson, 27 Sept. 1860, CU, R 791. There is an indication that Maxwell considered applying; Joule to Thomson, 12 Jul. 1860, GUL. Joule remarked: 'I am sorry Maxwell is not coming and am taking it in consideration whether or no I should apply for the place. I have a week to make up my mind.'

30 Clifton held the Oxford Chair for fifty years (1865–1915), but did little. Oxford physics did not revive until the appointment of Professor Lindemann (Lord Cherwell). See Rakjkumari Williamson (ed.), *The making of Physicists* (Adam Hilger, Bristol, 1987), p. 114 and *passim*.
31 Joule to Thomson, 6 Aug. 1860, GUL. Invercloy is on the Isle of Arran. Benjamin described himself in the 1861 Census as 'proprietor of land and J.P.'.
32 Joule to Thomson, 8 Jan. 1861, CU, J 262; 25 Jan. 1861, CU, J 263. There were, of course, no X-rays available at that time. Thereafter Thomson walked with a limp.
33 Joule to Thomson, 22 Feb. 1861, CU, J 264. Lewis Gordon was, apparently, exempt from this sweeping condemnation.
34 The lecture was given on 5 Nov. 1860 to Birkenhead Literary and Scientific Society; it was printed in Liverpool.
35 Joule to Thomson, 6 Mar. 1861, CU, J 265. Nasmyth's 'willow-leaf' patterns on the sun proved to be an illusion.
36 *Ibid.*
37 Undated letter, CU, J 305.
38 Joule to Thomson, 20 Mar. 1861, CU, J 266.
39 Joule to Thomson, 28 Apr. 1861, CU, 268.
40 Joule to Thomson, 13 May 1861, CU, 269.
41 Joule to Thomson, 25 Jun. 1861, CU, J 270.
42 Joule to Thomson, 16 Aug. 1861, CU, J 272.
43 *Ibid.* The plug had asbestos packed between two short, concentric tubes perforated by many holes. It was inside a wider, short tube, connected to the pipe from the coil. The U-shape of the plug minimised the conduction of heat to the side of the wider tube (see L. J. Hoxton, *Physical Review*, vol. 13 (1919), p. 438). The pump had a solid piston, to dispense with leathers.
44 Werner Siemens *Inventor and Entrepreneur; Recollections of Werner Siemens* (Lund Humphries, London and Prestel-Verlag, Munich, 1966), p. 119.
45 BA *Report* (1861), pp. xxxix, 37.
46 A. C. Lynch, *Institution of Electrical Engineers, Proceedings A*, vol. 132, pt A, no. 8 (Dec. 1985), pp. 564–73.
47 J. Cawood, 'Terrestrial magnetism and the development of international collaboration in the early nineteenth century', *Annals of Science*, vol. 34 (1977), pp. 551–87; and 'The magnetic crusade: science and politics in early Victorian Britain', *Isis*, vol. 70 (1979), pp. 493–518. The setting-up of magnetic observations all round the world raised the acute problem of standardising the magnets used in the observatories. Gauss pointed out that this could only be done by using the unit of dynamical force. The strength of the magnets should be defined in terms of dynamical force and this would not change from place to place, nor from continent to continent.
48 BA *Report* (1862), p. 125.
49 Joule to Thomson, 10 Sept. 1861, CU, J 274.
50 Joule to Roscoe, 26 Sept. 1861, Royal Society of Chemistry.
51 Joule to Frances Charlotte Tappenden, 5 Oct. 1861, GMMSI.
52 Joule to Thomson, 5 Oct. 1861, CU, J 275.
53 Robin Fox, *The Tory Islanders, a People of the Celtic Fringe* (CUP, 1978), pp. 8–10.
54 *Tory Island Letters* (between the Revd James O'Donnell, CC, resident priest of Tory and B. St J. B. Joule, JP for the County of Lancaster, to the editor of the *Liverpool Daily Post*). In Joule family papers, Archives Department, Manchester Central Reference Library.
55 Fox, *The Tory Islanders*. Professor Fox mentions that there is another copy of *Tory Island Letters* in the LSE Library. The Congested Districts Board cannot have purchased the island from Benjamin in 1903 since he was dead by then. Most probably it was sold by Joule's daughter and son-in-law.
56 Joule to Thomson, 8 Jan. 1862, CU, J 277.
57 Joule to Thomson, 13 Jan. 1862, CU, J 278. It is surprising that Joule's intuition that

there must be a 'neutral point', or inversion temperature, was apparently not accepted by Thomson. Joule's figures for the effect, in degrees calculated from a temperature of $-200°$ are:

Temp	Exptl	Calc^d	Temp	Exptl	Calc^d
7.3	4.367	4.367	7.4	4.37	4.4
35.6	3.407	3.37	35.6	3.41	3.63
54	2.951	2.9	54	2.95	3.23
95.5	2.15	2.152	97.5	2.14	2.52

The second table is printed in *JSP* (ii), p. 359 and *MPP* (i), p. 429. There is no mention of Joule's hypothesis although it was conceded that the results for carbon dioxide needed further investigation.

If a perfect gas, obeying the law p.v = R.T. is assumed the Joule–Thomson expression, [op. cit., (20)] reduces to $\triangle T = O$.

Thomson's inferred law was $\triangle T = A(\frac{273.7}{T})^2$, where A was a constant.

By equating these expressions an equation of state for the gas can be obtained.

If, conversely, we assume van der Waal's equation for a real gas we get for the cooling effect:

$$\triangle T = (\frac{2a}{RT} - b).\frac{p}{Cp} \quad \text{(a, b, are small)}$$

This allows for an inversion temperature.

58 Joule to Thomson, 4 Dec. 1861, CU, J 276.
59 *JSP* (i), pp. 490–500.
60 Joule to Thomson, 4 Dec. 1861, CU, J 276.
61 Joule to Thomson, 7 Apr. 1862, GUL.
62 *Proceedings*, Lit & Phil, vol. 2 (1862), p. 170.
63 Joule to Thomson, 8 Jan. 1862, CU, J 277. 'Have you considered the effect of condensation of vapour?' wrote Joule. 'Do you not think this the principal reason that the observed decrease of temperature on ascending the atmosphere is less than the theoretical on the convection theory?'
64 Joule to Thomson, 27 Jan. 1862, CU, J 280.
65 *JSP* (i), pp. 500–2; *Proceedings*, Lit & Phil, vol. 2 (1862), p. 208; letter to Thomson, 11 Feb. 1862, CU, J 281.
66 BA *Report* (1863), p. 111; and Appendix D.
67 Joule to Thomson, 30 May 1862, CU, J 283.
68 *Phil. Mag.*, vol. 24 (1862), p. 52.
69 Joule to Thomson, 9 Jul. 1862, GUL; *Phil. Mag.*, vol. 24 (1862), p. 121. Joule referred to 'my friend Professor Tyndall'. The ensuing debate/brawl was fully reported in the ensuing pages of the *Philosophical Magazine* and has been very adequately discussed by later writers.
70 Only in one respect was Thomson unsuccessful: he had no children. His two marriages were barren, his first wife being a more or less permanent invalid.
71 Joule to Tyndall, 21 Jul. 1862, Royal Institution.
72 Joule to Thomson, 27 Aug. 1862, GUL. He had just returned from his summer holiday at Llandudno.
73 The letter, dated 25 Nov. 1862, was printed in *Proceedings*, Lit & Phil, vol. 3 (1864), p. 21.
74 Joule to Thomson, 8 Oct. 1862, GUL.
75 Joule to Thomson, 21 Dec. 1862, GUL. Boiler explosions were an increasing hazard in a town so dependent on steam power as Manchester. This led to the formation of the Manchester Steam User's Association and subsequently to two leading industrial insurance companies. Joule devised an hydraulic pressure test for boilers, *JSP* (i), pp. 480–1.

76 Joule to Thomson, 27 Aug. 1862, GUL.
77 Joule to Roscoe, 26 Oct. 1862, Royal Society of Chemistry.
78 Joule to Thomson, 26 Jan. 1863, GUL.
79 J. R. Ashworth, 'Fragment of autobiography', in 'List of apparatus now in Manchester which belonged to Dr J. P. Joule, F.R.S.; with remarks on his MSS, letters and autobiography', *Manchester Memoirs*, vol. 75 (1930–1931), pp. 105–17. Joule's letter was dated 23 Jan. 1863.
80 *JSP* (i), pp. 531–4.
81 Joule to Thomson, 5 Mar. 1863, GUL.; *JSP* (i), pp. 535–6.
82 Joule to Tyndall, 23 Mar. 1863, Royal Institution.
83 Dyer had extended his criticisms to include Rankine, Tyndall and Armstrong (e.g. in *Proceedings*, Lit & Phil, vol. 1, p. 91; vol. 2, p. 43; vol. 3, p. 77; vol. 6, p. 52; and vol. 7, p. 165). See *op. cit.*, Ch 6 (34). Dyer was a versatile and energetic man; S. McKenna, 'Joseph Chessborough Dyer', *Manchester Memoirs*, vol. 117 (1974–1975), pp. 104–11.
84 Joule to Tait, 25 Jul. 1863, GUL. Joule commented on Tyndall's assertion that Mayer was the first to use the expression 'mechanical equivalent of heat'. He was also very critical of Mayer, who rushed into print with unsupported speculation whose influence 'was to retard the advance of sciene' (he did not explain how it would do so). 'This is my candid opinion although I feel far too great respect and kindness for Mayer to say so in print.'
85 Thomson to Joule, 12 Jan. 1864, GUL.
86 Joule to Margaret Thomson, 30 Mar. 1864, GUL. For details of Joule's deflecting magnets see *JSP* (i), pp. 540–2.
87 Joule first planned to use Thomson's current balance to measure i in mechanical units but found a tangent galvanometer more convenient.
    The apparatus used by Maxwell, Balfour Stewart and Fleeming Jenkin consisted of a vertical, closed coil of wire rotating rapidly round a compass needle at its centre. The current induced as the coil cut the earth's magnetic field generated another magnetic field that turned the needle through an angle that again depended on the earth's magnetic field. The double role of the earth's magnetic field cancelled out any need to measure the current induced (it was, of course, an alternating current, but not as viewed from the needle). The experimenters needed to know only the number of revolutions per minute, the deflection of the needle, the dimensions and number of turns of wire of the coil and the strength of the earth's magnetic field.
88 Joule to Thomson, 15 Oct. 1866, CU, J 284.
89 Joule to Thomson, 14 Jan. 1867, GUL.
90 Joule to Fleeming Jenkin, 14 Jan. 1867, GUL. He made the same suggestion, writing to Thomson, on the same day; 14 Jan. 1867, GUL.
91 Joule to Thomson, 9 Jul. 1867, GUL.
92 'Fifth report of B.A. committee on standards of electrical Resistance', BA *Report* (1867), p. 474; Appendix 5: J. P. Joule, 'Determination of the dynamical equivalent of heat from the thermal effects of an electric current', pp. 542–57.
93 Joule to Thomson, 28 Nov. 1867, GUL.
94 Joule to Thomson, 16 Feb. 1865, GUL.
95 Joule to Thomson, 30 Dec. 1865, GUL.
96 Joule to Thomson, 4 Jan. 1866, GUL.
97 Joule to Thomson, 13 Apr. 1866, GUL.
98 Joule to Thomson, 14 Jan. 1867, GUL.
99 Joule to Thomson, 30 Mar. 1867, GUL.

Chapter 11

1 The first intimation of the theory of dimensions is in Lazare Carnot's *Essay on the General Theory of Machines* (Paris, 1783, 1786). It was developed by J. B. J. Fourier, *Analytical*

Theory of Heat (Paris, 1822). The background to the theory is dealt with by J. R. Ravetz, 'The representation of physical quantities in eighteenth-century mathematical physics', *Isis*, vol. 52 (1961), pp. 7–20. Only after the work of the BA Committee could the theory be extended to cover electricity and magnetism.

2 Dionysus Lardner, in his widely read book on the steam-engine *Popular Lectures on the Steam Engine* (London, 1828, and subsequent editions), had speculated on the exhaustion of British coal mines. W. G. Armstrong raised the question in the course of his Presidential address to the British Association in Newcastle in 1863. W. S. Jevons joined the Lit & Phil in 1866 when Joule was a Vice-President.

3 Sinsteden seems to have had a promising idea (1951), and Soren Hjorth, of Liverpool, came close to the principle of the dynamo in 1854. Unfortunately there is little available information about Hjorth.

4 W. W. Haldane Gee, 'Obituary of Henry Wilde', *Manchester Memoirs*, vol. 63 (1920), 5, pp. 1–16. The list of benefactions given is by no means exhaustive.

5 H. Wilde, 'Experimental researches in electricity and magnetism, *Proc. Roy. Soc.* (1866), pp. 107–11. Received 20 Mar. 1866.

6 W. Siemens, *Inventor and Entrepreneur; Recollections of Werner Siemens* (Lund Humphries, London and Prestel-Verlag, Munich, 1966), p. 230; C. Wheatstone, *Proc. Roy. Soc.* (1867), pp. 367–9; C. F. Varley, *Proc. Roy. Soc.* (1867), pp. 403–4.

7 C. W. Siemens, *Pro. Roy. Soc.* (1867), pp. 367–9.

8 Messrs Elkington's, of Birmingham, were early users of Wilde's machines; Gee, 'Obituary'.

9 By the same token it might be – and indeed has been – argued that Newcomen's atmospheric steam-engine could have been invented without prior knowledge of atmospheric pressure. But what made it feasible was the well-publicised information about such pressure – its nature and extent – through, for example, von Guericke's graphic and most suggestive illustrations in his *Experimenta Nova* (Amsterdam, 1672).

10 He lived out in what was and is the affluent dormitory suburb of Alderly Edge. Katherine Chorley gives a most evocative account of life there in the early years of the present century in her *Manchester Made Them* (MUP, 1951).

11 Wilde had his correspondence with Sir Henry Truman Wood, Secretary of the Society of Arts, printed and published (Manchester, 1900). The award was finally given and accepted with minimal courtesies.

12 W. J. M. Rankine, *The Steam-Engine and Other Prime Movers* (Glasgow, 1859), covered steam-engines, water power, gas-engines and electric battery power. The help of Joule and Thomson was acknowledged in the preface.

13 G. Chrystal to W. Thomson, quoted in S. P. Thompson, *The Life of William Thompson, Baron Kelvin of Largs* (London, 1910), vol. 1, pp. 451–2.

14 The full title is *Exposition Analytique et Expérimentale de la Théorie Mécanique de la Chaleur.* Hirn presented a copy of the third edition (Paris, 1875–1876) to Joule, inscribing it 'Homage amicale à Joule'.

15 Like the Lit & Phil, the Société Industrielle is active today.

16 Hirn was a pioneer of the use of mineral oil as a lubricant.

17 A. Kastler, 'L'oeuvre scientifique de Gustave-Adolphe Hirn, 1815–1890', *Révue Générale des Sciences*, vol. 65 (1958), p. 277–97.

18 G-A. Hirn, 'Sur les principaux phénomènes qui presentait les frottements mediats, *Bulletin de la Société Industrielle de Mulhouse*, vol. 26 (1854), p. 188.

19 Library, Société Industrielle de Mulhouse (560/19).

20 *Gustave-Adolphe Hirn, 1815–1890*, notice biographique, M. le docteur Fadel et M. Emile Schwoerer (Colmar, 1891). Library, Société Industrielle de Mulhouse (Folio, 3894).

21 A. J. Pacey, 'Some early heat-engine concepts and the conservation of heat', *B.J.H.S.*, vol. 7 (1974), pp. 135–45. George Lee was pleased to discover that, as far as he could see, his engine gave out as much heat as it received!

22 A copy of Clausius's report is in the Library of the Société Industrielle de Mulhouse.

Clausius was, at the time, a professor at the Federal Polytechnic, Zurich.

23 Hirn showed that a Woolf compound engine without a steam jacket used little more steam but lost 25% of its power; an unjacketed single-cylinder engine lost little power but used much more steam; a single-cylinder, unjacketed engine using superheated steam was more powerful and more economic. He explained that, in the first case, the small, high-pressure cylinder determined the steam consumption and used little more when unjacketed, the loss of power was due to condensation in the big, low-pressure cylinder; the single-cylinder engine needed a lot of steam to heat the cylinder up but, that done, the full boiler pressure was available and normal power was delivered. With superheated steam there was full pressure and little condensation.

Hirn's ingenious experimental demonstration of the negative specific heat capacity of saturated steam has its place in textbooks.

24 R. L. Hills, 'Thermodynamics and practical engineering in the nineteenth century', *History of Technology*, vol. 1 (1976), pp. 1–20.

25 D. K. Clark, *The Steam-Engine: A Treatise on the Steam-Engine and Boiler*, 2 vols. (London, 1889–1890). Clark made many references to papers in the Bulletin de la Société Industrielle de Mulhouse.

26 Hirn, *Exposition*, p. 138.

27 *Ibid.*, p. 143. Hirn added that Mayer's metaphysical starting point led nowhere ('n'eut absolument conduit qu'à des élucubrations vide de sens'), unless supported by solid experimental evidence.

28 Thomson, 'On a universal tendency in nature to the dissipation of mechanical energy', *MPP* (i), pp. 511–14.

29 For a fuller account, see D. S. L. Cardwell, *From Watt to Clausius* (Heinemann, London, 1970).

30 Thomson, 'On the dynamical theory of heat', *MPP* (i), pp. 236–7. He envisaged a complex cycle; heat, Q, entering at temperature, T, is taken as positive; leaving as negative. The cycle is reversible and the sum of all Q/T is therefore zero.

31 When a body undergoes a thermodynamic change the change in entropy is independent of the route followed; it depends only on the first and final state. The entropy change can therefore be calculated by supposing the body to have followed a reversible change to bring it from the first to the last state.

32 When heat Q flows from a hot body, at temperature T_1, to a cooler body at T_2, the fall in entropy of the hot body (Q/T_1) must be smaller than the gain in entropy (Q/T_2) of the cooler body. The net change is, therefore, a gain in entropy.

33 Clausius introduced the concept of the mean free path (1857–8); Maxwell promulgated the distribution law (1859), which Boltzmann established on a systematic basis (1868 onward).

Chapter 12

1 S. P. Thomson, *The Life of William Thomson, Baron Kelvin of Largs* (London, 1910), vol. 1, pp. 238–305. The lecture was not published. Thompson's account (corrected by W. T.) was taken from the *Cambridge Chronicle*.

2 Joule to Roscoe, 12 Apr. 1867, Royal Society of Chemistry. In this letter he suggests that the Lit & Phil should give a special award to Thomson for his work on the Atlantic cable.

3 Joule to Thomson, 20 Dec. 1867, GUL. More than half the time needed for the 1849 experiments was devoted to winding up the weights; this doubled the errors of observation. Joule considered using tap water to drive a small water-wheel as the source of power.

4 Joule to Thomson, 7 Feb. 1868, GUL; Joule to Stokes, 26 Aug. 1868, CU, J 80; *JSP* (i), pp. 559–61, 574–5.

5 Joule to Thomson, 14 Oct. 1868, GUL.

6 J. V. Pickstone, *Medicine and Industrial Society* (MUP, 1985).

7 Ibid., pp. 110, 130. See D. S. L. Cardwell and J. Mottram, 'Fresh light on John Dalton',

Notes and Records of the Royal Society of London, vol. 39, no. 1 (1984), pp. 29–40, for details of John Roberton, a dedicated and highly effective pioneer of public health.

8 Joule to Thomson, 1 Dec. 1868, GUL.

9 I am indebted to Mr J. F. Clarke for this information.

10 Joule to Thomson, 12 Dec. 1868, GUL.

11 Joule to Thomson, 30 Jan. 1869, GUL. Dr Crompton was a grandson of Samuel Crompton, inventor of the spinning mule.

12 Joule to Thomson, 3 Mar. 1869, GUL.

13 Joule to Thomson, 18 Apr. 1869, GUL.

14 Joule to Margaret Thomson, 10 Jun. 1869, CU, J 285.

15 Joule to G. Griffith, 4 Aug. 1869, written from 60 Brighton Terrace, Promenade, Southport. The source is not known.

16 Joule to Thomson, 15 Sept. 1869, CU, J 286.

17 This was the view he expressed to Thomson in a letter of 6 Apr. 1869, CU, J 289. He first learned of the resignation when Jack resigned from the Lit & Phil; letter to Thomson, 17 Apr. 1870, CU, J 290.

18 Joule to Thomson, 17 Apr. 1870, CU, J 290.

19 Stewart to Roscoe, 20 May 1870, Royal Society of Chemistry.

20 Joule to Tyndall, 8 Jun. 1870, Royal Institution.

21 Cf. his letter to Grove, 21 Oct. 1870, Royal Institution.

22 For an account of these movements see D. S. L. Cardwell, *The Organisation of Science in England* (2nd edn, Heinemann, London, 1972), pp. 53–5.

23 Joule to Frances Charlotte Tappenden, 21 Nov. 1870, Physics Department, UMIST.

24 *JSP* (i), pp. 558–9.

25 J. R. Ashworth, 'Fragment of autobiography', in 'List of apparatus now in Manchester which belonged to Dr J. P. Joule, F.R.S., with remarks on his MSS, letters and autobiography', *Manchester Memoirs,* vol. 75 (1930–1931), pp. 105–17.

26 *JSP* (i), pp. 589–604.

27 *Ibid.,* pp. 607–13.

28 O. Reynolds, *Memoirs of James Prescott Joule* (Manchester Lit & Phil, 1892), p. 26.

29 John Roberton recollected that Dalton used to dominate the Society; Cardwell and Mottram, 'Fresh light on John Dalton'.

30 Highton first published his views in *Chemical News,* vol. 22 (1870), pp. 224, 238 and vol 23 (1971), *passim.* Other papers were in the *Pharmaceutical Journal* (1873), pp. 515–18 and *Quarterly Journal of Science,* vol. 1 (1871), pp. 77–94. He had an ally in the Revd J. M. Heath who published in *Phil. Mag.* (1870) and (1971), *passim.* Highton was not a member of the Lit & Phil but he was allowed to put his points to the Society.
    Joule was usually scornful of the scientific views of clergymen.

31 J. Hopkinson, 'The overthrow of the science of electro-dynamics', *Proceedings,* Lit & Phil, vol. 10 (1871). Joule had prior knowledge of Highton's attack. 'This is surely the time for new proofs now that the Jesuitical conclave are proposing to put down the dynamical theory as heretical.': letter to Thomson, 29 Dec. 1869, CU, J 287.

32 Rev H. Highton, 'On the mechanical equivalent of heat', *Proceedings,* Lit & Phil, vol. 10 (1871), p. 147. Hopkinson, *ibid.,* p. 150.

33 Joule, 'Examples of the performance of the electromagnetic engine', *Proceedings,* Lit & Phil, vol. 10 (1871), p. 151; *JSP* (i), pp. 613–19.

34 Revd H. Highton, 'Performance of the electromagnetic engine', *Proceedings,* Lit & Phil, vol. 10 (1871), p. 183. In fact, less heat is evolved, less work is done in unit time (less total energy is evolved), but the work done per unit weight of zinc (the duty) is greater.

35 Joule, *Proceedings,* Lit & Phil, vol. 10 (1871), p. 193; Apjohn, *Chemical News,* vol. 23 (1871), p. 105; *Nature* (1871), *passim.*

36 Joule to Tyndall, 6 Jan. 1872, Royal Institution. Later in the year he thanked Tyndall for the gift of a volume of Tyndall's researches; 24 Jun. 1872, Royal Institution.

37 Joule to Roscoe, 10 Mar. 1872, Royal Society of Chemistry.

38 *Report of Royal Commission on Scientific Instruction and the Advancement of Science, 1872–1875*, vol. 2, pp. 100–5.
39 Compare Lowe's comments on aid for tidal observations: 'I am in principle opposed to all the grants', quoted in Cardwell, *The Organisation of Science*.
40 *Report of Royal Commission*, Minute 10, 667.
41 The membership figures for the Lit & Phil ran as follows: 1831 – 134; 1842 – 176; 1852 – 172; 1862 – 207; 1871 – 169; 1882 – 140. By 1901 they had recovered slightly, to 161.
42 Joule, evidence to Devonshire Commission.
43 S. Mills, 'Thomas Kirkman – the mathematical cleric of Croft', *Manchester Memoirs*, vol. 120 (1977–1980), pp. 100–9.
44 R. A. Smith, *A Centenary of Science in Manchester* (Manchester Lit & Phil, 1883).
45 J. L. Heilbron, *H. G. J. Moseley: The Life and Letters of an English Physicist, 1887–1915* (University of California Press, 1974), p. 196.
46 Roscoe to Tyndall, 30 Jan. 1872, Royal Institution.
47 R. MacLeod, 'Science and the civil list, 1824–1914', *Technology and Society*, vol. 2 (1970), pp. 47–55.
48 Joule to Roscoe, 15 Nov. 1872, Royal Society of Chemistry.
49 Reynolds, *Memoir*.
50 Joule to Stokes, 14 Jun. 1873, Royal Society.
51 Reynolds, *Memoir* and BA *Report* (1873).
52 Reynolds, *Memoir*, p. 162.
53 *Ibid.*, pp. 162–3. Dixon Mann (1840–1912) was a leading member of the medical profession in Manchester. He was professor of forensic medicine in the Victoria University, 1892–1912.
54 *JSP* (i), pp. 623–7.
55 *JSP* (i), pp. 632–57. *Philosophical Transactions*, vol. 169 (1878), pp. 365–83.
56 Joule to Stokes, 16 Jan. 1878, Royal Society.
57 Dated 15 Aug. 1877 and directed to the Lords of Committee of Council on Education. The signatories were J. C. Adams, T. Andrews, J. A. Brown, A. Buchan, W. B. Carpenter, D. M. Home, J. P. Joule, J. C. Maxwell, A. Mitchell, J. Prestwich, H. E. Roscoe, B. Stewart and W. Thomson.
58 Joule to Frances C. Dancer, 24 Jan. 1878, Physics Department, UMIST. Lord Derby was Foreign Secretary at that time.
59 I am indebted to Mr Robert W. J. Derby for information on this point. One of Mr Derby's grandfathers, Benjamin James Tappenden, was a brother of Frances Charlotte and was, it is understood, named after the Joule brothers. Nathanael Dancer's family owned Little Sutton House, Chiswick, from 1623 to 1914 when Benjamin Tappenden's family bought it from Mrs C. F. Dancer, having rented it from 1886. Frederick Tappenden died in May 1879, aged 70; his wife, Joule's aunt, died in March 1887, aged 85. Sutton Court, the school house, was rented from 1882 and sold in 1887. Frances Charlotte died in 1923. It was her justifiable pride to have been so close to a great man of science.
   I am also indebted to Mrs Carolyn Hammond, of Chiswick District Library.
60 Public Record Office, T/1 7673A file 10491.
61 PRO, 16 May 1878. Sir Francis Sandford, CB, was Secretary of the Committee of the Council on Education.
62 Hooker to Corry, 16 May 1878, PRO; P. Currie to A. Turner, 21 May 1878, PRO. Lord Salisbury had replaced Lord Derby as Foreign Secretary.
63 Tyndall to Hooker, 19 May 1878, PRO.
64 D. S. L. Cardwell, *From Watt to Clausius* (Heinemann, London, 1970), p. 283.
65 Hooker to Roscoe, n.d., Royal Society of Chemistry.
66 Roscoe to Hooker, 24 May 1878, PRO.
67 Hooker to Turner, 24 May 1878, PRO. The second letter was written on the same day.
68 The second letter ends with the request that Lord Beaconsfield give urgent attention to the earlier opening of Kew Gardens to the public – a matter that would presumably cost

more money.
69 Minute in PRO. It was registered at the Treasury on 24 Jun. 1878. The pension was paid
from the £1,200 voted annually by Parliament.
70 Tyndall to Roscoe, 30 Jul. 1878, Royal Society of Chemistry.

Chapter 13

1 In Rowland's experiment a rapidly moving electric charge was found to generate a
(changing) magnetic field. V. Crémieu, who repeated the experiment in 1900, claimed
that no such effect was produced. There followed an international debate that was only
resolved when an explanation was found that confirmed Rowland's reputation as an
experimenter of genius, secured Maxwell's theory and preserved Crémieu's honour.
2 H. A. Rowland, 'On the mechanical equivalent of heat and subsidiary remarks on the
variation of the mercury from the air thermometer and on the variation of the specific heat
of water', *Proceedings of the American Academy of Arts and Sciences*, vol. 7 (1880), pp.
75–200.
3 J. H. Poynting, Presidential Address to Section A, British Association, BA *Report* (1899);
Nature, vol. 60 (1899), p. 470.
4 Joule to Thomson, 25 May 1879, CU, J 291. But in a letter dated 11 Aug. 1879, CU, J
292, Joule remarked: 'I only heard of Rowland's work the other day.'
5 Joule to Rowland, 23 Jul. 1879, Johns Hopkins University Library.
6 Rowland to Joule, 3 Aug. 1879, CU, J 292a.
7 Joule to Thomson, 19 Aug. 1879, CU, J 293.
8 Joule to Thomson, 21 Aug. 1879, CU, J 294.
9 Joule to Thomson, 2 Sept. 1879, CU, J 295.
10 *Ibid.*
11 Joule to Thomson, 16 Sept. 1879, CU, J 296. Joule later recalled that on being
introduced to Gladstone at the Royal Society, the latter extended his hand as if 'it were an
unpleasant duty', while the Prince of Wales, at the Society of Arts, gave a firm and manly
handshake and offered cordial greetings. Joule family records, Archives Department,
Manchester Central Reference Library.
12 Joule to Rowland, 21 Oct. 1879, Johns Hopkins University Library.
13 Joule to Rowland, 8 Dec. 1879, Johns Hopkins University Library.
14 Joule to Thomson, 25 May, 11 Aug. and 16 Sept. 1879.
15 Joule to Rowland, 9 Apr. 1880, Johns Hopkins University Library.
16 Reynolds to Stokes, 6 Nov. 1879, CU, Add.MS.
17 Joule to Thomson, 15 Dec. 1879, CU, J 297.
18 R. J. Strutt, *John William Strutt, Third Baron Rayleigh* (Edward Arnold, London, 1924), p.
180.
19 Joule to Rayleigh, 6 Jan. 1882, Strutt, *John William Strutt*.
20 Joule to Schuster, 16 Oct. 1885, Royal Society.
21 Sir A. Schuster, *Biographical Fragments* (MacMillan, London, 1932).
22 Early in 1880 the *S.S. Strathleven*, the first British refrigerated ship, docked at Tilbury
with a cargo of frozen meat from 'the antipodes'. It was in excellent condition and fetched
a good price at Smithfield. Sea transport received a further boost in the 1880s with the
arrival of the light and strong steel ship. By the end of the century exotic tropical fruit, like
bananas, reached British markets. By 1914 Britain was so dependent on imported food
that the German U-boat campaign almost brought the country to defeat. The great and
progressive farming industry of fifty years before was left in a state of depression that
lasted until 1939.
23 O. Reynolds, *Memoir of James Prescott Joule* (Manchester Lit & Phil, 1892), p. 166.
24 Joule to Thomson, 28 Jul. 1880, CU, J 298.
25 *Ibid.*
26 *The Nineteenth Century*, vol. 11 (1882), pp. 493, 657. Other men of science who signed the

petition included Huxley, Lubbock and Grove.

27 Joule to Roscoe, 7 Feb. 1882, Royal Society.

28 Joule to Thomson, 4 Mar. 1882, CU, J 299.

29 *Ibid.*

30 *Nature*, vol. 72 (1905), p. 612.

31 The transformer, based on Faraday's discovery of 1831, was being developed at that time by Gaulard and Gibbs.

32 O. Reynolds, 'The transmission of energy', *Journal of the Society of Arts*, vol. 32 (18830, pp. 973–9, 985–9, 995–9.

33 Ritter invented the secondary cell, or storage battery, at the end of the eighteenth century. But it was only of academic interest until the invention of the dynamo.

34 K. A. Barlow, 'A history of gas engines, 1791–1900', 2 vols, (Ph.D.thesis, Manchester University, 1979). In fact large numbers of gas-engines were manufactured and proved extremely useful. The gas-engine was also a natural stage in the development of the automobile engine.

35 William Siemens had suggested that the energy of Niagara could be harnessed to supply electricity to New York, Philadelphia, Boston and Toronto (1876). Thomson's paper was the Presidential Address to Section A of the BA meeting of 1881.

36 Engels to Bernstein, 1883.

37 *Nature*, vol. 26 (1882), p. 618.

38 Joule to Thomson, 15 Nov. 1882, CU, J 301. There are lock gates on the Manchester Ship Canal. Once again Joule's gloomy prophecy was not to be fulfilled.

39 Joule to Thomson, 16 Dec. 1883, CU, J 302.

40 Reynolds, *Memoir.*

41 Joule to Roscoe, 13 Mar. 1884, Royal Society of Chemistry.

42 Joule to Roscoe, 7 Jul. 1884, Royal Society of Chemistry.

43 Joule to Tyndall, 26 Nov. 1887, Royal Institution.

44 Joule to F. Tappenden, jun., 22 Jul. 1886, Physics Department, UMIST. Sir Charles Dilke, a radical member of Gladstone's administration, resigned following a particularly lurid sex scandal.

45 Reynolds, *Memoir.*

46 *Proceedings*, Lit & Phil, vol. 22 (1882–3), pp. 19, 104.

47 Account in Local History Library, Manchester Central Reference Library (942.73 MP 22). H. A. Rowland also attended the Manchester meeting. He would surely have wanted to talk to Joule.

48 Joule to Thomson, 23 May 1887, CU, J 304.

49 Reynolds, *Memoir.* My friend, Dr A. G. Hesling, FRCP, suggests that a cause of Joule's decline could have been a brain tumour; but the evidence is extremely thin and he stresses that this is no more than a possibility. On the other hand mercury, or any other form of 'vocational poisoning', seems most unlikely.

50 *Manchester Guardian*, 26 Jun. 1889. Hirn, had he lived, might well have been elected a Foreign Member of the Royal Society. Writing to Stokes on 6 Jan. 1889, Tyndall remarked: 'Were he chosen I am quite persuaded that the choice would be everywhere applauded' (CU, Add. MS). But Hirn died a year later.

51 Anon. In Joule family papers, Archives Department, Manchester Central Reference Library.

52 Undated fragment of letter, Physics Department, UMIST.

53 *Manchester Courier*, 19 Nov. 1889.

54 *Manchester Courier*, 14 Dec. 1889.

55 Reynolds, *Memoir.* The Chairman of the national committee for the Joule memorial in Westminster Abbey was Sir G. G. Stokes; Roscoe was the Secretary.

56 Joule's will was dated 27 Apr. 1881; the Married Woman's Property Act did not pass into law until 1 Jan. 1883. The executors of the will were Benjamin Arthur and Benjamin St J. B. Joule.

57 Newspaper cutting, Joule family papers, Archives Department, Manchester Central Reference Library.
58 Will of B. St J. B. Joule, Scottish Record Office, Edinburgh.
59 The *Joule* was one of a class of submarines named after French and British men of science.

Chapter 14

1 Joule was one of the three distinguished men of science – the other two being Brewster and Sedgwick – who signed the 'Declaration of students of natural and physical sciences' (1865), proclaiming that there could be no conflict between the findings of science and the truths of religion. See W. H. Brock, and R. MacLeod, 'The "scientists' declaration": reflexions on science and belief in the wake of *Essays and Reviews*, 1864–1865', *B.J.H.S.*, vol. 9 (1976), pp. 39–66. Joule's action was criticised by Tyndall, who remarked that he had not raised himself to the 'real region of philosophy to which his experiments point'. But to have done so would have been inconsistent with his iterated refusal to speculate. He was a physicist and the nuances and subtleties of the great debates about religious belief were not for him. *Per contra*, he had no time for clergyman who expressed uninformed opinions about scientific matters.
2 Cf. J. T. Desaguliers, *A Course of Experimental Philosophy*, 2 vols. (London, 1734, 1744). This popular and influential work – it went through a number of editions – maybe taken as indicating the scope of 'experimental philosophy'. The author dealt with the science of mechanics and included detailed accounts of water-wheels, pumps, 'fire engines' (Newcomen engines), etc., as exemplars of the experimental philosophy.
3 B. Stewart, *The Conservation of Energy: Being an Elementary Treatise on Energy and its Laws* (London, 1873). The work was translated and published in French.
4 Bagehot was an early graduate of London University. The requirements for the B.A. degree then included an adequate knowledge of mathematics, the classics, natural philosophy and biology.
5 It is said that the youthful Planck was advised against a career in physics on the grounds that the science was virtually complete and that there was nothing left to do, apart from tidying up a few loose ends.
6 Dr R. L. Pocock uses this expression in assessing the strength of Marconi's claim, *vis-à-vis* dubious rivals, to have invented wireless (private communication).
7 Physics Department, UMIST.

Index of names

Index of subjects

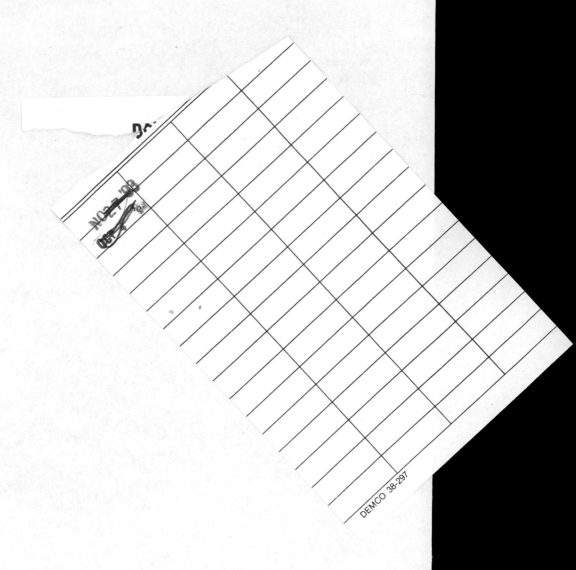

DEMCO 38-297